Generation X

AMERICANS AGED 18 TO 34

Generation X

X

AMERICANS AGED 18 TO 34

3rd EDITION

BY SUSAN MITCHELL

New Strategist Publications, Inc.
Ithaca, New York

New Strategist Publications, Inc.
P.O. Box 242, Ithaca, New York 14851
800/848-0841; 607/273-0913
www.newstrategist.com

ISBN 1-885070-36-5

Printed in the United States of America

Table of Contents

Chapter 4. Income

Chapter 5. Labor Force

Tables

Chapter 1. Attitudes and Behavior

Chapter 2. Education

Chapter 3. Health

Chapter 4. Income

Chapter 5. Labor Force

Chapter 6. Living Arrangements

Chapter 7. Population

Chapter 8. Spending

Chapter 9. Wealth

Illustrations

Chapter 7. Population

Chapter 9. Wealth

Introduction

The baby boom was the original "youth generation." Its large size insured that businesses, the media, and society in general would have to take notice. But as boomers grew older, the nation's attention shifted with it, tracking the generation into middle age. Businesses that had once served young adults retooled to meet the demands of older Americans. Politicians who had catered to the concerns of the young began to focus on Social Security, health care, and crime—issues that worry middle-aged and older adults. Now the nation's young-adult population is growing again, and the interests and needs of young people are commanding more attention.

In 2001, there were 76 million people aged 15 to 34, up from 75 million in 1999. By 2010, there will be nearly 82 million people in the age group because the Millennial generation—the children of the original baby boom—is entering the age group.

In 2001, the young adult population consists of Generation Xers and Millennials. Those aged 15 to 24 belong to the Millennial generation while those aged 25 to 34 are Gen Xers. By 2010, nearly all young adults will be Millennials.

Population aged 15 to 34

(percent of people aged 15 to 34 in the population, 1920 to 2020)

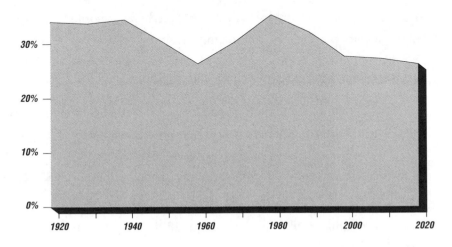

In the early part of the 19th century, young adults accounted for more than one-third of the American population. The share fell below the one-third level during the 1950s, bottoming out at 26 percent in 1960. But as the original baby boom came of age, the young-adult share of the population expanded once again. By 1980, the 15-to-34 age group accounted for 35 percent of the population. Then, as the small Generation X filled the young-adult age group, the proportion fell. By 2000, only 28 percent of Americans were between the ages of 15 and 34. The share will continue to edge downward, falling to 26 percent by 2020.

Regardless of the number of 15-to-34-year-olds, lifestage dictates that young adults are a vital part of the nation's commerce and culture. People in the age group go to college, get married, have children, embark on a career, and buy their first home. Each of these transitions creates distinct wants and needs, problems and opportunities.

Although today's young adults are not as quick to settle down as earlier generations, most still marry and have children in their twenties. Young adults head one-quarter of family households and fully 60 percent of households with children under age 6.

People under age 35 are more likely than older adults to move from one residence to another. Twenty-six percent of people aged 15 to 34 moved between March 1998 and March 1999 compared with only 16 percent of all Americans. Most young adults live in rental apartments. Only among 30-to-34-year-olds do the majority own a home.

Young adults are attending college in record proportions. More than 60 percent of people aged 18 or 19 and more than 40 percent of those aged 20 or 21 are still in school. One in four 22-to-24-year-olds is enrolled in college. Twenty-nine percent of men and 30 percent of women aged 25 to 34 have at least a bachelor's degree.

Three-quarters of young adults are in the labor force. In fact, people under age 35 make up 39 percent of the nation's workers. But unemployment is relatively high among people under age 25. Seven percent of people aged 20 to 24 and 13 percent of those aged 16 to 19 were looking for work in 2000 compared with an overall unemployment rate of just 4 percent.

Although households headed by people under age 25 have relatively low incomes (a median of $25,171 in 1999), the median income of households headed by 25-to-34-year-olds is higher than the overall median ($42,174 versus $40,816 for all households). Married couples aged 25 to 34 have a median income that is well above average, at $53,169 in 1999.

For many organizations—both public and private—young adults are the best, if not the only, customers. As the Millennial generation fills the 18-to-34 age group during the decade, the cultural and economic influence of young adults is once again on the rise.

How to Use This Book

We designed *Generation X: Americans Aged 18 to 34* for easy use. Its nine chapters—Attitudes and Behavior, Education, Health, Income, Labor Force, Living Arrangements, Population, Spending, and Wealth—appear in alphabetical order.

Most of the tables rely on data collected and published by the federal government, in particular the Bureau of the Census, the Bureau of Labor Statistics, the National Center for Education Statistics, the National Center for Health Statistics, and the Federal Reserve Board. The federal government continues to be the best source of up-to-date, reliable information about the changing characteristics of Americans.

To explore the attitudes of young adults, most of the tables in the Attitudes and Behavior chapter rely on data from the nationally representative General Social Survey of the University of Chicago's National Opinion Research Center. Attitudinal data for all age groups appear for comparative purposes. NORC had conducted the General Social Survey annually from 1972 through 1994, except for the years 1979, 1981, and 1992. It now conducts the survey every two years, 1998 being the latest year for which data are available.

While the federal government has produced most of the data reported in this book, the tables in *Generation X* are not simply reprints of government spreadsheets—as is the case in many reference books. Instead, we compiled and created each table individually, the calculations designed to reveal trends and highlight important information. Each chapter of *Generation X* includes the demographic and lifestyle data most important to researchers. Each table tells a story about people aged 18 to 34, a story fleshed out by the accompanying text, which analyzes the data and identifies future trends. Should you need even more statistical detail than the tables provide, try plumbing the source listed at the bottom of each table.

The book contains a comprehensive list of tables to help you locate the information you need. For a more detailed search, use the index at the back of the book. There is also a glossary, which defines the terms and describes the surveys appearing in tables and text. A list of telephone and Internet contacts also appears at the end of the book, enabling you to access government specialists and web sites.

Young adults will always be the nation's trendsetters. With *Generation X: Americans Aged 18 to 34* on your bookshelf, an in-depth understanding of this influential age group is at hand.

—Susan Mitchell

1

Attitudes and Behavior

♦ Today's young adults are skeptical of other people's motives. Few believe most people can be trusted.

♦ Young people worry about the future of Social Security. The majority think the Social Security program needs major changes, but most don't want to scrap the current system.

♦ Fewer than one-quarter of people under age 35 read the newspaper daily compared with the great majority of people aged 45 or older.

♦ Religious diversity is much greater among young adults than among older Americans. Those under age 35 are less likely to have a religious affiliation or to attend religious services regularly.

♦ Nearly three-quarters of people under age 35 believe working mothers can have as good a relationship with their children as mothers who do not have jobs. They speak from experience: more than three-quarters had mothers who worked for a year or more while they were growing up.

♦ People under age 35 are more likely to consider themselves political independents than Democrats or Republicans. As the Millennial generation joins the young-adult age group, liberals and moderates now substantially outnumber conservatives.

♦ Most young adults use the Internet, but a surprisingly large proportion—two out of five—are not wired. Many will go online when their income rises.

Youngest Adults Are Most Likely to Find Life Exciting

But they are least likely to say they are very happy.

Reaching adulthood and striking out on one's own is an exciting adventure. More than half of people aged 18 to 24 (51 percent) say they find their lives exciting compared with 45 percent of all adults. But excitement is not necessarily the path to happiness. Only 23 percent of the youngest adults are "very happy" versus 32 percent of all adults. Fifteen percent of 18-to-24-year-olds say they are "not too happy."

As people get older and their lives settle down, the proportion of those who are very happy rises. One-third of people aged 25 to 34 say they are very happy. Forty-five percent say their lives are exciting, while half say life is pretty routine.

♦ The transition to adulthood is exciting, but fraught with difficulty. The excitement wanes as young people settle into adult roles, but they're happier for it.

As excitement falls, happiness rises

(percent of people aged 18 to 34 who say life is "exciting" and who say they are "very happy," by age, 1998)

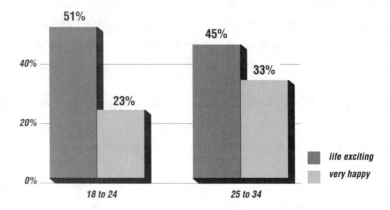

Personal Happiness, 1998

"Taken all together, how would you say things are these days—would you say that you are very happy, pretty happy, or not too happy?"

(percent of people aged 18 or older responding, by age, 1998)

	very happy	*pretty happy*	*not too happy*
Total people	**32%**	**56%**	**12%**
Aged 18 to 24	23	62	15
Aged 25 to 34	33	56	11
Aged 35 to 44	30	58	11
Aged 45 to 54	30	59	11
Aged 55 to 64	36	53	12
Aged 65 or older	36	51	13

Note: Numbers may not add to 100 because "don't know" is not shown.
Source: 1998 General Social Survey, National Opinion Research Center, University of Chicago; calculations by the author

Is Life Exciting? 1998

"In general, do you find life exciting, pretty routine, or dull?"

(percent of people aged 18 or older responding, by age, 1998)

	exciting	pretty routine	dull
Total people	**45%**	**49%**	**5%**
Aged 18 to 24	51	41	8
Aged 25 to 34	45	50	4
Aged 35 to 44	49	46	4
Aged 45 to 54	46	50	4
Aged 55 to 64	43	51	5
Aged 65 or older	35	53	10

Note: Numbers may not add to 100 because "no opinion" is not shown.
Source: 1998 General Social Survey, National Opinion Research Center, University of Chicago; calculations by the author

Young Adults Are Not Trusting

Most believe people are selfish and untrustworthy.

Americans are losing faith in the trustworthiness, helpfulness, and fairness of other people. Young adults are most likely to be suspicious of others.

Nearly three-quarters of people aged 18 to 24 and 65 percent of those aged 25 to 34 say one can't be too careful in dealing with other people. These shares are considerably higher than the 56 percent of all adults who feel that way.

Young adults are also inclined to believe that most people are just looking out for themselves. Half of people aged 25 to 34 and 59 percent of those aged 18 to 24 think most people are selfish compared with 43 percent of all adults. Similarly, about half of young adults believe most people will try to take advantage rather than being fair compared with 38 percent of all adults.

♦ Politicians and advertisers deserve some of the blame for the cynicism of today's young adults, who learned at the feet of their boomer parents that the claims made by advertisers and politicians should be viewed with suspicion.

Young adults are skeptical of the motives of other people

(percent of people aged 18 or older who say most people would try to take advantage rather than try to be fair, by age, 1998)

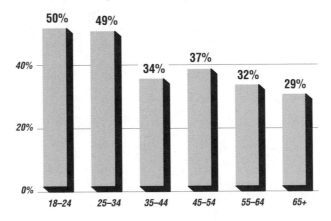

Opinion of Other People, 1998

"Generally speaking, would you say that most people can be trusted or that you can't be too careful in dealing with people?"

"Do you think most people would try to take advantage of you if they got a chance, or would they try to be fair?"

"Would you say that most of the time people try to be helpful, or that they are mostly just looking out for themselves?"

(percent of people aged 18 or older responding by age, 1998)

	trust		helpfulness		fairness	
	can be trusted	can't be too careful	try to be helpful	look out for themselves	try to be fair	would try to take advantage
Total people	**38%**	**56%**	**48%**	**43%**	**52%**	**38%**
Aged 18 to 24	20	73	34	59	38	50
Aged 25 to 34	27	65	39	50	41	49
Aged 35 to 44	39	56	48	42	58	34
Aged 45 to 54	46	48	50	44	56	37
Aged 55 to 64	52	45	52	38	59	32
Aged 65 or older	40	53	60	27	59	29

Note: Numbers may not add to 100 percent because "don't know" is not shown.
Source: 1998 General Social Survey, National Opinion Research Center, University of Chicago; calculations by the author

Most Young Adults Were Raised in Two-Parent Families

But a sizable minority are the children of single mothers.

Young adults are less likely than older generations to have been living with both parents when they were age 16, although the majority were. Only half of people aged 18 to 24 and 62 percent of those aged 25 to 34 lived with both parents at that age compared with three-quarters of people aged 45 or older.

Most of those who did not live with both parents lived with their mothers. Twenty-seven percent of people aged 18 to 24 and 18 percent of those aged 25 to 34 lived with only their mother at age 16.

Parental divorce is the most common reason why young adults did not live with both parents at age 16. This is a sea-change from decades ago, when the most common reason why a young person didn't live with both parents was the death of a parent.

♦ Young adults' experience of divorce during childhood may explain their tendency to delay marriage as well as their caution in making commitments.

The share of people raised by both parents is declining

(percent of people aged 18 or older who were living with both parents at age 16, by age, 1998)

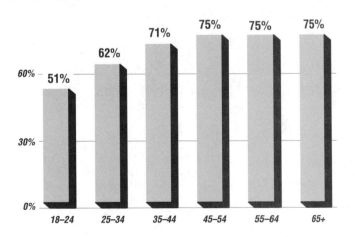

Living with Both Parents at Age 16, 1998

"Were you living with both your own mother and father around the time you were 16? If not, with whom were you living around that time?"

(percent of people aged 18 or older responding by age, 1998)

	both parents	parent and stepparent	mother only	father only	other
Total people	**69%**	**9%**	**14%**	**2%**	**6%**
Aged 18 to 24	51	11	27	3	7
Aged 25 to 34	62	12	18	2	6
Aged 35 to 44	71	8	13	2	7
Aged 45 to 54	75	8	8	2	7
Aged 55 to 64	76	7	9	1	7
Aged 65 or older	75	6	11	2	6

Source: 1998 General Social Survey, National Opinion Research Center, University of Chicago; calculations by the author

Reason Not Living with Both Parents, 1998

"If you were not living with both parents at age 16, what happened?"

(percent of people aged 18 or older responding by age, 1998)

	divorced/separated	parent died	other
Total people	**52%**	**28%**	**18%**
Aged 18 to 24	71	10	19
Aged 25 to 34	63	17	17
Aged 35 to 44	55	28	17
Aged 45 to 54	46	33	21
Aged 55 to 64	36	43	18
Aged 65 or older	25	54	18

Note: Numbers may not add to 100 because "don't know" is not shown.
Source: 1998 General Social Survey, National Opinion Research Center, University of Chicago; calculations by the author

Most Young Couples Are Happy

But for some, it won't always be that way.

Most Americans under age 25 are not married. Those who are, however, are more likely than older people to say their marriages are "very happy." Seventy percent of married people aged 18 to 24 say their marriage is very happy. Among married people aged 25 to 34, a slightly smaller 66 percent say their marriage is very happy. This share is nonetheless higher than the 59 to 61 percent of middle-aged couples who say they have very happy marriages.

Most married people under age 25 have not been married long. As they encounter the challenges of keeping a marriage happy and healthy over time, the percentage of those who say their marriage is very happy will decline; some will end up in divorce court. The 5 percent of married people under age 35 who say their marriage is "not too happy" are already facing high odds for divorce.

♦ Most young couples have a very happy marriage, as do most married people of any age. People who are in unhappy marriages don't usually stay married long.

Youngest adults are most likely to have very happy marriages

(percent of people aged 18 or older who say their marriage is "very happy," by age, 1998)

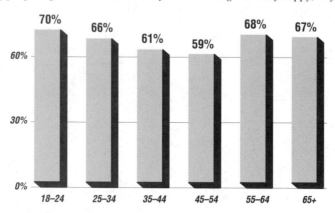

Marital Happiness, 1998

"Taking things all together, how would you describe your marriage? Would you say that your marriage is very happy, pretty happy, or not too happy?"

(percent of people aged 18 or older responding by age, 1998)

	very happy	pretty happy	not too happy
Total people	**64%**	**33%**	**3%**
Aged 18 to 24	70	24	5
Aged 25 to 34	66	33	1
Aged 35 to 44	61	35	3
Aged 45 to 54	59	38	3
Aged 55 to 64	68	28	4
Aged 65 or older	67	30	3

Note: Numbers may not add to 100 because "don't know" is not shown.
Source: 1998 General Social Survey, National Opinion Research Center, University of Chicago; calculations by the author

Greater Acceptance of Working Women

Young adults believe a woman's career is as important as a man's.

Younger generations are more likely than the oldest Americans to believe a woman's career is as important as a man's. Young adults are in agreement with baby boomers on this issue. Only 11 to 13 percent of people under age 55 believe it is more important for a wife to help her husband's career than to have one herself. In contrast, a slightly larger 20 percent of people aged 55 to 64 and a substantially higher 44 percent of those aged 65 or older think a woman's career should take a back seat to her husband's.

Young adults are much less likely than the oldest Americans to believe traditional sex roles—the wife taking care of the home and the husband working—are best. More than three-quarters of young adults do not favor the traditional arrangement compared with only 34 percent of people aged 65 or older.

♦ Young women are more ambitious and self-confident than previous generations, and young men are supportive of their aspirations. Today's young adults are likely to advance equality between the sexes.

Young adults don't believe traditional gender roles are best

(percent of people aged 18 or older who do not agree that "it is better for everyone if the man is the achiever outside the home and the woman takes care of the home and family," by age, 1998)

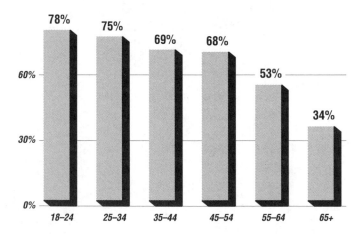

Female Homemakers and Male Breadwinners, 1998

"It is much better for everyone involved if the man is
the achiever outside the home and the woman takes care of
the home and family—do you agree or disagree?"

(percent of people aged 18 or older responding by age, 1998)

	strongly agree	agree	disagree	strongly disagree	agree, total	disagree, total
Total people	7%	27%	45%	18%	34%	63%
Aged 18 to 24	4	16	55	23	20	78
Aged 25 to 34	4	19	48	27	23	75
Aged 35 to 44	7	22	51	18	29	69
Aged 45 to 54	5	25	48	20	30	68
Aged 55 to 64	8	37	37	16	45	53
Aged 65 or older	14	49	29	5	63	34

Note: Numbers may not add to 100 because "don't know" is not shown.
Source: 1998 General Social Survey, National Opinion Research Center, University of Chicago; calculations by the author

Whose Career Is More Important? 1998

"It is more important for a wife to help her husband's career than to have one herself. Do you agree or disagree?"

(percent of people aged 18 or older responding by age, 1998)

	strongly agree	agree	disagree	strongly disagree	agree, total	disagree, total
Total people	**2%**	**16%**	**54%**	**25%**	**18%**	**79%**
Aged 18 to 24	1	12	54	32	13	86
Aged 25 to 34	2	9	53	33	11	86
Aged 35 to 44	2	11	56	29	13	85
Aged 45 to 54	2	11	57	27	13	84
Aged 55 to 64	2	18	58	20	20	78
Aged 65 or older	5	39	45	5	44	50

Note: Numbers may not add to 100 because "don't know" is not shown.
Source: 1998 General Social Survey, National Opinion Research Center, University of Chicago; calculations by the author

Children of Working Mothers

Young adults are comfortable with working mothers.

Today's young adults are the children of working mothers. Fully 83 percent of people aged 18 to 24 and 76 percent of those aged 25 to 34 say their mother worked for at least one year while they were growing up. In contrast, only 62 to 67 percent of people aged 35 to 54 and fewer than half of those aged 65 or older had mothers who worked for a year or more while they were children.

The experience with their own working mothers has not turned young adults into advocates for stay-at-home moms. Rather, it seems to have had the opposite effect. Young adults are most likely to believe that working mothers can have as good a relationship with their children as mothers who don't work. Three-quarters of people aged 18 to 24 and 71 percent of those aged 25 to 34 think working mothers have just as good a relationship with their children, compared with 67 percent of all adults.

♦ For young adults, working mothers are the norm. They grew up with them, and they intend to continue the trend when they have children.

Younger generations were raised by working mothers

(percent of people aged 18 or older whose mother worked for at least one year when they were growing up, by age, 1998)

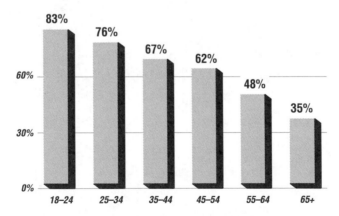

Opinion of Working Mothers, 1998

"A working mother can establish just as warm and secure a relationship with her children as a mother who does not work—do you agree or disagree?"

(percent of people aged 18 or older responding by age, 1998)

	strongly agree	agree	disagree	strongly disagree	agree, total	disagree, total
Total people	**22%**	**45%**	**25%**	**7%**	**67%**	**32%**
Aged 18 to 24	24	51	23	1	75	24
Aged 25 to 34	23	48	22	5	71	27
Aged 35 to 44	26	44	24	5	70	29
Aged 45 to 54	25	44	23	7	69	30
Aged 55 to 64	19	44	26	10	63	36
Aged 65 or older	12	42	33	10	54	43

Note: Numbers may not add to 100 because "don't know" is not shown.
Source: 1998 General Social Survey, National Opinion Research Center, University of Chicago; calculations by the author

Did Your Mother Work? 1998

"Did your mother ever work for pay for as long as one year
after you were born and before you were 14?"

(percent of people aged 18 or older responding by age, 1998)

	yes	no
Total people	**62%**	**37%**
Aged 18 to 24	83	17
Aged 25 to 34	76	23
Aged 35 to 44	67	32
Aged 45 to 54	62	37
Aged 55 to 64	48	50
Aged 65 or older	35	64

Note: Numbers may not add to 100 because "don't know" is not shown.
Source: 1998 General Social Survey, National Opinion Research Center, University of Chicago; calculations by the author

Financial Satisfaction Rises with Age

Young adults are most likely to say they are dissatisfied with their finances.

Older Americans are more satisfied with their financial situation than young people because they have had a lifetime to buy what they need, pay off their debts, and build wealth. Thirty-eight percent of people aged 18 to 24 say they are not at all satisfied with their financial situation compared with just 12 percent of people aged 65 or older. Conversely, while only 24 percent of 18-to-24-year-olds are "pretty well satisfied" with their finances, the proportion is a much higher 41 percent among people aged 65 or older.

People aged 25 to 34 are not much more satisfied with their financial situation than those aged 18 to 24. While the share of those who say they are dissatisfied is smaller, the share of those who are "pretty well satisfied" is also smaller. As young adults develop careers, earn more money, and build wealth, their satisfaction is likely to grow.

♦ Even young adults with college degrees and good salaries tend to be dissatisfied with their finances. Their dissatisfaction is due to the costs of setting up a household and starting a family.

Few young adults are happy with their finances

(percent of people aged 18 or older who say they are "pretty well satisfied" with their finances, by age, 1998)

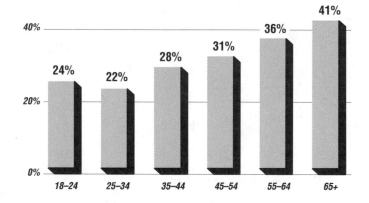

Satisfaction with Financial Situation, 1998

"So far as you and your family are concerned, would you say that you are pretty well satisfied with your present financial situation, more or less satisfied, or not satisfied at all?"

(percent of people aged 18 or older responding by age, 1998)

	pretty well satisfied	more or less satisfied	not at all satisfied
Total people	**30%**	**44%**	**25%**
Aged 18 to 24	24	37	38
Aged 25 to 34	22	48	30
Aged 35 to 44	28	42	30
Aged 45 to 54	31	44	24
Aged 55 to 64	36	45	19
Aged 65 or older	41	46	12

Note: Numbers may not add to total because "don't know" is not shown.
Source: 1998 General Social Survey, National Opinion Research Center, University of Chicago; calculations by the author

Young People Want More Time with Friends and Family

Those under age 25 are most likely to want to spend more time at work.

Like most Americans, young adults would like to spend more time with friends and family as well as enjoying leisure activities. Fully 81 percent of people aged 25 to 34 and 77 percent of those aged 18 to 24 would like to spend more time with family. Among people aged 18 to 24, 73 percent want more time with friends. The figure is a smaller 66 percent among people aged 25 to 34. At this age, priorities are beginning to shift because many people are starting families.

The youngest adults are more likely than other Americans to want to spend more time on the job. Forty-four percent would like to put in more work hours compared with 27 percent of people aged 25 to 34 and 23 percent of all adults. The reason for this desire is simple—money. Many young adults work part-time and most have relatively low incomes. More time at work would mean a larger paycheck.

♦ As young adults enter middle age, their enthusiasm for work will wane as their involvement in family life grows.

Young adults want to work more

*(percent of people aged 18 or older and aged 18 to 34
who want to spend more time in a paid job, 1998)*

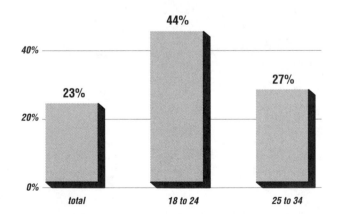

Preferred Use of Time, 1998

"Suppose you could change the way you spend your time, spending more on some things and less on others. Which of these things on the following list would you like to spend more time on, which would you like to spend less time on, and which would you like to spend the same amount of time as now? Time in a paid job; time doing household work; time with your family; time with your friends; time in leisure activities."

(percent of people aged 18 or older responding by age, 1998)

	paid job		household work		with family		with friends		leisure activities	
	more	less	more	less	more	less	more	less	more	less
Total people	**23%**	**27%**	**25%**	**40%**	**79%**	**2%**	**65%**	**4%**	**72%**	**4%**
Aged 18 to 24	44	14	35	28	77	4	73	5	72	6
Aged 25 to 34	27	24	27	37	81	0	66	3	73	3
Aged 35 to 44	22	39	26	45	85	2	69	5	82	4
Aged 45 to 54	20	32	22	50	84	1	66	2	81	1
Aged 55 to 64	17	31	17	44	75	0	64	3	67	3
Aged 65 or older	12	10	20	33	65	4	50	4	47	5

Note: Numbers may not add to 100 because "same amount of time" and "can't choose" are not shown.
Source: 1998 General Social Survey, National Opinion Research Center, University of Chicago; calculations by the author

The Young Would Rather Watch Than Read

Daily newspaper readership is lowest among people under age 35.

The amount of time young adults spend watching television is similar to that of older people, but they read the newspaper less frequently. Only 22 percent of people aged 18 to 24 and 25 percent of those aged 25 to 34 read the newspaper daily compared with more than one-half of those aged 45 or older. But young adults haven't given up on print media. Most read the paper at least once a week; only 8 to 10 percent never read the paper.

Forty-five percent of 18-to-24-year-olds and 50 percent of those aged 25 to 34 watch one to two hours of television a day, similar to the average for all adults. People aged 18 to 24 have more free time than the middle aged, so it is not surprising that a larger percentage of them watch five or more hours of television daily (18 percent versus 11 to 12 percent of those aged 35 to 54). People aged 25 to 34 are also heavy television watchers; 15 percent watch five or more hours a day.

♦ Although young adults are spending time on the Internet, it hasn't yet cut their television viewing significantly. Print media, on the other hand, will have to work hard to increase readership among young adults.

Young adults don't have the daily newspaper habit

(percent of people aged 18 or older who read the newspaper every day, by age, 1998)

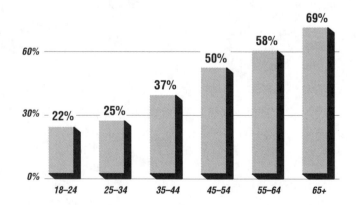

Newspaper Readership, 1998

"How often do you read the newspaper?"

(percent of people aged 18 or older responding by age, 1998)

	every day	a few times a week	once a week	less than once a week	never
Total people	43%	22%	16%	11%	8%
Aged 18 to 24	22	34	17	17	10
Aged 25 to 34	25	27	24	16	8
Aged 35 to 44	37	28	16	12	7
Aged 45 to 54	50	19	17	6	9
Aged 55 to 64	58	17	9	10	5
Aged 65 or older	69	10	7	3	10

Source: 1998 General Social Survey, National Opinion Research Center, University of Chicago; calculations by the author

Television Viewing, 1998

"On the average day, about how many hours
do you personally watch television?"

(percent of people aged 18 or older responding by age, 1998)

	none	1 to 2	3 to 4	5 or more
Total people	**5%**	**49%**	**31%**	**15%**
Aged 18 to 24	6	45	30	18
Aged 25 to 34	7	50	28	15
Aged 35 to 44	5	55	27	11
Aged 45 to 54	5	57	26	12
Aged 55 to 64	3	47	33	17
Aged 65 or older	4	32	41	23

Note: Numbers may not add to 100 because "don't know" is not shown.
Source: 1998 General Social Survey, National Opinion Research Center, University of Chicago; calculations by the author

Most Young Adults Are Online

But more than two out of five still don't use the Internet.

Today's young people are sometimes referred to as the "net generation," but they are not quite as wired as generally believed. Between 43 and 44 percent of adults under age 35 do not currently use the Internet.

More young adults would be online, especially those in the 18-to-24 age group, if computers and Internet access were less expensive. While prices for both have fallen to levels that make them accessible to the average middle-class household, many young adults have low incomes. Those with young children also have substantial expenses that prevent them from investing in online access.

♦ As the Internet evolves and the incomes of young adults rise, many more will find themselves on the information superhighway.

Young adults are not much more likely than boomers to go online

(percent of people aged 18 or older using the Internet, by age, 2000)

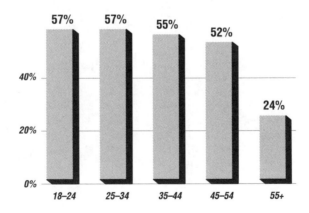

Internet Use, 2000

(percent of people aged 18 or older using the internet, by age, 2000)

	use the Internet	don't use Internet
Aged 18 to 24	57%	43%
Aged 25 to 34	57	44
Aged 35 to 44	55	45
Aged 45 to 54	52	48
Aged 55 or older	24	77

Source: National Telecommunications and Information Administration, Falling through the Net: Toward Digital Inclusion—A Report on Americans' Access to Technology Tools, *October 2000*

Young Adults Have a Different Concept of God

They are more likely then older generations to believe in a higher power.

The majority of young adults say they believe in God without a doubt. But the proportion is not as high as it is among older generations. Only 54 to 56 percent of adults under age 35 have no doubts about the existence of God. The proportion rises to 71 percent among people aged 65 or older. Fifteen percent of people aged 18 to 24 and 11 percent of those aged 25 to 34 do not believe in a "personal God," but instead believe in a "higher power of some kind." Only 3 to 5 percent of young adults do not believe in God.

Most 18-to-24-year-olds "definitely believe" in Heaven and Hell, but only 41 percent say they definitely believe in religious miracles, as do 42 percent of those aged 25 to 34. The 25-to-34 age group is slightly less likely than the youngest adults to believe in Heaven and Hell.

♦ Traditional religious organizations have been struggling to attract young adults into the fold—a problem that is likely to persist given the individualistic beliefs of the young.

Young adults are less likely than their elders to have no doubts about God

*(percent of people aged 18 or older who agree with the statement,
"I know God really exists and I have no doubts about it," by age, 1998)*

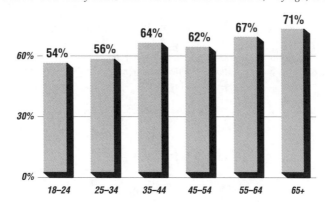

Belief in God, 1998

"Please tell me which of these statements comes closest
to expressing what you believe about God.
- I don't believe in God.
- I don't know whether there is a God and I don't
believe there is any way to find out.
- I don't believe in a personal God, but I do believe
in a Higher Power of some kind.
- I find myself believing in God some of the time, but not at others.
- While I have doubts, I feel that I do believe in God.
- I know God really exists and I have no doubts about it."

(percent of people aged 18 or older responding by age, 1998)

	don't know, don't believe	no way to find out	believe in Higher Power	believe only some of the time	believe, but have doubts	believe, have no doubts
Total people	3%	5%	10%	5%	15%	63%
Aged 18 to 24	3	8	15	3	17	54
Aged 25 to 34	5	5	11	2	21	56
Aged 35 to 44	3	5	9	5	12	64
Aged 45 to 54	3	5	10	4	15	62
Aged 55 to 64	1	4	9	6	12	67
Aged 65 or older	3	4	6	8	9	71

Note: Numbers may not add to 100 because "don't know" is not shown.
Source: 1998 General Social Survey, National Opinion Research Center, University of Chicago; calculations by the author

Belief in Heaven, Hell, and Miracles, 1998

(percent of people aged 18 or older who say they "definitely believe" in Heaven, Hell, and religious miracles, by age, 1998)

	believe in Heaven	believe in Hell	believe in miracles
Total people	**63%**	**51%**	**47%**
Aged 18 to 24	64	54	41
Aged 25 to 34	58	50	42
Aged 35 to 44	69	56	52
Aged 45 to 54	56	45	47
Aged 55 to 64	63	52	51
Aged 65 or older	65	49	48

Source: 1998 General Social Survey, National Opinion Research Center, University of Chicago; calculations by the author

Young and Old Differ on Religion

One-quarter of people aged 18 to 24 do not identify with a specific religion.

Religious differences between older and younger generations are widening. Young adults are less likely than older generations to be Protestant or to attend religious services regularly. They are more likely to say they have no religious preference.

Fewer than half of people under age 35 are Protestant. In contrast, fully 67 percent of people aged 65 or older are Protestant. Young adults are also less likely to be Jewish and more likely to be of "other" religion, such as Islam.

Fully one-quarter of people aged 18 to 24 say they have no religious preference as do 19 percent of those aged 25 to 34. This does not mean they are atheists, however. Many young people are mixing the beliefs and practices of different religions to create their own personal faith.

This trend helps explain the decline in attendance at religious services. Only 16 percent of people aged 18 to 24 and 22 percent of those aged 25 to 34 attend religious services at least once a week. More than half attend less often than once a month or not at all.

♦ The individualistic perspective of the young means they prefer to pick and choose among different belief systems to create a personalized religion.

Religious Preference, 1998

"What is your religious preference?"

(percent of people aged 18 or older responding by age, 1998)

	Protestant	Catholic	Jewish	other	none
Total people	**54%**	**25%**	**2%**	**4%**	**14%**
Aged 18 to 24	43	24	1	6	25
Aged 25 to 34	45	27	1	7	19
Aged 35 to 44	52	26	1	5	15
Aged 45 to 54	60	22	3	4	11
Aged 55 to 64	59	27	3	2	9
Aged 65 or older	67	23	2	1	6

Note: Numbers may not add to 100 because "don't know" is not shown.
Source: 1998 General Social Survey, National Opinion Research Center, University of Chicago; calculations by the author

Attendance at Religious Services, 1998

"How often do you attend religious services?"

(percent of people aged 18 or older responding by age, 1998)

	at least weekly	at least monthly, but less than once a week	once to several times a year	less than once a year or never
Total people	**32%**	**16%**	**22%**	**30%**
Aged 18 to 24	16	19	26	39
Aged 25 to 34	22	18	28	31
Aged 35 to 44	31	17	22	30
Aged 45 to 54	35	16	21	28
Aged 55 to 64	34	13	21	31
Aged 65 or older	50	13	12	25

Source: 1998 General Social Survey, National Opinion Research Center, University of Chicago; calculations by the author

Young Adults Are Politically Independent

Those with a party affiliation are most likely to be Democrats.

Today's young adults are more likely to identify themselves as political independents than as Republicans or Democrats. More than half the people aged 18 to 24 and 41 percent of those aged 25 to 34 say they are independent compared with 38 percent of all adults.

Among young adults who do have a political party affiliation, Democrats claim the larger share. Only 19 percent of people aged 18 to 24 consider themselves Republicans while 28 percent say they are Democrats. Among people aged 25 to 34, only 24 percent are Republicans compared with 31 percent Democrats.

Only 25 to 39 percent of adults under age 35 consider themselves conservative. The remainder are almost evenly split between moderates and liberals. Liberalism has had a bad run during the last couple of decades, but in general, the generations born after World War II are still more liberal than older Americans.

♦ As the Millennial generation began entering the young-adult age group, the proportions of young adults who say they are liberals and Democrats have grown slightly. This shift may represent another swing of the pendulum in American politics.

Young adults are more liberal than their elders

(percent of people aged 18 or older who consider themselves slightly to extremely liberal, by age, 1998)

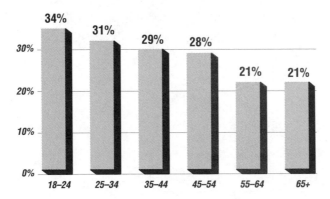

Political Leaning, 1998

"We hear a lot of talk these days about liberals and conservatives.
On a seven-point scale from extremely liberal to extremely conservative,
where would you place yourself?"

(percent of people aged 18 or older responding by age, 1998)

	slightly to extremely liberal	moderate, middle of the road	slightly to extremely conservative
Total people	**27%**	**35%**	**33%**
Aged 18 to 24	34	34	25
Aged 25 to 34	31	35	29
Aged 35 to 44	29	31	36
Aged 45 to 54	28	36	32
Aged 55 to 64	21	38	37
Aged 65 or older	21	37	36

Note: Numbers may not add to 100 because "don't know" is not shown.
Source: 1998 General Social Survey, National Opinion Research Center, University of Chicago; calculations by the author

Political Party Identification, 1998

"Generally speaking, do you usually think of yourself as a
Republican, Democrat, independent, or what?"

(percent of people aged 18 or older responding by age, 1998)

	Democrat	Independent	Republican
Total people	**34%**	**38%**	**26%**
Aged 18 to 24	28	52	19
Aged 25 to 34	31	41	24
Aged 35 to 44	31	40	27
Aged 45 to 54	35	39	25
Aged 55 to 64	39	33	27
Aged 65 or older	43	27	29

Note: Numbers may not add to 100 because "don't know" and other are shown.
Source: 1998 General Social Survey, National Opinion Research Center, University of Chicago; calculations by the author

Confidence in Education Is Highest among the Youngest Adults

Two out of five 18-to-24-year-olds have confidence in the leaders of the educational establishment.

The youngest adults are more likely than average to say they have a "great deal of confidence" in most of the nation's government and industry leaders. The biggest difference of opinion surrounds the educational system. Forty percent of people aged 18 to 24 have a great deal of confidence in education compared with only 27 percent of all adults. A smaller 25 percent of people aged 25 to 34 (many of whom have children in school) have a great deal of confidence in education.

The youngest adults are also more likely to have a great deal of confidence in medicine. Fifty-five percent of people aged 18 to 24 have a great deal of confidence in medical leaders compared with 43 percent of people aged 25 to 34 and 44 percent of all adults.

♦ The higher confidence of young adults in the nation's leaders likely reflects the general optimism of Millennials, in contrast to the more cynical view of Generation Xers. It remains to be seen whether young adults will become more pessimistic as they gain experience.

Confidence in education drops off sharply beginning at age 25

(percent of people aged 18 or older who have a "great deal of confidence" in the people running the educational system, by age, 1998)

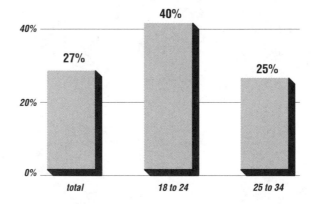

Confidence in Leaders, 1998

"As far as the people running the following institutions are concerned, would you say you have a great deal of confidence, only some confidence, or hardly any confidence at all in them?"

(percent of people aged 18 or older and aged 18 to 34 responding, by age, 1998)

	a great deal of confidence			only some confidence			hardly any confidence		
	total	18 to 24	25 to 34	total	18 to 24	25 to34	total	18 to 24	25 to 34
Medicine	44%	55%	43%	45%	35%	47%	9%	7%	9%
Scientific community	40	49	43	45	38	43	8	5	9
Military	36	41	30	49	40	52	12	16	14
Supreme Court	31	43	30	50	41	50	14	10	17
Religion	27	27	24	51	49	51	19	20	22
Education	27	40	25	55	46	57	17	13	17
Banks and financial institutions	26	38	24	56	46	58	16	13	17
Major companies	26	29	28	56	59	57	13	9	12
Executive branch of government	14	16	13	48	49	50	35	30	35
Organized labor	11	15	12	52	60	58	29	16	23
Congress	11	16	11	56	54	57	30	26	29
Television	10	14	11	49	55	54	39	30	33
The press	9	13	10	46	44	47	42	39	42

Note: Numbers may not add to 100 because "don't know" is not shown.
Source: 1998 General Social Survey, National Opinion Research Center, University of Chicago; calculations by the author

Young People Are Pessimistic about Social Security

Most expect to get fewer benefits than today's retirees do.

The majority of people under age 35 believe the Social Security system is in serious trouble. Among people aged 18 to 24, fully 45 percent think the system needs major changes and 16 percent believe it is beyond repair and should be replaced. But 27 percent think only minor changes are required to preserve the program's viability.

People aged 25 to 34 have less confidence in the possibility of fixing Social Security. Only 17 percent think minor changes will solve the problems, while 53 percent believe a major overhaul is needed. Twenty-one percent believe the current system needs to be scrapped.

Few young adults believe they will receive better Social Security benefits than today's retirees. Most believe their benefits will be lower. People aged 25 to 34 are especially pessimistic—fully 46 percent believe future benefits will be much worse.

◆ Young adults are likely to benefit from today's concern over Social Security regardless of what happens to the program because the attention on Social Security's problems has prompted many to begin saving for retirement at a much earlier age than older generations did.

How Serious Is the Social Security Problem? 1998

"Please tell me which of the following statements comes closest to your opinion about the Social Security program. The Social Security program has no serious problems, certainly none that require changing the current system; has minor problems that can be fixed with minor changes; problems are serious and can be fixed only with major changes; problems are so bad the current system should be replaced."

(percent of people aged 18 or older responding by age, 1998)

	no serious problems	minor problems	need major changes	need to replace current system
Total people	**5%**	**22%**	**52%**	**16%**
Aged 18 to 24	3	27	45	16
Aged 25 to 34	5	17	53	21
Aged 35 to 44	2	15	57	21
Aged 45 to 54	3	23	53	18
Aged 55 to 64	5	25	54	8
Aged 65 or older	11	34	42	4

Note: Numbers may not add to 100 because "don't know" is not shown.
Source: 1998 General Social Survey, National Opinion Research Center, University of Chicago; calculations by the author

Future Social Security Benefits, 1998

"When you retire, do you think Social Security benefits will be
much better than those now paid to retirees, somewhat better,
about the same, somewhat worse, or much worse?"

(percent of people aged 18 or older responding, by age, 1998)

	much better	somewhat better	about the same	somewhat worse	much worse
Total people	2%	7%	24%	27%	32%
Aged 18 to 24	5	8	22	28	29
Aged 25 to 34	3	6	13	25	46
Aged 35 to 44	1	4	13	34	44
Aged 45 to 54	1	7	23	34	31
Aged 55 to 64	1	2	55	28	8
Aged 65 or older	5	13	42	10	5

Note: Numbers may not add to 100 because "don't know" is not shown.
Source: 1998 General Social Survey, National Opinion Research Center, University of Chicago; calculations by the author

Young Adults Are More Likely to Condone Cheating

Many think it's not seriously wrong to cheat on taxes.

Today's young people are often undeservedly maligned, but in one area they may be living down to their reputation. People under age 35 are more likely than their elders to believe it is OK to underreport income in order to pay less tax. One-third of people aged 35 or older believe it is "seriously wrong" to lie on a tax return compared with a smaller 27 percent of people aged 25 to 34 and just 19 percent of those aged 18 to 24.

Young adults are less likely to approve of lying to receive government benefits. Fifty-three percent of people aged 18 to 34 say it is seriously wrong, equal to the percentage of all adults who say so. But while only 1 to 4 percent of people aged 35 or older say it is not wrong or only "a bit wrong" to lie to receive benefits, a larger 6 to 8 percent of young adults feel this way.

♦ Young adults often don't have the money to make ends meet. This struggle is one factor in their greater likelihood of believing it is OK to fudge the truth. Perhaps their ethics will improve as they grow older.

Young adults think it's worse to lie for benefits than to save on taxes

(percent of people aged 18 to 34 who say it is "seriously wrong" to underreport income to reduce taxes or to give false information to receive government benefits, 1998)

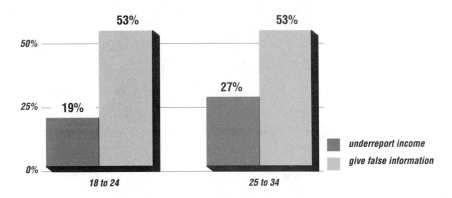

■ underreport income
■ give false information

Wrong to Cheat on Taxes? 1998

"Do you feel it is wrong or not wrong if a taxpayer does not report all of his income in order to pay less income taxes?"

(percent of people aged 18 or older responding by age, 1998)

	not wrong	a bit wrong	wrong	seriously wrong
Total people	5%	10%	50%	31%
Aged 18 to 24	7	11	52	19
Aged 25 to 34	7	17	45	27
Aged 35 to 44	3	9	50	34
Aged 45 to 54	6	9	49	33
Aged 55 to 64	3	6	55	33
Aged 65 or older	2	6	51	33

Note: Numbers may not add to 100 because "can't choose" is not shown.
Source: 1998 General Social Survey, National Opinion Research Center, University of Chicago; calculations by the author

Wrong to Lie to Receive Government Benefits? 1998

"Do you feel it is wrong or not wrong if a person gives
the government incorrect information about himself
to get government benefits that he is not entitled to?"

(percent of people aged 18 or older responding, by age, 1998)

	not wrong	a bit wrong	wrong	seriously wrong
Total people	**2%**	**3%**	**41%**	**53%**
Aged 18 to 24	2	6	34	53
Aged 25 to 34	2	4	38	53
Aged 35 to 44	2	2	40	55
Aged 45 to 54	2	2	43	53
Aged 55 to 64	2	1	43	54
Aged 65 or older	0	1	46	49

Note: Numbers may not add to 100 because "don't know" is not shown.
Source: 1998 General Social Survey, National Opinion Research Center, University of Chicago; calculations by the author

Changing Sexual Mores

Younger generations have more liberal attitudes about sex.

Although today's young adults grew up in the era of AIDS, they generally share their parents' "free-love" era attitudes about sexuality. Young adults are less likely than their elders to believe homosexuality is wrong. Only 39 percent of adults under age 25 and 43 percent of those aged 25 to 34 believe it is "always wrong" for adults of the same sex to engage in sexual relations. In contrast, a much larger 62 to 74 percent of people aged 55 or older believe it is always wrong. Four out of ten adults under age 35 believe homosexuality is not wrong compared with one-quarter of those aged 35 to 44 and only 12 percent of people aged 65 or older.

The opinions of young adults and baby boomers about premarital sex are similar. Slightly fewer than one-quarter of people aged 18 to 24 and aged 35 to 54 believe premarital sex is always wrong. Among young adults aged 25 to 34, the share is an even smaller 17 percent. These opinions stand in contrast to those of people aged 65 or older, 41 percent of whom say premarital sex is always wrong.

♦ Young adults' more liberal position on sexuality puts them at odds with many of the members of the World War II generation who still hold power in government and industry.

Premarital Sex, 1998

"If a man and woman have sex relations before marriage,
do you think it is always wrong, almost always wrong,
wrong only sometimes, or not wrong at all?"

(percent of people aged 18 or older responding by age, 1998)

	always wrong	almost always wrong	wrong only sometimes	not wrong at all
Total people	**25%**	**9%**	**20%**	**42%**
Aged 18 to 24	22	8	26	43
Aged 25 to 34	17	7	19	55
Aged 35 to 44	23	9	20	46
Aged 45 to 54	24	6	17	50
Aged 55 to 64	27	13	22	33
Aged 65 or older	41	13	23	16

Note: Numbers may not add to 100 because "don't know" is not shown.
Source: 1998 General Social Survey, National Opinion Research Center, University of Chicago; calculations by the author

Homosexual Sex, 1998

"What about sexual relations between two adults of the same sex—
do you think it is always wrong, almost always wrong,
wrong only sometimes, or not wrong at all?"

(percent of people aged 18 or older responding by age, 1998)

	always wrong	almost always wrong	wrong only sometimes	not wrong at all
Total people	**54%**	**5%**	**6%**	**27%**
Aged 18 to 24	39	7	7	39
Aged 25 to 34	43	4	7	39
Aged 35 to 44	56	6	7	25
Aged 45 to 54	49	7	8	31
Aged 55 to 64	62	5	4	21
Aged 65 or older	74	4	5	12

Note: Numbers may not add to 100 because "don't know" is not shown.
Source: 1998 General Social Survey, National Opinion Research Center, University of Chicago; calculations by the author

Popular Culture Is "The Arts" for Young Adults

They are most likely to go to movies and popular music concerts.

Young adults' attendance at "high culture" art events is at or below average. Offer them a movie or a popular music concert, however, and their attendance will be significantly above average.

Young adults are less likely than average to visit an art museum or gallery, attend a play, or take in a ballet or classical dance performance. They are just as likely as the average adult to attend a classical music or opera performance—but few adults of any age attend those types of events.

What brings young adults out in droves are movies and popular music. Fully 87 percent of people aged 18 to 24 and 79 percent of those aged 25 to 34 have attended at least one movie in the past year. In contrast, a smaller 66 percent of all adults went to see a movie. Only 38 percent of all adults attended a popular music performance in the past year compared with 53 percent of people aged 18 to 24 and 46 percent of those aged 25 to 34.

♦ Young adults are more likely to attend movies and popular music concerts because those forms of entertainment are targeted directly at their age group. Many will broaden their interests as they age and come to view popular culture as "too youthful."

Arts and Entertainment, 1998

"Here are some leisure or recreational activities that people do during their free time. Is this something you have done in the past 12 months?"

(percent of people aged 18 or older and people aged 18 to 34 who say they have participated in selected arts and entertainment events, 1998)

	total	18 to 24	25 to 34
Read novels, poems, or plays	68%	64%	70%
Go out to see a movie	66	87	79
Attend popular music performance	38	53	46
Visit art museum or gallery	37	32	33
Attend nonmusical stage play	24	21	21
Attend live ballet or dance performance	20	16	18
Attend classical music or opera performance	17	16	17

Note: Events do not include school performances or reading required for work or school.
Source: 1998 General Social Survey, National Opinion Research Center, University of Chicago; calculations by the author

Education

♦ Today's young women are better educated than any previous generation of women. Thirty percent of women aged 25 to 34 have at least a bachelor's degree.

♦ Young women are pulling ahead of men in educational attainment. Sixty percent of women aged 25 to 34 have at least some college experience compared with 55 percent of their male counterparts.

♦ Among young adults, Asians have the highest educational attainment. More than half of non-Hispanic Asians aged 25 to 34 have a college degree.

♦ Hispanics are the least educated young adults. Among Hispanics aged 25 to 34, only 59 percent of men and 64 percent of women are high school graduates.

♦ The number of 25-to-34-year-olds participating in adult education grew from 48 percent in 1995 to the 56 percent majority in 1999.

More Than One-Quarter of Young Men Are College Graduates

Many of those without a college degree will get one later in life.

Eighty-seven percent of men aged 25 to 34 are high school graduates. The proportion of young men who did not finish high school has hovered around 13 percent for decades. While this is a much smaller proportion than the 50 percent who had not completed high school in 1950, it still represents a substantial number of young men who will have difficulty making ends meet in an economic environment that rewards the well-educated.

More than half of men aged 25 to 34 have attended college, while 29 percent have a college degree. Although about half of young men who start college drop out, some are likely to return to school and complete their education.

It now takes six years, on average, to obtain an undergraduate degree, so it is understandable that few men in their twenties have postgraduate degrees. Among men aged 30 to 34, 8 percent have advanced degrees.

♦ Most young men are aware of the importance of education for their careers. Even if they do not obtain a college degree, attending college for a year or two will boost their earnings significantly.

Most men aged 25 to 34 have at least some college experience

(educational attainment of men aged 25 to 34, in percent, 2000)

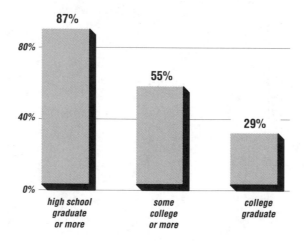

Educational Attainment of Men Aged 25 to 34, 2000

(number and percent distribution of men aged 25 or older and aged 25 to 34 by highest level of education, 2000; numbers in thousands)

	total	25 to 34	25 to 29	30 to 34
Total men	**83,611**	**18,563**	**8,942**	**9,621**
Not a high school graduate	13,215	2,386	1,186	1,200
High school graduate only	26,651	5,989	2,831	3,158
Some college, no degree	14,540	3,483	1,770	1,713
Associate's degree	5,953	1,387	657	730
Bachelor's degree	14,909	4,134	2,079	2,055
Master's degree	5,166	801	287	514
Professional degree	1,752	241	96	145
Doctoral degree	1,425	142	36	106
High school graduate or more	70,396	16,177	7,756	8,421
Some college or more	43,745	10,188	4,925	5,263
Bachelor's degree or more	23,252	5,318	2,498	2,820
Total men	**100.0%**	**100.0%**	**100.0%**	**100.0%**
Not a high school graduate	15.8	12.9	13.3	12.5
High school graduate only	31.9	32.3	31.7	32.8
Some college, no degree	17.4	18.8	19.8	17.8
Associate's degree	7.1	7.5	7.3	7.6
Bachelor's degree	17.8	22.3	23.2	21.4
Master's degree	6.2	4.3	3.2	5.3
Professional degree	2.1	1.3	1.1	1.5
Doctoral degree	1.7	0.8	0.4	1.1
High school graduate or more	84.2	87.1	86.7	87.5
Some college or more	52.3	54.9	55.1	54.7
Bachelor's degree or more	27.8	28.6	27.9	29.3

Source: Bureau of the Census, detailed tables from Educational Attainment in the United States (Update): March 2000, *Current Population Reports, P20-536, 2000; Internet site <www.census.gov/population/www/socdemo/educ-attn.html>; calculations by the author*

Young Women Are Better Educated Than Young Men

Young women are more likely than young men to attend and complete college.

As educational opportunities for women broadened over the years, increasing numbers of women took advantage. Women aged 25 to 34 have not only caught up to the high school and college completion rates of their male counterparts, they have surpassed them.

Women aged 25 to 34 are the best educated women in the nation's history. Thirty percent have at least a bachelor's degree, and 60 percent have at least some college experience. Among men aged 25 to 34, a smaller 29 percent have a bachelor's degree while 55 percent have college experience.

The higher educational attainment of women born after World War II has contributed greatly to the changing roles of women in society. With greater education, young women expect more opportunity in the workplace. While many will still encounter obstacles to advancement, young women will continue to expand the boundaries of women's achievements.

♦ With well over half of young women entering college after high school, the share with a college degree is likely to increase in the coming years, as will the proportion with advanced or professional degrees.

Young women are better educated than young men

(educational attainment of women aged 25 to 34, in percent, 2000)

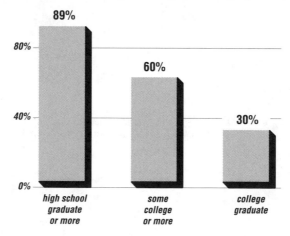

Educational Attainment of Women Aged 25 to 34, 2000

(number and percent distribution of women aged 25 or older and aged 25 to 34 by highest level of education, 2000; numbers in thousands)

	total	*25 to 34*	*25 to 29*	*30 to 34*
Total women	**91,620**	**19,222**	**9,326**	**9,896**
Not a high school graduate	14,638	2,084	987	1,097
High school graduate only	31,435	5,557	2,604	2,953
Some college, no degree	16,213	3,893	1,992	1,901
Associate's degree	7,740	1,938	932	1,006
Bachelor's degree	14,931	4,428	2,234	2,194
Master's degree	5,230	978	449	529
Professional degree	834	238	89	149
Doctoral degree	599	106	39	67
High school graduate or more	76,982	17,138	8,339	8,799
Some college or more	45,547	11,581	5,735	5,846
Bachelor's degree or more	21,594	5,750	2,811	2,939
Total women	**100.0%**	**100.0%**	**100.0%**	**100.0%**
Not a high school graduate	16.0	10.8	10.6	11.1
High school graduate only	34.3	28.9	27.9	29.8
Some college, no degree	17.7	20.3	21.4	19.2
Associate's degree	8.4	10.1	10.0	10.2
Bachelor's degree	16.3	23.0	24.0	22.2
Master's degree	5.7	5.1	4.8	5.3
Professional degree	0.9	1.2	1.1	1.5
Doctoral degree	0.7	0.6	0.4	0.7
High school graduate or more	84.0	89.2	89.4	88.9
Some college or more	49.7	60.2	61.5	59.1
Bachelor's degree or more	23.6	29.9	30.1	29.7

Source: Bureau of the Census, detailed tables from Educational Attainment in the United States (Update): March 2000, *Current Population Reports, P20-536, 2000; Internet site <www.census.gov/population/www/socdemo/educ-attn.html>; calculations by the author*

Asian-American Men Have the Highest Educational Attainment

Hispanics are least likely to have completed high school.

There are substantial socioeconomic differences between Americans of different racial and ethnic backgrounds. Differences in educational attainment are the primary reason for the disparity.

Among young-adult men, non-Hispanic whites and Asian Americans have considerably more education than non-Hispanic blacks and Hispanics. Fully 93 percent of Asian and white men aged 25 to 34 are high school graduates compared with 89 percent of blacks and only 59 percent of Hispanics.

Asian-American men also have a considerably higher college graduation rate. Three-quarters have attended college compared with 61 percent of whites and fewer than half of blacks and Hispanics. Half of Asian-American men aged 25 to 34 have at least a bachelor's degree, as do one-third of white men in the age group. In contrast, only 18 percent of black men and 9 percent of Hispanic men are college graduates.

◆ Many young Hispanic men are recent immigrants who did not have the opportunity to complete high school in their native country. As the Hispanic population grows to include more second- and third-generation immigrants, educational attainment among Hispanics is likely to increase.

Education gaps point to continued socioeconomic differences

(percent of men aged 25 to 34 with a bachelor's degree or more, by race and Hispanic origin, 2000)

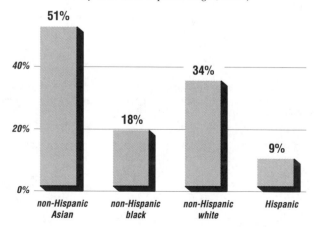

Educational Attainment of Men Aged 25 to 34 by Race and Hispanic Origin, 2000

(number and percent distribution of men aged 25 to 34 by educational attainment, race, and Hispanic origin, 2000; numbers in thousands)

	non-Hispanic			
	Asian	*black*	*white*	*Hispanic*
Total men	**932**	**2,196**	**12,454**	**2,855**
Not a high school graduate	69	247	866	1,172
High school graduate only	157	925	3,988	870
Some college, no degree	170	499	2,380	414
Associate's degree	65	127	1,036	153
Bachelor's degree	289	335	3,303	197
Master's degree	121	54	587	30
Professional degree	35	6	187	13
Doctoral degree	26	3	107	6
High school graduate or more	863	1,949	11,588	1,683
Some college or more	706	1,024	7,600	813
Bachelor's degree or more	471	398	4,184	246
Total men	**100.0%**	**100.0%**	**100.0%**	**100.0%**
Not a high school graduate	7.4	11.2	7.0	41.1
High school graduate only	16.8	42.1	32.0	30.5
Some college, no degree	18.2	22.7	19.1	14.5
Associate's degree	7.0	5.8	8.3	5.4
Bachelor's degree	31.0	15.3	26.5	6.9
Master's degree	13.0	2.5	4.7	1.1
Professional degree	3.8	0.3	1.5	0.5
Doctoral degree	2.8	0.1	0.9	0.2
High school graduate or more	92.6	88.8	93.0	58.9
Some college or more	75.8	46.6	61.0	28.5
Bachelor's degree or more	50.5	18.1	33.6	8.6

Note: Hispanics may be of any race.
Source: Bureau of the Census, detailed tables from Educational Attainment in the United States (Update):
March 2000, *Current Population Reports, P20-536, 2000; Internet site <www.census.gov/population/www/
socdemo/educ-attn.html>; calculations by the author*

Hispanic Women Are Least Likely to Finish High School

Women's educational attainment is rising, but Hispanic women still lag behind.

Although the educational attainment of women has been rising for decades, substantial gaps persist by race and ethnicity. Only 5 to 6 percent of non-Hispanic white and Asian-American women aged 25 to 34 did not complete high school compared with 12 percent of non-Hispanic black women in the age group. But fully 36 percent of Hispanic women aged 25 to 34 did not complete high school.

There are large differences by race and ethnicity in college graduation rates as well. Among 25-to-34-year-old women, more than half of Asian Americans and more than one-third of whites have at least a bachelor's degree. In contrast, a smaller 18 percent of blacks and 11 percent of Hispanics are college graduates.

♦ The aspirations of today's young women are evidenced by their high rate of college attendance. Their educational investment is likely to be rewarded as they advance in their careers.

Young Asian women have the highest educational attainment

(percent of women aged 25 to 34 with a bachelor's degree or more, by race and Hispanic origin, 2000)

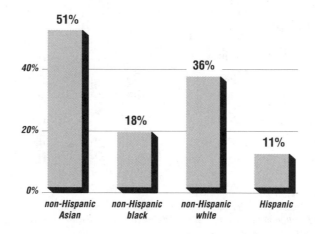

Educational Attainment of Women Aged 25 to 34 by Race and Hispanic Origin, 2000

(number and percent distribution of women aged 25 to 34 by educational attainment, race, and Hispanic origin, 2000; numbers in thousands)

	non-Hispanic			Hispanic
	Asian	*black*	*white*	*Hispanic*
Total women	**964**	**2,740**	**12,526**	**2,805**
Not a high school graduate	60	339	653	1,003
High school graduate only	172	926	3,567	830
Some college, no degree	169	709	2,483	491
Associate's degree	68	284	1,373	180
Bachelor's degree	328	340	3,515	228
Master's degree	107	113	708	45
Professional degree	38	22	159	19
Doctoral degree	22	7	68	9
High school graduate or more	904	2,401	11,873	1,802
Some college or more	732	1,475	8,306	972
Bachelor's degree or more	495	482	4,450	301
Total women	**100.0%**	**100.0%**	**100.0%**	**100.0%**
Not a high school graduate	6.2	12.4	5.2	35.8
High school graduate only	17.8	33.8	28.5	29.6
Some college, no degree	17.5	25.9	19.8	17.5
Associate's degree	7.1	10.4	11.0	6.4
Bachelor's degree	34.0	12.4	28.1	8.1
Master's degree	11.1	4.1	5.7	1.6
Professional degree	3.9	0.8	1.3	0.7
Doctoral degree	2.3	0.3	0.5	0.3
High school graduate or more	93.8	87.6	94.8	64.2
Some college or more	75.9	53.8	66.3	34.7
Bachelor's degree or more	51.3	17.6	35.5	10.7

Note: Hispanics may be of any race.
Source: Bureau of the Census, detailed tables from Educational Attainment in the United States (Update): March 2000, *Current Population Reports, P20-536, 2000; Internet site <www.census.gov/population/www/socdemo/educ-attn.html>; calculations by the author*

Many Young Adults Are Still in School

Three out of ten people aged 16 to 34 are students.

For young adults, school is a major part of life. The majority of 16-to-19-year-olds are in school, as are 45 percent of people aged 20 to 21. The proportion drops to a still-substantial 25 percent among those aged 22 to 24. Even among people aged 25 to 29, 11 percent are students. The enrollment rate falls well below 10 percent among people aged 30 to 34, however.

For the past few decades, the proportion of women who go to college has been rising. Women are now more likely than men to be college students. Of the 12.5 million people aged 16 to 34 enrolled in college, 47 percent are men and 53 percent are women.

♦ As the number of young adults grows, competition for enrollment slots at the nation's colleges is increasing.

The share of young adults enrolled in school drops sharply with age

(percent of people aged 16 to 34 enrolled in school, 1999)

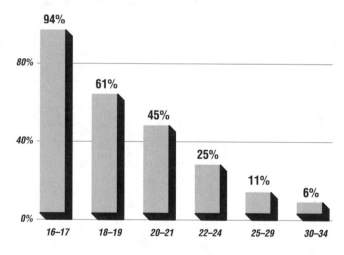

School Enrollment of People Aged 16 to 34 by Sex, 1999

(number and percent of people aged 16 or older and aged 16 to 34 enrolled in school by sex and age, 1999; numbers in thousands)

| | | enrolled in school | | | | | |
| | | total | | below college level | | in college | |
	total	number	percent	number	percent	number	percent
Total, aged 16 or older	**208,483**	**24,398**	**11.7%**	**9,204**	**4.4%**	**15,194**	**7.3%**
Total, aged 16 to 34	71,924	21,604	30.0	9,108	12.7	12,496	17.4
Aged 16 to 17	8,131	7,611	93.6	7,470	91.9	141	1.7
Aged 18 to 19	7,991	4,840	60.6	1,320	16.5	3,520	44.0
Aged 20 to 21	7,196	3,256	45.2	137	1.9	3,119	43.3
Aged 22 to 24	10,855	2,664	24.5	44	0.4	2,620	24.1
Aged 25 to 29	18,250	2,018	11.1	78	0.4	1,940	10.6
Aged 30 to 34	19,501	1,215	6.2	59	0.3	1,156	5.9
Aged 35 or older	136,559	2,794	2.0	96	0.1	2,698	2.0
Total men, aged 16 or older	**100,089**	**11,782**	**11.8**	**4,828**	**4.8**	**6,954**	**6.9**
Total, aged 16 to 34	35,583	10,724	30.1	4,794	13.5	5,930	16.7
Aged 16 to 17	4,201	3,935	93.7	3,860	91.9	75	1.8
Aged 18 to 19	4,026	2,428	60.3	780	19.4	1,648	40.9
Aged 20 to 21	3,590	1,604	44.7	79	2.2	1,525	42.5
Aged 22 to 24	5,290	1,250	23.6	26	0.5	1,224	23.1
Aged 25 to 29	8,881	951	10.7	40	0.5	911	10.3
Aged 30 to 34	9,595	556	5.8	9	0.1	547	5.7
Aged 35 or older	64,506	1,058	1.6	34	0.1	1,024	1.6
Total women, aged 16 or older	**108,395**	**12,615**	**11.6**	**4,374**	**4.0**	**8,241**	**7.6**
Total, aged 16 to 34	36,341	10,878	29.9	4,312	11.9	6,566	18.1
Aged 16 to 17	3,930	3,675	93.5	3,609	91.8	66	1.7
Aged 18 to 19	3,965	2,413	60.9	541	13.6	1,872	47.2
Aged 20 to 21	3,606	1,652	45.8	57	1.6	1,595	44.2
Aged 22 to 24	5,565	1,414	25.4	18	0.3	1,396	25.1
Aged 25 to 29	9,369	1,066	11.4	37	0.4	1,029	11.0
Aged 30 to 34	9,906	658	6.6	50	0.5	608	6.1
Aged 35 or older	72,054	1,737	2.4	62	0.1	1,675	2.3

Source: Bureau of the Census, detailed tables for School Enrollment in the United States—Social and Economic Characteristics of Students: October 1999, *Current Population Reports, P20-533, 2001; calculations by the author*

Most College Students Are under Age 25

One-quarter are aged 30 or older, however.

Although college enrollment among people aged 35 or older has grown over the years, young adults still dominate the nation's college campuses. In 1999, fully 62 percent of college students were aged 15 to 24.

Few students begin college before age 18, and a remarkably large number are still plugging away in their late twenties and early thirties. While 44 percent of college students are aged 18 to 21, another 20 percent are aged 25 to 34.

While most college students attend four-year institutions, a sizable number are enrolled in two-year colleges. Of the nation's 12 million undergraduates, 31 percent are enrolled in two-year colleges.

Undergraduates are most likely to be under age 25, while graduate students are more commonly aged 25 or older. In fact, many of today's young adults will be pursuing an education until they are in their late thirties or early forties. Thirty-eight percent of graduate students are aged 35 or older.

♦ Two-year institutions are becoming more important as low-income young adults attempt to improve their employment prospects through higher education. Although many stop with an associate's degree, some will go on to complete a bachelor's degree at a four-year institution.

College Students Aged 15 to 34 by Level of Enrollment, 1999

(number and percent of people aged 15 or older and aged 15 to 34 enrolled in college by age and level of enrollment, 1999: numbers in thousands)

		enrolled in college			
		total	undergraduate		graduate
	total		two-year college	four-year college	
Total, aged 15 or older	**212,400**	**15,203**	**3,794**	**8,252**	**3,157**
Total, aged 15 to 34	75,841	12,507	3,043	7,509	1,953
Aged 15 to 17	12,048	151	45	102	3
Aged 18 to 19	7,991	3,520	1141	2337	42
Aged 20 to 21	7,196	3,120	715	2329	77
Aged 22 to 24	10,855	2,620	460	1539	620
Aged 25 to 29	18,250	1,940	407	785	747
Aged 30 to 34	19,501	1,156	275	417	464
Aged 35 or older	136,559	2,698	752	746	1204
Percent distribution by age					
Total people	**100.0%**	**100.0%**	**100.0%**	**100.0%**	**100.0%**
Total, aged 15 to 34	35.7	82.3	80.2	91.0	61.9
Aged 15 to 17	5.7	1.0	1.2	1.2	0.1
Aged 18 to 19	3.8	23.2	30.1	28.3	1.3
Aged 20 to 21	3.4	20.5	18.8	28.2	2.4
Aged 22 to 24	5.1	17.2	12.1	18.7	19.6
Aged 25 to 29	8.6	12.8	10.7	9.5	23.7
Aged 30 to 34	9.2	7.6	7.2	5.1	14.7
Aged 35 or older	64.3	17.7	19.8	9.0	38.1
Percent distribution by type of school					
Total people	**100.0%**	**7.2%**	**1.8%**	**3.9%**	**1.5%**
Total, aged 15 to 34	100.0	16.5	4.0	9.9	2.6
Aged 15 to 17	100.0	1.3	0.4	0.8	0.0
Aged 18 to 19	100.0	44.0	14.3	29.2	0.5
Aged 20 to 21	100.0	43.4	9.9	32.4	1.1
Aged 22 to 24	100.0	24.1	4.2	14.2	5.7
Aged 25 to 29	100.0	10.6	2.2	4.3	4.1
Aged 30 to 34	100.0	5.9	1.4	2.1	2.4
Aged 35 or older	100.0	2.0	0.6	0.5	0.9

Source: Bureau of the Census, detailed tables for School Enrollment in the United States—Social and Economic Characteristics of Students: October 1999, *Current Population Reports, P20-533, 2001; calculations by the author*

College Campuses Are Becoming More Youthful

The large Millennial generation is beginning to reverse the aging of the student body.

For years, college students have been getting older along with the population as a whole. But thanks to the Millennial generation (the children of baby boomers), colleges are about to get a little younger again. In 2001, a substantial 21 percent of college students were aged 35 or older. By 2010, the figure will have dropped to 18 percent. The percentage of students under age 35 will rise from 79 to 82 percent.

Continuing a trend that is already underway, the gender balance on college campuses will tip even more to females. In 2001, fully 57 percent of college students were women, a figure that will increase slightly to 58 percent by 2010.

♦ With the student body getting younger, colleges may face more disciplinary problems from rowdy teens.

A smaller share of students will be aged 35 or older

(percent distribution of college students by age, 2001 and 2010)

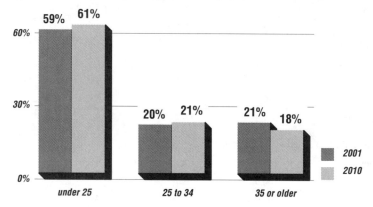

Projections of College Students by Age, 2001 and 2010

(number and percent distribution of people aged 14 or older enrolled in institutions of higher education, by age, 2001 to 2010; numbers in thousands)

	2001			2010		
	total	*men*	*women*	*total*	*men*	*women*
Total students	**15,361**	**6,565**	**8,796**	**17,490**	**7,320**	**10,169**
Aged 14 to 17	206	99	107	258	113	145
Aged 18 to 19	3,473	1,544	1,929	4,077	1,761	2,316
Aged 20 to 21	3,037	1,408	1,629	3,569	1,607	1,962
Aged 22 to 24	2,397	1,161	1,236	2,831	1,342	1,488
Aged 25 to 29	1,922	898	1,023	2,383	1,089	1,294
Aged 30 to 34	1,139	431	708	1,258	443	815
Aged 35 or older	3,188	1,024	2,165	3,115	965	2,150
Percent distribution by age						
Total students	**100.0%**	**100.0%**	**100.0%**	**100.0%**	**100.0%**	**100.0%**
Aged 14 to 17	1.3	1.5	1.2	1.5	1.5	1.4
Aged 18 to 19	22.6	23.5	21.9	23.3	24.1	22.8
Aged 20 to 21	19.8	21.4	18.5	20.4	22.0	19.3
Aged 22 to 24	15.6	17.7	14.1	16.2	18.3	14.6
Aged 25 to 29	12.5	13.7	11.6	13.6	14.9	12.7
Aged 30 to 34	7.4	6.6	8.0	7.2	6.1	8.0
Aged 35 or older	20.8	15.6	24.6	17.8	13.2	21.1
Percent distribution by sex						
Total students	**100.0%**	**42.7%**	**57.3%**	**100.0%**	**41.9%**	**58.1%**
Aged 14 to 17	100.0	48.1	51.9	100.0	43.8	56.2
Aged 18 to 19	100.0	44.5	55.5	100.0	43.2	56.8
Aged 20 to 21	100.0	46.4	53.6	100.0	45.0	55.0
Aged 22 to 24	100.0	48.4	51.6	100.0	47.4	52.6
Aged 25 to 29	100.0	46.7	53.2	100.0	45.7	54.3
Aged 30 to 34	100.0	37.8	62.2	100.0	35.2	64.8
Aged 35 or older	100.0	32.1	67.9	100.0	31.0	69.0

Source: National Center for Education Statistics, Projections of Education Statistics to 2010, *2000; Internet site <www.nces.ed.gov/edstats>; calculations by the author*

Young Adults Are Most Likely to Participate in Adult Education

Because of their already-high level of education, young adults are likely to be lifelong learners.

As Americans have become more educated, they have become more appreciative of education. Young adults are no exception. Fifty-two percent of people aged 16 to 24 participated in adult education in 1999, up 5 percentage points from 1995. Among 25-to-34-year-olds, 56 percent participated in adult education, 8 percentage points more than in 1995.

Young adults are more likely than their elders to participate in adult education, primarily because young adults are seeking training and education to further their careers. As people grow older, their reasons for participating in adult education shift to more personal ones.

♦ The share of young adults seeking education opportunities is likely to increase. As the economy becomes even more information-based, lifelong learning will become increasingly necessary for success.

Participation in adult education is highest among young adults

(percent of people aged 16 or older participating in adult education, by age, 1999)

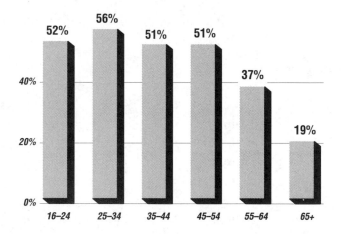

Participation in Adult Education by Age, 1995 and 1999

(percent of people aged 16 or older participating in adult education activities, by age, 1995 and 1999; percentage point change, 1995–99)

	1999	*1995*	*percentage point change*
Total people	**46%**	**40%**	**6**
Aged 16 to 24	52	47	5
Aged 25 to 34	56	48	8
Aged 35 to 44	51	49	2
Aged 45 to 54	51	46	5
Aged 55 to 64	37	28	9
Aged 65 or older	19	15	4

Note: Adult education activities include apprenticeships, courses for basic skills, personal development, English as a second language, work-related courses, and credential programs in organizations other than postsecondary institutions. Excludes full-time participation in postsecondary institutions leading to a college degree, diploma, or certificate.
Source: National Center for Education Statistics, unpublished data from the National Household Education Survey, 1999; and Statistical Abstract of the United States, *1999; calculations by the author*

3

Health

♦ Despite attention the media give to older mothers, 87 percent of babies were born to women under age 35 in 1999.

♦ Most twentysomethings exercise vigorously at least once a week, but the percentage is lower among people in their thirties.

♦ Young men are less concerned about nutrition than young women are. Men are more likely to eat fast food and less likely to take vitamins.

♦ Young adults are more likely than other age groups to be without health insurance. Twenty-nine percent of people aged 18 to 24 do not have health insurance versus 16 percent of all Americans.

♦ Binge drinking is increasing among young adults. Fully 38 percent of people aged 18 to 25 and 31 percent of those aged 26 to 29 drank five or more drinks on at least one occasion during the past month.

♦ Young adults are more likely than older age groups to smoke cigarettes. Smoking peaks in the 18-to-25 age group at 40 percent.

♦ Accidents claim the most lives among people aged 15 to 34. Murder is the second-most common cause of death for people aged 15 to 24, while suicide is the second-most common cause among those aged 25 to 34.

Most Young Adults Say Their Health Is Good or Excellent

The proportion of people in good or excellent health declines with age.

People feel better today than their counterparts two decades ago did. The proportion of people aged 18 to 24 who say they are in excellent health increased from 38 to 42 percent between 1977 and 1998. The share saying their health is poor or fair declined from 27 to 22 percent during those years. The proportion of 25-to-34-year-olds who feel their health is excellent, however, fell from 43 percent in 1977 to 37 percent in 1998, while the share saying their health is good rose from 43 percent to 51 percent.

Young adults are more likely than their elders to say their health is good or excellent for good reason. Although many of the conditions and diseases associated with aging have diminished in severity thanks to better lifestyles and medical care, health usually deteriorates with age.

♦ Basic biology dictates that young adults will always feel more fit than their elders.

More than four out of ten people aged 18 to 24 say their health is excellent

(percent of people aged 18 or older who say their health is excellent, by age, 1998)

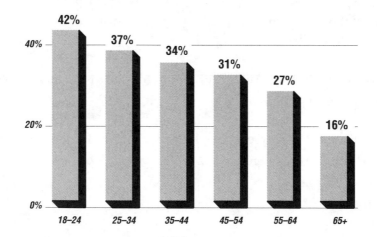

Health Status, 1977 and 1998

"Would you say your own health, in general, is excellent, good, fair, or poor?"

(percent of people aged 18 or older responding by age, 1977 and 1998)

	excellent		good		fair		poor	
	1990	1977	1998	1077	1998	1977	1998	1977
Total people	**31%**	**32%**	**48%**	**41%**	**17%**	**20%**	**5%**	**7%**
Aged 18 to 24	42	38	44	44	14	17	1	2
Aged 25 to 34	37	43	51	43	11	11	1	3
Aged 35 to 44	34	37	49	47	14	13	2	4
Aged 45 to 54	31	32	45	42	18	20	6	5
Aged 55 to 64	27	22	46	36	18	30	9	12
Aged 65 or older	16	14	46	32	26	35	11	18

Note: Numbers may not add to 100 because "don't know" is not shown.
Source: 1977 and 1998 General Social Surveys, National Opinion Research Center, University of Chicago; calculations by the author

Diets of Young Men and Women Differ

Young men are more likely to eat meat and potatoes.

Young adults are more likely than the average person to eat French fries, cheese, tomatoes, and lettuce on an average day. They are less likely to consume cereal and fruit. Behind these differences is young adults' above-average consumption of fast food.

The eating habits of young men and women differ. Men aged 20 to 39 are more likely than their female counterparts to eat bread, meat, potatoes, and tomatoes on an average day. Young women are more likely to eat cereal, fruit, dark green and yellow vegetables, sugars and sweets.

The drinking habits of men and women differ as well. Young women are more likely to drink milk, tea, and diet soft drinks. Young men are more likely to drink beer and regular soft drinks.

♦ The health problems that accompany aging will encourage young adults to adopt a healthier diet later in life. Until then, they will continue to opt for the convenience of fast food.

Food Consumption of Men Aged 20 to 39, 1994–96

(percent of total people aged 20 or older and men aged 20 to 39 consuming selected types of food on an average day, 1994–96)

		men	
	total, both sexes	20 to 29	30 to 39
Grain products	**96.9%**	**94.4%**	**96.6%**
Yeast breads and rolls	66.3	62.3	67.5
Cereals and pastas	46.8	34.1	37.6
Ready-to-eat cereals	28.5	17.5	20.1
Rice	11.0	11.8	13.0
Pasta	7.4	8.5	6.8
Quick breads, pancakes, French toast	22.7	18.6	22.7
Cakes, cookies, pastries, pies	41.2	32.2	37.8
Crackers, popcorn, pretzels, corn chips	27.8	27.7	25.4
Mixtures, mainly grain	35.9	41.6	39.4
Vegetables	**82.8**	**83.7**	**87.9**
White potatoes	44.3	49.7	49.9
Fried	27.0	37.0	33.0
Dark-green vegetables	9.8	6.7	11.5
Deep-yellow vegetables	12.9	7.2	11.2
Tomatoes	38.8	45.5	42.2
Lettuce, lettuce-based salads	24.9	26.0	27.0
Green beans	7.7	4.6	6.1
Corn, green peas, lima beans	11.7	8.4	9.9
Other vegetables	42.5	41.1	50.4
Fruits	**53.7**	**41.6**	**40.0**
Citrus fruits and juices	26.5	23.8	21.3
Juices	20.4	21.0	16.1
Other fruits, mixtures, and juices	39.3	25.2	26.5
Apples	12.2	7.4	8.3
Bananas	13.4	7.3	11.2
Melons and berries	7.8	4.7	4.6
Other fruits and mixtures, mainly fruit	13.7	7.2	10.0
Noncitrus juices and nectars	8.5	5.0	3.8
Milk and milk products	**78.9**	**67.9**	**74.3**
Milk, milk drinks, yogurt	60.5	42.7	51.2
Fluid milk	55.6	39.6	47.5
Whole	19.4	13.2	17.0

(continued)

(continued from previous page)

	total, both sexes	men	
		20 to 29	30 to 39
Low fat	26.3%	19.4%	23.5%
Skim	11.0	7.0	6.8
Yogurt	4.0	1.9	3.6
Milk desserts	17.4	12.4	16.7
Cheese	32.6	37.7	36.7
Meat, poultry, and fish	**86.2**	**89.1**	**90.0**
Beef	20.9	22.8	27.9
Pork	15.8	13.3	15.4
Frankfurters, sausages, luncheon meats	28.6	30.9	31.9
Poultry	22.6	24.1	23.0
Chicken	19.2	19.6	20.3
Fish and shellfish	8.0	6.6	10.8
Mixtures, mainly meat, poultry, fish	36.2	44.9	39.8
Eggs	19.1	18.7	19.6
Legumes	13.6	12.0	16.9
Nuts and seeds	9.6	7.0	7.6
Fats and oils	54.5	46.3	56.7
Table fats	30.4	18.8	28.7
Salad dressings	29.3	29.7	30.6
Sugars and sweets	53.2	39.4	49.9
Sugars	28.1	18.7	32.4
Candy	15.4	14.9	12.1
Beverages	**86.9**	**91.5**	**94.0**
Alcoholic	12.5	27.8	23.4
Wine	3.5	3.1	3.5
Beer and ale	7.6	24.3	19.1
Nonalcoholic	85.8	87.1	92.5
Coffee	39.5	24.6	51.9
Tea	22.8	17.6	26.9
Fruit drinks and ades	19.7	20.5	13.2
Carbonated soft drinks	50.4	68.3	62.9
Regular	39.3	62.9	51.0
Low calorie	12.8	6.7	14.2

Source: USDA, ARS Food Surveys Research Group, Supplementary Data Tables: USDA's 1994–96 Continuing Survey of Food Intakes by Individuals, *Internet site <www.barc.usda.gov/bhnrc/foodsurvey/home.htm>*

Food Consumption of Women Aged 20 to 39, 1994–96

(percent of total people aged 20 or older and women aged 20 to 39 consuming selected types of foods on an average day, 1994–96)

		women	
	total, both sexes	20 to 29	30 to 39
Grain products	**96.9%**	**95.6%**	**96.1%**
Yeast breads and rolls	66.3	59.7	64.6
Cereals and pastas	46.8	41.7	38.8
Ready-to-eat cereals	28.5	23.6	20.5
Rice	11.0	13.5	11.5
Pasta	7.4	6.8	8.2
Quick breads, pancakes, French toast	22.7	19.7	21.3
Cakes, cookies, pastries, pies	41.2	35.9	38.1
Crackers, popcorn, pretzels, corn chips	27.8	24.6	29.8
Mixtures, mainly grain	35.9	40.2	38.0
Vegetables	**82.8**	**81.2**	**82.6**
White potatoes	44.3	42.3	41.9
Fried	27.0	28.1	23.5
Dark-green vegetables	9.8	9.2	10.8
Deep-yellow vegetables	12.9	11.3	15.3
Tomatoes	38.8	40.6	40.4
Lettuce, lettuce-based salads	24.9	25.5	28.8
Green beans	7.7	7.1	7.4
Corn, green peas, lima beans	11.7	7.6	12.4
Other vegetables	42.5	40.9	42.8
Fruits	**53.7**	**46.5**	**47.2**
Citrus fruits and juices	26.5	24.3	21.4
Juices	20.4	18.9	15.5
Other fruits, mixtures, and juices	39.3	28.9	34.3
Apples	12.2	6.8	9.9
Bananas	13.4	9.0	12.5
Melons and berries	7.8	4.5	8.1
Other fruits and mixtures, mainly fruit	13.7	10.7	10.8
Noncitrus juices and nectars	8.5	6.0	5.4
Milk and milk products	**78.9**	**73.1**	**75.9**
Milk, milk drinks, yogurt	60.5	51.2	53.3
Fluid milk	55.6	46.1	49.0
Whole	19.4	17.7	14.2

(continued)

(continued from previous page)

	total, both sexes	women 20 to 29	women 30 to 39
Low fat	26.3%	16.3%	24.0%
Skim	11.0	12.1	11.2
Yogurt	4.0	3.5	6.7
Milk desserts	17.4	11.2	14.0
Cheese	32.6	34.4	35.9
Meat, poultry, and fish	**86.2**	**79.7**	**84.4**
Beef	20.9	16.3	20.4
Pork	15.8	12.8	15.2
Frankfurters, sausages, luncheon meats	28.6	22.5	26.9
Poultry	22.6	23.4	19.3
Chicken	19.2	20.6	16.8
Fish and shellfish	8.0	6.2	7.1
Mixtures, mainly meat, poultry, fish	36.2	36.9	36.1
Eggs	19.1	17.7	17.2
Legumes	13.6	15.0	15.9
Nuts and seeds	9.6	7.0	7.1
Fats and oils	54.5	48.5	59.1
Table fats	30.4	23.0	29.2
Salad dressings	29.3	27.9	32.0
Sugars and sweets	53.2	47.0	56.5
Sugars	28.1	26.7	36.7
Candy	15.4	13.2	12.2
Beverages	**86.9**	**90.3**	**90.0**
Alcoholic	12.5	13.0	12.8
Wine	3.5	2.9	4.8
Beer and ale	7.6	8.1	5.7
Nonalcoholic	85.8	88.4	89.3
Coffee	39.5	24.7	45.9
Tea	22.8	25.8	29.3
Fruit drinks and ades	19.7	20.3	15.6
Carbonated soft drinks	50.4	63.2	56.0
Regular	39.3	50.3	39.2
Low calorie	12.8	15.7	18.6

Source: USDA, ARS Food Surveys Research Group, Supplementary Data Tables: USDA's 1994–96 Continuing Survey of Food Intakes by Individuals, *Internet site <www.barc.usda.gov/bhnrc/foodsurvey/home.htm>*

Fast Food Rules with Young Men

Young men and women eat away from home more often than average.

People in their twenties and thirties are more likely than the average adult to eat out. Young men are especially likely to get their meals away from home. Fully 71 percent of men aged 20 to 29 and 67 percent of those aged 30 to 39 eat at least one meal away from home on a typical day. Among all men aged 20 or older, 61 percent eat out on a typical day.

Only about half of women aged 20 or older eat out on an average day. Among women aged 20 to 29, however, a considerably higher 63 percent eat out. Among those aged 30 to 39, 57 percent eat out on an average day.

Young adults most commonly frequent fast-food restaurants. Thirty-six percent of men and women in their thirties and 38 percent of women in their twenties eat at a fast-food restaurant on a typical day. Men in their twenties are the fast-food kings—44 percent eat at a fast-food restaurant on an average day.

♦ Home cooked meals, especially those made "from scratch," are becoming less common in American households. Today's young adults, raised on fast food and take out, are unlikely to reverse this trend.

Twentysomethings are most likely to eat out

(percent of people aged 20 or older and aged 20 to 39 who eat out at least once on an average day, by sex, 1994–96)

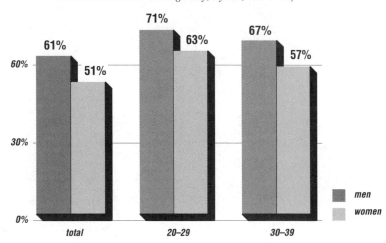

People Aged 20 to 39 Consuming Food Away from Home by Location, 1994–96

(percent of people aged 20 or older and aged 20 to 39 eating away from home on an average day, and percent distribution of those eating away from home by location, by sex, 1994–96)

	men			women		
	total	*20 to 29*	*30 to 39*	*total*	*20 to 29*	*30 to 39*
Percent eating away from home	61.2%	71.2%	66.9%	51.0%	63.0%	56.5%
Percent distribution by location						
Total eating away from home	100.0	100.0	100.0	100.0	100.0	100.0
Fast-food restaurant	35.6	43.7	35.5	30.3	37.5	35.7
Sit-down restaurant	32.2	29.7	26.5	34.1	35.6	27.3
Store	27.7	31.9	31.7	22.3	25.8	23.8
Someone else/gift	17.3	19.0	19.1	23.5	22.5	22.4
School cafeteria	1.7	2.3	1.1	2.5	2.6	2.3
Other cafeteria	8.5	6.8	9.5	9.9	10.0	11.4
Day care	0.1	0.3	0.0	0.9	1.2	1.3
Other	29.1	30.6	32.9	25.6	27.3	27.5

Note: Numbers will not add to 100 because food may be eaten at more than one location during the day.
Source: USDA, ARS Food Surveys Research Group, Data Tables: Results from USDA's 1994–96 Continuing Survey of Food Intakes by Individuals and 1994–96 Diet and Health Knowledge Survey, 1999; Internet site <www.barc.usda.gov/bhnrc/foodsurvey/home.htm>

Men and Women Differ in Food Buying

Young women have more concerns about food.

Young men and women have different opinions about what is important when buying food. For women aged 20 to 39, food safety is the most important consideration, although taste runs a close second. Young men, on the other hand, consider taste the most important factor.

In general, women's standards are higher than men's when it comes to buying food. Women aged 20 to 39 are more likely than their male counterparts to say food safety, taste, nutrition, and how well the food keeps are very important considerations. The issue of nutrition provides the biggest difference: 65 percent of women say nutrition is very important versus only 49 percent of men.

♦ Young men and women agree on one issue. Forty-five percent of both sexes say price is a very important consideration when buying food.

Young women are more concerned about nutrition

(percent of people aged 20 to 39 saying nutrition is "very important" when buying food, by sex, 1994–96)

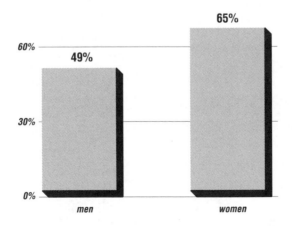

What Matters When Buying Food, 1994–96

"When you buy food, how important is…"

(percent of people aged 20 or older and aged 20 to 39 saying the following are "very important," by sex, 1994–96)

		aged 20 to 39	
	total	men	women
Food safety	84.0%	75.9%	86.1%
Taste	83.0	79.0	85.1
Nutrition	62.3	49.4	64.6
How well the food keeps	57.1	48.1	57.5
Price	43.7	44.8	45.4
Easy to prepare	37.5	35.2	39.1

Source: USDA, ARS Food Surveys Research Group, USDA's 1994–96 Diet and Health Knowledge Survey: Table Set 19, *Internet site <www.barc.usda.gov/bhnrc/foodsurvey/home.htm>*

Most Young Women Take Vitamin or Mineral Supplements

Young men are far less likely to take supplements.

Young women are more likely than the average American to take vitamin supplements, and they are far more likely than young men to take them. Forty-seven percent of Americans of all ages take a vitamin or mineral supplement on an average day. An even larger 52 percent of women aged 20 to 29 and 54 percent of those aged 30 to 39 take supplements.

Young men are far less likely than young women to take supplements. Only 36 percent of men aged 20 to 29 and 40 percent of those aged 30 to 39 take vitamin or mineral supplements.

♦ Not only are young men less likely than young women to take vitamin or mineral supplements, they are less likely to eat a healthy diet. Over time, this will contribute to a continued difference in the longevity of men and women.

Supplement use increases with age

(percent of people aged 20 to 39 who take vitamin/mineral supplements, by sex, 1994–96)

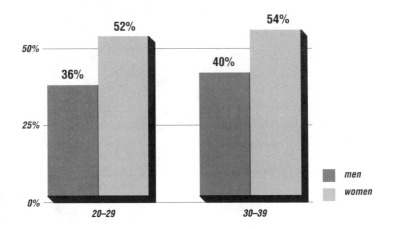

Use of Vitamin and Mineral Supplements by People Aged 20 to 39, 1994–96

(percent of total people and people aged 20 to 39 taking vitamin/mineral supplements, by sex and type of supplement, 1994–96)

			type of supplement		
	total	*multivitamin*	*multivitamin with iron or other minerals*	*combination of vitamin C and iron*	*single vitamins or minerals*
Total, both sexes	**46.8%**	**20.7%**	**16.8%**	**2.9%**	**15.3%**
Men					
Aged 20 to 29	36.4	18.8	9.7	3.2	9.6
Aged 30 to 39	39.7	20.6	14.1	3.1	10.2
Women					
Aged 20 to 29	52.0	22.7	21.9	3.9	13.7
Aged 30 to 39	54.4	19.8	25.6	3.5	17.5

Source: USDA, ARS Food Surveys Research Group, Supplementary Data Tables: USDA's 1994–96 Continuing Survey of Food Intakes by Individuals*; Internet site <www.barc.usda.gov/bhnrc/foodsurvey/home.htm>*

Twentysomethings Are Less Likely Than Average to Be Overweight

The proportion is higher among those in their thirties.

Almost one-third of Americans aged 20 or older are overweight. Young adults are less likely than average to be overweight, however. Only 22 percent of men and women aged 20 to 29 are overweight.

The lifestyle of the average American makes it difficult to keep the weight off forever. Labor-saving devices have proliferated and Americans now burn fewer calories. At the same time, we take in more calories than ever by eating larger meals and snacking between meals. One-third of men in their thirties are overweight, as are 27 percent of women in the age group.

♦ Although most young adults keep their weight down by being active, their eating habits insure that as their activity level falls later in life, the pounds will rise.

Keeping the pounds off gets harder as people get older

(percent of people aged 20 to 39 who are overweight, by sex, 1994–96)

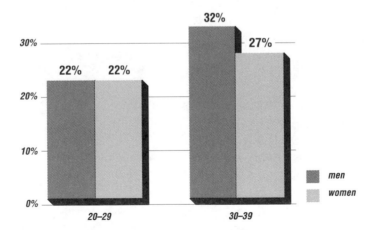

Overweight People Aged 20 to 39, 1994–96

(percent of people aged 20 or older and aged 20 to 39 who are overweight, by sex, 1994–96)

Total people	**31.7%**
Total men	**31.8**
Aged 20 to 29	21.5
Aged 30 to 39	32.3
Total women	**31.5**
Aged 20 to 29	22.1
Aged 30 to 39	27.4

Note: Overweight is defined as having a body mass index (BMI) equal to or greater than 27.8 for men and 27.3 for women, excluding pregnant women.
Source: USDA, ARS Food Surveys Research Group, Data Tables: Results from USDA's 1994–96 Continuing Survey of Food Intakes by Individuals and 1994–96 Diet *and* Health Knowledge Survey, *1999; Internet site <www.barc.usda.gov/bhnrc/foodsurvey/home.htm>*

More Than Three out of Ten Young Adults Want to Lose Weight

But fewer than 10 percent of young adults are cutting calories.

Most young adults are not dieting, but are trying to maintain their current weight. The proportion battling the bulge increases with age, however. Thirty-five percent of people aged 25 to 34 are trying to lose weight compared with 30 percent of those aged 18 to 24.

Many of today's young adults likely will enter middle age carrying extra pounds. Although 25-to-34-year-olds are more likely than younger adults to say they are trying to lose weight, they are no more likely to be cutting calories and they're less likely to exercise—the two tried-and-true weight loss methods. Those aged 25 to 34 are only slightly more likely than 18-to-24-year-olds to be limiting both fat and calories.

Thirty-two percent of people aged 25 to 34 are eating less fat, slightly higher than the 29 percent of people aged 18 to 24 who are doing so. While there are good health reasons for reducing fat consumption, without also cutting calories this dietary change will have no impact on weight.

♦ As the incidence of obesity increases in the U.S., so do associated illnesses such as diabetes. Young adults will need to step up their weight-control efforts to avoid contributing to this trend.

Extra pounds pile on early in life

(percent of people aged 18 to 34 who are trying to lose weight, 1998)

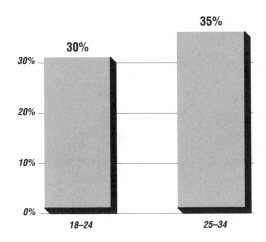

Weight Loss Behavior of People Aged 18 to 34, 1998

(percent of people aged 18 or older and aged 18 to 34 engaging in selected weight loss behaviors, 1998)

	total	18 to 24	25 to 34
Trying to lose weight	36.2%	29.6%	35.1%
Trying to maintain weight	55.6	50.1	54.3
Eating fewer calories	10.7	9.5	9.1
Eating less fat	31.6	28.6	32.4
Eating fewer calories and less fat	31.7	27.2	29.5
Exercising	59.9	72.6	67.8
Advised by health professional to lose weight	11.1	3.7	7.3

Source: Centers for Disease Control and Prevention, Behavioral Risk Factor Surveillance System Online Prevalence Data, *1995–1998; Internet site <www2.cdc.gov/nccdphp/brfss/index.asp>*

Most Young Men Exercise Regularly

Young women are less likely to get regular workouts.

Americans of all ages lead lives that are too sedentary for good health. Twenty-eight percent of men and 44 percent of women aged 20 or older rarely get a vigorous physical workout.

Young men are more likely than average to exercise regularly. Forty percent of men in their twenties exercise vigorously at least five times a week compared with 32 percent of all men. Only 17 percent of men in their twenties rarely participate in vigorous physical exercise.

Young women are less likely to exercise than their male counterparts. Just 18 percent of women aged 20 to 29 and 20 percent of those aged 30 to 39 exercise vigorously five or more times a week. More than one-third rarely participate in vigorous physical exercise.

♦ Most young adults manage to fit exercise into their busy schedules. This bodes well for their health, especially if they stay physically active as they grow older.

Young men are more likely to exercise than young women

(percent of people aged 20 to 39 who exercise vigorously five or more times per week, by sex, 1994–96)

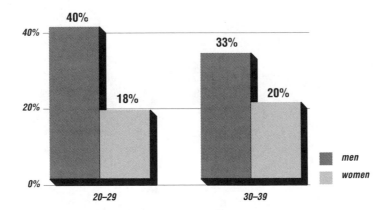

Vigorous Exercise by People Aged 20 to 39, 1994—96

(percent distribution of people aged 20 or older and aged 20 to 39 by sex and frequency of vigorous exercise, 1994–96)

	total	5 to 7 times per week	2 to 4 times per week	1 to 4 times per month	rarely
Total people	**100.0%**	**25.4%**	**23.8%**	**14.0%**	**36.5%**
Total men	**100.0**	**32.4**	**25.4**	**13.4**	**28.4**
Aged 20 to 29	100.0	39.6	29.0	14.5	16.6
Aged 30 to 39	100.0	32.5	29.7	16.0	21.8
Total women	**100.0**	**18.8**	**22.3**	**14.6**	**43.9**
Aged 20 to 29	100.0	18.3	27.1	18.4	35.8
Aged 30 to 39	100.0	19.6	26.5	19.3	34.6

Source: USDA, ARS Food Surveys Research Group, Data Tables: Results from USDA's 1996 Continuing Survey of Food Intakes by Individuals *and* 1996 Diet and Health Knowledge Survey, *1999, Internet site <www.barc.usda.gov/bhnrc/foodsurvey/home.htm>*

Birth Rate Is Rising

After decades of decline, the birth rate rose in the late 1990s.

The birth rate in the U.S. fell for decades, but in 1995 it began to rise again. The rate is still far lower than in 1960, however. The birth rate among women aged 20 to 24 in 1960 was 258 live births per 1,000 women. In 1998, the rate was 43 percent lower, at 111 births per 1,000 women. This figure is higher than in 1995, however, when the birth among women aged 20 to 24 was 110.

The only exception to the rise in birth rate since 1995 is among teenagers. The share of teens who give birth has fallen steadily since 1960. In that year, the birth rate for teenagers stood at 89. In 1998, it was a much lower 51.

♦ Efforts to lower the teen pregnancy rate are clearly showing results. If the trend continues, it promises a brighter future for more young women.

Birth rate is unlikely to return to 1960 level

(births per 1,000 women in age group)

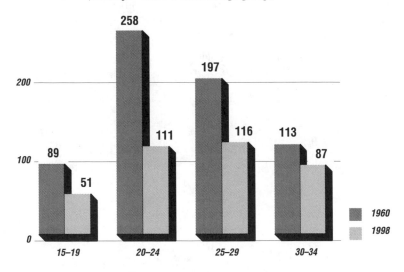

Birth Rates by Age of Mother, 1950 to 1998

(number of live births per 1,000 women in age group; percent change in rate for selected years, 1950 to 1998)

	15 to 19	20 to 24	25 to 29	30 to 34	35 to 39	40 to 44	45 to 54
1998	51.1	111.2	115.9	87.4	37.4	7.3	0.4
1997	52.3	110.4	113.8	85.3	36.1	7.1	0.4
1996	54.4	110.4	113.1	83.9	35.3	6.8	0.3
1995	56.8	109.8	112.2	82.5	34.3	6.6	0.3
1994	58.9	111.1	113.9	81.5	33.7	6.4	0.3
1993	59.6	112.6	115.5	80.8	32.9	6.1	0.3
1992	60.7	114.6	117.4	80.2	32.5	5.9	0.3
1991	62.1	115.7	118.2	79.5	32.0	5.5	0.2
1990	59.9	116.5	120.2	80.8	31.7	5.5	0.2
1980	53.0	115.1	112.9	61.9	19.8	3.9	0.2
1970	68.3	167.8	145.1	73.3	31.7	8.1	0.5
1960	89.1	258.1	197.4	112.7	56.2	15.5	0.9
1950	81.6	196.6	166.1	103.7	52.9	15.1	1.2
Percent change							
1990–1998	−14.7%	−4.5%	−3.6%	8.2%	18.0%	32.7%	100.0%
1950–1998	−37.4	−43.4	−30.2	−15.7	−29.3	−51.7	−66.7

Source: National Center for Health Statistics, Health, United States, 2000, *Internet site <www.cdc.gov/nchs/products/pubs/pubd/hus/hus.htm>; calculations by the author*

Most New Mothers Are Twentysomethings

More than half of women giving birth in 1999 were in their twenties.

The media have focused much attention on older mothers—women who postpone child-bearing until they are in their forties. Despite an increase in the number of older mothers during the past few decades, the majority of new mothers continue to be in their twenties. Only 7 percent of women having their first child in 1999 were aged 35 or older. Teenage mothers also get a lot of media attention, but only 12 percent of women giving birth in 1999 were under age 20.

Among women under age 35 who gave birth in 1999, 43 percent were having their first child and 33 percent were having a second. Only 9 percent were giving birth to a fourth or subsequent child.

About three-quarters of births to blacks, Native Americans, and Hispanics in 1999 were to women under age 30. Among non-Hispanic whites, a smaller 59 percent of births were to women under age 30. Asian women are most likely to delay childbearing; only 51 percent of births to Asians in 1999 were to women under age 30.

♦ Women are waiting longer to have their first child today than they did in the 1950s, but the prime childbearing years are still between the ages of 20 and 29.

Women are most likely to have children in their late twenties

(percent distribution of births by age of mother, 1999)

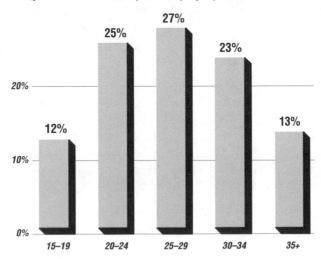

Births to Women under Age 35 by Race and Hispanic Origin, 1999

(number and percent distribution of births by age, race, and Hispanic origin of mother, 1999)

	total births	Asian	black	Native American	white	Hispanic	non-Hispanic white
				race		**Hispanic origin**	
Total births	**3,957,829**	**180,993**	**606,720**	**40,015**	**3,130,100**	**762,364**	**2,349,536**
Under age 35	3,436,829	147,961	549,497	36,555	2,702,816	692,487	1,996,989
Under age 15	9,049	142	3,981	203	4,723	2,721	2,046
Aged 15 to 19	475,745	9,255	121,262	7,905	337,323	124,352	213,223
Aged 20 to 24	981,207	27,304	193,483	13,203	747,217	230,881	515,026
Aged 25 to 29	1,078,350	56,040	139,175	9,549	873,586	203,399	665,018
Aged 30 to 34	892,478	55,220	91,596	5,695	739,967	131,134	601,676
Aged 35 or older	520,998	33,033	57,223	3,461	427,283	69,875	352,424

Percent distribution by race and Hispanic origin

	total births	Asian	black	Native American	white	Hispanic	non-Hispanic white
Total births	**100.0%**	**4.6%**	**15.3%**	**1.0%**	**79.1%**	**19.3%**	**59.4%**
Under age 35	100.0	4.3	16.0	1.1	78.6	20.1	58.1
Under age 15	100.0	1.6	44.0	2.2	52.2	30.1	22.6
Aged 15 to 19	100.0	1.9	25.5	1.7	70.9	26.1	44.8
Aged 20 to 24	100.0	2.8	19.7	1.3	76.2	23.5	52.5
Aged 25 to 29	100.0	5.2	12.9	0.9	81.0	18.9	61.7
Aged 30 to 34	100.0	6.2	10.3	0.6	82.9	14.7	67.4
Aged 35 or older	100.0	6.3	11.0	0.7	82.0	13.4	67.6

Percent distribution by age

	total births	Asian	black	Native American	white	Hispanic	non-Hispanic white
Total births	**100.0%**	**100.0%**	**100.0%**	**100.0%**	**100.0%**	**100.0%**	**100.0%**
Total, under age 35	86.8	81.7	90.6	91.4	86.3	90.8	85.0
Under age 15	0.2	0.1	0.7	0.5	0.2	0.4	0.1
Aged 15 to 19	12.0	5.1	20.0	19.8	10.8	16.3	9.1
Aged 20 to 24	24.8	15.1	31.9	33.0	23.9	30.3	21.9
Aged 25 to 29	27.2	31.0	22.9	23.9	27.9	26.7	28.3
Aged 30 to 34	22.5	30.5	15.1	14.2	23.6	17.2	25.6
Aged 35 or older	13.2	18.3	9.4	8.6	13.7	9.2	15.0

Note: Numbers will not add to total because Hispanics may be of any race and "not stated" is not shown.
Source: National Center for Health Statistics, Births: Preliminary Data for 1999, *National Vital Statistics Reports, Vol. 48, No. 14, 2000, Internet site <www.cdc.gov/nchs>; calculations by the author*

Births to Women under Age 35 by Birth Order, 1999

(number and percent distribution of births by age of mother and birth order, 1999)

	total births	first child	second child	third child	fourth or later child
Total births	**3,957,829**	**1,587,971**	**1,285,974**	**652,380**	**413,012**
Under age 35	3,436,829	1,473,758	1,120,612	533,054	293,637
Under age 15	9,049	8,818	160	8	0
Aged 15 to 19	475,745	370,749	85,455	14,643	2,148
Aged 20 to 24	981,207	448,102	338,720	137,232	52,762
Aged 25 to 29	1,078,350	392,762	373,887	194,879	112,263
Aged 30 to 34	892,478	253,327	322,390	186,292	126,464
Aged 35 or older	520,998	114,213	165,363	119,326	119,374

Percent distribution by birth order

Total births	**100.0%**	**40.1%**	**32.5%**	**16.5%**	**10.4%**
Under age 35	100.0	42.9	32.6	15.5	8.5
Under age 15	100.0	97.4	1.8	0.1	0.0
Aged 15 to 19	100.0	77.9	18.0	3.1	0.5
Aged 20 to 24	100.0	45.7	34.5	14.0	5.4
Aged 25 to 29	100.0	36.4	34.7	18.1	10.4
Aged 30 to 34	100.0	28.4	36.1	20.9	14.2
Aged 35 or older	100.0	21.9	31.7	22.9	22.9

Percent distribution by age

Total births	**100.0%**	**100.0%**	**100.0%**	**100.0%**	**100.0%**
Under age 35	86.8	92.8	87.1	81.7	71.1
Under age 15	0.2	0.6	0.0	0.0	0.0
Aged 15 to 19	12.0	23.3	6.6	2.2	0.5
Aged 20 to 24	24.8	28.2	26.3	21.0	12.8
Aged 25 to 29	27.2	24.7	29.1	29.9	27.2
Aged 30 to 34	22.5	16.0	25.1	28.6	30.6
Aged 35 or older	13.2	7.2	12.9	18.3	28.9

Note: Numbers will not add to total because "not stated" is not shown.
Source: National Center for Health Statistics, Births: Preliminary Data for 1999, *National Vital Statistics Reports, Vol. 48, No. 14, 2000, Internet site <www.cdc.gov/nchs>; calculations by the author*

Most Teen Mothers Are Not Married

The percentage of births to unmarried women falls with age.

One-third of women who gave birth in 1998 were not married. There are sharp differences by age in the percentage of new mothers who are not married, however. The younger the woman, the more likely she is to give birth out of wedlock.

Virtually all girls under age 15 who gave birth in 1998 were not married. Three-quarters of births among women aged 15 to 19 were out of wedlock as well. The share drops to less than half (48 percent) among women in their early twenties. It declines further to 23 percent among those in their late twenties. Only 14 percent of babies born to mothers aged 30 to 34 were out of wedlock.

Black women are most likely to be single mothers. Fully 72 percent of babies born to black women under age 35 in 1998 were out of wedlock. Among Hispanics, the share was 43 percent. Among non-Hispanic whites, it was a much smaller 24 percent.

♦ Women who have children out of wedlock are at high risk for long-term poverty. The demands of motherhood make it difficult for single mothers to gain the educational credentials necessary for a middle-class lifestyle.

Births to Women under Age 35 by Marital Status, 1998

(total number of births and number and percent to unmarried women, by age, race, and Hispanic origin of mother, 1998)

| | total | race | | Hispanic origin | |
		white	black	non-Hispanic white	Hispanic
Total births	**3,941,553**	**3,118,727**	**609,902**	**2,361,462**	**734,661**
Under age 35	3,431,945	2,700,379	553,401	2,014,268	668,931
Under age 15	9,462	4,801	4,289	2,132	2,716
Aged 15 to 19	484,895	340,694	126,937	219,169	121,388
Aged 20 to 24	965,122	736,664	189,088	511,101	223,113
Aged 25 to 29	1,083,101	880,688	139,302	678,227	196,012
Aged 30 to 34	889,365	737,532	93,785	603,639	125,702
Aged 35 or older	509,699	418,348	56,501	347,194	65,730
Births to unmarried women					
Total births	**1,293,567**	**821,441**	**421,383**	**517,153**	**305,442**
Under age 35	1,218,276	773,216	397,902	485,537	288,869
Under age 15	9,137	4,514	4,270	2,044	2,516
Aged 15 to 19	380,868	245,832	121,458	157,517	88,529
Aged 20 to 24	460,367	291,677	151,903	185,985	106,020
Aged 25 to 29	243,280	153,310	79,344	92,542	61,079
Aged 30 to 34	124,624	77,883	40,927	47,449	30,725
Aged 35 or older	75,291	48,225	23,481	31,616	16,573
Percent of births to unmarried women					
Total births	**32.8%**	**26.3%**	**69.1%**	**21.9%**	**41.6%**
Under age 35	35.5	28.6	71.9	24.1	43.2
Under age 15	96.6	94.0	99.6	95.9	92.6
Aged 15 to 19	78.5	72.2	95.7	71.9	72.9
Aged 20 to 24	47.7	39.6	80.3	36.4	47.5
Aged 25 to 29	22.5	17.4	57.0	13.6	31.2
Aged 30 to 34	14.0	10.6	43.6	7.9	24.4
Aged 35 or older	14.8	11.5	41.6	9.1	25.2

Note: Births by race and Hispanic origin will not add to total because Hispanics may be of any race, not all races are shown, and "not stated" is not shown.
Source: National Center for Health Statistics, Births: Final Data for 1998, National Vital Statistics Report, Vol. 48, No. 3, 2000, Internet site <www.cdc.gov/nchs/data/nvs48_3.pdf>; calculations by the author

Younger Women Have Fewer Childbirth Complications

Caesareans are more common among older women.

Delayed childbearing frequently has an unanticipated cost. The older a woman is when she has a child, the greater the likelihood of complications that necessitate Caesarean delivery.

Among babies born in 1998, one-fifth were Caesarean deliveries. Only 14 percent of babies born to women under age 20 were delivered by Caesarean section, but the share stood at 29 percent among women aged 35 or older.

Many women whose first child is delivered by Caesarean hope that subsequent children can be delivered vaginally. Age influences the likelihood of a subsequent Caesarean delivery, however. Repeat Caesareans are more common among older women.

♦ As women have delayed childbearing, the rate of Caesarean delivery has increased. With new fertility technologies enabling more women to have children later in life, the rate is likely to rise further.

Young women are least likely to require Caesarean deliveries

(percent of births delivered by Caesarean section, by age of mother, 1998)

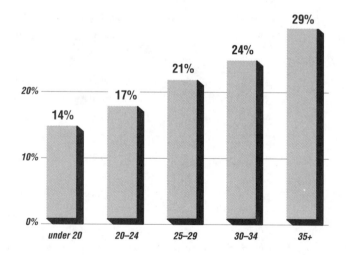

Birth Delivery Method for Women under Age 35, 1998

(number and percent distribution of births by age and method of delivery, 1998)

		vaginal		Caesarean		
	total	total	after previous Caesarean	total	first	repeat
Total births	**3,941,553**	**3,078,537**	**108,903**	**825,870**	**519,975**	**305,895**
Under age 35	3,431,854	2,722,200	88,614	677,486	439,422	238,064
Under age 20	494,357	418,743	3,614	71,195	63,425	7,770
Aged 20 to 24	965,122	789,395	20,742	166,403	114,822	51,581
Aged 25 to 29	1,083,010	847,952	31,292	224,878	140,031	84,847
Aged 30 to 34	889,365	666,110	32,966	215,010	121,144	93,866
Aged 35 or older	509,699	356,337	20,289	148,384	80,553	67,831

Percent distribution by delivery method

Total births	**100.0%**	**78.1%**	**2.8%**	**21.0%**	**13.2%**	**7.8%**
Under age 35	100.0	79.3	2.6	19.7	12.8	6.9
Under age 20	100.0	84.7	0.7	14.4	12.8	1.6
Aged 20 to 24	100.0	81.8	2.1	17.2	11.9	5.3
Aged 25 to 29	100.0	78.3	2.9	20.8	12.9	7.8
Aged 30 to 34	100.0	74.9	3.7	24.2	13.6	10.6
Aged 35 or older	100.0	69.9	4.0	29.1	15.8	13.3

Percent distribution by age

Total births	**100.0%**	**100.0%**	**100.0%**	**100.0%**	**100.0%**	**100.0%**
Under age 35	87.1	88.4	81.4	82.0	84.5	77.8
Under age 20	12.5	13.6	3.3	8.6	12.2	2.5
Aged 20 to 24	24.5	25.6	19.0	20.1	22.1	16.9
Aged 25 to 29	27.5	27.5	28.7	27.2	26.9	27.7
Aged 30 to 34	22.6	21.6	30.3	26.0	23.3	30.7
Aged 35 or older	12.9	11.6	18.6	18.0	15.5	22.2

Note: Numbers will not add to total because "not stated" is not shown.
Source: National Center for Health Statistics, Births: Final Data for 1998, *National Vital Statistics Report, Vol. 48, No. 3, 2000, Internet site <www.cdc.gov/nchs/data/nvs48_3.pdf>; calculations by the author*

Young Adults Are Most Likely to Smoke

Smoking peaks among 18-to-25-year-olds.

Most Americans have smoked at some point in their lives, but only 26 percent are current smokers. Among young adults, however, the proportion is considerably higher. Forty percent of people aged 18 to 25 are smokers—a larger share than in any other age group. One-third of people aged 26 to 29 smoke. The proportion of people who smoke drops to 30 percent among people in their early thirties.

Many young adults are former smokers. Fully 69 to 71 percent of people aged 18 to 34 have ever smoked. This means that more than half of people aged 26 to 34 who ever smoked have been able to quit. A smaller share of people aged 18 to 25 have managed to quit smoking, but more will give it up in the next 10 years.

♦ Despite strong antismoking campaigns, many young adults are still taking up the habit. Although most eventually kick it, many will find it difficult to quit.

Many adults have kicked the habit

(percent of people aged 18 to 34 who are current smokers or have ever smoked, 1999)

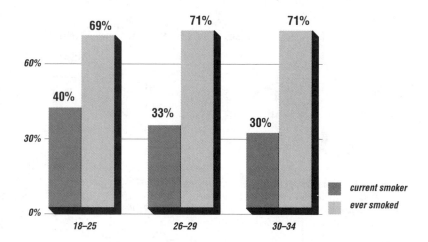

Current and Lifetime Cigarette Smoking by Age, 1999

(percent of people aged 12 or older who smoked cigarettes during the past month and who have ever smoked cigarettes, by age, 1999)

	current smoker	ever smoked
Total people	**25.8%**	**68.2%**
12 to 17	14.9	37.1
18 to 25	39.7	68.9
26 to 29	33.1	70.7
30 to 34	30.3	71.2
35 to 39	30.3	75.0
40 to 44	32.1	76.5
45 to 49	27.9	73.6
50 to 64	22.5	74.9
65 or older	10.7	64.9

Source: U.S. Substance Abuse and Mental Health Services Administrations, National Household Survey on Drug Abuse, *1999, Internet site <www.DrugAbuseStatistics.samhsa.gov>*

Young Adults Are the Heaviest Drinkers

College-aged young people are most likely to binge drink.

Most adults enjoy having a drink now and then. Many young adults do not stop with one or two drinks, however. Binge drinking is an increasingly serious problem among young people, especially those in their late teens (who are not even old enough to purchase alcohol legally) and early twenties.

Fully 38 percent of 18-to-25-year-olds had five or more drinks on at least one occasion in the 30 days prior to the 1999 survey, as had 31 percent of people aged 26 to 29. Thirteen percent of people aged 18 to 25 were heavy drinkers, binging on five or more occasions in the past month.

As people get older they become less likely to binge drink or drink heavily. Among those aged 35 to 39, a smaller 24 percent had been binging in the prior month, and only 7 percent were heavy drinkers.

♦ The sizable percentage of 18-to-25-year-olds who are binge drinkers shows the clear need for continued efforts to curb excessive drinking in the age group.

Young adults are binge drinking at alarming rates

(percent of people aged 12 or older and aged 18 to 29 who binged at least once in the prior month, 1999)

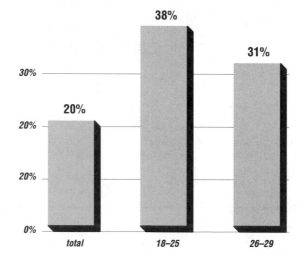

Alcohol Use by Age and Level of Use, 1999

(percent of people aged 12 or older who drank alcohol during the past month, by age and level of alcohol use, 1999)

	any drinking	binge drinking	heavy drinking
Total people	**47.3%**	**20.2%**	**5.6%**
Aged 12 to 17	18.6	10.9	2.5
Aged 18 to 25	58.0	38.3	13.3
Aged 26 to 29	59.5	31.3	8.2
Aged 30 to 34	56.6	28.0	6.8
Aged 35 to 39	56.5	24.0	6.5
Aged 40 to 44	55.1	21.1	6.0
Aged 45 to 49	52.8	20.7	6.0
Aged 50 to 64	47.2	13.8	2.9
Aged 65 or older	32.7	5.6	1.6

Note: Binge drinking is defined as having had five or more drinks on the same occasion on at least one day in the 30 days prior to the survey. Heavy drinking is having had five or more drinks on the same occasion on each of five or more days in 30 days prior to the survey.
Source: U.S. Substance Abuse and Mental Health Services Administrations, National Household Survey on Drug Abuse, *1999, Internet site <www.DrugAbuseStatistics.samhsa.gov>*

Drug Use Is Highest among Young Adults

Most young adults have never used drugs, however.

People aged 18 to 25 are most likely to be current drug users. Seventeen percent use illicit drugs, most commonly marijuana. The percentage of current users fall to 9 percent among 26-to-29-year-olds and to 6 percent among those aged 30 to 44.

Boomers aged 35 to 39 still hold the record for lifetime drug use. Sixty percent of the age group have used illicit drugs at some point. A smaller 51 percent of people aged 26 to 29 and 55 percent of those aged 30 to 34 have ever used illicit drugs.

◆ Although drug use among the young is a serious concern, today's teens are more likely to be drug free than previous generations were.

Today's young adults are less likely than boomers to have used drugs

(percent of people aged 12 or older who have ever used any illicit drug, by age, 1999)

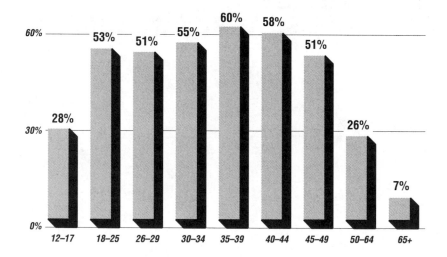

Drug Use by Age, 1999

(percent of people aged 12 or older who ever used and currently use illicit drugs, by age, 1999)

	any illicit drug	
	current user	*ever used*
Total people	**6.7%**	**39.7%**
Aged 12 to 17	10.9	27.6
Aged 18 to 25	17.1	52.6
Aged 26 to 29	8.5	50.8
Aged 30 to 34	6.3	55.0
Aged 35 to 39	6.6	59.5
Aged 40 to 44	8.6	58.0
Aged 45 to 49	4.1	51.1
Aged 50 to 64	1.7	25.9
Aged 65 or older	0.6	7.1

Note: Current users are those who used the drug at least once during the month prior to the survey.
Source: U.S. Substance Abuse and Mental Health Services Administrations, National Household Survey on Drug Abuse, *1999; Internet site <www.DrugAbuseStatistics.samhsa.gov>*

Youngest Adults Have Highest Opinion of Medical Leaders

Fewer people aged 25 to 34 hold medical leaders in high regard.

The majority of 18-to-24-year-olds have a "great deal" of confidence in the leaders of the medical profession. Among older adults, including 25-to-34-year-olds, a smaller 42 to 44 percent have the same confidence in medicine's leaders. Thirty-five percent of people aged 18 to 24 say they have "only some" confidence in medicine compared with a much larger 47 percent of people aged 25 to 34.

♦ The youngest adults have had little contact with the medical profession. Their confidence may wane as they encounter more health problems requiring medical attention.

The young have the most confidence in medicine

(percent of people aged 18 or older who have a "great deal" of confidence in medical leaders, 1998)

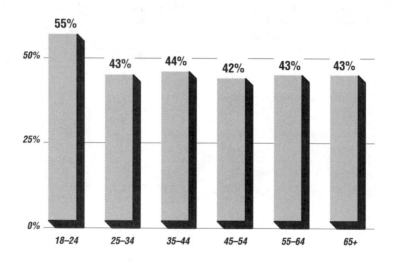

Confidence in Medicine, 1998

"As far as the people running medicine are concerned, would you say
you have a great deal of confidence, only some confidence,
or hardly any confidence at all in them?"

(percent of people aged 18 or older responding by age, 1998)

	a great deal	*only some*	*hardly any*
Total people	**44%**	**45%**	**9%**
Aged 18 to 24	55	35	7
Aged 25 to 34	43	47	9
Aged 35 to 44	44	47	7
Aged 45 to 54	42	48	9
Aged 55 to 64	43	46	9
Aged 65 or older	43	43	11

Note: Numbers may not add to 100 because "don't know" is not included.
Source: 1998 General Social Survey, National Opinion Research Center, University of Chicago; calculations by the author

Young Adults Are Most Likely to Be Uninsured

Twenty-nine percent of 18-to-24-year-olds lack health insurance.

People aged 18 to 34 are more likely than any other age group to be without health insurance. Reaching adulthood usually means health insurance coverage through a parent's plan is no longer available. Twenty-nine percent of people aged 18 to 24 and 23 percent of those aged 25 to 34 lack health insurance, much larger proportions than the 16 percent of all Americans who are uninsured.

Most Americans obtain health insurance coverage through employers, but many young adults are unemployed or have jobs that do not offer health insurance coverage. While 63 percent of all Americans have employment-based coverage, this is true for only 51 percent of 18-to-24-year-olds. One-quarter of the population is covered by government insurance, such as Medicaid or Medicare, compared with only 11 percent of people under age 35.

♦ The health insurance needs of young adults are a problem without an easy solution since few can afford to buy private insurance.

More than one-quarter of young adults do not have health insurance

(percent of people aged 18 to 34 who do not have health insurance, 1999)

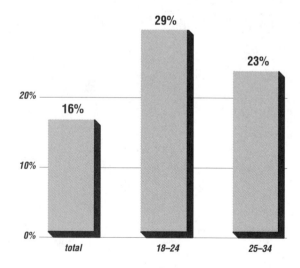

Health Insurance Coverage of People Aged 18 to 34, 1999

(number and percent distribution of total people and people aged 18 to 34 by health insurance coverage status, 1999; numbers in thousands)

| | | covered by private or government health insurance | | | | | | | |
| | | private health insurance | | | government health insurance | | | | |
	total	total	total	employ- ment based	total	Medicaid	Medicare	military	not covered
Total	**274,087**	**231,533**	**194,599**	**172,023**	**66,176**	**27,890**	**36,066**	**8,530**	**42,554**
18 to 34	64,318	47,875	43,005	38,685	6,879	4,987	475	1,738	16,443
18 to 24	26,532	18,844	16,438	13,535	3,450	2,643	152	798	7,688
25 to 34	37,786	29,031	26,567	25,150	3,429	2,344	323	940	8,755

Percent distribution by type of coverage

Total	**100.0%**	**84.5%**	**71.0%**	**62.8%**	**24.1%**	**10.2%**	**13.2%**	**3.1%**	**15.5%**
18 to 34	100.0	74.4	66.9	60.1	10.7	7.8	0.7	2.7	25.6
18 to 24	100.0	71.0	62.0	51.0	13.0	10.0	0.6	3.0	29.0
25 to 34	100.0	76.8	70.3	66.6	9.1	6.2	0.9	2.5	23.2

Percent distribution by age

Total	**100.0%**	**100.0%**	**100.0%**	**100.0%**	**100.0%**	**100.0%**	**100.0%**	**100.0%**	**100.0%**
18 to 34	23.5	20.7	22.1	22.5	10.4	17.9	1.3	20.4	38.6
18 to 24	9.7	8.1	8.4	7.9	5.2	9.5	0.4	9.4	18.1
25 to 34	13.8	12.5	13.7	14.6	5.2	8.4	0.9	11.0	20.6

Note: Numbers may not add to total because people may have more than one type of health insurance coverage.
Source: Bureau of the Census, Internet site <www.census.gov/hhes/hlthins/historic/hihistt2.html>; calculations by the author

Acute Conditions Are More Common among Young Adults

Young adults account for a large share of many illnesses and injuries.

But for a few exceptions, acute conditions afflict the young more than the old, a result of both physiology and lifestyle. As people age, they build immunity through exposure to a wide variety of viruses, reducing the instance of many respiratory and gastrointestinal illnesses. Injuries also decline as the risk-taking of youth gives way to a more careful middle age.

Respiratory problems are the most common acute affliction of young adults. Forty-one percent of people aged 18 to 24 and 38 percent of those aged 25 to 44 caught the flu in 1996. Twenty-four percent of 18-to-24-year-olds caught colds severe enough to restrict their activity or send them to a doctor, as did 19 percent of those aged 25 to 44.

Nearly one-third of people aged 18 to 24 and one-quarter of those aged 25 to 44 suffered an injury in 1996 that required medical care or restricted their activity.

♦ Acute illnesses are rarely life threatening, but this is small consolation to the afflicted. Young adults are important customers of over-the-counter medicines as well as herbal and other alternative therapies.

Acute Health Conditions Experienced by People Aged 18 to 44, 1996

(total number of acute conditions, number and rate per 100 people aged 18 to 44, and share of total acute conditions accounted for by age group, by type of condition, 1996; numbers in thousands)

		aged 18 to 24			aged 25 to 44		
	total	number	rate	share of total	number	rate	share of total
Total acute conditions	**432,001**	**45,272**	**184.2**	**10.5%**	**120,332**	**144.3**	**27.9%**
Infective and parasitic diseases	54,192	5,695	23.2	10.5	10,138	12.2	18.7
Common childhood diseases	3,118	221	0.9	7.1	325	0.4	10.4
Intestinal virus	15,980	1,530	6.2	9.6	3,932	4.7	24.6
Viral infections	15,067	688	2.8	4.6	2,183	2.6	14.5
Other	20,027	3,256	13.2	16.3	3,698	4.4	18.5
Respiratory conditions	**208,623**	**21,150**	**86.0**	**10.1**	**64,114**	**76.9**	**30.7**
Common cold	62,251	5,839	23.8	9.4	15,630	18.7	25.1
Other acute upper respiratory infections	29,866	3,961	16.1	13.3	9,642	11.6	32.3
Influenza	95,049	9,946	40.5	10.5	31,803	38.1	33.5
Acute bronchitis	12,116	947	3.9	7.8	4,270	5.1	35.2
Pneumonia	4,791	347	1.4	7.2	1,084	1.3	22.6
Other respiratory conditions	4,550	110	0.4	2.4	1,685	2.0	37.0
Digestive system conditions	**17,646**	**1,584**	**6.4**	**9.0**	**4,212**	**5.1**	**23.9**
Dental conditions	2,970	274	1.1	9.2	714	0.9	24.0
Indigestion, nausea, and vomiting	7,963	617	2.5	7.7	1,796	2.2	22.6
Other digestive conditions	6,713	693	2.8	10.3	1,702	2.0	25.4
Injuries	**57,279**	**7,736**	**31.5**	**13.5**	**20,742**	**24.9**	**36.2**
Fractures and dislocations	8,465	736	3.0	8.7	1,506	1.8	17.8
Sprains and strains	12,977	1,790	7.3	13.8	6,907	8.3	53.2
Open wounds and lacerations	9,027	1,634	6.6	18.1	3,635	4.4	40.3
Contusions & superficial injuries	9,979	1,433	5.8	14.4	3,691	4.4	37.0
Other current injuries	16,832	2,143	8.7	12.7	5,004	6.0	29.7
Selected other acute conditions	**63,090**	**6,243**	**25.4**	**9.9**	**13,994**	**16.8**	**22.2**
Eye conditions	3,478	384	1.6	11.0	334	0.4	9.6
Acute ear infections	21,766	937	3.8	4.3	2,397	2.9	11.0
Other ear conditions	3,833	185	0.8	4.8	986	1.2	25.7
Acute urinary conditions	8,405	707	2.9	8.4	2,523	3.0	30.0
Disorders of menstruation	839	169	0.7	20.1	537	0.6	64.0

(continued)

(continued from previous page)

		aged 18 to 24			aged 25 to 44		
	total	number	rate	share of total	number	rate	share of total
Other disorders of female genital tract	1,597	446	1.8	27.9%	613	0.7	38.4%
Delivery and other conditions of pregnancy	3,279	1,096	4.5	33.4	1,871	2.2	57.1
Skin conditions	4,986	493	2.0	9.9	1,182	1.4	23.7
Acute musculoskeletal conditions	8,461	1,321	5.4	15.6	2,514	3.0	29.7
Headache, excluding migraine	1,738	282	1.1	16.2	586	0.7	33.7
Fever, unspecified	4,708	224	0.9	4.8	451	0.5	9.6
Other acute conditions	**31,170**	**2,863**	**11.6**	**9.2**	**7,131**	**8.6**	**22.9**

Note: The acute conditions shown here are those that caused people to seek medical attention or to restrict their activity for at least half a day.
Source: National Center for Health Statistics, Current Estimates from the National Health Interview Survey, *1996, Series 10, No. 200, 1999, Internet site <www.cdc.gov/nchs/data/nvs48_3.pdf>; calculations by the author*

Chronic Conditions Are Uncommon among Young Adults

Young adults account for the majority of some chronic conditions, however.

Chronic conditions are more common among older Americans than among young adults. The most common chronic conditions among people under age 45 are allergies and hay fever, chronic sinusitis, and deformities or orthopedic impairments.

Asthma is one of the most serious chronic conditions afflicting young adults. Unlike most other chronic conditions suffered by the young, asthma is life-threatening.

A few chronic conditions become less common as people grow older. People aged 18 to 44 are more likely than older adults to suffer from acne, dermatitis, migraines, diseases of the female reproductive system, hay fever, chronic sinusitis, and chronic disease of the tonsils or adenoids. The age group accounted for more than one-half of those suffering from acne, subaceous skin cysts, migraines, anemias, and diseases of the female reproductive system.

♦ The incidence of asthma in children and young adults is growing, although no one knows why. If this trend continues, asthma will become a serious public health issue.

Chronic Health Conditions Experienced by People Aged 18 to 44, 1996

(total number of chronic conditions, number and rate per 1,000 people aged 18 to 44, and share of total chronic conditions accounted for by age group, by type of conditions, 1996; numbers in thousands)

		18 to 44		
	total	number	rate	share of total
Skin and musculoskeletal conditions				
Arthritis	33,638	5,409	50.1	16.1%
Gout, including gouty arthritis	2,487	320	3.0	12.9
Intervertebral disc disorders	6,700	2,275	21.1	34.0
Bonespur or tendinitis	2,934	1,181	10.9	40.3
Disorders of bone or cartilage	1,730	334	3.1	19.3
Bunions	2,360	704	6.5	29.8
Bursitis	5,006	1,410	13.1	28.2
Sebaceous skin cyst	1,190	616	5.7	51.8
Acne	4,952	2,968	27.5	59.9
Psoriasis	2,940	1,134	10.5	38.6
Dermatitis	8,249	3,251	30.1	39.4
Dry, itching skin	6,627	2,636	24.4	39.8
Ingrown nails	5,807	2,810	26.0	48.4
Corns and calluses	3,778	1,404	13.0	37.2
Impairments				
Visual impairment	8,280	2,592	24.0	31.3
Color blindness	2,811	1,075	10.0	38.2
Cataracts	7,022	299	2.8	4.3
Glaucoma	2,595	214	2.0	8.2
Hearing impairment	22,044	4,522	41.9	20.5
Tinnitus	7,866	1,728	16.0	22.0
Speech impairment	2,720	839	7.8	30.8
Absence of extremities	1,285	293	2.7	22.8
Paralysis of extremities	2,138	550	5.1	25.7
Deformity or orthopedic impairment	29,499	13,216	122.4	44.8
Back	16,905	8,705	80.6	51.5
Upper extremities	4,170	1,438	13.3	34.5
Lower extremities	12,696	4,669	43.2	36.8

(continued)

(continued from previous page)

	total	18 to 44		
		number	rate	share of total
Digestive conditions				
Ulcer	3,709	1,270	11.8	34.2%
Hernia of abdominal cavity	4,470	1,166	10.8	26.1
Gastritis or duodenitis	3,729	1,461	13.5	39.2
Frequent indigestion	6,420	2,882	26.7	44.9
Enteritis or colitis	1,686	745	6.9	44.2
Spastic colon	2,083	849	7.9	40.8
Diverticula of intestines	2,529	263	2.4	10.4
Frequent constipation	3,149	913	8.5	29.0
Genitourinary, nervous, endocrine, metabolic, and blood conditions				
Goiter or other thyroid disorders	4,598	1,405	13.0	30.6
Diabetes	7,627	1,270	11.8	16.7
Anemias	3,457	1,798	16.7	52.0
Epilepsy	1,335	478	4.4	35.8
Migraine headache	11,546	6,477	60.0	56.1
Neuralgia or neuritis, unspecified	353	30	0.3	8.5
Kidney trouble	2,553	1,272	11.8	49.8
Bladder disorders	3,139	1,215	11.3	38.7
Diseases of prostate	2,803	241	2.2	8.6
Disease of female genital organs	4,420	2,615	24.2	59.2
Circulatory conditions				
Rheumatic fever	1,759	745	6.9	42.4
Heart disease	20,653	4,246	39.3	20.6
Ischemic heart disease	7,672	453	4.2	5.9
Heart rhythm disorders	8,716	3,140	29.1	36.0
Tachycardia or rapid heart	2,310	687	6.4	29.7
Heart murmurs	4,783	2,034	18.8	42.5
Other heart rhythm disorders	1,624	420	3.9	25.9
Other selected diseases of heart	4,265	653	6.0	15.3
High blood pressure (hypertension)	28,314	5,355	49.6	18.9
Cerebrovascular disease	2,999	221	2.0	7.4
Hardening of the arteries	1,556	–	–	–
Varicose veins of lower extremities	7,399	2,397	22.2	32.4
Hemorrhoids	8,531	3,716	34.4	45.1

(continued)

(continued from previous page)

	total	18 to 44		
		number	rate	share of total
Respiratory conditions				
Chronic bronchitis	14,150	4,904	45.4	34.7%
Asthma	14,596	6,141	56.9	42.1
Hay fever or allergic rhinitis	23,721	11,809	109.4	49.8
Chronic sinusitis	33,161	15,628	144.7	47.1
Deviated nasal septum	1,985	868	8.0	43.7
Chronic disease of tonsils and adenoids	2,513	885	8.2	35.2
Emphysema	1,821	90	0.8	4.9

Note: Chronic conditions are those that last at least three months or belong to a group of conditions that are considered to be chronic regardless of when they begin. (–) means sample is too small to make a reliable estimate.
Source: National Center for Health Statistics, Current Estimates from the National Health Interview Survey, 1996, *Series 10, No. 200, 1999, Internet site <www.cdc.gov/nchs/data/nvs48_3.pdf>; calculations by the author*

Most Deaths of Young Adults Are Preventable

Accidents are the leading killers of 15-to-34-year-olds.

When young adults die, it is most commonly from a preventable cause. Accidents claim the most lives among both 15-to-24-year-olds and 25-to-34-year-olds. Murder is the second-most common cause of death among people aged 15 to 24, while suicide is the second-most common cause among those aged 25 to 34.

People aged 15 to 24 are most likely to die a violent death. Three-quarters of deaths in the age group in 1998 were the result of accidents, murder, or suicide. The fourth leading cause of death for this age group—cancer—accounted for only 6 percent of deaths.

Among 25-to-34-year-olds, diseases resulting from HIV infection were the second-leading cause of death for many years. This cause fell to number six in 1998, thanks to new treatments.

Although more could be done to reduce the death rate of young adults, some progress has been made. The life expectancy of Americans continues to rise. At age 25, life expectancy is another 53 years. At age 35, another 44 years of life remain on average. If middle age is defined as the point at which people have lived half their lives, then 35-year-olds are not there yet since they have, on average, more than 40 years left to live.

♦ Young adults are not as safety-conscious as middle-aged and older adults, the ones pushing the auto industry to produce safer cars. As cars become safer, young adults may benefit the most since automobile accidents are the most common cause of accidental death in the age group.

Leading Causes of Death for People Aged 15 to 24, 1998

(number and percent distribution of deaths for the ten leading causes of death for people aged 15 to 24, 1998)

		number	percent
All causes		**30,627**	**100.0%**
1.	Accidents	13,349	43.6
2.	Homicide and legal intervention	5,506	18.0
3.	Suicide	4,135	13.5
4.	Cancer	1,699	5.5
5.	Heart disease	1,057	3.5
6.	Congenital anomalies	450	1.5
7.	Chronic obstructive pulmonary diseases	239	0.8
8.	Pneumonia and influenza	215	0.7
9.	Human immunodeficiency virus	194	0.6
10.	Cerebrovascular diseases	178	0.6
All other causes		3,605	11.8

Source: National Center for Health Statistics, Deaths: Final Data for 1998, *National Vital Statistics Report, Vol. 48, No. 11, 2000, Internet site <www.cdc.gov/nchs/data/nvs48_11.pdf>; calculations by the author*

Leading Causes of Death for People Aged 25 to 34, 1998

(number and percent distribution of deaths for the ten leading causes of death for people aged 25 to 34, 1998)

		number	percent
All causes		**42,516**	**100.0%**
1.	Accidents	12,045	28.3
2.	Suicide	5,365	12.6
3.	Homicide and legal intervention	4,565	10.7
4.	Cancer	4,385	10.3
5.	Heart diseases	3,207	7.5
6.	Human immunodeficiency virus	2,912	6.8
7.	Cerebrovascular diseases	670	1.6
8.	Diabetes mellitus	636	1.5
9.	Pneumonia and influenza	531	1.2
10.	Chronic liver diseases and cirrhosis	506	1.2
	All other causes	7,694	18.1

Source: National Center for Health Statistics, Deaths: Final Data for 1998, *National Vital Statistics Report, Vol. 48, No. 11, 2000, Internet site <www.cdc.gov/nchs/data/nvs48_11.pdf>; calculations by the author*

Life Expectancy of People Aged 35 or Younger by Sex and Race, 1998

(years of life remaining at birth to age 35, by sex and race, 1998)

	total	men			women		
	total	total	black	white	total	black	white
At birth	76.7	73.8	67.6	74.5	79.5	74.8	80.0
Aged 1	76.3	73.4	67.7	74.0	79.0	74.8	79.4
Aged 5	72.4	69.5	63.9	70.1	75.1	70.9	75.5
Aged 10	67.4	64.6	59.0	65.2	70.2	66.0	70.6
Aged 15	62.5	59.7	54.1	60.2	65.2	61.1	65.6
Aged 20	57.7	55.0	49.5	55.5	60.3	56.2	60.8
Aged 25	53.0	50.3	45.1	50.8	55.5	51.4	55.9
Aged 30	48.2	45.7	40.6	46.1	50.6	46.7	51.0
Aged 35	43.5	41.0	36.2	41.5	45.8	42.0	46.2

Source: National Center for Health Statistics, Deaths: Final Data for 1998, *National Vital Statistics Report, Vol. 48, No. 18, 2000, Internet site <www.cdc.gov/nchs/data/nvs48_18.pdf>*

4

Income

♦ After years of decline, the incomes of households headed by young adults rose substantially during the 1990s. Among householders aged 15 to 24, median income rose 10 percent between 1990 and 1999, after adjusting for inflation.

♦ Among young-adult households, married couples have the highest incomes. The median income of married couples headed by people aged 15 to 34 was $50,123 compared with a median of $38,105 for all households in the age group.

♦ Households headed by non-Hispanic whites under age 35 had a median income of $43,169 in 1999. The median income of black households in the age group was a much lower $25,219 because few black households are headed by married couples.

♦ The median income of men aged 15 to 34 who work full-time stood at $29,463 in 1999, less than the $37,574 for all men who work full-time. The incomes of young women who work full-time are lower than those of men—a median of only $24,432 in 1999.

♦ The youngest adults are more likely to be poor than the average American. Overall, 12 percent of Americans lived in poverty in 1999. Among people aged 18 to 24, however, 17 percent were poor.

Household Incomes of Young Adults Are on the Rise

During the 1990s, the incomes of young-adult households have grown faster than inflation.

Between 1990 and 1999, the median income of households headed by people aged 15 to 24 rose 10 percent, after adjusting for inflation. The median for households headed by people aged 25 to 34 rose 9 percent. During those years, the median income of all households rose a smaller 7 percent.

Although the fortunes of the youngest households have improved, their median income is still below the level of 1980. In that year, the median income of householders aged 15 to 24 was $25,731, versus $25,171 in 1999.

The median income of households headed by people aged 25 to 34 was lower in the early 1990s than in 1980. By 1997, however, their median had finally exceeded the 1980 level. In 1999, the median income of householders aged 25 to 34 was $42,174—8 percent higher than in 1980.

♦ For most young adults, rising incomes mean more spending, although concern about the future of Social Security is prompting many in the age group to begin saving earlier than previous generations did.

Incomes of young adults rose substantially in the 1990s

(median income of households headed by people aged 15 to 34, 1990 and 1999; in 1999 dollars)

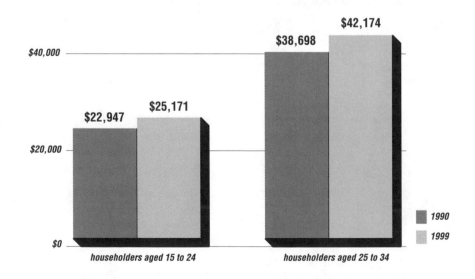

Median Income of Households Headed by People Aged 15 to 34, 1980 to 1999

(median income of total households and households headed by people aged 15 to 34, 1980–99; percent change for selected years; in 1999 dollars)

		householders aged 15 to 34	
	total	15 to 24	25 to 34
1999	$40,816	$25,171	$42,174
1998	39,744	24,084	40,954
1997	38,411	23,441	39,625
1996	37,686	22,763	38,107
1995	37,251	22,934	37,934
1994	36,270	21,741	37,267
1993	36,019	22,290	36,065
1992	36,379	20,974	37,095
1991	36,850	22,400	37,726
1990	38,168	22,947	38,698
1989	38,837	25,075	40,069
1988	38,341	23,997	40,007
1987	38,220	24,120	39,547
1986	37,845	23,272	39,367
1985	36,568	23,301	38,840
1984	35,942	22,493	38,058
1983	34,934	22,417	36,374
1982	35,152	24,077	37,086
1981	35,269	24,485	37,930
1980	35,850	25,731	39,144
Percent change			
1998–1999	2.7%	4.5%	3.0%
1990–1999	6.9	9.7	9.0
1980–1999	13.9	–2.2	7.7

Source: Bureau of the Census, Internet site <www.census.gov/hhes/income/histinc/h10.html>; calculations by the author

Incomes Start Low, but Rise Rapidly

Household income jumps sharply after age 25.

Many young adults are still in school. Even if they have jobs, their incomes tend to be low because they are in entry-level positions. Half of households headed by people aged 15 to 24 have incomes of less than $25,171.

Incomes rise rapidly, however, as young adults complete school and gain job experience. Among households headed by people aged 25 to 29, median income stood at $38,282 in 1999. Households headed by people aged 30 to 34 had an even higher median of $45,756.

Among young adults, two incomes are the norm. Consequently, a substantial 19 percent of households headed by people aged 30 to 34 have incomes of at least $80,000 and 11 percent have incomes of $100,000 or more.

♦ As more young men and women attend college, the proportion of young-adult households with relatively high incomes may increase in the coming years.

Many young householders have substantial incomes

(median income of households headed by people under age 35, 1999)

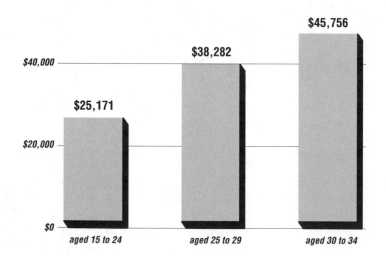

Income Distribution of Households Headed by People Aged 15 to 34, 1999: Total Households

(number and percent distribution of total households and households headed by people aged 15 to 34 by income, 1999; households in thousands as of 2000)

| | | aged 15 to 34 | | | aged 25 to 34 | |
| | | | | | aged 25 to 34 | |
	total	total	15 to 24	total	25 to 29	30 to 34
Total households	**104,705**	**24,487**	**5,860**	**18,627**	**8,520**	**10,107**
Under $10,000	9,656	2,272	1,043	1,229	655	574
$10,000 to $19,999	15,142	3,519	1,239	2,280	1,164	1,117
$20,000 to $29,999	14,128	3,801	1,236	2,565	1,325	1,240
$30,000 to $39,999	12,398	3,468	799	2,669	1,262	1,408
$40,000 to $49,999	10,524	2,751	565	2,186	990	1,196
$50,000 to $59,999	8,853	2,264	371	1,893	866	1,027
$60,000 to $69,999	7,492	1,819	202	1,617	731	885
$70,000 to $79,999	5,830	1,280	113	1,167	477	689
$80,000 to $89,999	4,549	873	84	789	309	480
$90,000 to $99,999	3,303	574	53	521	189	332
$100,000 or more	12,831	1,865	154	1,711	554	1,157
Median income	$40,816	$38,105	$25,171	$42,174	$38,282	$45,756
Total households	**100.0%**	**100.0%**	**100.0%**	**100.0%**	**100.0%**	**100.0%**
Under $10,000	9.2	9.3	17.8	6.6	7.7	5.7
$10,000 to $19,999	14.5	14.4	21.1	12.2	13.7	11.1
$20,000 to $29,999	13.5	15.5	21.1	13.8	15.6	12.3
$30,000 to $39,999	11.8	14.2	13.6	14.3	14.8	13.9
$40,000 to $49,999	10.1	11.2	9.6	11.7	11.6	11.8
$50,000 to $59,999	8.5	9.2	6.3	10.2	10.2	10.2
$60,000 to $69,999	7.2	7.4	3.4	8.7	8.6	8.8
$70,000 to $79,999	5.6	5.2	1.9	6.3	5.6	6.8
$80,000 to $89,999	4.3	3.6	1.4	4.2	3.6	4.7
$90,000 to $99,999	3.2	2.3	0.9	2.8	2.2	3.3
$100,000 or more	12.3	7.6	2.6	9.2	6.5	11.4

Source: Bureau of the Census, data from the 2000 Current Population Survey, Internet site <http://ferret.bls.census.gov/macro/03200/hhinc/new02_001.htm>; calculations by the author

Incomes Are Highest for Non-Hispanic White Households

Among young householders, the incomes of non-Hispanic whites are far higher than those of blacks or Hispanics.

The median income of households headed by non-Hispanic whites under age 35 was $43,169 in 1999. For black householders in the age group, median income was a much lower $25,219. For Hispanics, it was $29,528. Fully 41 percent of non-Hispanic white households headed by 15-to-34-year-olds have incomes of $50,000 or more. In contrast, only 20 percent of black and 22 percent of Hispanic households had incomes that high.

The primary reason for income differences by race and Hispanic origin is the number of earners per household. Because non-Hispanic white households are more likely to be two-earner married couples than black or Hispanic households, their incomes are considerably higher. Education also accounts for some of the gap. Non-Hispanic whites are more likely to have completed college than blacks or Hispanics.

♦ The fortunes of minority householders are not likely to improve until dual-earner couples make up a larger share of their households and college graduation rates approach those of non-Hispanic whites.

Incomes of young householders vary by race and Hispanic origin

(median income of households headed by people aged 15 to 34 by race and Hispanic origin, 1999)

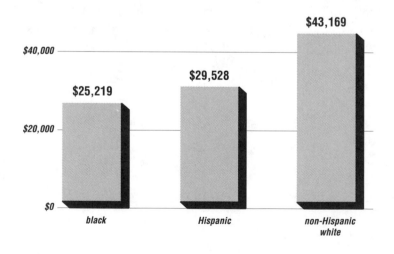

Income Distribution of Households Headed by People Aged 15 to 34, 1999: Black Households

(number and percent distribution of total black households and households headed by blacks aged 15 to 34 by income, 1999; households in thousands as of 2000)

| | | aged 15 to 34 | | | aged 25 to 34 | |
	total	total	15 to 24	total	25 to 29	30 to 34
Total black households	**12,849**	**3,726**	**1,002**	**2,724**	**1,291**	**1,433**
Under $10,000	2,368	764	375	389	202	188
$10,000 to $19,999	2,428	726	196	530	296	236
$20,000 to $29,999	1,973	696	201	495	233	263
$30,000 to $39,999	1,498	514	97	417	170	246
$40,000 to $49,999	1,150	286	47	239	108	130
$50,000 to $59,999	930	236	46	190	103	87
$60,000 to $69,999	687	167	14	153	71	83
$70,000 to $79,999	428	97	5	92	47	43
$80,000 to $89,999	325	56	0	56	14	43
$90,000 to $99,999	275	53	17	36	19	18
$100,000 or more	788	129	3	126	29	97
Median income	$27,910	$25,219	$15,576	$28,766	$26,702	$31,259
Total black households	**100.0%**	**100.0%**	**100.0%**	**100.0%**	**100.0%**	**100.0%**
Under $10,000	18.4	20.5	37.4	14.3	15.6	13.1
$10,000 to $19,999	18.9	19.5	19.6	19.5	22.9	16.5
$20,000 to $29,999	15.4	18.7	20.1	18.2	18.0	18.4
$30,000 to $39,999	11.7	13.8	9.7	15.3	13.2	17.2
$40,000 to $49,999	9.0	7.7	4.7	8.8	8.4	9.1
$50,000 to $59,999	7.2	6.3	4.6	7.0	8.0	6.1
$60,000 to $69,999	5.3	4.5	1.4	5.6	5.5	5.8
$70,000 to $79,999	3.3	2.6	0.5	3.4	3.6	3.0
$80,000 to $89,999	2.5	1.5	0.0	2.1	1.1	3.0
$90,000 to $99,999	2.1	1.4	1.7	1.3	1.5	1.3
$100,000 or more	6.1	3.5	0.3	4.6	2.2	6.8

Source: Bureau of the Census, data from the 2000 Current Population Survey, Internet site <http://ferret.bls .census.gov/macro/03200/hhinc/new02_001.htm>; calculations by the author

Income Distribution of Households Headed by People Aged 15 to 34, 1999: Hispanic Households

(number and percent distribution of total Hispanic households and households headed by Hispanics aged 15 to 34 by income, 1999; households in thousands as of 2000)

| | | aged 15 to 34 | | | | |
| | | | | aged 25 to 34 | | |
	total	total	15 to 24	total	25 to 29	30 to 34
Total households	**9,319**	**3,348**	**871**	**2,477**	**1,133**	**1,344**
Under $10,000	1107	345	128	217	103	112
$10,000 to $19,999	1813	735	226	509	250	258
$20,000 to $29,999	1617	644	193	451	234	216
$30,000 to $39,999	1281	484	109	375	150	225
$40,000 to $49,999	974	392	82	310	136	174
$50,000 to $59,999	645	216	44	172	70	101
$60,000 to $69,999	550	164	30	134	67	66
$70,000 to $79,999	389	123	18	105	43	62
$80,000 to $89,999	254	67	12	55	25	30
$90,000 to $99,999	203	66	8	58	20	39
$100,000 or more	488	107	17	90	31	60
Median income	$30,735	$29,528	$24,268	$31,377	$28,858	$33,126
Total Hispanic households	**100.0%**	**100.0%**	**100.0%**	**100.0%**	**100.0%**	**100.0%**
Under $10,000	11.9	10.3	14.7	8.8	9.1	8.3
$10,000 to $19,999	19.5	22.0	25.9	20.5	22.1	19.2
$20,000 to $29,999	17.4	19.2	22.2	18.2	20.7	16.1
$30,000 to $39,999	13.7	14.5	12.5	15.1	13.2	16.7
$40,000 to $49,999	10.5	11.7	9.4	12.5	12.0	12.9
$50,000 to $59,999	6.9	6.5	5.1	6.9	6.2	7.5
$60,000 to $69,999	5.9	4.9	3.4	5.4	5.9	4.9
$70,000 to $79,999	4.2	3.7	2.1	4.2	3.8	4.6
$80,000 to $89,999	2.7	2.0	1.4	2.2	2.2	2.2
$90,000 to $99,999	2.2	2.0	0.9	2.3	1.8	2.9
$100,000 or more	5.2	3.2	2.0	3.6	2.7	4.5

Source: Bureau of the Census, data from the 2000 Current Population Survey, Internet site <http://ferret.bls .census.gov/macro/03200/hhinc/new02_001.htm>; calculations by the author

Income Distribution of Households Headed by People Aged 15 to 34, 1999: White Households

(number and percent distribution of total white households and households headed by whites aged 15 to 34 by income, 1999; households in thousands as of 2000)

| | | aged 15 to 34 | | | | |
| | | | | aged 25 to 34 | | |
	total	*total*	*15 to 24*	*total*	*25 to 29*	*30 to 34*
Total white households	**87,671**	**19,412**	**4,541**	**14,871**	**6,744**	**8,127**
Under $10,000	6,856	1,356	599	757	400	355
$10,000 to $19,999	12,231	2,618	968	1,650	827	822
$20,000 to $29,999	11,701	2,925	975	1,950	1,025	925
$30,000 to $39,999	10,414	2,748	665	2,083	1,010	1,074
$40,000 to $49,999	8,976	2,344	495	1,849	836	1,012
$50,000 to $59,999	7,576	1,911	302	1,609	718	891
$60,000 to $69,999	6,547	1,558	184	1,374	607	766
$70,000 to $79,999	5,135	1,098	105	993	393	600
$80,000 to $89,999	4,039	786	79	707	288	420
$90,000 to $99,999	2895	494	36	458	160	298
$100,000 or more	11,298	1,579	135	1,444	482	962
Median income	$42,504	$40,916	$26,787	$45,230	$41,066	$48,452
Total white households	**100.0%**	**100.0%**	**100.0%**	**100.0%**	**100.0%**	**100.0%**
Under $10,000	7.8	7.0	13.2	5.1	5.9	4.4
$10,000 to $19,999	14.0	13.5	21.3	11.1	12.3	10.1
$20,000 to $29,999	13.3	15.1	21.5	13.1	15.2	11.4
$30,000 to $39,999	11.9	14.2	14.6	14.0	15.0	13.2
$40,000 to $49,999	10.2	12.1	10.9	12.4	12.4	12.5
$50,000 to $59,999	8.6	9.8	6.7	10.8	10.6	11.0
$60,000 to $69,999	7.5	8.0	4.1	9.2	9.0	9.4
$70,000 to $79,999	5.9	5.7	2.3	6.7	5.8	7.4
$80,000 to $89,999	4.6	4.0	1.7	4.8	4.3	5.2
$90,000 to $99,999	3.3	2.5	0.8	3.1	2.4	3.7
$100,000 or more	12.9	8.1	3.0	9.7	7.1	11.8

Source: Bureau of the Census, data from the 2000 Current Population Survey, Internet site <http://ferret.bls .census.gov/macro/03200/hhinc/new02_001.htm>; calculations by the author

Income Distribution of Households Headed by People Aged 15 to 34, 1999: Non-Hispanic White Households

(number and percent distribution of total non-Hispanic white households and households headed by non-Hispanic whites aged 15 to 34 by income, 1999; households in thousands as of 2000)

| | | aged 15 to 34 | | | | |
| | | | | aged 25 to 34 | | |
	total	total	15 to 24	total	25 to 29	30 to 34
Total non-Hispanic white households	**78,819**	**16,254**	**3,721**	**12,533**	**5,678**	**6,855**
Under $10,000	5,813	1,040	485	555	303	251
$10,000 to $19,999	10,513	1,926	758	1,168	596	572
$20,000 to $29,999	10,152	2,304	785	1,519	800	719
$30,000 to $39,999	9,179	2,280	557	1,723	863	860
$40,000 to $49,999	8,050	1,979	421	1,558	705	852
$50,000 to $59,999	6,975	1,714	262	1,452	653	798
$60,000 to $69,999	6,025	1,404	154	1,250	549	701
$70,000 to $79,999	4,764	979	86	893	350	542
$80,000 to $89,999	3,795	720	66	654	263	392
$90,000 to $99,999	2,714	435	29	406	144	263
$100,000 and over	10,841	1,473	118	1,355	451	904
Median income	$44,366	$43,169	$27,237	$47,899	$43,510	$51,769
Total non-Hispanic white households	**100.0%**	**100.0%**	**100.0%**	**100.0%**	**100.0%**	**100.0%**
Under $10,000	7.4	6.4	13.0	4.4	5.3	3.7
$10,000 to $19,999	13.3	11.8	20.4	9.3	10.5	8.3
$20,000 to $29,999	12.9	14.2	21.1	12.1	14.1	10.5
$30,000 to $39,999	11.6	14.0	15.0	13.7	15.2	12.5
$40,000 to $49,999	10.2	12.2	11.3	12.4	12.4	12.4
$50,000 to $59,999	8.8	10.5	7.0	11.6	11.5	11.6
$60,000 to $69,999	7.6	8.6	4.1	10.0	9.7	10.2
$70,000 to $79,999	6.0	6.0	2.3	7.1	6.2	7.9
$80,000 to $89,999	4.8	4.4	1.8	5.2	4.6	5.7
$90,000 to $99,999	3.4	2.7	0.8	3.2	2.5	3.8
$100,000 and over	13.8	9.1	3.2	10.8	7.9	13.2

Source: Bureau of the Census, Internet site <http://ferret.bls.census.gov/macro/03200/hhinc/new02_005.htm>; calculations by the author

Two Incomes Give Young Marrieds Higher Incomes

Young single mothers have the lowest incomes.

The incomes of households headed by people aged 15 to 34 vary dramatically by household type. Married couples have the highest incomes among households headed by people aged 25 to 34, a median of $53,169 in 1999. Among householders aged 15 to 24, however, the median income of male-headed families slightly exceeds that of married couples ($35,692 versus $30,399).

Female-headed families in the 15-to-34 age group had a median income of only $18,944 in 1999. Most are single parents. The median income of male-headed families ($38,749) is more than twice that of female-headed families. The median income of male nonfamily householders (those who live alone or with nonrelatives) was $33,946 in 1999, compared with $29,274 for their female counterparts.

♦ The lack of affordable and reliable day care is one factor behind the lower incomes of young single mothers. Many also interrupted their education when they had children, which makes it difficult for them to get higher paying jobs.

Incomes of young couples are above average

(median income of total households and married couples headed by people aged 15 to 34, 1999)

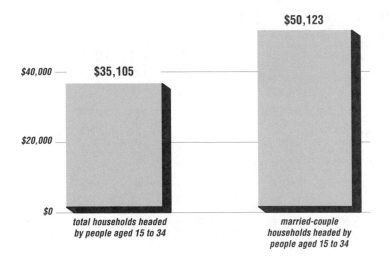

Income Distribution of Households by Household Type, 1999: Aged 15 to 34

(number and percent distribution of households headed by people aged 15 to 34, by income and household type, 1999; households in thousands as of 2000)

| | | family households | | | nonfamily households | | | |
| | | | | | female householder | | male householder | |
	total	married couples	female hh no spouse present	male hh no spouse present	total	living alone	total	living alone
Total households	**24,487**	**10,839**	**4,074**	**1,446**	**3,393**	**2,156**	**4,734**	**2,835**
Under $10,000	2,272	288	1,098	81	409	348	395	315
$10,000 to $19,999	3,519	873	1,028	201	631	497	784	578
$20,000 to $29,999	3,801	1,305	746	230	654	462	865	588
$30,000 to $39,999	3,468	1,501	452	241	566	402	711	497
$40,000 to $49,999	2,751	1,436	281	189	320	165	526	292
$50,000 to $59,999	2,264	1,334	134	144	262	105	391	188
$60,000 to $69,999	1,819	1,184	87	83	150	47	316	123
$70,000 to $79,999	1,280	827	71	70	87	28	223	99
$80,000 to $89,999	873	545	61	50	66	15	148	37
$90,000 to $99,999	574	376	42	38	40	11	81	21
$100,000 or more	1,865	1,167	74	119	540	76	298	99
Median income	$38,105	$50,123	$18,944	$38,749	$29,274	$25,688	$33,946	$28,733
Total households	**100.0%**	**100.0%**	**100.0%**	**100.0%**	**100.0%**	**100.0%**	**100.0%**	**100.0%**
Under $10,000	9.3	2.7	27.0	5.6	12.1	16.1	8.3	11.1
$10,000 to $19,999	14.4	8.1	25.2	13.9	18.6	23.1	16.6	20.4
$20,000 to $29,999	15.5	12.0	18.3	15.9	19.3	21.4	18.3	20.7
$30,000 to $39,999	14.2	13.8	11.1	16.7	16.7	18.6	15.0	17.5
$40,000 to $49,999	11.2	13.2	6.9	13.1	9.4	7.7	11.1	10.3
$50,000 to $59,999	9.2	12.3	3.3	10.0	7.7	4.9	8.3	6.6
$60,000 to $69,999	7.4	10.9	2.1	5.7	4.4	2.2	6.7	4.3
$70,000 to $79,999	5.2	7.6	1.7	4.8	2.6	1.3	4.7	3.5
$80,000 to $89,999	3.6	5.0	1.5	3.5	1.9	0.7	3.1	1.3
$90,000 to $99,999	2.3	3.5	1.0	2.6	1.2	0.5	1.7	0.7
$100,000 or more	7.6	10.8	1.8	8.2	6.1	3.5	6.3	3.5

Source: Bureau of the Census, data from the 2000 Current Population Survey, Internet site <http://ferret.bls.census.gov/macro/03200/hhinc/new02_000.htm>; calculations by the author

Income Distribution of Households by Household Type, 1999: Aged 15 to 24

(number and percent distribution of households headed by people aged 15 to 24, by income and household type, 1999; households in thousands as of 2000)

| | | family households | | | nonfamily households | | | |
| | | | | | female householder | | male householder | |
	total	married couples	female hh no spouse present	male hh no spouse present	total	living alone	total	living alone
Total households	**5,860**	**1,450**	**1,342**	**560**	**1,221**	**587**	**1,286**	**556**
Under $10,000	1,043	83	468	44	254	204	192	131
$10,000 to $19,999	1,239	249	313	66	297	193	313	184
$20,000 to $29,999	1,236	380	225	108	251	119	272	117
$30,000 to $39,999	799	269	116	103	138	43	173	59
$40,000 to $49,999	565	190	86	74	96	9	119	27
$50,000 to $59,999	371	103	49	53	79	10	89	23
$60,000 to $69,999	202	73	26	31	35	2	37	7
$70,000 to $79,999	113	43	18	11	16	–	24	7
$80,000 to $89,999	84	16	10	19	16	–	22	–
$90,000 to $99,999	53	9	13	21	5	–	6	–
$100,000 or more	154	32	19	30	34	9	40	–
Median income	$25,171	$30,399	$16,071	$35,692	$21,962	$14,587	$24,361	$17,553
Total households	**100.0%**	**100.0%**	**100.0%**	**100.0%**	**100.0%**	**100.0%**	**100.0%**	**100.0%**
Under $10,000	17.8	5.7	34.9	7.9	20.8	34.8	14.9	23.6
$10,000 to $19,999	21.1	17.2	23.3	11.8	24.3	32.9	24.3	33.1
$20,000 to $29,999	21.1	26.2	16.8	19.3	20.6	20.3	21.2	21.0
$30,000 to $39,999	13.6	18.6	8.6	18.4	11.3	7.3	13.5	10.6
$40,000 to $49,999	9.6	13.1	6.4	13.2	7.9	1.5	9.3	4.9
$50,000 to $59,999	6.3	7.1	3.7	9.5	6.5	1.7	6.9	4.1
$60,000 to $69,999	3.4	5.0	1.9	5.5	2.9	0.3	2.9	1.3
$70,000 to $79,999	1.9	3.0	1.3	2.0	1.3	–	1.9	1.3
$80,000 to $89,999	1.4	1.1	0.7	3.4	1.3	–	1.7	–
$90,000 to $99,999	0.9	0.6	1.0	3.8	0.4	–	0.5	–
$100,000 or more	2.6	2.2	1.4	5.4	2.8	1.5	3.1	–

Note: (–) means sample is too small to make a reliable estimate.
Source: Bureau of the Census, data from the 2000 Current Population Survey, Internet site <http://ferret.bls
.census.gov/macro/03200/hhinc/new02_000.htm>; calculations by the author

Income Distribution of Households by Household Type, 1999: Aged 25 to 34

(number and percent distribution of households headed by people aged 25 to 34 by income and household type, 1999; households in thousands as of 2000)

		family households			nonfamily households			
					female householder		male householder	
	total	married couples	female hh no spouse present	male hh no spouse present	total	living alone	total	living alone
Total households	**18,627**	**9,389**	**2,732**	**886**	**2,172**	**1,569**	**3,448**	**2,279**
Under $10,000	1,229	205	630	37	155	144	203	184
$10,000 to $19,999	2,280	624	715	135	334	304	471	394
$20,000 to $29,999	2,565	925	521	122	403	343	593	471
$30,000 to $39,999	2,669	1,232	336	138	428	359	538	438
$40,000 to $49,999	2,186	1,246	195	115	224	156	407	265
$50,000 to $59,999	1,893	1,231	85	91	183	95	302	165
$60,000 to $69,999	1,617	1,111	61	52	115	45	279	116
$70,000 to $79,999	1,167	784	53	59	71	28	199	92
$80,000 to $89,999	789	529	51	31	50	15	126	37
$90,000 to $99,999	521	367	29	17	35	11	75	21
$100,000 or more	1,711	1,135	55	89	174	67	258	99
Median income	$42,174	$53,169	$20,356	$40,681	$33,385	$29,841	$37,521	$31,461
Total households	**100.0%**	**100.0%**	**100.0%**	**100.0%**	**100.0%**	**100.0%**	**100.0%**	**100.0%**
Under $10,000	6.6	2.2	23.1	4.2	7.1	9.2	5.9	8.1
$10,000 to $19,999	12.2	6.6	26.2	15.2	15.4	19.4	13.7	17.3
$20,000 to $29,999	13.8	9.9	19.1	13.8	18.6	21.9	17.2	20.7
$30,000 to $39,999	14.3	13.1	12.3	15.6	19.7	22.9	15.6	19.2
$40,000 to $49,999	11.7	13.3	7.1	13.0	10.3	9.9	11.8	11.6
$50,000 to $59,999	10.2	13.1	3.1	10.3	8.4	6.1	8.8	7.2
$60,000 to $69,999	8.7	11.8	2.2	5.9	5.3	2.9	8.1	5.1
$70,000 to $79,999	6.3	8.4	1.9	6.7	3.3	1.8	5.8	4.0
$80,000 to $89,999	4.2	5.6	1.9	3.5	2.3	1.0	3.7	1.6
$90,000 to $99,999	2.8	3.9	1.1	1.9	1.6	0.7	2.2	0.9
$100,000 or more	9.2	12.1	2.0	10.0	8.0	4.3	7.5	4.3

Source: Bureau of the Census, data from the 2000 Current Population Survey, Internet site <http://ferret.bls .census.gov/macro/03200/hhinc/new02_000.htm>; calculations by the author

Income Distribution of Households by Household Type, 1999: Aged 25 to 29

(number and percent distribution of households headed by people aged 25 to 29, by income and household type, 1999; households in thousands as of 2000)

| | | family households | | | nonfamily households | | | |
| | | | | | female householder | | male householder | |
	total	married couples	female hh no spouse present	male hh no spouse present	total	living alone	total	living alone
Total households	**8,520**	**3,775**	**1,289**	**426**	**1,249**	**848**	**1,782**	**1,079**
Under $10,000	655	119	314	23	93	81	105	94
$10,000 to $19,999	1,164	284	382	67	186	162	247	201
$20,000 to $29,999	1,325	456	228	62	255	211	324	251
$30,000 to $39,999	1,262	545	146	59	245	187	267	196
$40,000 to $49,999	990	536	76	57	125	77	195	118
$50,000 to $59,999	866	490	51	46	111	52	166	80
$60,000 to $69,999	731	475	21	36	68	19	133	50
$70,000 to $79,999	477	281	28	33	35	13	100	31
$80,000 to $89,999	309	190	23	8	26	9	60	9
$90,000 to $99,999	189	113	5	0	24	6	48	8
$100,000 or more	554	289	13	34	81	29	137	40
Median income	$38,282	$49,018	$18,484	$40,319	$32,120	$28,454	$37,455	$29,705
Total households	**100.0%**	**100.0%**	**100.0%**	**100.0%**	**100.0%**	**100.0%**	**100.0%**	**100.0%**
Under $10,000	7.7	3.2	24.4	5.4	7.4	9.6	5.9	8.7
$10,000 to $19,999	13.7	7.5	29.6	15.7	14.9	19.1	13.9	18.6
$20,000 to $29,999	15.6	12.1	17.7	14.6	20.4	24.9	18.2	23.3
$30,000 to $39,999	14.8	14.4	11.3	13.8	19.6	22.1	15.0	18.2
$40,000 to $49,999	11.6	14.2	5.9	13.4	10.0	9.1	10.9	10.9
$50,000 to $59,999	10.2	13.0	4.0	10.8	8.9	6.1	9.3	7.4
$60,000 to $69,999	8.6	12.6	1.6	8.5	5.4	2.2	7.5	4.6
$70,000 to $79,999	5.6	7.4	2.2	7.7	2.8	1.5	5.6	2.9
$80,000 to $89,999	3.6	5.0	1.8	1.9	2.1	1.1	3.4	0.8
$90,000 to $99,999	2.2	3.0	0.4	0.0	1.9	0.7	2.7	0.7
$100,000 or more	6.5	7.7	1.0	8.0	6.5	3.4	7.7	3.7

Source: Bureau of the Census, data from the 2000 Current Population Survey, Internet site <http://ferret.bls .census.gov/macro/03200/hhinc/new02_000.htm>; calculations by the author

Income Distribution of Households by Household Type, 1999: Aged 30 to 34

(number and percent distribution of households headed by people aged 30 to 34, by income and household type, 1999; households in thousands as of 2000)

| | | family households | | | nonfamily households | | | |
| | | | | | female householder | | male householder | |
	total	married couples	female hh no spouse present	male hh no spouse present	total	living alone	total	living alone
Total households	**10,107**	**5,615**	**1,443**	**460**	**923**	**720**	**1,666**	**1,200**
Under $10,000	574	86	315	13	62	62	96	89
$10,000 to $19,999	1,117	341	334	68	149	141	226	193
$20,000 to $29,999	1,240	471	294	60	148	132	268	221
$30,000 to $39,999	1,408	686	189	79	182	172	271	241
$40,000 to $49,999	1,196	709	118	59	98	80	212	147
$50,000 to $59,999	1,027	741	34	44	72	43	137	84
$60,000 to $69,999	885	638	39	17	47	26	146	68
$70,000 to $79,999	689	503	26	27	36	16	97	60
$80,000 to $89,999	480	340	27	22	23	6	67	28
$90,000 to $99,999	332	255	24	17	10	5	27	13
$100,000 or more	1,157	846	42	55	93	38	121	59
Median income	$45,756	$56,799	$22,184	$40,993	$35,442	$31,354	$37,693	$32,876
Total households	**100.0%**	**100.0%**	**100.0%**	**100.0%**	**100.0%**	**100.0%**	**100.0%**	**100.0%**
Under $10,000	5.7	1.5	21.8	2.8	6.7	8.6	5.8	7.4
$10,000 to $19,999	11.1	6.1	23.1	14.8	16.1	19.6	13.6	16.1
$20,000 to $29,999	12.3	8.4	20.4	13.0	16.0	18.3	16.1	18.4
$30,000 to $39,999	13.9	12.2	13.1	17.2	19.7	23.9	16.3	20.1
$40,000 to $49,999	11.8	12.6	8.2	12.8	10.6	11.1	12.7	12.3
$50,000 to $59,999	10.2	13.2	2.4	9.6	7.8	6.0	8.2	7.0
$60,000 to $69,999	8.8	11.4	2.7	3.7	5.1	3.6	8.8	5.7
$70,000 to $79,999	6.8	9.0	1.8	5.9	3.9	2.2	5.8	5.0
$80,000 to $89,999	4.7	6.1	1.9	4.8	2.5	0.8	4.0	2.3
$90,000 to $99,999	3.3	4.5	1.7	3.7	1.1	0.7	1.6	1.1
$100,000 or more	11.4	15.1	2.9	12.0	10.1	5.3	7.3	4.9

Source: Bureau of the Census, data from the 2000 Current Population Survey, Internet site <http://ferret.bls .census.gov/macro/03200/hhinc/new02_000.htm>; calculations by the author

Incomes of Young Men Are Still below 1980 Levels

Their incomes have risen since 1990, but they have not yet fully recovered.

The incomes of young men have risen and fallen during the past two decades, but as of 1999 they remained below the level of 1980. Overall, the median income of men aged 15 to 24 fell 11 percent between 1980 and 1999, after adjusting for inflation. The income of men aged 25 to 34 dropped 5 percent during those years. In contrast, the median income of all men rose 8 percent between 1980 and 1999, after adjusting for inflation.

Although young men's incomes have still not regained the level of 1980, the past few years have been promising thanks to the strong economy of the late 1990s. The median income of men aged 25 to 34 rose 4 percent between 1998 and 1999, while that of men aged 15 to 24 rose 1 percent, after adjusting for inflation.

♦ The tight labor market has enabled young men to command higher wages, but it is unclear whether the gains will continue. As the economy slows, young men's income gains may slow with it.

Young men's incomes have risen since 1990

(median income of men aged 15 to 34 with income, 1990 and 1999; in 1999 dollars)

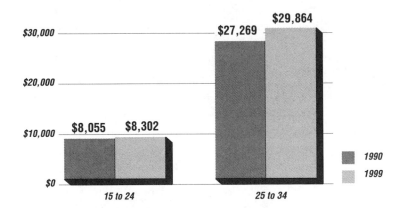

Median Income of Men Aged 15 to 34, 1980 to 1999

(median income of men with income, for total men and men aged 15 to 34, 1980 to 1999, and percent change for selected years; in 1999 dollars)

	total men	men aged 15 to 34	
		15 to 24	25 to 34
1999	$27,275	$8,302	$29,864
1998	27,077	8,371	28,738
1997	26,170	7,752	26,984
1996	25,307	7,390	26,736
1995	24,664	7,557	25,809
1994	24,417	7,923	25,413
1993	24,329	7,412	25,281
1992	24,289	7,477	25,527
1991	25,038	7,683	26,415
1990	25,867	8,055	27,269
1989	26,727	8,482	28,708
1988	26,628	8,229	29,267
1987	26,084	8,003	29,224
1986	26,015	8,031	29,128
1985	25,255	7,734	28,895
1984	25,014	7,551	29,011
1983	24,473	7,166	28,110
1982	24,310	7,715	28,608
1981	24,912	5,680	29,755
1980	25,364	9,306	31,539
Percent change			
1998–1999	0.7%	1.4%	3.9%
1990–1999	5.4	3.1	9.5
1980–1999	7.5	−10.8	−5.3

Source: Bureau of the Census, Internet site <www.census.gov/hhes/income/histinc/p08.html>; calculations by the author

Young Men's Incomes Are below Average

Nearly one-quarter of men aged 30 to 34 have incomes of $50,000 or more, however.

The median income of young men is much lower than that of older men because many are still in school, and among those who do work, many are in entry-level positions. One if four men aged 15 to 24 had no income in 1999. Most of those without income were full-time students, although some were unemployed. Overall, only 49 percent of men aged 15 to 34 work full-time, ranging from just 23 percent of men aged 15 to 24 to 76 percent of those aged 30 to 34.

The median income of men aged 15 to 24 who work full-time was just $19,515—much lower than the $37,574 median for all men who work full-time. Among men in their early thirties, however, median income ($35,873) is close to the median of all men who work full-time.

Among men aged 15 to 34, non-Hispanic whites have the highest incomes. Non-Hispanic white men had a median income of $21,331 in 1999 versus about $16,000 for black and Hispanic men. Among full-time workers, non-Hispanic whites have a median income of $32,490, compared with only $25,134 for blacks and $20,665 for Hispanics.

♦ Men in their thirties have higher incomes than younger men, but they also have more financial responsibilities. This means some younger men have more discretionary income

Non-Hispanic white men have the highest incomes

(median income of men aged 15 to 34 by race and Hispanic origin, 1999)

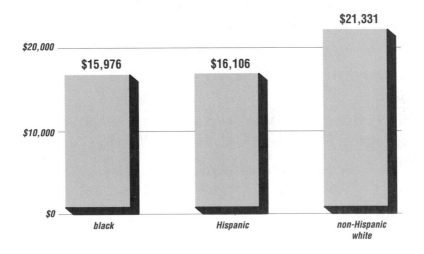

Income Distribution of Men Aged 15 to 34, 1999: Total Men

(number and percent distribution of men aged 15 or older and aged 15 to 34 by income, 1999; median income by work status, and percent working year-round, full-time; men in thousands as of 2000)

| | | aged 15 to 34 | | | | |
| | | | | aged 25 to 34 | | |
	total	*total*	*15 to 24*	*total*	*25 to 29*	*30 to 34*
Total men	**103,114**	**38,066**	**19,503**	**18,563**	**8,942**	**9,621**
Without income	7,091	5,664	5,075	589	374	215
With income	96,023	32,402	14,428	17,974	8,568	9,406
Under $10,000	17,036	9,646	7,966	1,680	945	734
$10,000 to $19,999	18,366	7,084	3,585	3,499	1,901	1,598
$20,000 to $29,999	15,982	5,667	1,818	3,849	2,035	1,814
$30,000 to $39,999	12,874	4,012	630	3,382	1,623	1,760
$40,000 to $49,999	9,345	2,446	224	2,222	923	1,299
$50,000 to $74,999	12,559	2,378	148	2,230	793	1,437
$75,000 to $99,999	4,520	637	41	596	182	415
$100,000 or more	5,346	532	16	516	168	348
Median income of men with income	$27,275	$20,263	$8,302	$29,864	$26,510	$32,273
Median income of full-time workers	37,574	29,463	19,515	32,599	39,600	35,873
Percent working full-time	55.8%	48.9%	22.9%	76.2%	72.1%	80.0%
Total men	**100.0%**	**100.0%**	**100.0%**	**100.0%**	**100.0%**	**100.0%**
Without income	6.9	14.9	26.0	3.2	4.2	2.2
With income	93.1	85.1	74.0	96.8	95.8	97.8
Under $10,000	16.5	25.3	40.8	9.1	10.6	7.6
$10,000 to $19,999	17.8	18.6	18.4	18.8	21.3	16.6
$20,000 to $29,999	15.5	14.9	9.3	20.7	22.8	18.9
$30,000 to $39,999	12.5	10.5	3.2	18.2	18.2	18.3
$40,000 to $49,999	9.1	6.4	1.1	12.0	10.3	13.5
$50,000 to $74,999	12.2	6.2	0.8	12.0	8.9	14.9
$75,000 to $99,999	4.4	1.7	0.2	3.2	2.0	4.3
$100,000 or more	5.2	1.4	0.1	2.8	1.9	3.6

Source: Bureau of the Census, data from the 2000 Current Population Survey, Internet site <http://ferret.bls .census.gov/macro/03200/perinc/new01_000.htm>; calculations by the author

Income Distribution of Men Aged 15 to 34, 1999: Black Men

(number and percent distribution of black men aged 15 or older and aged 15 to 34 by income, 1999; median income by work status, and percent working year-round, full-time; men in thousands as of 2000)

| | | aged 15 to 34 | | | | |
| | | | | aged 25 to 34 | | |
	total	total	15 to 24	total	25 to 29	30 to 34
Total black men	**11,687**	**5,114**	**2,809**	**2,305**	**1,102**	**1,203**
Without income	1,620	1,289	1,120	169	117	52
With income	10,067	3,825	1,689	2,136	985	1,151
Under $10,000	2,621	1,349	1,071	278	163	115
$10,000 to $19,999	2,253	896	354	542	285	258
$20,000 to $29,999	1,817	707	176	531	247	281
$30,000 to $39,999	1,267	433	70	363	131	232
$40,000 to $49,999	804	181	12	169	71	100
$50,000 to $74,999	864	170	6	164	58	104
$75,000 to $99,999	244	46	0	46	21	25
$100,000 or more	192	44	0	44	9	35
Median income of men with income	$20,579	$15,976	$6,691	$23,318	$21,106	$26,376
Median income of full-time workers	30,297	25,134	17,176	27,577	25,478	30,540
Percent working full-time	48.3%	38.8%	16.6%	65.9%	59.4%	71.7%
Total black men	**100.0%**	**100.0%**	**100.0%**	**100.0%**	**100.0%**	**100.0%**
Without income	13.9	25.2	39.9	7.3	10.6	4.3
With income	86.1	74.8	60.1	92.7	89.4	95.7
Under $10,000	22.4	26.4	38.1	12.1	14.8	9.6
$10,000 to $19,999	19.3	17.5	12.6	23.5	25.9	21.4
$20,000 to $29,999	15.5	13.8	6.3	23.0	22.4	23.4
$30,000 to $39,999	10.8	8.5	2.5	15.7	11.9	19.3
$40,000 to $49,999	6.9	3.5	0.4	7.3	6.4	8.3
$50,000 to $74,999	7.4	3.3	0.2	7.1	5.3	8.6
$75,000 to $99,999	2.1	0.9	0.0	2.0	1.9	2.1
$100,000 or more	1.6	0.9	0.0	1.9	0.8	2.9

Source: Bureau of the Census, data from the 2000 Current Population Survey, Internet site <http://ferret.bls .census.gov/macro/03200/perinc/new01_000.htm>; calculations by the author

Income Distribution of Men Aged 15 to 34, 1999: Hispanic Men

(number and percent distribution of Hispanic men aged 15 or older and aged 15 to 34 by income, 1999; median income by work status, and percent working year-round, full-time; men in thousands as of 2000)

| | | aged 15 to 34 | | | aged 25 to 34 | |
	total	total	15 to 24	total	25 to 29	30 to 34
Total Hispanic men	**11,327**	**5,817**	**2,962**	**2,855**	**1,416**	**1,439**
Without income	1,282	1,033	932	101	57	44
With income	10,045	4,784	2,030	2,754	1,359	1,395
Under $10,000	2,189	1,295	909	386	216	170
$10,000 to $19,999	3,275	1,743	739	1,004	505	499
$20,000 to $29,999	1,956	892	263	629	313	317
$30,000 to $39,999	1,096	414	70	344	160	185
$40,000 to $49,999	625	216	30	186	91	95
$50,000 to $74,999	616	161	13	148	49	98
$75,000 to $99,999	158	38	3	35	15	20
$100,000 or more	129	24	3	21	9	12
Median income of men with income	$18,234	$16,106	$11,048	$19,834	$18,986	$20,664
Median income of full-time workers	23,342	20,665	16,664	22,379	21,581	23,632
Percent working full-time	57.2%	51.5%	30.4%	73.5%	71.3%	75.7%
Total Hispanic men	**100.0%**	**100.0%**	**100.0%**	**100.0%**	**100.0%**	**100.0%**
Without income	11.3	17.8	31.5	3.5	4.0	3.1
With income	88.7	82.2	68.5	96.5	96.0	96.9
Under $10,000	19.3	22.3	30.7	13.5	15.3	11.8
$10,000 to $19,999	28.9	30.0	24.9	35.2	35.7	34.7
$20,000 to $29,999	17.3	15.3	8.9	22.0	22.1	22.0
$30,000 to $39,999	9.7	7.1	2.4	12.0	11.3	12.9
$40,000 to $49,999	5.5	3.7	1.0	6.5	6.4	6.6
$50,000 to $74,999	5.4	2.8	0.4	5.2	3.5	6.8
$75,000 to $99,999	1.4	0.7	0.1	1.2	1.1	1.4
$100,000 or more	1.1	0.4	0.1	0.7	0.6	0.8

Source: Bureau of the Census, data from the 2000 Current Population Survey, Internet site <http://ferret.bls .census.gov/macro/03200/perinc/new01_000.htm>; calculations by the author

Income Distribution of Men Aged 15 to 34, 1999: White Men

(number and percent distribution of white men aged 15 or older and aged 15 to 34 by income, 1999; median income by work status, and percent working year-round, full-time; men in thousands as of 2000)

| | | aged 15 to 34 | | | | |
| | | | | aged 25 to 34 | | |
	total	**total**	**15 to 24**	**total**	**25 to 29**	**30 to 34**
Total white men	**86,443**	**30,687**	**15,543**	**15,144**	**7,274**	**7,870**
Without income	4,869	3,885	3,520	365	221	144
With income	81,574	26,802	12,023	14,779	7,053	7,726
Under $10,000	13,498	7,785	6,492	1,293	720	574
$10,000 to $19,999	15,276	5,836	3,057	2,779	1,529	1,249
$20,000 to $29,999	13,493	4,657	1,557	3,100	1,669	1,430
$30,000 to $39,999	11,040	3,363	536	2,827	1,382	1,446
$40,000 to $49,999	8,202	2,149	206	1,943	807	1,135
$50,000 to $74,999	11,130	2,025	120	1,905	666	1,241
$75,000 to $99,999	4,056	540	41	499	139	360
$100,000 or more	4,876	447	16	431	142	289
Median income of men with income	$28,564	$20,727	$8,689	$30,520	$27,114	$33,626
Median income of full-time workers	39,331	30,211	19,650	33,618	30,901	36,628
Percent working full-time	56.9%	50.9%	24.6%	78.0%	74.3%	81.5%
Total white men	**100.0%**	**100.0%**	**100.0%**	**100.0%**	**100.0%**	**100.0%**
Without income	5.6	12.7	22.6	2.4	3.0	1.8
With income	94.4	87.3	77.4	97.6	97.0	98.2
Under $10,000	15.6	25.4	41.8	8.5	9.9	7.3
$10,000 to $19,999	17.7	19.0	19.7	18.4	21.0	15.9
$20,000 to $29,999	15.6	15.2	10.0	20.5	22.9	18.2
$30,000 to $39,999	12.8	11.0	3.4	18.7	19.0	18.4
$40,000 to $49,999	9.5	7.0	1.3	12.8	11.1	14.4
$50,000 to $74,999	12.9	6.6	0.8	12.6	9.2	15.8
$75,000 to $99,999	4.7	1.8	0.3	3.3	1.9	4.6
$100,000 or more	5.6	1.5	0.1	2.8	2.0	3.7

Source: Bureau of the Census, data from the 2000 Current Population Survey, Internet site <http://ferret.bls .census.gov/macro/03200/perinc/new01_000.htm>; calculations by the author

Income Distribution of Men Aged 15 to 34, 1999: Non-Hispanic White Men

(number and percent distribution of non-Hispanic white men aged 15 or older and aged 15 to 34 by income, 1999; median income by work status, and percent working year-round, full-time; men in thousands as of 2000)

| | | aged 15 to 34 | | | | |
| | | | | aged 25 to 34 | | |
	total	total	15 to 24	total	25 to 29	30 to 34
Total non-Hispanic white men	**75,692**	**25,169**	**12,715**	**12,454**	**5,940**	**6,514**
Without income	3,665	2,908	2,635	273	168	105
With income	72,027	22,261	10,080	12,181	5,772	6,409
Under $10,000	11,433	6,568	5,631	937	520	415
$10,000 to $19,999	12,140	4,170	2,345	1,825	1,053	772
$20,000 to $29,999	11,635	3,814	1,307	2,507	1,368	1,139
$30,000 to $39,999	9,992	2,972	467	2,505	1,233	1,272
$40,000 to $49,999	7,615	1,939	174	1,765	721	1,044
$50,000 to $74,999	10,551	1,872	106	1,766	618	1,150
$75,000 to $99,999	3,908	503	38	465	126	339
$100,000 or more	4,752	423	13	410	133	277
Median income of men with income	$30,594	$21,331	$8,091	$32,288	$29,467	$36,444
Median income of full-time workers	41,406	32,490	20,609	36,054	32,228	39,420
Percent working full-time	56.8%	50.7%	23.2%	78.8%	74.8%	82.6%
Total non-Hispanic white men	**100.0%**	**100.0%**	**100.0%**	**100.0%**	**100.0%**	**100.0%**
Without income	4.8	11.6	20.7	2.2	2.8	1.6
With income	95.2	88.4	79.3	97.8	97.2	98.4
Under $10,000	15.1	26.1	44.3	7.5	8.8	6.4
$10,000 to $19,999	16.0	16.6	18.4	14.7	17.7	11.9
$20,000 to $29,999	15.4	15.2	10.3	20.1	23.0	17.5
$30,000 to $39,999	13.2	11.8	3.7	20.1	20.8	19.5
$40,000 to $49,999	10.1	7.7	1.4	14.2	12.1	16.0
$50,000 to $74,999	13.9	7.4	0.8	14.2	10.4	17.7
$75,000 to $99,999	5.2	2.0	0.3	3.7	2.1	5.2
$100,000 or more	6.3	1.7	0.1	3.3	2.2	4.3

Source: Bureau of the Census, data from the 2000 Current Population Survey, Internet site <http://ferret.bls .census.gov/macro/03200/perinc/new01_000.htm>; calculations by the author

Women's Incomes Keep Rising

The median income of women aged 25 to 34 is 37 percent higher than in 1980.

Women's incomes have been rising for decades, thanks to their growing educational attainment and participation in the labor force. The median income of women rose 54 percent between 1980 and 1999, after adjusting for inflation. Although most of this gain occurred prior to 1990, women's incomes have increased 19 percent during the past decade.

The median income of women aged 25 to 34 increased 37 percent between 1980 and 1999, from $14,115 to $19,396, after adjusting for inflation. During the 1990s, the median income of women in the 25-to-34 age group grew faster than the median for all women. Between 1990 and 1999, the median income of women aged 25 to 34 rose 21 percent.

Gains have not been as great for women under age 25, however. Between 1980 and 1999, the median income of women aged 15 to 24 rose only 6 percent, after adjusting for inflation.

♦ The incomes of women will continue to rise, but the rate of growth will likely be smaller than it was in the past.

Incomes rose sharply for 25-to-34-year-old women

(median income of women aged 15 to 34, 1980 and 1999; in 1999 dollars)

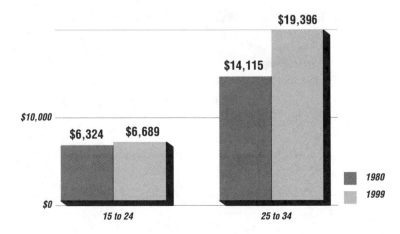

Median Income of Women Aged 15 to 34, 1980 to 1999

(median income of women with income, for total women and women aged 15 to 34, 1980 to 1999, and percent change for selected years; in 1999 dollars)

	total women	women aged 15 to 34	
		15 to 24	25 to 34
1999	$15,311	$6,689	$19,396
1998	14,749	6,678	18,660
1997	14,224	6,583	18,318
1996	13,607	6,245	17,397
1995	13,260	5,805	17,007
1994	12,890	6,192	16,732
1993	12,735	6,169	16,127
1992	12,722	6,139	16,186
1991	12,814	6,357	15,858
1990	12,836	6,248	16,047
1989	12,930	6,367	16,433
1988	12,511	6,316	16,287
1987	12,165	6,465	16,101
1986	11,568	6,147	15,672
1985	11,174	5,870	15,296
1984	11,013	5,787	15,060
1983	10,570	5,782	14,223
1982	10,259	5,841	13,893
1981	10,092	3,691	14,049
1980	9,960	6,324	14,115
Percent change			
1998–1999	3.8%	0.2%	3.9%
1990–1999	19.3	7.1	20.9
1980–1999	53.7	5.8	37.4

Source: Bureau of the Census, Internet site <www.census.gov/hhes/income/histinc/p08.html>; calculations by the author

Incomes of Young Women Are Low as They Prepare for Careers

Only one-third of young women work full-time.

Young women's incomes are low in part because so many are in school. More than 60 percent of women go to college after high school and few work full-time. Consequently, the median income of women aged 15 to 24 was only $6,689 in 1999. Among those aged 25 to 34, most of whom are no longer in school, median income was a much higher $19,396.

Among young women, non-Hispanic whites have the highest incomes. The median income of non-Hispanic white women aged 15 to 34 was $14,319 in 1999, compared with $13,269 for black women and just $10,896 for Hispanics. The income differences are similar among women who work full-time: $19,467 for Hispanics, $22,868 for blacks, and $25,668 for non-Hispanic whites. Among women aged 15 to 24, Hispanics have the highest incomes because they are more likely to work full-time rather than go to school. This costs them later, as evidenced by the fact that Hispanic women in the next older age group, 25 to 34, have the lowest incomes.

♦ Young women know that getting an education is the key to a better future, and they are attending college in record numbers. Although this choice depresses their incomes while they are in their teens and early twenties, it assures higher incomes later in life.

Income Distribution of Women Aged 15 to 34, 1999: Total Women

(number and percent distribution of women aged 15 or older and aged 15 to 34 by income, 1999; median income by work status, and percent working year-round, full-time; women in thousands as of 2000)

| | | aged 15 to 34 | | | | |
| | | | | aged 25 to 34 | | |
	total	total	15 to 24	total	25 to 29	30 to 34
Total women	**110,660**	**38,263**	**19,040**	**19,223**	**9,326**	**9,896**
Without income	11,047	6,895	5,083	1,812	930	881
With income	99,613	31,368	13,957	17,411	8,396	9,015
Under $10,000	35,356	13,337	8,754	4,583	2,126	2,458
$10,000 to $19,999	24,607	7,668	3,322	4,346	2,242	2,105
$20,000 to $29,999	16,038	4,971	1,302	3,669	1,935	1,732
$30,000 to $39,999	9,839	2,730	377	2,353	1,126	1,227
$40,000 to $49,999	5,632	1,270	112	1,158	489	668
$50,000 to $74,999	5,466	900	56	844	323	521
$75,000 to $99,999	1491	269	12	257	90	167
$100,000 or more	1,185	223	22	201	65	136
Median income of women with income	$15,311	$13,742	$6,689	$19,396	$19,111	$19,698
Median income of full-time workers	$27,370	$24,432	$17,851	$26,670	$25,877	$27,789
Percent working full-time	36.5%	34.3%	17.5%	50.9%	51.1%	50.7%
Total women	**100.0%**	**100.0%**	**100.0%**	**100.0%**	**100.0%**	**100.0%**
Without income	10.0	18.0	26.7	9.4	10.0	8.9
With income	90.0	82.0	73.3	90.6	90.0	91.1
Under $10,000	32.0	34.9	46.0	23.8	22.8	24.8
$10,000 to $19,999	22.2	20.0	17.4	22.6	24.0	21.3
$20,000 to $29,999	14.5	13.0	6.8	19.1	20.7	17.5
$30,000 to $39,999	8.9	7.1	2.0	12.2	12.1	12.4
$40,000 to $49,999	5.1	3.3	0.6	6.0	5.2	6.8
$50,000 to $74,999	4.9	2.4	0.3	4.4	3.5	5.3
$75,000 to $99,999	1.3	0.7	0.1	1.3	1.0	1.7
$100,000 or more	1.1	0.6	0.1	1.0	0.7	1.4

Source: Bureau of the Census, data from the 2000 Current Population Survey, Internet site <http://ferret.bls .census.gov/macro/03200/perinc/new01_000.htm>; calculations by the author

Income Distribution of Women Aged 15 to 34, 1999: Black Women

(number and percent distribution of black women aged 15 or older and aged 15 to 34 by income, 1999; median income by work status, and percent working year-round, full-time; women in thousands as of 2000)

| | | aged 15 to 34 | | | | |
| | | | | aged 25 to 34 | | |
	total	total	15 to 24	total	25 to 29	30 to 34
Total black women	**14,167**	**5,869**	**3,011**	**2,858**	**1,418**	**1,439**
Without income	1,735	1,196	995	201	95	105
With income	12,432	4,673	2,016	2,657	1,323	1,334
Under $10,000	4,504	1,987	1,332	655	329	325
$10,000 to $19,999	3,172	1,190	412	778	426	350
$20,000 to $29,999	2,110	812	188	624	293	328
$30,000 to $39,999	1,289	436	58	378	193	185
$40,000 to $49,999	623	132	17	115	39	75
$50,000 to $74,999	542	72	6	66	26	40
$75,000 to $99,999	99	34	3	31	13	17
$100,000 or more	91	12	0	12	0	12
Median income of women with income	$14,771	$13,269	$6,497	$18,407	$17,394	$19,674
Median income of full-time workers	25,142	22,868	18,539	24,018	23,371	24,533
Percent working full-time	41.6%	36.2%	14.8%	58.7%	56.2%	61.2%
Total black women	**100.0%**	**100.0%**	**100.0%**	**100.0%**	**100.0%**	**100.0%**
Without income	12.2	20.4	33.0	7.0	6.7	7.3
With income	87.8	79.6	67.0	93.0	93.3	92.7
Under $10,000	31.8	33.9	44.2	22.9	23.2	22.6
$10,000 to $19,999	22.4	20.3	13.7	27.2	30.0	24.3
$20,000 to $29,999	14.9	13.8	6.2	21.8	20.7	22.8
$30,000 to $39,999	9.1	7.4	1.9	13.2	13.6	12.9
$40,000 to $49,999	4.4	2.2	0.6	4.0	2.8	5.2
$50,000 to $74,999	3.8	1.2	0.2	2.3	1.8	2.8
$75,000 to $99,999	0.7	0.6	0.1	1.1	0.9	1.2
$100,000 or more	0.6	0.2	0.0	0.4	0.0	0.8

Source: Bureau of the Census, data from the 2000 Current Population Survey, Internet site <http://ferret.bls .census.gov/macro/03200/perinc/new01_000.htm>; calculations by the author

Income Distribution of Women Aged 15 to 34, 1999: Hispanic Women

(number and percent distribution of Hispanic women aged 15 or older and aged 15 to 34 by income, 1999; median income by work status, and percent working year-round, full-time; women in thousands as of 2000)

	total	total	15 to 24	aged 15 to 34 / aged 25 to 34 total	25 to 29	30 to 34
Total Hispanic women	**11,466**	**5,486**	**2,681**	**2,805**	**1,415**	**1,390**
Without income	2,717	1,762	1,129	633	329	305
With income	8,749	3,724	1,552	2,172	1,086	1,085
Under $10,000	3,901	1,748	936	812	414	398
$10,000 to $19,999	2,514	1,077	432	645	337	307
$20,000 to $29,999	1,148	505	137	368	187	182
$30,000 to $39,999	552	213	28	185	71	113
$40,000 to $49,999	304	90	10	80	43	40
$50,000 to $74,999	230	58	5	53	22	33
$75,000 to $99,999	45	18	2	16	9	7
$100,000 or more	52	14	3	11	5	7
Median income of women with income	$11,314	$10,896	$7,189	$13,545	$13,091	$13,994
Median income of full-time workers	20,051	19,467	15,602	21,082	20,517	21,692
Percent working full-time	56.5%	28.6%	33.5%	74.8%	71.4%	78.3%
Total Hispanic women	**100.0%**	**100.0%**	**100.0%**	**100.0%**	**100.0%**	**100.0%**
Without income	23.7	32.1	42.1	22.6	23.3	21.9
With income	76.3	67.9	57.9	77.4	76.7	78.1
Under $10,000	34.0	31.9	34.9	28.9	29.3	28.6
$10,000 to $19,999	21.9	19.6	16.1	23.0	23.8	22.1
$20,000 to $29,999	10.0	9.2	5.1	13.1	13.2	13.1
$30,000 to $39,999	4.8	3.9	1.0	6.6	5.0	8.1
$40,000 to $49,999	2.7	1.6	0.4	2.9	3.0	2.9
$50,000 to $74,999	2.0	1.1	0.2	1.9	1.6	2.4
$75,000 to $99,999	0.4	0.3	0.1	0.6	0.6	0.5
$100,000 or more	0.5	0.3	0.1	0.4	0.4	0.5

Source: Bureau of the Census, data from the 2000 Current Population Survey, Internet site <http://ferret.bls .census.gov/macro/03200/perinc/new01_000.htm>; calculations by the author

Income Distribution of Women Aged 15 to 34, 1999: White Women

(number and percent distribution of white women aged 15 or older and aged 15 to 34 by income, 1999; median income by work status, and percent working year-round, full-time; women in thousands as of 2000)

| | | aged 15 to 34 | | | | |
| | | | | aged 25 to 34 | | |
	total	*total*	*15 to 24*	*total*	*25 to 29*	*30 to 34*
Total white women	**91,138**	**30,147**	**14,971**	**15,176**	**7,282**	**7,894**
Without income	8,357	5,104	3,676	1,428	730	698
With income	82,781	25,043	11,295	13,748	6,552	7,196
Under $10,000	29,233	10,696	7,028	3,668	1,673	1,995
$10,000 to $19,999	20,486	6,061	2,747	3,314	1,675	1,637
$20,000 to $29,999	13,262	3,908	1,050	2,858	1,537	1,321
$30,000 to $39,999	8,130	2,143	308	1,835	860	976
$40,000 to $49,999	4,733	1,078	93	985	419	567
$50,000 to $74,999	4,591	754	42	712	259	450
$75,000 to $99,999	1,294	205	9	196	62	132
$100,000 or more	1,048	198	17	181	65	116
Median income of women with income	$15,362	$13,804	$6,723	$19,622	$19,488	$19,757
Median income of full-time workers	28,023	24,655	17,699	27,190	26,268	28,928
Percent working full-time	35.7%	34.3%	18.5%	50.0%	51.0%	49.1%
Total white women	**100.0%**	**100.0%**	**100.0%**	**100.0%**	**100.0%**	**100.0%**
Without income	9.2	16.9	24.6	9.4	10.0	8.8
With income	90.8	83.1	75.4	90.6	90.0	91.2
Under $10,000	32.1	35.5	46.9	24.2	23.0	25.3
$10,000 to $19,999	22.5	20.1	18.3	21.8	23.0	20.7
$20,000 to $29,999	14.6	13.0	7.0	18.8	21.1	16.7
$30,000 to $39,999	8.9	7.1	2.1	12.1	11.8	12.4
$40,000 to $49,999	5.2	3.6	0.6	6.5	5.8	7.2
$50,000 to $74,999	5.0	2.5	0.3	4.7	3.6	5.7
$75,000 to $99,999	1.4	0.7	0.1	1.3	0.9	1.7
$100,000 or more	1.1	0.7	0.1	1.2	0.9	1.5

Source: Bureau of the Census, data from the 2000 Current Population Survey, Internet site <http://ferret.bls .census.gov/macro/03200/perinc/new01_000.htm>; calculations by the author

Income Distribution of Women Aged 15 to 34, 1999: Non-Hispanic White Women

(number and percent distribution of non-Hispanic white women aged 15 or older and aged 15 to 34 by income, 1999; median income by work status, and percent working year-round, full-time; women in thousands as of 2000)

| | | aged 15 to 34 | | | aged 25 to 34 | |
	total	total	15 to 24	total	25 to 29	30 to 34
Total non-Hispanic white women	**80,228**	**24,948**	**12,422**	**12,526**	**5,950**	**6,576**
Without income	5,732	3,403	2,588	815	408	407
With income	74,496	21,545	9,834	11,711	5,542	6,169
Under $10,000	25,521	9,053	6,147	2,906	1,287	1,618
$10,000 to $19,999	18,121	5,061	2,346	2,715	1,372	1,343
$20,000 to $29,999	12,173	3,431	920	2,511	1,360	1,152
$30,000 to $39,999	7,608	1,939	280	1,659	793	866
$40,000 to $49,999	4,443	994	84	910	376	534
$50,000 to $74,999	4,380	697	37	660	241	419
$75,000 to $99,999	1,251	188	7	181	53	127
$100,000 or more	1,000	184	14	170	60	110
Median income of women with income	$15,922	$14,319	$6,665	$20,747	$20,707	$20,787
Median income of full-time workers	29,369	25,668	18,220	28,303	26,958	30,339
Percent working full-time	36.1%	35.5%	18.7%	52.3%	53.9%	50.8%
Total non-Hispanic white women	**100.0%**	**100.0%**	**100.0%**	**100.0%**	**100.0%**	**100.0%**
Without income	7.1	13.6	20.8	6.5	6.9	6.2
With income	92.9	86.4	79.2	93.5	93.1	93.8
Under $10,000	31.8	36.3	49.5	23.2	21.6	24.6
$10,000 to $19,999	22.6	20.3	18.9	21.7	23.1	20.4
$20,000 to $29,999	15.2	13.8	7.4	20.0	22.9	17.5
$30,000 to $39,999	9.5	7.8	2.3	13.2	13.3	13.2
$40,000 to $49,999	5.5	4.0	0.7	7.3	6.3	8.1
$50,000 to $74,999	5.5	2.8	0.3	5.3	4.1	6.4
$75,000 to $99,999	1.6	0.8	0.1	1.4	0.9	1.9
$100,000 or more	1.2	0.7	0.1	1.4	1.0	1.7

Source: Bureau of the Census, data from the 2000 Current Population Survey, Internet site <http://ferret.bls .census.gov/macro/03200/perinc/new01_000.htm>; calculations by the author

Jobs Are the Most Important Source of Income for Young Adults

A substantial proportion receive educational grants and loans.

Earnings are the most common source of income for young adults. Eighty-nine percent of people aged 15 to 24 and 92 percent of those aged 25 to 44 receive income from a job.

The second most common source of income for young adults is interest. More than half of people aged 25 to 44 and 29 percent of those aged 15 to 24 receive interest income, albeit small amounts. Twenty percent of people aged 25 to 44 receive dividend income.

Fourteen percent of people aged 15 to 24 received educational grants and scholarships in 1999. On average, they received more than $4,000 from this source, accounting for a substantial portion of the income of many young adults.

♦ Earnings from employment will remain young adults' primary source of income. For many, however, educational support is significant.

Sources of Income for People Aged 15 to 44, 1999

(number and percent distribution of people aged 15 to 44 with income and average income for those with income, by selected sources of income and age, 1999; people in thousands as of 2000)

	aged 15 to 24			aged 25 to 44		
	number	percent distribution	average	number	percent distribution	average
Total people	**28,384**	**100.0%**	**$10,670**	**78,138**	**100.0%**	**$33,243**
Earnings	25,211	88.8	10,422	71,859	92.0	33,690
Wages and salary	24,890	87.7	10,333	68,110	87.2	33,675
Nonfarm self-employment	587	2.1	8,586	5,457	7.0	22,428
Unemployment compensation	434	1.5	1,771	2,896	3.7	2,633
Social Security	783	2.8	5,012	1,732	2.2	7,668
Supplement Security Income (SSI)	491	1.7	4,756	1,434	1.8	5,113
Public Assistance	817	2.9	2,485	1,413	1.8	3,428
Veterans' benefits	36	0.1	–	374	0.5	5,977
Survivors' benefits	59	0.2	–	210	0.3	16,715
Disability benefits	62	0.2	–	464	0.6	9,422
Pensions	22	0.1	–	458	0.6	11,307
Interest	8,315	29.3	387	41,278	52.8	991
Dividends	1,841	6.5	1,501	15,669	20.1	2,331
Rents, royalties, estates, trusts	212	0.7	2,920	3,808	4.9	3,229
Education	4,068	14.3	4,273	2,883	3.7	3,917
Pell grants only	776	2.7	2,163	503	0.6	1,786
Scholarships only	1,622	5.7	4,010	434	0.6	4,452
Child support	520	1.8	2,578	3,814	4.9	4,106
Alimony	7	0.0	–	184	0.2	9,669

Note: (–) means sample too small to make a reliable estimate.
Source: Bureau of the Census, Money Income in the United States: 1999, *Current Population Reports, P60-209, 2000; calculations by the author*

Many Young Adults Are Poor

After age 25, poverty falls below average.

The youngest adults are more likely to be poor than the average American. Overall, 12 percent of Americans lived in poverty in 1999. Among people aged 18 to 24, however, 17 percent were poor. After age 25, the percentage of people in poverty declines substantially. Eleven percent of people aged 25 to 34 are poor.

Young adults make up a substantial portion of America's poor. Twenty-seven percent of people living in poverty are aged 18 to 34. Regardless of age, whites are less likely than Hispanics or blacks to be poor. Nine percent of non-Hispanic whites aged 18 to 34 are poor, compared with 21 percent of Hispanics and 23 percent of blacks.

♦ Many young adults are poor because they attend school rather than work full-time. Another factor is the low pay of entry-level jobs. Poverty declines as people age and earnings rise.

Young adults are more likely to be poor

(percent of total people and people aged 15 to 34 with incomes below poverty level, 1999)

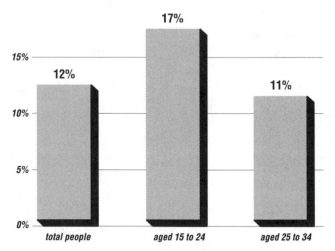

People Aged 15 to 34 below Poverty Level by Race and Hispanic Origin, 1999

(number, percent, and percent distribution of total people and people aged 15 to 34 with incomes below poverty level, by race and Hispanic origin, 1999; people in thousands as of 2000)

	total	black	Hispanic	white	non-Hispanic white
Number of people in poverty					
Total people	**32,258**	**8,360**	**7,439**	**21,922**	**14,875**
Aged 18 to 34	8,571	2,058	2,062	5,917	3,968
Aged 18 to 24	4,603	1,165	941	3,125	2,236
Aged 25 to 34	3,968	893	1,121	2,792	1,732
Percent of people in poverty					
Total people	**11.8%**	**23.6%**	**22.8%**	**9.8%**	**7.7%**
Aged 18 to 34	13.3	22.5	21.4	11.5	9.4
Aged 18 to 24	17.3	29.3	23.8	14.8	12.9
Aged 25 to 34	10.5	17.3	19.8	9.2	6.9
Percent distribution of poor by age					
Total people	**100.0%**	**100.0%**	**100.0%**	**100.0%**	**100.0%**
Aged 18 to 34	26.6	24.6	27.7	27.0	26.7
Aged 18 to 24	14.3	13.9	12.6	14.3	15.0
Aged 25 to 34	12.3	10.7	15.1	12.7	11.6
Percent distribution of poor by race and Hispanic origin					
Total people	**100.0%**	**25.9%**	**23.1%**	**68.0%**	**46.1%**
Aged 18 to 34	100.0	24.0	24.1	69.0	46.3
Aged 18 to 24	100.0	25.3	20.4	67.9	48.6
Aged 25 to 34	100.0	22.5	28.3	70.4	43.6

Note: Numbers will not add to total because Hispanics may be of any race and not all races are shown.
Source: Bureau of the Census, Poverty in the United States: 1999, *Current Population Reports, P60-210, 2000, Internet site <www.census.gov/hhes/www/povty99.html>; calculations by the author*

5

Labor Force

♦ The labor force participation of young women has increased sharply since 1970. In 2000, 76 percent of women aged 25 to 34 were in the labor force, up from only 45 percent in 1970.

♦ The labor force participation rate of young men fell during the past three decades. In 2000, 93 percent of men aged 25 to 34 were in the labor force, down from 96 percent in 1970.

♦ Among men aged 16 to 34, whites and Hispanics are more likely than blacks to be in the labor force. Among women in the age group, whites are considerably more likely to work than blacks or Hispanics.

♦ Dual incomes are the norm for young married couples. Among couples aged 20 to 24, 65 percent are dual earners. The dual-earner share stands at 73 percent among couples aged 25 to 29 and at 70 percent among those aged 30 to 34.

♦ Most young people who work are employed full-time. Among workers aged 25 to 34, 95 percent of men and 82 percent of women have full-time jobs.

♦ The number of 25-to-34-year-olds in the labor force will fall slightly between 1998 and 2008. But as the children of the baby boom reach adulthood, the number of workers aged 16 to 24 will increase substantially.

More Young Women Are Working

Women's labor force participation has grown while men's has declined.

The proportion of men aged 16 to 34 who are in the labor force is smaller today than it was in 1970. In that year, 83 percent of men aged 20 to 24 and 96 percent of those aged 25 to 34 were in the labor force. By 2000, however, a smaller 83 percent of the younger and 93 percent of the older age group were in the labor force. Behind the decline is an increase in the proportion of young men attending college.

A bigger story, however, is the rise in the proportion of young women who work. Fewer than half of women aged 16 to 19 and 25 to 34 were in the labor force in 1970. By 2000, however, 51 percent of women aged 16 to 19, 73 percent of women aged 20 to 24, and 76 percent of those aged 25 to 34 were in the labor force.

♦ Media reports to the contrary, young women are not leaving the workforce to care for home and family. They are pursuing education and careers in record proportions.

The share of women in the labor force is higher than ever

(percent of women aged 16 to 34 in the civilian labor force, 1970 and 2000)

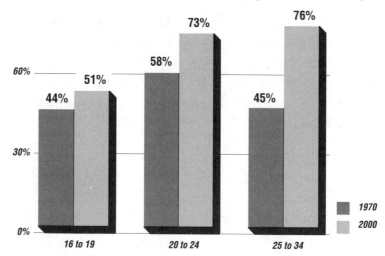

Labor Force Participation of People Aged 16 to 34 by Sex, 1970 to 2000

(civilian labor force participation rate for people aged 16 or older and aged 16 to 34, by sex, 1970–2000; percentage point change, 1970–2000)

	2000	1990	1980	1970	percentage point change 1970–2000
Men aged 16 or older	**74.7%**	**76.1%**	**77.4%**	**79.7%**	**–5.0**
Aged 16 to 19	53.0	55.7	60.5	56.1	–3.1
Aged 20 to 24	82.6	84.3	85.9	83.3	–0.7
Aged 25 to 34	93.4	94.2	95.2	96.4	–3.0
Women aged 16 or older	**60.2**	**57.5**	**51.5**	**43.3**	**16.9**
Aged 16 to 19	51.3	51.8	52.9	44.0	7.3
Aged 20 to 24	73.3	71.6	68.9	57.7	15.6
Aged 25 to 34	76.3	73.6	65.5	45.0	31.3

Sources: Bureau of Labor Statistics, Employment and Earnings, *January 2001; and* Handbook of Labor Statistics, *Bulletin 2340, 1989; and Bureau of the Census,* Statistical Abstract, *1999*

Three-Quarters of Young Adults Are in the Labor Force

Despite the tight labor market, teens had an unemployment rate of 13 percent in 2000.

Three quarters of people aged 16 to 34 were in the labor force in 2000. But the labor force participation rate varies greatly by age within the young-adult population. Only 52 percent of people aged 16 to 19 (most of whom are still in school) are in the labor force compared with 78 percent of people aged 20 to 24 and 85 percent of those aged 25 to 34.

Young men are more likely than young women to be in the labor force. Fully 93 percent of men aged 25 to 34 are in the labor force compared with 76 percent of women in the age group. The gap is smallest among 16-to-19-year-olds. Fifty-three percent of men in that age group are in the labor force compared with 51 percent of women.

Although the majority of people aged 16 to 19 are in the labor force, a minority (45 percent) are employed. Teenagers have the highest unemployment rate among all age groups. Unemployment is also above average among people aged 20 to 24, at 7 percent. The unemployment rate of people aged 25 to 34 is slightly below average.

♦ Although unemployment has been exceptionally low in recent years, it remains relatively high among the youngest adults. Lack of experience, the need to schedule work around school and extracurricular activities, and, in some cases, insufficient education are behind the higher rate.

Employment Status of People Aged 16 to 34 by Sex, 2000

(number and percent of people aged 16 or older and aged 16 to 34 in the civilian labor force by sex and employment status, 2000; numbers in thousands)

| | civilian noninstitutional population | civilian labor force | | | | | |
| | | total | percent of population | employed | percent of population | unemployed | |
						number	percent of labor force
Total, aged 16 or older	**209,699**	**140,863**	**67.2%**	**135,208**	**64.5%**	**5,655**	**4.0%**
Total, aged 16 to 34	71,870	54,384	75.7	51,098	71.1	3,287	6.0
Aged 16 to 24	34,453	22,715	65.9	20,597	59.8	2,118	9.3
Aged 25 to 34	37,417	31,669	84.6	30,501	81.5	1,169	3.7
Aged 16 to 19	16,042	8,369	52.2	7,276	45.4	1,093	13.1
Aged 20 to 24	18,411	14,346	77.9	13,321	72.4	1,025	7.1
Aged 25 to 29	17,972	15,196	84.6	14,570	81.1	626	4.1
Aged 30 to 34	19,445	16,473	84.7	15,930	81.9	543	3.3
Men, aged 16 or older	**100,731**	**75,247**	**74.7**	**72,293**	**71.8**	**2,954**	**2.9**
Men, aged 16 to 34	35,594	28,948	81.3	27,216	76.5	1,731	6.0
Aged 16 to 24	17,305	11,875	68.6	10,722	62.0	1,153	9.7
Aged 25 to 34	18,289	17,073	93.4	16,494	90.2	578	3.4
Aged 16 to 19	8,151	4,317	53.0	3,713	45.6	604	14.0
Aged 20 to 24	9,154	7,558	82.6	7,009	76.6	549	7.3
Aged 25 to 29	8,746	8,085	92.4	7,766	88.8	318	3.9
Aged 30 to 34	9,543	8,988	94.2	8,728	91.5	260	2.9
Women, aged 16 or older	**108,968**	**65,616**	**60.2**	**62,915**	**57.7**	**2,701**	**4.1**
Women, aged 16 to 34	36,275	25,435	70.1	23,881	65.8	1,554	6.1
Aged 16 to 24	17,147	10,839	63.2	9,875	57.6	965	8.9
Aged 25 to 34	19,128	14,596	76.3	14,006	73.2	589	4.0
Aged 16 to 19	7,890	4,051	51.3	3,563	45.2	489	12.1
Aged 20 to 24	9,257	6,788	73.3	6,312	68.2	476	7.0
Aged 25 to 29	9,226	7,111	77.1	6,804	73.7	307	4.3
Aged 30 to 34	9,902	7,485	75.6	7,202	72.7	282	3.8

Source: Bureau of Labor Statistics, Employment and Earnings, *January 2001, Internet site <http://stats.bls.gov/cpsaatab.htm>; calculations by the author*

White Men Are Least Likely to Be Unemployed

One out of five black men aged 16 to 24 is unemployed.

Most young men are in the labor force, but there are substantial differences in labor force participation and unemployment by race and Hispanic origin. Fully 94 percent of white and Hispanic men aged 25 to 34 are in the labor force compared with a smaller 88 percent of black men in the age group. Among men aged 16 to 24, a similar gap exists: 72 percent of whites and Hispanics are in the labor force compared with 56 percent of blacks.

Young white and Hispanic men are less likely than young black men to be unemployed. Only 3 percent of white men and 4 percent of Hispanic men aged 25 to 34 were unemployed in 2000 compared with 7 percent of black men. The difference is even greater among men aged 16 to 24. Eight percent of whites were unemployed compared with 10 percent of Hispanics and 20 percent of blacks.

♦ The high unemployment rate among young black men contributes to their lower labor force participation rate. Discouraged by the lack of prospects for work in their communities, some young black men are not even looking for jobs.

Unemployment rate differs sharply by race and Hispanic origin

(percent of men aged 16 to 34 who are unemployed, by age, race, and Hispanic origin, 2000)

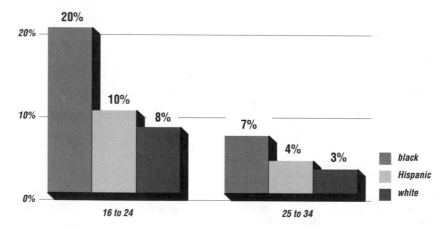

Employment Status of Men Aged 16 to 34 by Race and Hispanic Origin, 2000

(number and percent of men aged 16 or older and aged 16 to 34 in the civilian labor force by race, Hispanic origin, and employment status, 2000; numbers in thousands)

| | civilian noninstitutional population | civilian labor force | | | | | |
| | | total | percent of population | employed | percent of population | unemployed | |
						number	percent of labor force
White men, aged							
16 or older	**84,647**	**63,861**	**75.4%**	**61,696**	**72.9%**	**2,165**	**3.4%**
Total, aged 16 to 34	28,785	24,030	83.5	22,800	79.2	1,230	5.1
Aged 16 to 24	13,916	9,987	71.8	9,166	65.9	821	8.2
Aged 25 to 34	14,869	14,043	94.4	13,634	91.7	409	2.9
Aged 16 to 19	6,496	3,679	56.6	3,227	49.7	452	12.3
Aged 20 to 24	7,420	6,308	85.0	5,939	80.0	369	5.9
Aged 25 to 29	7,074	6,646	93.9	6,426	90.8	220	3.3
Aged 30 to 34	7,795	7,397	94.9	7,208	92.5	189	2.6
Black men, aged							
16 or older	**11,320**	**7,816**	**69.0**	**7,180**	**63.4**	**636**	**8.1**
Total, aged 16 to 34	4,749	3,397	71.5	2,985	62.9	412	12.1
Aged 16 to 24	2,448	1,379	56.3	1,103	45.1	276	20.0
Aged 25 to 34	2,301	2,018	87.7	1,882	81.8	136	6.7
Aged 16 to 19	1,213	473	39.0	348	28.7	125	26.4
Aged 20 to 24	1,235	906	73.4	755	61.2	151	16.7
Aged 25 to 29	1,115	948	85.0	868	77.9	80	8.4
Aged 30 to 34	1,186	1,070	90.3	1,014	85.5	56	5.3
Hispanic men, aged							
16 or older*	**11,064**	**8,919**	**80.6**	**8,478**	**76.6**	**441**	**4.9**
Total, aged 16 to 34	5,482	4,564	83.3	4,284	78.1	279	6.1
Aged 16 to 24	2,662	1,912	71.8	1,730	65.0	181	9.5
Aged 25 to 34	2,820	2,652	94.0	2,554	90.6	98	3.7
Aged 16 to 19	1,205	613	50.9	517	42.9	96	15.7
Aged 20 to 24	1,457	1,299	89.2	1,214	83.3	85	6.5

* Data on employment status by five-year age group are not available for Hispanics aged 25 or older.
Source: Bureau of Labor Statistics, Employment and Earnings, *January 2000, Internet site <http://stats.bls.gov/cpsaatab.htm>; calculations by the author*

Labor Force Participation of Women Varies by Race and Ethnicity

Young white women are more likely than blacks or Hispanics to be in the labor force.

White women aged 16 to 34 are more likely than black or Hispanic women to be in the labor force. Seventy-one percent of white women aged 16 to 34 are in the labor force compared with 69 percent of blacks and 60 percent of Hispanics. One reason for their greater labor force participation is that young whites are less likely to have children.

Differences in labor force participation are most pronounced among women aged 16 to 24. Within this age group, 66 percent of white women are in the labor force compared with 56 percent of blacks and 54 percent of Hispanics. The situation is reversed in the 25-to-34 age group, in which black women are more likely than white women to be in the labor force (81 versus 76 percent). A much smaller 65 percent of Hispanic women that age are in the labor force.

♦ Among young adults, Hispanic women are less likely to work than black or white women because a much larger proportion of them are married and caring for young children.

Employment Status of Women Aged 16 to 34 by Race and Hispanic Origin, 2000

(number and percent of women aged 16 or older and aged 16 to 34 in the civilian labor force by race, Hispanic origin, and employment status, 2000; numbers in thousands)

| | | civilian labor force | | | | | |
| | | | | | | unemployed | |
	civilian noninstitutional population	total	percent of population	employed	percent of population	number	percent of labor force
White women, aged 16 or older	**89,781**	**53,714**	**59.8%**	**51,780**	**57.7%**	**1,934**	**3.6%**
Total, aged 16 to 34	28,592	20,291	71.0	19,227	67.2	1,064	5.2
Aged 16 to 24	13,511	8,851	65.5	8,183	60.6	668	7.5
Aged 25 to 34	15,081	11,440	75.9	11,044	73.2	396	3.5
Aged 16 to 19	6,211	3,396	54.7	3,043	49.0	353	10.4
Aged 20 to 24	7,300	5,455	74.7	5,140	70.4	315	5.8
Aged 25 to 29	7,195	5,532	76.9	5,332	74.1	200	3.6
Aged 30 to 34	7,886	5,908	74.9	5,712	72.4	196	3.3
Black women, aged 16 or older	**13,898**	**8,787**	**63.2**	**8,154**	**58.7**	**633**	**7.2**
Total, aged 16 to 34	5,554	3,830	69.0	3,421	61.6	409	10.7
Aged 16 to 24	2,710	1,520	56.1	1,267	46.8	253	16.6
Aged 25 to 34	2,844	2,310	81.2	2,154	75.7	156	6.8
Aged 16 to 19	1,255	494	39.4	380	30.3	114	23.0
Aged 20 to 24	1,455	1,026	70.5	887	60.9	139	13.5
Aged 25 to 29	1,410	1,148	81.4	1,061	75.2	87	7.6
Aged 30 to 34	1,434	1,162	81.0	1,093	76.2	69	5.9
Hispanic women, aged 16 or older*	**11,329**	**6,449**	**56.9**	**6,014**	**53.1**	**435**	**6.7**
Total, aged 16 to 34	5,261	3,159	60.0	2,881	54.8	279	8.8
Aged 16 to 24	2,455	1,326	54.0	1,165	47.5	162	12.2
Aged 25 to 34	2,806	1,833	65.3	1,716	61.1	117	6.4
Aged 16 to 19	1,136	470	41.4	385	33.9	85	18.1
Aged 20 to 24	1,319	856	64.9	780	59.1	77	8.9

* Employment status by five-year age group for Hispanics aged 25 or older is not available.
Source: Bureau of Labor Statistics, Employment and Earnings, *January 2000, Internet site <http://stats.bls.gov/cpsaatab.htm>; calculations by the author*

The Two-Income Couple Is the Norm

Seven out of ten young couples have two incomes.

Among young married couples, it is the norm for both husband and wife to work. Seventy percent of couples headed by someone under age 30 are dual earners.

Among the handful of married couples aged 15 to 19, only 56 percent are dual earners. The share stands at 65 percent among couples aged 20 to 24, rising to 73 percent among couples aged 25 to 29. The dual-earner share drops slightly, to 70 percent, among couples aged 30 to 34. Many in this age group have two or more young children, making it difficult for both spouses to work.

♦ While men and women now share breadwinning and housekeeping responsibilities, the old-fashioned division of labor is far from extinct. Most couples say the woman still does most of the household chores.

The share of dual-earner couples rises with age

(percent of married couples headed by people aged 15 to 34 in which both husband and wife are in the labor force, by age, 1998)

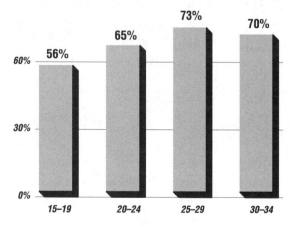

Dual-Earner Couples Aged 15 to 34, 1998

(number and percent distribution of total married couples and couples headed by people aged 15 to 34, by labor force status of husband and wife, 1998; numbers in thousands)

	total	husband and wife in labor force	husband only in labor force	wife only in labor force	husband and wife not in labor force
Total couples	**54,317**	**30,591**	**11,582**	**3,087**	**9,057**
Total, aged 15 to 34	11,259	7,887	3,014	228	128
Aged 15 to 19	86	48	37	–	–
Aged 20 to 24	1,287	841	392	24	30
Aged 25 to 29	3,967	2,880	992	62	33
Aged 30 to 34	5,919	4,118	1,593	142	65
Total couples	**100.0%**	**56.3%**	**21.3%**	**5.7%**	**16.7%**
Total, aged 15 to 34	100.0	70.1	26.8	2.0	1.1
Aged 15 to 19	100.0	55.8	43.0	–	–
Aged 20 to 24	100.0	65.3	30.5	1.9	2.3
Aged 25 to 29	100.0	72.6	25.0	1.6	0.8
Aged 30 to 34	100.0	69.6	26.9	2.4	1.1

Note: (–) means sample is too small to make a reliable estimate.
Source: Bureau of the Census, detailed tables from Household and Family Characteristics: March 1998, *Current Population Reports, P20-515, 1998; calculations by the author*

Young Adults Staff the Service Industry

Nearly half of service-industry workers are under age 35.

Thirty-eight percent of employed people are under age 35, but the share of young workers varies widely by occupation. Nearly half (47 percent) of service workers are aged 16 to 34, for example. Not surprisingly, young adults are underrepresented in managerial occupations, accounting for just 27 percent of executives, administrators, and managers.

Young adults make up a large share of employees in entry-level jobs. Sixty-eight percent of stock handlers and baggers are under age 35, as are 72 percent of waiters and waitresses and 68 percent of cashiers. They account for more than half of file clerks and construction laborers. But they also account for a sizable portion of some technical occupations: 45 percent of computer programmers are under age 35.

Thirty-one percent of employed 16-to-19-year-olds are in service occupations. The proportion falls to 19 percent among 20-to-24-year-olds. People aged 25 to 34 are moving up the career ladder. Thirty-one percent are in managerial or professional specialty occupations, while only 13 percent are in service occupations.

♦ Young adults will always staff the nation's entry-level positions. Since many of these jobs require customer contact, which is increasingly important to business success, customer-service training for young people is a worthwhile investment.

Occupations of Workers Aged 16 to 34, 2000

(number of employed people aged 16 or older and aged 16 to 34 by occupation, 2000; numbers in thousands)

	total	aged 16 to 34 total	aged 16 to 24 total	16 to 19	20 to 24	25 to 34
Total employed	**135,208**	**51,098**	**20,597**	**7,276**	**13,321**	**30,501**
Managerial and professional specialty	40,887	12,067	2,486	346	2,140	9,581
Executive, administrative, and managerial	19,774	5,289	1,008	121	887	4,281
Professional specialty	21,113	6,779	1,479	225	1,254	5,300
Technical, sales, and administrative support	39,442	16,196	7,486	2,731	4,755	8,710
Technicians and related support	4,385	1,779	583	92	491	1,196
Sales	16,340	7,021	3,635	1,737	1,898	3,386
Administrative support, including clerical	18,717	7,397	3,268	902	2,366	4,129
Service	18,278	8,668	4,760	2,274	2,486	3,908
Private household	792	289	171	83	88	118
Protective service	2,399	937	305	89	216	632
Other service	15,087	7,441	4,284	2,102	2,182	3,157
Precision production, craft, repair	14,882	5,223	1,709	364	1,345	3,514
Mechanics and repairers	4,875	1,665	533	97	436	1,132
Construction trades	6,120	2,389	830	193	637	1,559
Extractive occupations	128	32	10	2	8	22
Precision production	3,759	1,138	336	72	264	802
Operators, fabricators, and laborers	18,319	7,689	3,535	1,279	2,256	4,154
Machine operators, assemblers, and inspectors	7,319	2,788	1,045	251	794	1,743
Transportation and material moving	5,557	1,858	623	151	472	1,235
Handlers, equipment cleaners, helpers, and laborers	5,443	3,043	1,867	877	990	1,176
Farming, forestry, and fishing	3,399	1,253	619	281	338	634
Farm operators and managers	1,125	151	33	8	25	118
Other agricultural and related occupations	2,115	1,045	562	268	294	483
Forestry and logging	109	39	15	3	12	24
Fishers, hunters, and trappers	51	18	9	2	7	9

Source: Bureau of Labor Statistics, unpublished data from the 2000 Current Population Survey

Distribution of Workers Aged 16 to 34 by Occupation, 2000

(percent distribution of employed people aged 16 or older and aged 16 to 34 by occupation, 2000)

| | total | aged 16 to 34 | | | | |
| | | total | aged 16 to 24 | | | 25 to 34 |
			total	16 to 19	20 to 24	
Total workers	**100.0%**	**100.0%**	**100.0%**	**100.0%**	**100.0%**	**100.0%**
Managerial and professional specialty	30.2	23.6	12.1	4.8	16.1	31.4
Executive, administrative, and managerial	14.6	10.4	4.9	1.7	6.7	14.0
Professional specialty	15.6	13.3	7.2	3.1	9.4	17.4
Technical, sales, and administrative support	29.2	31.7	36.3	37.5	35.7	28.6
Technicians and related support	3.2	3.5	2.8	1.3	3.7	3.9
Sales	12.1	13.7	17.6	23.9	14.2	11.1
Administrative support, including clerical	13.8	14.5	15.9	12.4	17.8	13.5
Service	13.5	17.0	23.1	31.3	18.7	12.8
Private household	0.6	0.6	0.8	1.1	0.7	0.4
Protective service	1.8	1.8	1.5	1.2	1.6	2.1
Other service	11.2	14.6	20.8	28.9	16.4	10.4
Precision production, craft, repair	11.0	10.2	8.3	5.0	10.1	11.5
Mechanics and repairers	3.6	3.3	2.6	1.3	3.3	3.7
Construction trades	4.5	4.7	4.0	2.7	4.8	5.1
Extractive occupations	0.1	0.1	0.0	0.0	0.1	0.1
Precision production	2.8	2.2	1.6	1.0	2.0	2.6
Operators, fabricators, and laborers	13.5	15.0	17.2	17.6	16.9	13.6
Machine operators, assemblers and inspectors	5.4	5.5	5.1	3.4	6.0	5.7
Transportation and material moving	4.1	3.6	3.0	2.1	3.5	4.0
Handlers, equipment cleaners, helpers, and laborers	4.0	6.0	9.1	12.1	7.4	3.9
Farming, forestry, and fishing	2.5	2.5	3.0	3.9	2.5	2.1
Farm operators and managers	0.8	0.3	0.2	0.1	0.2	0.4
Other agricultural and related occupations	1.6	2.0	2.7	3.7	2.2	1.6
Forestry and logging	0.1	0.1	0.1	0.0	0.1	0.1
Fishing, hunters, and trappers	0.0	0.0	0.0	0.0	0.1	0.0

Source: Bureau of Labor Statistics, unpublished data from the 2000 Current Population Survey; calculations by the author

Share of Workers Aged 16 to 34 by Occupation, 2000

(employed persons aged 16 to 34 as a percent of total employed people aged 16 or older by occupation, 2000

	total	aged 16 to 34	aged 16 to 24			25 to 34
		total	total	16 to 19	20 to 24	
Total workers	**100.0%**	**37.8%**	**15.2%**	**5.4%**	**9.9%**	**22.6%**
Managerial and professional specialty	100.0	29.5	6.1	0.8	5.2	23.4
Executive, administrative, and managerial	100.0	26.7	5.1	0.6	4.5	21.6
Professional specialty	100.0	32.1	7.0	1.1	5.9	25.1
Technical, sales, and administrative support	100.0	41.1	19.0	6.9	12.1	22.1
Technicians and related support	100.0	40.6	13.3	2.1	11.2	27.3
Sales	100.0	43.0	22.2	10.6	11.6	20.7
Administrative support, including clerical	100.0	39.5	17.5	4.8	12.6	22.1
Service	100.0	47.4	26.0	12.4	13.6	21.4
Private household	100.0	36.5	21.6	10.5	11.1	14.9
Protective service	100.0	39.1	12.7	3.7	9.0	26.3
Other service	100.0	49.3	28.4	13.9	14.5	20.9
Precision production, craft, repair	100.0	35.1	11.5	2.4	9.0	23.6
Mechanics and repairers	100.0	34.2	10.9	2.0	8.9	23.2
Construction trades	100.0	39.0	13.6	3.2	10.4	25.5
Extractive occupations	100.0	25.0	7.8	1.6	6.3	17.2
Precision production	100.0	30.3	8.9	1.9	7.0	21.3
Operators, fabricators, and laborers	100.0	42.0	19.3	7.0	12.3	22.7
Machine operators, assemblers, and inspectors	100.0	38.1	14.3	3.4	10.8	23.8
Transport and material moving	100.0	33.4	11.2	2.7	8.5	22.2
Handlers, equipment cleaners, helpers, and laborers	100.0	55.9	34.3	16.1	18.2	21.6
Farming, forestry, and fishing	100.0	36.9	18.2	8.3	9.9	18.7
Farm operators and managers	100.0	13.4	2.9	0.7	2.2	10.5
Other agricultural and related occupations	100.0	49.4	26.6	12.7	13.9	22.8
Forestry and logging	100.0	35.8	13.8	2.8	11.0	22.0
Fishing, hunters, and trappers	100.0	35.3	17.6	3.9	13.7	17.6

Source: Bureau of Labor Statistics, unpublished data from the 2000 Current Population Survey; calculations by the author

Workers Aged 16 to 34 by Detailed Occupation, 2000

(number of employed workers aged 16 or older and number and percent aged 16 to 34 by selected detailed occupation; 2000; numbers in thousands)

	total workers	aged 16 to 34 number	aged 16 to 34 percent of total
Total workers	**135,208**	**51,098**	**37.8%**
Managers, food service and lodging establishments	1,446	553	38.2
Accountants and auditors	1,592	600	37.7
Computer systems analysts and scientists	1,797	768	42.7
Actors and directors	139	57	41.0
Editors and reporters	288	125	43.4
Public relations specialists	205	91	44.4
Athletes	90	56	62.2
Health technologists and technicians	1,724	692	40.1
Computer programmers	699	314	44.9
Securities and financial services sales	600	244	40.7
Sales workers, apparel	411	281	68.4
Sales workers, shoes	114	84	73.7
Sales workers, radio, TV, and appliances	258	168	65.1
Sales workers, hardware and building supplies	328	138	42.1
Sales counter clerks	185	107	57.8
Cashiers	2,939	1,992	67.8
Computer equipment operators	323	141	43.7
Information clerks	2,071	1,033	49.9
Receptionists	1,017	520	51.1
File clerks	338	191	56.5
Telephone operators	156	73	46.8
Dispatchers	269	111	41.3
Traffic, shipping, and receiving clerks	661	288	43.6
Insurance adjusters, examiners, and investigators	451	199	44.1
General office clerks	864	382	44.2
Bank tellers	431	259	60.1
Data-entry keyers	749	356	47.5
Child care workers, private household	275	180	65.5
Firefighters	233	95	40.8
Bartenders	365	209	57.3

(continued)

(continued from previous page)

	total workers	aged 16 to 34	
		number	percent of total
Waiters and waitresses	1,440	1,038	72.1%
Cooks	2,076	1,149	55.3
Kitchen workers, food preparation	317	189	59.6
Dental assistants	218	134	61.5
Nursing aides, orderlies, attendants	1,983	771	38.9
Hairdressers, cosmetologists	820	362	44.1
Attendants, amusement and recreation facilities	246	155	63.0
Automobile mechanics	860	362	42.1
Data processing equipment repairers	342	164	48.0
Brickmasons and stonemasons	242	96	39.7
Carpenters	1,467	634	43.2
Electricians	860	334	38.8
Painters, construction and maintenance	624	244	39.1
Roofers	215	118	54.9
Butchers and meat cutters	265	108	40.8
Bakers	154	67	43.5
Paint and paint-spraying machine operators	187	92	49.2
Assemblers	1,299	552	42.5
Parking lot attendants	60	39	65.0
Industrial truck and tractor equipment operators	569	266	46.7
Construction laborers	1,015	537	52.9
Garbage collectors	54	26	48.1
Stock handlers and baggers	1,125	763	67.8
Garage and service station-related occupations	184	128	69.6
Vehicle washers and equipment cleaners	313	197	62.9
Laborers, except construction	1,307	606	46.4
Farm workers	768	382	49.7
Groundskeepers and gardeners	870	451	51.8

Source: Bureau of Labor Statistics, unpublished tables from the 2000 Current Population Survey; calculations by the author

Most 16- and 17-Year-Olds Work Part-Time

Among workers aged 18 to 34, full-time work is the norm.

The majority of workers aged 18 or older have full-time jobs. Among employed 16 and 17 year olds, however, part-time work is most common. Eighty-one percent of men aged 16 to 17 work part-time, while only 19 percent work full-time. Among women in the age group, 86 percent work full-time and 14 percent work part-time.

Slightly more than half of employed 18- and 19-year-olds work full-time. The proportion rises sharply among workers aged 20 to 24, however. Fully 81 percent of employed men and 70 percent of employed women in the age group work full-time. Among employed people aged 25 to 34, 95 percent of men and 82 percent of women are full-time workers.

♦ Although a large proportion of young adults work only part-time, many have plenty of money to spend. Living with their parents or in college dorm rooms paid for by Mom and Dad means they can spend their earnings as they choose.

School prevents younger people from working full-time

(percent of employed people aged 16 to 34 who work part-time, by sex, 2000)

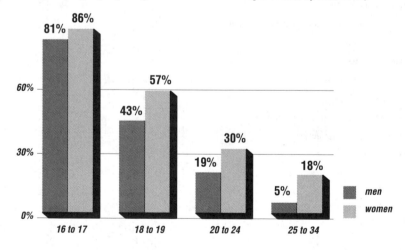

Full- and Part-Time Workers Aged 16 to 34 by Sex, 2000

(number and percent distribution of people aged 16 or older and aged 16 to 34 in the civilian labor force by full- and part-time employment status, 2000; numbers in thousands)

	men			women		
	total	full-time	part-time	total	full-time	part-time
Total employed	**75,248**	**67,403**	**7,845**	**65,615**	**49,390**	**16,225**
Total, aged 16 to 34	28,949	24,232	4,717	25,435	17,963	7,472
Aged 16 to 17	1,688	319	1,369	1,596	217	1,379
Aged 18 to 19	2,629	1,488	1,141	2,456	1,064	1,392
Aged 20 to 24	7,559	6,137	1,422	6,788	4,747	2,041
Aged 25 to 34	17,073	16,288	785	14,595	11,935	2,660
Percent distribution by employment status						
Total employed	**100.0%**	**89.6%**	**10.4%**	**100.0%**	**75.3%**	**24.7%**
Total, aged 16 to 34	100.0	83.7	16.3	100.0	70.6	29.4
Aged 16 to 17	100.0	18.9	81.1	100.0	13.6	86.4
Aged 18 to 19	100.0	56.6	43.4	100.0	43.3	56.7
Aged 20 to 24	100.0	81.2	18.8	100.0	69.9	30.1
Aged 25 to 34	100.0	95.4	4.6	100.0	81.8	18.2
Percent distribution by age						
Total employed	**100.0%**	**100.0%**	**100.0%**	**100.0%**	**100.0%**	**100.0%**
Total, aged 16 to 34	38.5	36.0	60.1	38.8	36.4	46.1
Aged 16 to 17	2.2	0.5	17.5	2.4	0.4	8.5
Aged 18 to 19	3.5	2.2	14.5	3.7	2.2	8.6
Aged 20 to 24	10.0	9.1	18.1	10.3	9.6	12.6
Aged 25 to 34	22.7	24.2	10.0	22.2	24.2	16.4

Source: unpublished data from the Bureau of Labor Statistics; calculations by the author

Most Young Adults Want to Be Their Own Boss

Few are able to realize this dream, however.

The entrepreneurial spirit is alive and well in young adults. Overall, 63 percent of adults would prefer self-employment. Fully 72 percent of 18-to-24-year-olds and 70 percent of 25-to-34-year-olds would prefer to be self-employed.

Although many may dream of self-employment, only 7 percent of all workers are self-employed. Among workers aged 16 to 24, fewer than 4 percent work for themselves. Only 5 percent of workers aged 25 to 34 are self-employed.

As people age, the share of those who want to be self-employed declines. Many prefer the security of working for someone else, while others don't want the responsibility of being the top dog.

♦ The desire for self-employment shared by most young adults reflects the independence and individualism of younger generations.

Young adults want to be entrepreneurs

(percent of people aged 18 or older who would prefer to be self-employed, 1998)

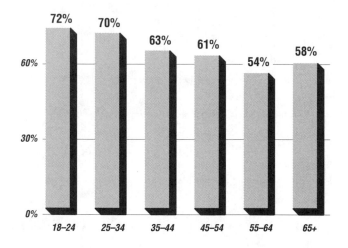

Self-Employed Workers Aged 16 to 34 by Sex, 2000

(number of employed workers aged 16 or older and aged 16 to 34, number and percent who are self-employed, and percent distribution of self-employed by age, 2000; numbers in thousands)

	total	self-employed		percent distribution
		number	percent	
Total, aged 16 or older	**135,208**	**9,907**	**7.3%**	**100.0%**
Total, aged 16 to 34	51,098	1,879	3.7	19.0
Aged 16 to 19	7,276	82	1.1	0.8
Aged 20 to 24	13,321	262	2.0	2.6
Aged 25 to 34	30,501	1,535	5.0	15.5
Total men, aged 16 or older	**72,293**	**6,154**	**8.5**	**100.0**
Total, aged 16 to 34	27,216	1,110	4.1	18.0
Aged 16 to 19	3,713	53	1.4	0.9
Aged 20 to 24	7,009	163	2.3	2.6
Aged 25 to 34	16,494	894	5.4	14.5
Total women, aged 16 or older	**62,915**	**3,753**	**6.0**	**100.0**
Total, aged 16 to 34	23,881	768	3.2	20.5
Aged 16 to 19	3,563	28	0.8	0.7
Aged 20 to 24	6,312	99	1.6	2.6
Aged 25 to 34	14,006	641	4.6	17.1

Source: Bureau of Labor Statistics, Employment and Earnings, *January 2000, Internet site <http://stats.bls.gov/cpsaatab.htm>; calculations by the author*

Prefer Self-Employment? 1998

"Suppose you were working and could choose between different kinds of jobs.
Which of the following would you personally choose:
being an employee or self-employed?"

(percent of people aged 18 or older responding by age, 1998)

	employee	self-employed	can't choose
Total people	**26%**	**63%**	**11%**
Aged 18 to 24	18	72	9
Aged 25 to 34	19	70	11
Aged 35 to 44	27	63	10
Aged 45 to 54	28	61	11
Aged 55 to 64	35	54	11
Aged 65 or older	30	58	11

Source: 1998 General Social Survey, National Opinion Research Center, University of Chicago; calculations by the author

Most Temps Are Young Adults

Young adults make up almost one-third of alternative workers.

Most working Americans are in traditional jobs. But 9 percent work in alternative arrangements as independent contractors, on-call workers, temporary-help agency workers, or workers supplied by contract firms.

Young adults are less likely than average to work in alternative arrangements, but they account for a sizable share of some types of alternative workers. People aged 16 to 34 make up 56 percent of the nation's temporary-help agency workforce. They account for 42 percent of on-call workers and 47 percent of workers provided by contract firms.

♦ Although many young adults complain about their "dead-end" jobs, alternative work arrangements often serve a useful purpose. For people who attend school or have young children at home, the flexibility offered by alternative jobs is a necessity.

Young people account for a large share of alternative workers

(percent of alternative workers aged 16 to 34, by type of alternative work, 1999)

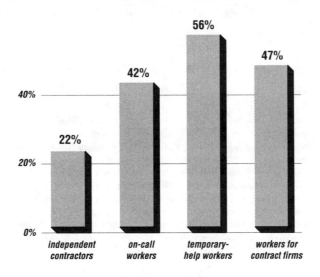

Workers Aged 16 to 34 in Alternative Work Arrangements, 1999

(number and percent distribution of workers aged 16 or older and aged 16 to 34 employed in alternative work arrangements, 1999; numbers in thousands)

| | total employed | alternative workers | | | | |
		total	independent contractors	on-call workers	temporary-help agency workers	workers provided by contract firms
Total workers	**131,494**	**12,385**	**8,247**	**2,032**	**1,188**	**769**
Total, aged 16 to 34	50,092	3,780	1,807	851	665	359
Aged 16 to 19	6,662	397	76	179	68	37
Aged 20 to 24	12,462	825	252	202	249	87
Aged 25 to 34	30,968	2,558	1,479	470	348	235
Percent distribution by alternative work status						
Total workers	**100.0%**	**9.4%**	**6.3%**	**1.5%**	**0.9%**	**0.6%**
Total, aged 16 to 34	100.0	7.5	3.6	1.7	1.3	0.7
Aged 16 to 19	100.0	6.0	1.1	2.7	1.0	0.6
Aged 20 to 24	100.0	6.6	2.0	1.6	2.0	0.7
Aged 25 to 34	100.0	8.3	4.8	1.5	1.1	0.8
Percent distribution by age						
Total workers	**100.0%**	**100.0%**	**100.0%**	**100.0%**	**100.0%**	**100.0%**
Total, aged 16 to 34	38.1	30.5	21.9	41.9	56.0	46.7
Aged 16 to 19	5.1	3.2	0.9	8.8	5.7	4.8
Aged 20 to 24	9.5	6.7	3.1	9.9	21.0	11.3
Aged 25 to 34	23.6	20.7	17.9	23.1	29.3	30.6

Note: Numbers may not add to total because total employed includes day laborers, an alternative arrangement not shown separately, and because a small number of workers were both on call and provided by contract firms. Independent contractors are self-employed (except when incorporated) or wage and salary workers who obtain customers on their own to provide a product or service. On-call workers are in a pool of workers who are called to work only as needed, such as substitute teachers and construction workers supplied by a union hiring hall. Temporary-help agency workers are those who said they are paid by a temporary help agency. Workers provided by contract firms are employed by a company that provides employees or their services to others under contract, such as security, landscaping, and computer programming.
Source: Bureau of Labor Statistics, Contingent and Alternative Employment Arrangements, *February 1999, USDL 99-362, Internet site <www.bls.gov/news.release/conemp.toc.htm>; calculations by the author*

Number of Young Workers Will Increase by 3 Million

The labor force participation rate of young adults is not expected to change, however.

The number of 16-to-34-year-olds in the labor force in 2008 is expected to be about 3 million greater than it was in 1998, an increase of 5 percent. The reason for the increase is the large Millennial generation's entry into the labor force.

The number of people aged 16 to 19 who are in the labor force will increase 14 percent, while the number of workers aged 20 to 24 will increase 16 percent. The number of workers aged 25 to 34 will decline slightly because small Generation X accounts for much of the age group during the period.

The labor force participation rate of young men is expected to continue its downward trend, dropping a little more than 1 percentage point. Young women, on the other hand, are expected to enter the labor force at a greater rate. Their labor force participation rate is expected to rise 1 percentage point between 1998 and 2008.

♦ The labor shortages of the past several years should ease somewhat in the near future, even if the unemployment rate remains low. An expanding pool of young workers will provide much-needed entry level workers.

Young Millennials will boost the number of young adults in the workforce

(percent change in the number of people aged 16 to 34 in the labor force, 1998–2008)

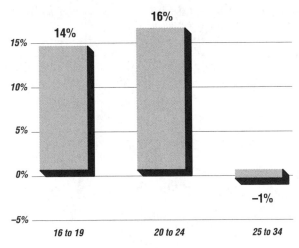

Projections of Labor Force Aged 16 to 34 by Sex, 1998 to 2008

(number and percent of people aged 16 or older and aged 16 to 34 in the civilian labor force by sex and age, 1998 and 2008; percent change in number and percentage point change in rate, 1998–2008; numbers in thousands)

	number			participation rate		
	1998	*2008*	*percent change 1998–2008*	*1998*	*2008*	*percentage point change 1998–2008*
Total labor force	**137,673**	**154,576**	**12.3%**	**67.1%**	**67.6%**	**0.5**
Total, aged 16 to 34	54,707	57,608	5.3	76.0	76.0	0.0
Aged 16 to 19	8,256	9,396	13.8	52.8	52.7	–0.1
Aged 20 to 24	13,638	15,814	16.0	77.5	78.0	0.5
Aged 25 to 34	32,813	32,398	–1.3	84.6	85.9	1.3
Total men	**73,959**	**81,132**	**9.7**	**74.9**	**73.7**	**–1.2**
Total, aged 16 to 34	29,261	30,193	3.2	81.6	80.3	–1.2
Aged 16 to 19	4,244	4,769	12.4	53.3	52.9	–0.4
Aged 20 to 24	7,221	8,279	14.7	82.0	81.4	–0.6
Aged 25 to 34	17,796	17,145	–3.7	93.2	93.2	0.0
Total women	**63,714**	**73,444**	**15.3**	**59.8**	**61.9**	**2.1**
Total, aged 16 to 34	25,447	27,415	7.7	70.4	71.7	1.3
Aged 16 to 19	4,012	4,627	15.3	52.3	52.4	0.1
Aged 20 to 24	6,418	7,535	17.4	73.0	74.6	1.6
Aged 25 to 34	15,017	15,253	1.6	76.3	79.0	2.7

Source: Bureau of Labor Statistics, Monthly Labor Review, *November 1999, Internet site <www.bls.gov/opub/mlr/1999/11/contents.htm>; calculations by the author*

Youngest Workers Are Most Likely to Want a New Career

Career contentment is higher among older workers.

Two out of five adults would like to change careers. Among the youngest workers (aged 18 to 24), however, fully 57 percent want to change the type of work they do.

Most young adults are not yet settled into a career that suits them. Many are in entry-level jobs with low pay and little autonomy or responsibility. As they age, they will move into different jobs that provide more satisfaction. The proportion of people who want to change careers drops to 39 percent among people aged 25 to 34.

♦ Although younger generations are sometimes portrayed as chronic job-hoppers, most eventually will settle into a career.

Workers aged 18 to 24 are least satisfied with their careers

(percent of workers aged 18 or older and aged 18 to 34 who want to change their present type of work, 1998)

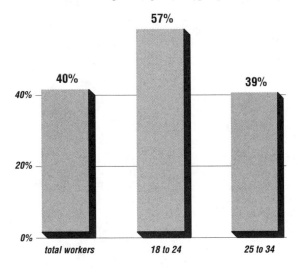

Would Like Different Work, 1998

"To what extent do you agree or disagree with this statement? Given the chance, I would change my present type of work for something different."

(percent of people aged 18 or older responding by age, 1998)

	strongly agree	agree	neither	disagree	strongly disagree
Total people	**14%**	**26%**	**23%**	**26%**	**11%**
18 to 24	25	32	31	8	4
25 to 34	14	25	27	23	10
35 to 44	14	29	20	26	9
45 to 54	10	22	24	31	13
55 to 64	10	24	14	34	15
65 or older	4	7	19	48	22

Note: Asked of people currently working. Numbers may not add to 100 because "can't choose" is not shown.
Source: 1998 General Social Survey, National Opinion Research Center, University of Chicago; calculations by the author

Most Young Adults Think There's More to Life Than Work

Expect them to continue to push for a more balanced life.

Young adults are not the slackers they are often accused of being. Most are hard-working and ambitious. But there are some significant differences in the opinions of older and younger people about the appropriate balance between work and other areas of life.

The youngest workers (aged 18 to 24) are most likely to say they work hard, but don't let work interfere with the rest of their life (45 percent compared with 37 percent of all working adults). They are also most likely to say they don't work any harder than they have to.

This is not necessarily indicative of a dismissive attitude toward work that they will carry throughout their lives. For many, it reflects the fact that they have not yet settled into career-track jobs they value and enjoy. In fact, people aged 18 to 24 are more likely than those aged 25 to 54 to believe work is a person's most important activity.

As people age, their willingness to sacrifice for work increases. But younger generations are unlikely to ever agree with the oldest Americans that work is more important than anything else in life.

♦ Today's younger generations are hard-working and ambitious, but most do not see work as the ultimate source of satisfaction in life. Although many will become more involved in their jobs as they get older, they are likely to continue to seek a balance between work and personal life.

Young adults are least likely to let work interfere with life

(percent of workers aged 18 or older and aged 18 to 34 who say they do the best work they can, even if it interferes with the rest of life, 1998)

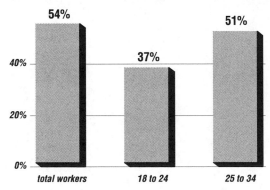

Work Is a Person's Most Important Activity, 1998

"Thinking of work in general, please indicate how much you agree or disagree: Work is a person's most important activity."

(percent of people aged 18 or older responding by age, 1998)

	agree	neither	disagree
Total people	**30%**	**19%**	**50%**
Aged 18 to 24	32	16	52
Aged 25 to 34	26	20	53
Aged 35 to 44	24	20	56
Aged 45 to 54	27	21	51
Aged 55 to 64	35	17	48
Aged 65 or older	43	16	38

Note: Numbers may not add to 100 because "can't choose" is not shown.
Source: 1998 General Social Survey, National Opinion Research Center, University of Chicago; calculations by the author

Work to Live or Live to Work? 1998

"Which of the following statements best describes your feelings about your job?
I work only as hard as I have to. I work hard but not so as to interfere with
the rest of my life. I make a point of doing the best work
I can, even if it sometimes does interfere with the rest of my life."

(percent of people aged 18 or older responding by age, 1998)

	work only as hard as I have to	work hard, but don't let it interfere with rest of life	do best work I can, even if it interferes with rest of life
Total people	**8%**	**37%**	**54%**
18 to 24	17	45	37
25 to 34	12	37	51
35 to 44	6	37	54
45 to 54	5	36	58
55 to 64	4	29	65
65 or older	3	33	63

Note: Asked of people working at least ten hours per week. Numbers may not add to 100 because "can't choose" is not shown.
Source: 1998 General Social Survey, National Opinion Research Center, University of Chicago; calculations by the author

6

Living Arrangements

♦ Married couples accounted for only 44 percent of households headed by adults under age 35 in 2000.

♦ Only 24 percent of black households headed by people under age 35 consist of married couples compared with 49 percent of white and 52 percent of Hispanic households in the age group.

♦ A 21 percent minority of households headed by 15-to-19-year-olds include children, but the proportion rises to 61 percent among householders aged 30 to 34.

♦ Sixty-six percent of Hispanic households and 60 percent of black households headed by people aged 15 to 34 include children under age 18. In contrast, only 49 percent of white households in the age group include children under age 18.

♦ Twenty percent of men aged 25 to 29 still live with their parents, as do 10 percent of those aged 30 to 34. In contrast, only 12 percent of women aged 25 to 29 and 5 percent of those aged 30 to 34 live with their parents.

♦ Most people are married by the time they reach age 35, but men marry at a later age than women. More than half of women aged 25 to 29 are married. Among men, the married share does not surpass 50 percent until the 30-to-34 age group.

Change Is the Norm for Young Adults

No other age group undergoes such dramatic lifestyle change.

For young adults, life is a series of changes. The lifestyle of Americans in their teens and early twenties is very different from that of people in their early thirties.

Two-thirds of households headed by people under age 35 were families in 2000. Among householders aged 15 to 24, however, only 57 percent are family heads. The proportion rises to 74 percent among householders aged 30 to 34.

Fully 43 percent of households headed by people aged 15 to 24 are nonfamily households—people living with nonrelatives or alone. Only 26 percent of households headed by people aged 30 to 34 are nonfamilies.

♦ Although most middle-aged people remember fondly their carefree youth, being a young adult can be as stressful as it is exciting. During their young adult years, most people graduate from high school, marry, have children, and launch careers.

Households Headed by People Aged 15 to 34
by Household Type, 2000: Total Households

(number and percent distribution of total households and households headed by people aged 15 to 34, by household type, 2000; numbers in thousands)

| | | aged 15 to 34 | | | | |
| | | | | | aged 25 to 34 | |
	total	total	15 to 24	total	25 to 29	30 to 34
Total households	**104,705**	**24,487**	**5,860**	**18,627**	**8,520**	**10,107**
Family households	**72,025**	**16,360**	**3,353**	**13,007**	**5,489**	**7,518**
Married couples	55,311	10,840	1,450	9,390	3,775	5,615
Female householder, no spouse present	12,687	4,074	1,342	2,732	1,289	1,443
Male householder, no spouse present	4,028	1,446	560	886	426	460
Nonfamily households	**32,680**	**8,128**	**2,508**	**5,620**	**3,031**	**2,589**
Female householder	18,039	3,393	1,221	2,172	1,249	923
Living alone	15,543	2,155	587	1,568	848	720
Male householder	14,641	4,734	1,286	3,448	1,782	1,666
Living alone	11,181	2,835	556	2,279	1,079	1,200
Percent distribution by age						
Total households	**100.0%**	**23.4%**	**5.6%**	**17.8%**	**8.1%**	**9.7%**
Family households	**100.0**	**22.7**	**4.7**	**18.1**	**7.6**	**10.4**
Married couples	100.0	19.6	2.6	17.0	6.8	10.2
Female householder, no spouse present	100.0	32.1	10.6	21.5	10.2	11.4
Male householder, no spouse present	100.0	35.9	13.9	22.0	10.6	11.4
Nonfamily households	**100.0**	**24.9**	**7.7**	**17.2**	**9.3**	**7.9**
Female householder	100.0	18.8	6.8	12.0	6.9	5.1
Living alone	100.0	13.9	3.8	10.1	5.5	4.6
Male householder	100.0	32.3	8.8	23.6	12.2	11.4
Living alone	100.0	25.4	5.0	20.4	9.7	10.7

(continued)

(continued from previous page)

	total	aged 15 to 34		aged 25 to 34		
		total	15 to 24	total	25 to 29	30 to 34
Percent distribution by household type						
Total households	100.0%	100.0%	100.0%	100.0%	100.0%	100.0%
Family households	**68.8**	**66.8**	**57.2**	**69.8**	**64.4**	**74.4**
Married couples	52.8	44.3	24.7	50.4	44.3	55.6
Female householder, no spouse present	12.1	16.6	22.9	14.7	15.1	14.3
Male householder, no spouse present	3.8	5.9	9.6	4.8	5.0	4.6
Nonfamily households	**31.2**	**33.2**	**42.8**	**30.2**	**35.6**	**25.6**
Female householder	17.2	13.9	20.8	11.7	14.7	9.1
Living alone	14.8	8.8	10.0	8.4	10.0	7.1
Male householder	14.0	19.3	21.9	18.5	20.9	16.5
Living alone	10.7	11.6	9.5	12.2	12.7	11.9

Source: Bureau of the Census, Internet site <http://ferret.bls.census.gov/macro/03200/hhinc/new02_000.htm>; calculations by the author

Female-Headed Families Are Most Common among Blacks

Married couples account for fewer than one-quarter of young-adult households headed by blacks.

While most black householders under age 35 are family heads, only 24 percent live with a spouse. The married-couple share ranges from only 9 percent of householders aged 15 to 24 to 33 percent of those aged 30 to 34.

People who live alone or with friends (nonfamily households) account for 29 percent of households headed by blacks aged 15 to 34. Families headed by men are the least common household type among blacks under age 35, accounting for only 7 percent of households in the age group.

♦ During the past few decades, the proportion of female-headed families has grown steadily among black households. Today, black children are more likely to be raised by a single parent than by two parents.

Married couples head few black households

(percent distribution of black households headed by people aged 15 to 34, by household type, 2000)

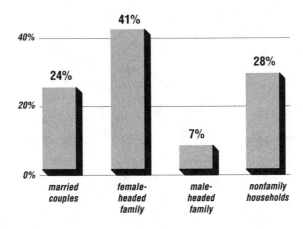

Households Headed by People Aged 15 to 34
by Household Type, 2000: Black Households

(number and percent distribution of total black households and households headed by blacks aged 15 to 34, by household type, 2000; numbers in thousands)

| | | aged 15 to 34 | | | | |
| | | | | aged 25 to 34 | | |
	total	total	15 to 24	total	25 to 29	30 to 34
Total black households	**12,849**	**3,726**	**1,002**	**2,724**	**1,291**	**1,433**
Family households	**8,664**	**2,669**	**709**	**1,960**	**871**	**1,089**
Married couples	4,144	876	93	783	312	471
Female householder, no spouse present	3,814	1,541	502	1,039	494	545
Male householder, no spouse present	706	254	115	139	65	74
Nonfamily households	**4,185**	**1,057**	**293**	**764**	**420**	**344**
Female householder	2,309	513	190	323	188	135
Living alone	2,025	399	126	273	152	121
Male householder	1,876	544	103	441	232	209
Living alone	1,580	429	76	353	175	178
Percent distribution by age						
Total black households	**100.0%**	**29.0%**	**7.8%**	**21.2%**	**10.0%**	**11.2%**
Family households	**100.0**	**30.8**	**8.2**	**22.6**	**10.1**	**12.6**
Married couples	100.0	21.1	2.2	18.9	7.5	11.4
Female householder, no spouse present	100.0	40.4	13.2	27.2	13.0	14.3
Male householder, no spouse present	100.0	36.0	16.3	19.7	9.2	10.5
Nonfamily households	**100.0**	**25.3**	**7.0**	**18.3**	**10.0**	**8.2**
Female householder	100.0	22.2	8.2	14.0	8.1	5.8
Living alone	100.0	19.7	6.2	13.5	7.5	6.0
Male householder	100.0	29.0	5.5	23.5	12.4	11.1
Living alone	100.0	27.2	4.8	22.3	11.1	11.3

(continued)

(continued from previous page)

	total	aged 15 to 34		aged 25 to 34		
		total	15 to 24	total	25 to 29	30 to 34
Percent distribution by household type						
Total black households	**100.0%**	**100.0%**	**100.0%**	**100.0%**	**100.0%**	**100.0%**
Family households	**67.4**	**71.6**	**70.8**	**72.0**	**67.5**	**76.0**
Married couples	32.3	23.5	9.3	28.7	24.2	32.9
Female householder, no spouse present	29.7	41.4	50.1	38.1	38.3	38.0
Male householder, no spouse present	5.5	6.8	11.5	5.1	5.0	5.2
Nonfamily households	**32.6**	**28.4**	**29.2**	**28.0**	**32.5**	**24.0**
Female householder	18.0	13.8	19.0	11.9	14.6	9.4
Living alone	15.8	10.7	12.6	10.0	11.8	8.4
Male householder	14.6	14.6	10.3	16.2	18.0	14.6
Living alone	12.3	11.5	7.6	13.0	13.6	12.4

Source: Bureau of the Census, Internet site <http://ferret.bls.census.gov/macro/03200/hhinc/new02_000.htm>; calculations by the author

Many Hispanics Marry Young

More than half of households headed by young Hispanics are married couples.

As the median age at first marriage has increased over the past few decades, the married-couple share of young-adult households has declined. Because Hispanics marry at a younger age than both blacks and whites, a larger share of Hispanic households in the age group are headed by married couples. Married couples account for 36 percent of households headed by Hispanics under age 25. In contrast, married couples head only 29 percent of white households and just 9 percent of black households in the age group.

Nonfamily households are much less common among young Hispanics than among their black and white counterparts. Only 18 percent of Hispanic households headed by 15-to-34-year-olds are nonfamilies compared with 28 percent of black and 34 percent of white households in the age group.

♦ The Hispanic population is growing faster than the black and white populations. Among young adults, this growth could result in a slight increase in the proportion of households headed by married couples during the next decade.

Young Hispanic householders are most likely to be married

(married-couple share of households headed by people aged 15 to 24, by race and Hispanic origin, 2000)

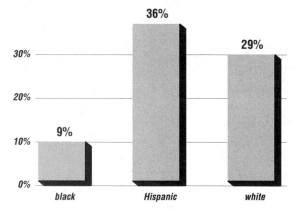

Households Headed by People Aged 15 to 34
by Household Type, 2000: Hispanic Households

(number and percent distribution of total Hispanic households and households headed by Hispanics aged 15 to 34, by household type, 2000; numbers in thousands)

		aged 15 to 34				
				aged 25 to 34		
	total	*total*	*15 to 24*	*total*	*25 to 29*	*30 to 34*
Total Hispanic households	**9,319**	**3,348**	**871**	**2,477**	**1,133**	**1,344**
Family households	**7,561**	**2,738**	**671**	**2,067**	**928**	**1,139**
Married couples	5,133	1,751	315	1,436	618	818
Female householder, no spouse present	1,769	646	213	433	204	229
Male householder, no spouse present	658	341	143	198	106	92
Nonfamily households	**1,758**	**609**	**200**	**409**	**204**	**205**
Female householder	783	193	81	112	64	48
Living alone	630	114	42	72	32	40
Male householder	974	417	119	298	141	157
Living alone	666	218	43	175	80	95
Percent distribution by age						
Total Hispanic households	**100.0%**	**35.9%**	**9.3%**	**26.6%**	**12.2%**	**14.4%**
Family households	**100.0**	**36.2**	**8.9**	**27.3**	**12.3**	**15.1**
Married couples	100.0	34.1	6.1	28.0	12.0	15.9
Female householder, no spouse present	100.0	36.5	12.0	24.5	11.5	12.9
Male householder, no spouse present	100.0	51.8	21.7	30.1	16.1	14.0
Nonfamily households	**100.0**	**34.6**	**11.4**	**23.3**	**11.6**	**11.7**
Female householder	100.0	24.6	10.3	14.3	8.2	6.1
Living alone	100.0	18.1	6.7	11.4	5.1	6.3
Male householder	100.0	42.8	12.2	30.6	14.5	16.1
Living alone	100.0	32.7	6.5	26.3	12.0	14.3

(continued)

(continued from previous page)

	total	aged 15 to 34				
		total	15 to 24	aged 25 to 34		
				total	25 to 29	30 to 34
Percent distribution by household type						
Total Hispanic households	100.0%	100.0%	100.0%	100.0%	100.0%	100.0%
Family households	**81.1**	**81.8**	**77.0**	**83.4**	**81.9**	**84.7**
Married couples	55.1	52.3	36.2	58.0	54.5	60.9
Female householder, no spouse present	19.0	19.3	24.5	17.5	18.0	17.0
Male householder, no spouse present	7.1	10.2	16.4	8.0	9.4	6.8
Nonfamily households	**18.9**	**18.2**	**23.0**	**16.5**	**18.0**	**15.3**
Female householder	8.4	5.8	9.3	4.5	5.6	3.6
Living alone	6.8	3.4	4.8	2.9	2.8	3.0
Male householder	10.5	12.5	13.7	12.0	12.4	11.7
Living alone	7.1	6.5	4.9	7.1	7.1	7.1

Source: Bureau of the Census, Internet site <http://ferret.bls.census.gov/macro/03200/hhinc/new02_000.htm>; calculations by the author

Many Young Whites Live with Friends or Alone

One-third of white householders under age 35 head nonfamily households.

Two-thirds of households headed by whites under age 35 are families. Among those headed by whites under age 25, however, households are almost evenly divided between families and nonfamilies—54 percent versus 46 percent, respectively.

Non-Hispanic whites are less likely than all whites (a category that includes most Hispanics) to be family householders. Only 63 percent of non-Hispanic white householders under age 35 are family heads.

♦ Among young adults, family households are less common among non-Hispanic whites than among blacks or Hispanics because whites are less likely to have children.

Half of non-Hispanic white householders under age 25 live alone or with friends

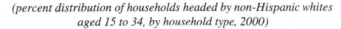

(percent distribution of households headed by non-Hispanic whites aged 15 to 34, by household type, 2000)

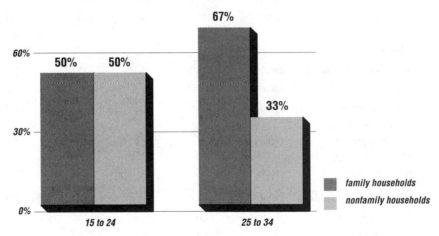

■ family households
■ nonfamily households

15 to 24   25 to 34

Households Headed by People Aged 15 to 34
by Household Type, 2000: White Households

(number and percent distribution of total white households and households headed by whites aged 15 to 34, by household type, 2000; numbers in thousands)

| | | | | aged 15 to 34 | | |
| | | | | | aged 25 to 34 | |
	total	*total*	*15 to 24*	*total*	*25 to 29*	*30 to 34*
Total white households	**87,671**	**19,412**	**4,541**	**14,871**	**6,744**	**8,127**
Family households	**60,251**	**12,846**	**2,470**	**10,376**	**4,349**	**6,027**
Married couples	48,790	9,426	1,298	8,128	3,293	4,835
Female householder, no spouse present	8,380	2,356	770	1,586	733	853
Male householder, no spouse present	3,081	1,064	402	662	323	339
Nonfamily households	**27,420**	**6,567**	**2,071**	**4,496**	**2,395**	**2,101**
Female householder	15,215	2,673	973	1,700	971	729
Living alone	13,109	1,613	421	1,192	629	563
Male householder	12,204	3,893	1,098	2,795	1,424	1,371
Living alone	9,198	2,207	440	1,767	813	954
Percent distribution by age						
Total white households	**100.0%**	**22.1%**	**5.2%**	**17.0%**	**7.7%**	**9.3%**
Family households	**100.0**	**21.3**	**4.1**	**17.2**	**7.2**	**10.0**
Married couples	100.0	19.3	2.7	16.7	6.7	9.9
Female householder, no spouse present	100.0	28.1	9.2	18.9	8.7	10.2
Male householder, no spouse present	100.0	34.5	13.0	21.5	10.5	11.0
Nonfamily households	**100.0**	**23.9**	**7.6**	**16.4**	**8.7**	**7.7**
Female householder	100.0	17.6	6.4	11.2	6.4	4.8
Living alone	100.0	12.3	3.2	9.1	4.8	4.3
Male householder	100.0	31.9	9.0	22.9	11.7	11.2
Living alone	100.0	24.0	4.8	19.2	8.8	10.4

(continued)

(continued from previous page)

	total	aged 15 to 34			aged 25 to 34	
		total	15 to 24	total	25 to 29	30 to 34
Percent distribution by household type						
Total white households	100.0%	100.0%	100.0%	100.0%	100.0%	100.0%
Family households	**68.7**	**66.2**	**54.4**	**69.8**	**64.5**	**74.2**
Married couples	55.7	48.6	28.6	54.7	48.8	59.5
Female householder, no spouse present	9.6	12.1	17.0	10.7	10.9	10.5
Male householder, no spouse present	3.5	5.5	8.9	4.5	4.8	4.2
Nonfamily households	**31.3**	**33.8**	**45.6**	**30.2**	**35.5**	**25.9**
Female householder	17.4	13.8	21.4	11.4	14.4	9.0
Living alone	15.0	8.3	9.3	8.0	9.3	6.9
Male householder	13.9	20.1	24.2	18.8	21.1	16.9
Living alone	10.5	11.4	9.7	11.9	12.1	11.7

Source: Bureau of the Census, Internet site <http://ferret.bls.census.gov/macro/03200/hhinc/new02_000.htm>; calculations by the author

Households Headed by People Aged 15 to 34
by Household Type, 2000: Non-Hispanic White Households

(number and percent distribution of total non-Hispanic white households and households headed by non-Hispanic whites aged 15 to 34, by household type, 2000; numbers in thousands)

| | | aged 15 to 34 | | | aged 25 to 34 | |
	total	total	15 to 24	total	25 to 29	30 to 34
Total non-Hispanic white households	78,819	16,254	3,721	12,533	5,678	6,855
Family households	53,066	10,267	1,844	8,423	3,481	4,942
Married couples	43,865	7,755	992	6,763	2,708	4,055
Female householder, no spouse present	6,732	1,772	587	1,185	550	635
Male householder, no spouse present	2,468	741	265	476	223	253
Nonfamily households	25,753	5,987	1,878	4,109	2,197	1,912
Female householder	14,475	2,490	897	1,593	907	686
Living alone	12,508	1,507	383	1,124	597	527
Male householder	11,278	3,497	981	2,516	1,290	1,226
Living alone	8,562	1,999	399	1,600	734	866
Percent distribution by age						
Total non-Hispanic white households	100.0%	20.6%	4.7%	15.9%	7.2%	8.7%
Family households	100.0	19.3	3.5	15.9	6.6	9.3
Married couples	100.0	17.7	2.3	15.4	6.2	9.2
Female householder, no spouse present	100.0	26.3	8.7	17.6	8.2	9.4
Male householder, no spouse present	100.0	30.0	10.7	19.3	9.0	10.3
Nonfamily households	100.0	23.2	7.3	16.0	8.5	7.4
Female householder	100.0	17.2	6.2	11.0	6.3	4.7
Living alone	100.0	12.0	3.1	9.0	4.8	4.2
Male householder	100.0	31.0	8.7	22.3	11.4	10.9
Living alone	100.0	23.3	4.7	18.7	8.6	10.1

(continued)

(continued from previous page)

	total	aged 15 to 34		aged 25 to 34		
		total	15 to 24	total	25 to 29	30 to 34
Percent distribution by household type						
Total non-Hispanic						
white households	100.0%	100.0%	100.0%	100.0%	100.0%	100.0%
Family households	**67.3**	**63.2**	**49.6**	**67.2**	**61.3**	**72.1**
Married couples	55.7	47.7	26.7	54.0	47.7	59.2
Female householder, no spouse present	8.5	10.9	15.8	9.5	9.7	9.3
Male householder, no spouse present	3.1	4.6	7.1	3.8	3.9	3.7
Nonfamily households	**32.7**	**36.8**	**50.5**	**32.8**	**38.7**	**27.9**
Female householder	18.4	15.3	24.1	12.7	16.0	10.0
Living alone	15.9	9.3	10.3	9.0	10.5	7.7
Male householder	14.3	21.5	26.4	20.1	22.7	17.9
Living alone	10.9	12.3	10.7	12.8	12.9	12.6

Source: Bureau of the Census, Internet site <http://ferret.bls.census.gov/macro/03200/hhinc/new02_000.htm>; calculations by the author

Household Size Expands during Young-Adult Years

Nearly half of people under age 35 live in one- or two-person households.

American households have been shrinking for more than a century. More than half of all households now include only one or two people. There is considerable variation in household size among young adults, however.

More than half of the households headed by people aged 15 to 19 include three or more people. Few of these households include children—their larger-than-average size (2.8 people versus 2.6 people in the average household) is due to the tendency of young people to room together while attending college.

Households headed by people in their early twenties are smaller, averaging only 2.4 people. Sixty percent include only one or two people. Most households headed by people in their thirties include children, which is why 60 percent are home to at least three people.

♦ Although the households of young adults start small, they grow quickly. But they don't get much larger after age 35. People aged 35 to 39 have the largest average household size— 3.3 people.

Householders aged 20 to 24 have smaller households than other young adults

(average household size by age of householder, 1998)

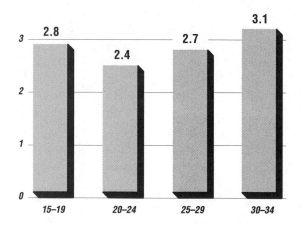

Households by Size, 1998

(number and percent distribution of total households and households headed by people aged 15 to 34, by size of household, 1998; numbers in thousands)

	total	aged 15 to 34						
		total	aged 15 to 24			aged 25 to 34		
	total	total	total	15 to 19	20 to 24	total	25 to 29	30 to 34
Total households	**102,528**	**24,468**	**5,435**	**705**	**4,730**	**19,033**	**8,463**	**10,570**
One person	26,327	4,930	1,251	139	1,112	3,679	1,687	1,992
Two people	32,965	6,844	1,906	199	1,707	4,938	2,726	2,212
Three people	17,331	5,287	1,289	167	1,122	3,998	1,793	2,205
Four people	15,358	4,458	634	111	523	3,824	1,415	2,409
Five people	7,048	1,976	247	57	190	1,729	586	1,143
Six people	2,232	655	76	24	52	579	157	422
Seven or more people	1,267	321	33	8	25	288	101	187
Percent distribution by age								
Total households	**100.0%**	**23.9%**	**5.3%**	**0.7%**	**4.6%**	**18.6%**	**8.3%**	**10.3%**
One person	100.0	18.7	4.8	0.5	4.2	14.0	6.4	7.6
Two people	100.0	20.8	5.8	0.6	5.2	15.0	8.3	6.7
Three people	100.0	30.5	7.4	1.0	6.5	23.1	10.3	12.7
Four people	100.0	29.0	4.1	0.7	3.4	24.9	9.2	15.7
Five people	100.0	28.0	3.5	0.8	2.7	24.5	8.3	16.2
Six people	100.0	29.3	3.4	1.1	2.3	25.9	7.0	18.9
Seven or more people	100.0	25.3	2.6	0.6	2.0	22.7	8.0	14.8
Percent distribution by household size								
Total households	**100.0%**	**100.0%**	**100.0%**	**100.0%**	**100.0%**	**100.0%**	**100.0%**	**100.0%**
One person	25.7	20.1	23.0	19.7	23.5	19.3	19.9	18.8
Two people	32.2	28.0	35.1	28.2	36.1	25.9	32.2	20.9
Three people	16.9	21.6	23.7	23.7	23.7	21.0	21.2	20.9
Four people	15.0	18.2	11.7	15.7	11.1	20.1	16.7	22.8
Five people	6.9	8.1	4.5	8.1	4.0	9.1	6.9	10.8
Six people	2.2	2.7	1.4	3.4	1.1	3.0	1.9	4.0
Seven or more people	1.2	1.3	0.6	1.1	0.5	1.5	1.2	1.8
Average number of people per household	2.6	2.8	2.5	2.8	2.4	2.9	2.7	3.1

Source: Bureau of the Census, detailed tables from Households and Family Characteristics: March 1998, *Current Population Reports, P20-515, 1998, Internet site <www.census.gov/population/www/socdemo/hh-fam.html>; calculations by the author*

Among Households Headed by Young Adults, Half include Children

Most households headed by people in their early thirties include children.

During their twenties and early thirties, most people become parents. Only 21 percent of the youngest householders, aged 15 to 19, have children at home. The proportion rises with age to 61 percent of households headed by people aged 30 to 34.

Only 26 percent of all young-adult households include school-aged children, but among those headed by people aged 30 to 34, a substantial 39 percent have children aged 6 to 17 at home. Thirty-eight percent of young-adult households include children under age 6, and 25 percent include children under age 3.

♦ During the young adult years, priorities and interests shift as people become parents. The youngest adults are looking for a good time, while those in their thirties are just looking for a good night's sleep.

Children are the norm for householders aged 30 to 34

(percent of households headed by people aged 15 to 34 with children under age 18 at home, 1998)

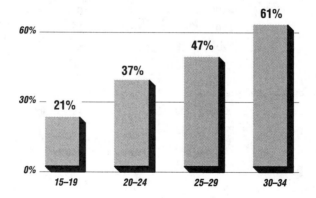

Households Headed by People Aged 15 to 34 by Presence and Age of Children, 1998

(number and percent distribution of total households and households headed by people aged 15 to 34, by presence and age of own children at home, 1998; numbers in thousands)

| | total | aged 15 to 34 | | | | | | |
| | | total | aged 15 to 24 | | | aged 25 to 34 | | |
			total	15 to 19	20 to 24	total	25 to 29	30 to 34
Total households	**102,528**	**24,468**	**5,435**	**705**	**4,730**	**19,033**	**8,463**	**10,570**
With children								
of any age	44,979	12,334	1,880	150	1,730	10,454	4,011	6,443
Under age 25	40,006	12,320	1,879	150	1,729	10,441	3,999	6,442
Under age 18	34,760	12,281	1,862	150	1,712	10,419	3,990	6,429
Under age 12	26,030	11,870	1,842	144	1,698	10,028	3,970	6,058
Under age 6	15,532	9,361	1,751	139	1,612	7,610	3,266	4,344
Under age 3	8,927	6,071	1,321	133	1,188	4,750	2,112	2,638
Under age 1	3,160	2,308	523	63	460	1,785	867	918
Aged 6 to 17	26,298	6,324	327	11	316	5,997	1,854	4,143
Total households	**100.0%**	**100.0%**	**100.0%**	**100.0%**	**100.0%**	**100.0%**	**100.0%**	**100.0%**
With children								
of any age	43.9	50.4	34.6	21.3	36.6	54.9	47.4	61.0
Under age 25	39.0	50.4	34.6	21.3	36.6	54.9	47.3	60.9
Under age 18	33.9	50.2	34.3	21.3	36.2	54.7	47.1	60.8
Under age 12	25.4	48.5	33.9	20.4	35.9	52.7	46.9	57.3
Under age 6	15.1	38.3	32.2	19.7	34.1	40.0	38.6	41.1
Under age 3	8.7	24.8	24.3	18.9	25.1	25.0	25.0	25.0
Under age 1	3.1	9.4	9.6	8.9	9.7	9.4	10.2	8.7
Aged 6 to 17	25.6	25.8	6.0	1.6	6.7	31.5	21.9	39.2

Source: Bureau of the Census, detailed tables from Households and Family Characteristics: March 1998, *Current Population Reports, P20-515, 1998, Internet site <www.census.gov/population/www/socdemo/hh-fam.html>; calculations by the author*

More Than 70 Percent of Young Couples Have Children at Home

Female-headed families are most likely to have children.

Half of the households headed by people aged 15 to 34 include children under age 18. The proportion of young-adult households that include children rises with age and varies by household type.

Seventy-two percent of young married couples have children at home. Families headed by single women are even more likely to have children. Fully 89 percent of families headed by women under age 35 include children. Only 48 percent of family households headed by men under age 35 include children, although the majority of those headed by men aged 25 to 34 have children at home.

♦ The presence of children drives much of the spending of households headed by 25-to-34-year-olds. But most 15-to-24-year-olds are still free to spend their money on themselves.

Male-headed families are least likely to have children at home

(percent of households headed by people aged 15 to 34 with children under age 18 at home, by household type1998)

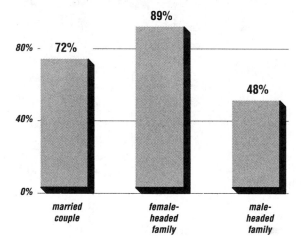

Householders Aged 15 to 34 by Type of Household and Presence of Children, 1998: Total Households

(number of total households and households headed by people aged 15 to 34, and number and percent with own children under age 18 at home, by household type, 1998; numbers in thousands)

		with children under age 18	
	total	*number*	*percent*
Total households	**102,528**	**34,760**	**33.9%**
Total, aged 15 to 34	24,468	12,281	50.2
Aged 15 to 19	705	150	21.3
Aged 20 to 24	4,730	1,712	36.2
Aged 25 to 29	8,463	3,990	47.1
Aged 30 to 34	10,570	6,429	60.8
Married couples	**54,317**	**25,269**	**46.5**
Total, aged 15 to 34	11,259	8,048	71.5
Aged 15 to 19	86	56	65.1
Aged 20 to 24	1,287	755	58.7
Aged 25 to 29	3,967	2,535	63.9
Aged 30 to 34	5,919	4,702	79.4
Female householder, no spouse present	**12,652**	**7,693**	**60.8**
Total, aged 15 to 34	3,982	3,559	89.4
Aged 15 to 19	152	76	50.0
Aged 20 to 24	943	790	83.8
Aged 25 to 29	1,305	1,204	92.3
Aged 30 to 34	1,582	1,489	94.1
Male householder, no spouse present	**3,911**	**1,798**	**46.0**
Total, aged 15 to 34	1,417	675	47.6
Aged 15 to 19	167	18	10.8
Aged 20 to 24	384	168	43.8
Aged 25 to 29	462	251	54.3
Aged 30 to 34	404	238	58.9

Source: Bureau of the Census, detailed tables from Households and Family Characteristics: March 1998, *Current Population Reports, P20-515, 1998, Internet site <www.census.gov/population/www/socdemo/hh-fam.html>; calculations by the author*

Hispanic Households Are Most Likely to include Children

Households headed by whites are least likely to include children.

Two-thirds of Hispanic households headed by 15-to-34-year-olds include children. The proportion is a smaller 60 percent for black households in the age group. Not quite half of households headed by whites aged 15 to 34 include children. Blacks and Hispanics have children at a younger age than whites, which accounts for these differences. Only after age 30 does the proportion of white households with children surpass 50 percent. Among black and Hispanic households, the majority include children by the 20-to-24 age group.

Regardless of race, the great majority of households headed by single women under age 35 include children. Just 1 out of 10 female-headed families does not include children. Families headed by single men aged 15 to 34 are least likely to include children. Only 50 percent of white, 47 percent of black, and 42 percent of Hispanic households headed by single men aged 15 to 34 include children.

◆ Because blacks and Hispanics are more likely to be raising children than whites, there are significant lifestyle differences among young adults by race and Hispanic origin.

Young whites are more likely to delay childbearing

(percent of households headed by people aged 15 to 34 with children under age 18 at home, by race and Hispanic origin, 1998)

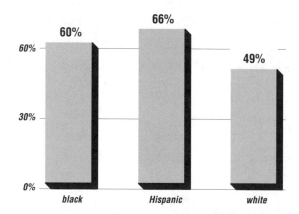

Householders Aged 15 to 34 by Type of Household and Presence of Children, 1998: Black Households

(number of total black households and households headed by blacks aged 15 to 34, and number and percent with own children under age 18 at home, by household type, 1998; numbers in thousands)

	total	with children under age 18	
		number	percent
Total black households	**12,474**	**4,847**	**38.9%**
Total, aged 15 to 34	3,687	2,201	59.7
Aged 15 to 19	134	22	16.4
Aged 20 to 24	801	451	56.3
Aged 25 to 29	1,200	754	62.8
Aged 30 to 34	1,552	974	62.8
Married couples	**3,921**	**2,055**	**52.4**
Total, aged 15 to 34	969	736	76.0
Aged 15 to 19	1	–	–
Aged 20 to 24	110	79	71.8
Aged 25 to 29	348	263	75.6
Aged 30 to 34	510	394	77.3
Female householder, no spouse present	**3,926**	**2,569**	**65.4**
Total, aged 15 to 34	1,514	1,372	90.6
Aged 15 to 19	49	20	40.8
Aged 20 to 24	380	348	91.6
Aged 25 to 29	498	462	92.8
Aged 30 to 34	587	542	92.3
Male householder, no spouse present	**562**	**223**	**39.7**
Total, aged 15 to 34	203	95	46.8
Aged 15 to 19	43	3	7.0
Aged 20 to 24	48	25	52.1
Aged 25 to 29	51	29	56.9
Aged 30 to 34	61	38	62.3

Note: (–) means sample is too small to make a reliable estimate.
Source: Bureau of the Census, detailed tables from Households and Family Characteristics: March 1998, *Current Population Reports, P20-515, 1998, Internet site <www.census.gov/population/www/socdemo/hh-fam.html>; calculations by the author*

Householders Aged 15 to 34 by Type of Household and Presence of Children, 1998: Hispanic Households

(number of Hispanic households and households headed by Hispanics aged 15 to 34, and number and percent with own children under age 18 at home, by household type, 1998; numbers in thousands)

		with children under age 18	
	total	*number*	*percent*
Total Hispanic households	**8,590**	**4,475**	**52.1%**
Total, aged 15 to 34	3,081	2,021	65.6
Aged 15 to 19	129	50	38.8
Aged 20 to 24	650	359	55.2
Aged 25 to 29	1,026	652	63.5
Aged 30 to 34	1,276	960	75.2
Married couples	**4,804**	**3,121**	**65.0**
Total, aged 15 to 34	1,645	1,333	81.0
Aged 15 to 19	29	18	62.1
Aged 20 to 24	271	197	72.7
Aged 25 to 29	578	433	74.9
Aged 30 to 34	767	685	89.3
Female householder, no spouse present	**1,612**	**1,121**	**69.5**
Total, aged 15 to 34	615	557	90.6
Aged 15 to 19	37	25	67.6
Aged 20 to 24	143	117	81.8
Aged 25 to 29	186	177	95.2
Aged 30 to 34	249	238	95.6
Male householder, no spouse present	**545**	**233**	**42.8**
Total, aged 15 to 34	311	132	42.4
Aged 15 to 19	37	7	18.9
Aged 20 to 24	110	45	40.9
Aged 25 to 29	95	42	44.2
Aged 30 to 34	69	38	55.1

Source: Bureau of the Census, detailed tables from Households and Family Characteristics: March 1998, *Current Population Reports, P20-515, 1998, Internet site <www.census.gov/population/www/socdemo/hh-fam.html>; calculations by the author*

Householders Aged 15 to 34 by Type of Household and Presence of Children, 1998: White Households

(number of white households and households headed by whites aged 15 to 34, and number and percent with own children under age 18 at home, by household type, 1998; numbers in thousands)

	total	with children under age 18	
		number	percent
Total white households	**88,106**	**28,336**	**32.2%**
Total, aged 15 to 34	19,586	9,645	49.2
Aged 15 to 19	530	125	23.6
Aged 20 to 24	3,712	1,220	32.9
Aged 25 to 29	6,891	3,137	45.5
Aged 30 to 34	8,453	5,163	61.1
Married couples	**48,066**	**21,910**	**45.6**
Total, aged 15 to 34	9,778	6,981	71.4
Aged 15 to 19	83	54	65.1
Aged 20 to 24	1,138	658	57.8
Aged 25 to 29	3,480	2,202	63.3
Aged 30 to 34	5,077	4,067	80.1
Female householder, no spouse present	**8,308**	**4,912**	**59.1**
Total, aged 15 to 34	2,337	2,105	90.1
Aged 15 to 19	95	56	58.9
Aged 20 to 24	517	422	81.6
Aged 25 to 29	778	717	92.2
Aged 30 to 34	947	910	96.1
Male householder, no spouse present	**3,137**	**1,514**	**48.3**
Total, aged 15 to 34	1,120	560	50.0
Aged 15 to 19	111	16	14.4
Aged 20 to 24	326	140	42.9
Aged 25 to 29	382	219	57.3
Aged 30 to 34	301	185	61.5

Source: Bureau of the Census, detailed tables from Households and Family Characteristics: March 1998, *Current Population Reports, P20-515, 1998, Internet site <www.census.gov/population/www/socdemo/hh-fam.html>; calculations by the author*

Two-Child Families Are Most Common

Few young couples have more than two children.

Smaller families have been growing in popularity for decades. Most Americans now consider two children the ideal number. But many young adults, who are still building their families, have had only one child so far. Overall, 29 percent of young married couples have two children, while 27 percent have just one. Another 29 percent are still childless.

Among couples aged 15 to 24, the plurality of 41 percent have no child. Thirty-four percent have one child, while 18 percent have two, and 7 percent have three or more. Two children are most common among couples aged 25 to 34. Thirty percent of couples in this age group have two children, while 26 percent have one, 17 percent have three or more, and 27 percent have none.

♦ Most young married couples eventually will have children, but only a minority will have more than two. Fewer children means parents can devote more resources to each child.

Few young married couples have more than two children

(percent of married couples headed by people aged 15 to 34, by number of children under age 18 at home, 1998)

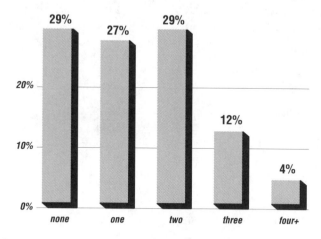

Married Couples Aged 15 to 34 by Presence and Number of Children, 1998

(number and percent distribution of total married couples and couples headed by 15-to-34-year-olds, by presence and number of own children under age 18 at home, 1998; numbers in thousands)

| | total | aged 15 to 34 | | | | | | |
| | | total | aged 15 to 24 | | | aged 25 to 34 | | |
	total	total	total	15 to 19	20 to 24	total	25 to 29	30 to 34
Total married couples	**54,317**	**11,259**	**1,373**	**86**	**1,287**	**9,886**	**3,967**	**5,919**
Without children < 18	29,048	3,211	562	30	532	2,649	1,432	1,217
With children < 18	25,269	8,048	811	56	755	7,237	2,535	4,702
One	9,507	3,037	471	32	439	2,566	1,033	1,533
Two	10,241	3,230	240	19	221	2,990	1,041	1,949
Three	4,124	1,323	82	3	79	1,241	357	884
Four or more	1,397	456	17	1	16	439	104	335
Total married couples	**100.0%**	**100.0%**	**100.0%**	**100.0%**	**100.0%**	**100.0%**	**100.0%**	**100.0%**
Without children < 18	53.5	28.5	40.9	34.9	41.3	26.8	36.1	20.6
With children < 18	46.5	71.5	59.1	65.1	58.7	73.2	63.9	79.4
One	17.5	27.0	34.3	37.2	34.1	26.0	26.0	25.9
Two	18.9	28.7	17.5	22.1	17.2	30.2	26.2	32.9
Three	7.6	11.8	6.0	3.5	6.1	12.6	9.0	14.9
Four or more	2.6	4.1	1.2	1.2	1.2	4.4	2.6	5.7

Source: Bureau of the Census, detailed tables from Households and Family Characteristics: March 1998, *Current Population Reports, P20-515, 1998, Internet site <www.census.gov/population/www/socdemo/hh-fam.html>; calculations by the author*

Most Female-Headed Families include Children

Most male-headed families do not.

Most young women who head families without a spouse are single mothers. Among female family householders under age 35, only 11 percent head families that do not include children. In contrast, most male family heads under age 35 do not have children at home—52 percent live with relatives such as siblings or parents rather than children.

Among female-headed families with a householder aged 20 to 24, 84 percent include children. The proportion rises to 93 percent among those headed by women aged 25 to 34. One-third of families headed by women aged 20 to 24 include at least two children, as do 52 percent of families headed by women aged 25 to 29 and 64 percent of those headed by women aged 30 to 34.

Only 34 percent of male family heads aged 15 to 24 have children at home, but among those aged 25 to 34, the 57 percent majority do. The largest share of these single parents have only one child.

♦ For young adults, the presence of children in the home can make it difficult to get the education necessary to earn a middle-class income.

Most young women who head families are single mothers

(percent of female- and male-headed families headed by people aged 15 to 34 with children under age 18 at home, 1998)

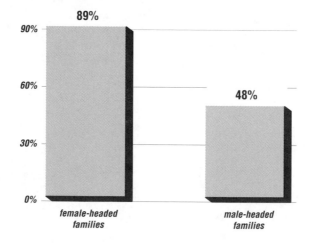

Female-Headed Families Aged 15 to 34 by Presence and Number of Children, 1998

(number and percent distribution of total female-headed families and families headed by women aged 15 to 34, by presence and number of own children under age 18 at home, 1998; numbers in thousands)

	total	aged 15 to 34						
		total	aged 15 to 24			aged 25 to 34		
			total	15 to 19	20 to 24	total	25 to 29	30 to 34
Total female-headed families	**12,652**	**3,982**	**1,095**	**152**	**943**	**2,887**	**1,305**	**1,582**
Without children < 18	4,960	423	229	76	153	194	101	93
With children <18	7,693	3,559	866	76	790	2,693	1,204	1,489
One	3,739	1,504	505	50	455	999	525	474
Two	2,425	1,190	270	22	248	920	409	511
Three	1,054	575	66	3	63	509	215	294
Four or more	475	287	23	2	23	264	55	209
Total female-headed families	**100.0%**	**100.0%**	**100.0%**	**100.0%**	**100.0%**	**100.0%**	**100.0%**	**100.0%**
Without children < 18	39.2	10.6	20.9	50.0	16.2	6.7	7.7	5.9
With children < 18	60.8	89.4	79.1	50.0	83.8	93.3	92.3	94.1
One	29.6	37.8	46.1	32.9	48.3	34.6	40.2	30.0
Two	19.2	29.9	24.7	14.5	26.3	31.9	31.3	32.3
Three	8.3	14.4	6.0	2.0	6.7	17.6	16.5	18.6
Four or more	3.8	7.2	2.1	1.3	2.4	9.1	4.2	13.2

Source: Bureau of the Census, detailed tables from Households and Family Characteristics: March 1998, *Current Population Reports, P20-515, 1998, Internet site <www.census.gov/population/www/socdemo/hh-fam.html>; calculations by the author*

Male-Headed Families Aged 15 to 34 by Presence and Number of Children, 1998

(number and percent distribution of total male-headed families and families headed by men aged 15 to 34, by presence and number of own children under age 18 at home, 1998; numbers in thousands)

| | | aged 15 to 34 | | | | | | |
| | | | aged 15 to 24 | | | aged 25 to 34 | | |
	total	total	total	15 to 19	20 to 24	total	25 to 29	30 to 34
Total male-headed families	**3,911**	**1,417**	**551**	**167**	**384**	**866**	**462**	**404**
Without children < 18	2,113	742	365	149	216	377	211	166
With children < 18	1,798	675	186	18	168	489	251	238
One	1,117	431	136	8	128	295	164	131
Two	456	160	34	10	24	126	55	71
Three	175	70	10	–	10	60	32	28
Four or more	50	14	5	–	5	9	–	9
Total male-headed families	**100.0%**	**100.0%**	**100.0%**	**100.0%**	**100.0%**	**100.0%**	**100.0%**	**100.0%**
Without children < 18	54.0	52.4	66.2	89.2	56.3	43.5	45.7	41.1
With children < 18	46.0	47.6	33.8	10.8	43.8	56.5	54.3	58.9
One	28.6	30.4	24.7	4.8	33.3	34.1	35.5	32.4
Two	11.7	11.3	6.2	6.0	6.3	14.5	11.9	17.6
Three	4.5	4.9	1.8	–	2.6	6.9	6.9	6.9
Four or more	1.3	1.0	0.9	–	1.3	1.0	–	2.2

Note: (–) means sample is too small to make a reliable estimate.
Source: Bureau of the Census, detailed tables from Households and Family Characteristics: March 1998, *Current Population Reports, P20-515, 1998, Internet site <www.census.gov/population/www/socdemo/hh-fam.html>; calculations by the author*

Women Leave the Nest Sooner Than Men

Two out of three men aged 15 to 24 still live in their parents' home.

Only 29 percent of men under age 35 are married and heading their own households. A much larger share of 41 percent still live with their parents. (This figure includes college students in dormitories because they are considered dependents.) The third most common living arrangement for young men is sharing a house with nonrelatives, such as roommates or a partner. Thirteen percent of men aged 15 to 34 live with nonrelatives.

Most women aged 15 to 19 live with their parents, but in their early twenties women begin to move out. Only 37 percent of women aged 20 to 24 still live with Mom and Dad. A nearly equal proportion head their own families, with or without a spouse. One-quarter live alone or with unrelated roommates.

Twenty percent of men aged 25 to 29 still live in their parents' home compared with only 12 percent of women in the age group. Among people aged 30 to 34, only 5 percent of women live with their parents, compared with 10 percent of men.

♦ Young women establish their own households sooner than young men because they marry at a younger age.

Many young adults still live with parents

(percent of people aged 15 to 34 who live with their parents, by sex, 1998)

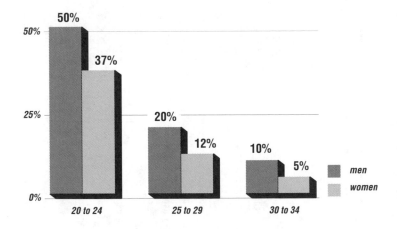

Living Arrangements of Men Aged 15 to 34, 1998

(number and percent distribution of men aged 15 or older and aged 15 to 34 by living arrangement, 1998; numbers in thousands)

	total	aged 15 to 34	aged 15 to 24				aged 25 to 34		
		total	total	15 to 17	18 to 19	20 to 24	total	25 to 29	30 to 34
Total men	101,123	38,273	18,747	6,114	3,807	8,826	19,526	9,450	10,076
Living with spouse	55,310	11,086	1,246	6	61	1,179	9,840	3,915	5,925
Other family householder	3,911	1,417	551	65	102	384	866	462	404
Living with parents	18,226	15,762	12,917	5,518	3,030	4,369	2,845	1,847	998
Living with other family member(s)	3,713	1,947	1,229	376	252	601	718	452	266
Living alone	11,010	2,944	722	10	63	649	2,222	987	1,235
Living with nonrelatives	8,953	5,115	2,081	139	298	1,644	3,034	1,786	1,248
Total men	100.0%	100.0%	100.0%	100.0%	100.0%	100.0%	100.0%	100.0%	100.0%
Living with spouse	54.7	29.0	6.6	0.1	1.6	13.4	50.4	41.4	58.8
Other family householder	3.9	3.7	2.9	1.1	2.7	4.4	4.4	4.9	4.0
Living with parents	18.0	41.2	68.9	90.3	79.6	49.5	14.6	19.5	9.9
Living with other family member(s)	3.7	5.1	6.6	6.1	6.6	6.8	3.7	4.8	2.6
Living alone	10.9	7.7	3.9	0.2	1.7	7.4	11.4	10.4	12.3
Living with nonrelatives	8.9	13.4	11.1	2.3	7.8	18.6	15.5	18.9	12.4

Note: (–) means sample too small to be reliable.
Source: Bureau of the Census, detailed tables from Marital Status and Living Arrangements: March 1998, Current Population Reports, P20-514, 1998, Internet site <www.census.gov/population/www/socdemo/ms-la.html>; calculations by the author

Living Arrangements of Women Aged 15 to 34, 1998

(number and percent distribution of women aged 15 or older and aged 15 to 34 by living arrangement, 1998; numbers in thousands)

	total	aged 15 to 34		aged 15 to 24				aged 25 to 34		
		total	total	15 to 17	18 to 19	20 to 24	total	25 to 29	30 to 34
Total women	**108,168**	**38,161**	**18,333**	**5,765**	**3,780**	**8,788**	**19,828**	**9,546**	**10,282**
Living with spouse	55,310	13,794	2,366	51	180	2,135	11,428	4,903	6,525
Other family householder	12,653	3,981	1,094	43	109	942	2,887	1,305	1,582
Living with parents	13,998	12,735	11,055	5,081	2,767	3,207	1,680	1,166	514
Living with other family member(s)	3,778	1,270	966	399	229	338	304	202	102
Living alone	15,317	1,984	528	5	60	463	1,456	699	757
Living with nonrelatives	7,113	4,396	2,324	186	435	1,703	2,072	1,271	801
Total women	**100.0%**	**100.0%**	**100.0%**	**100.0%**	**100.0%**	**100.0%**	**100.0%**	**100.0%**	**100.0%**
Living with spouse	51.1	36.1	12.9	0.9	4.8	24.3	57.6	51.4	63.5
Other family householder	11.7	10.4	6.0	0.7	2.9	10.7	14.6	13.7	15.4
Living with parents	12.9	33.4	60.3	88.1	73.2	36.5	8.5	12.2	5.0
Living with other family member(s)	3.5	3.3	5.3	6.9	6.1	3.8	1.5	2.1	1.0
Living alone	14.2	5.2	2.9	0.1	1.6	5.3	7.3	7.3	7.4
Living with nonrelatives	6.6	11.5	12.7	3.2	11.5	19.4	10.4	13.3	7.8

Source: Bureau of the Census, detailed tables from Marital Status and Living Arrangements: March 1998, Current Population Reports, P20-514, 1998, Internet site <www.census.gov/population/www/socdemo/ms-la.html>; calculations by the author

Most Young Adults Are Not Married

Young women are more likely than young men to be married.

Women marry at a younger age than men. Consequently, a larger percentage of men than women aged 15 to 34 have not yet married—65 percent of men versus 56 percent of women. But young women are more likely than their male counterparts to be divorced.

In the 1950s, when the median age at first marriage was just 20, half of women marrying for the first time were teenagers. In 1998, only 3 percent of women aged 15 to 19 had been to the altar. Men are waiting even longer to marry. Only 1 percent of men aged 15 to 19 have married.

Twenty-seven percent of women aged 20 to 24 are married. The proportion rises to more than half (56 percent) among women aged 25 to 29. For men, the married share does not surpass 50 percent until the 30-to-34 age group.

♦ Young adults are in no hurry to marry because many are finishing college and starting careers. Social scientists believe as many as 10 percent of today's young adults will never marry.

Young men are less likely to be married

(percent of people aged 15 to 34 who are married, by sex, 1998)

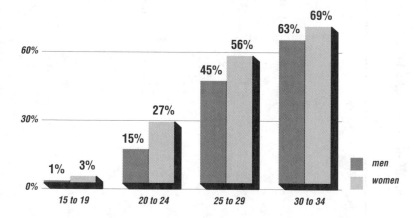

Marital Status of People Aged 15 to 34 by Sex, 1998: Total

(number and percent distribution of people aged 15 or older and aged 15 to 34 by marital status and sex, 1998; numbers in thousands)

	total	aged 15 to 34				
		total	*15 to 19*	*20 to 24*	*25 to 29*	*30 to 34*
Total men	**101,123**	**38,273**	**9,921**	**8,826**	**9,450**	**10,076**
Never married	31,591	24,899	9,778	7,360	4,822	2,939
Married	58,633	12,017	121	1,332	4,219	6,345
Divorced	8,331	1,323	19	133	398	773
Widowed	2,569	33	3	–	10	20
Total women	**108,168**	**38,161**	**9,545**	**8,788**	**9,546**	**10,282**
Never married	26,713	21,321	9,235	6,178	3,689	2,219
Married	59,333	15,003	289	2,372	5,298	7,044
Divorced	11,093	1,731	20	222	525	964
Widowed	11,029	109	2	17	35	55
Percent distribution						
Total men	**100.0%**	**100.0%**	**100.0%**	**100.0%**	**100.0%**	**100.0%**
Never married	31.2	65.1	98.6	83.4	51.0	29.2
Married	58.0	31.4	1.2	15.1	44.6	63.0
Divorced	8.2	3.5	0.2	1.5	4.2	7.7
Widowed	2.5	0.1	0.0	–	0.1	0.2
Total women	**100.0**	**100.0**	**100.0**	**100.0**	**100.0**	**100.0**
Never married	24.7	55.9	96.8	70.3	38.6	21.6
Married	54.9	39.3	3.0	27.0	55.5	68.5
Divorced	10.3	4.5	0.2	2.5	5.5	9.4
Widowed	10.2	0.3	0.0	0.2	0.4	0.5

Note: (–) means sample is too small to make a reliable estimate.
Source: Bureau of the Census, detailed tables from Marital Status and Living Arrangements: March 1998, *Current Population Reports, P20-514, 1998, Internet site <www.census.gov/population/www/socdemo/ms-la.html>*

Blacks Are Least Likely to Be Married

Whites are most likely to be divorced.

There are sharp differences in marital status by race and Hispanic origin. Similar percentages of white and Hispanic women aged 15 to 34 have never married—51 and 53 percent, respectively. Among black women aged 15 to 34, however, fully 73 percent have never been married.

Young men are more likely than young women not to have married. Sixty-three percent of white and Hispanic men aged 15 to 34 have never married. The proportion is even higher among young black men, 76 percent of whom have never married.

Whites are more likely than blacks or Hispanics to be divorced. Among white women aged 15 to 34, 5 percent are divorced compared with 3 percent of black and Hispanic women. Four percent of white men aged 15 to 34 are divorced compared with 3 percent of black and 2 percent of Hispanic men in the age group.

♦ As the nation has become more diverse racially and ethnically, it has also become more diverse in its living arrangements.

Hispanics under age 35 are most likely to be married

(percent of people aged 15 to 34 who are married, by race, Hispanic origin, and sex, 1998)

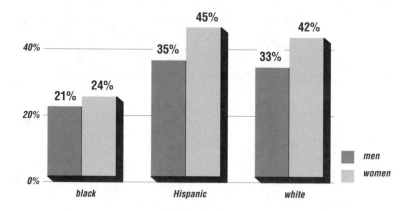

Marital Status of People Aged 15 to 34 by Sex, 1998: Blacks

(number and percent distribution of blacks aged 15 or older and aged 15 to 34 by marital status and sex, 1998; numbers in thousands)

	total	aged 15 to 34				
		total	15 to 19	20 to 24	25 to 29	30 to 34
Total black men	**11,283**	**5,094**	**1,522**	**1,183**	**1,177**	**1,212**
Never married	5,191	3,864	1,496	1,087	758	523
Married	4,675	1,075	20	96	385	574
Divorced	1,035	153	6	–	35	112
Widowed	382	3	–	–	–	3
Total black women	**13,715**	**5,826**	**1,536**	**1,380**	**1,425**	**1,485**
Never married	5,689	4,238	1,516	1,174	847	701
Married	4,983	1,381	19	189	521	652
Divorced	1,673	192	2	14	55	121
Widowed	1,370	15	–	2	2	11
Percent distribution						
Total black men	**100.0%**	**100.0%**	**100.0%**	**100.0%**	**100.0%**	**100.0%**
Never married	46.0	75.9	98.3	91.9	64.4	43.2
Married	41.4	21.1	1.3	8.1	32.7	47.4
Divorced	9.2	3.0	0.4	–	3.0	9.2
Widowed	3.4	0.1	–	–	–	0.2
Total black women	**100.0**	**100.0**	**100.0**	**100.0**	**100.0**	**100.0**
Never married	41.5	72.7	98.7	85.1	59.4	47.2
Married	36.3	23.7	1.2	13.7	36.6	43.9
Divorced	12.2	3.3	0.1	1.0	3.9	8.1
Widowed	10.0	0.3	–	0.1	0.1	0.7

Note: (–) means sample is too small to make a reliable estimate.
Source: Bureau of the Census, detailed tables from Marital Status and Living Arrangements: March 1998, *Current Population Reports, P20-514, 1998, Internet site <www.census.gov/population/www/socdemo/ms-la.html>*

Marital Status of People Aged 15 to 34 by Sex, 1998: Hispanics

(number and percent distribution of Hispanics aged 15 or older and aged 15 to 34 by marital status and sex, 1998; numbers in thousands)

	total	aged 15 to 34				
		total	*15 to 19*	*20 to 24*	*25 to 29*	*30 to 34*
Total Hispanic men	**10,944**	**5,808**	**1,435**	**1,455**	**1,510**	**1,408**
Never married	4,370	3,648	1,403	1,112	747	386
Married	5,797	2,041	28	337	733	943
Divorced	647	117	3	6	29	79
Widowed	131	2	–	–	2	–
Total Hispanic women	**10,485**	**5,065**	**1,287**	**1,209**	**1,285**	**1,284**
Never married	3,072	2,589	1,183	733	423	250
Married	5,911	2,282	100	447	810	925
Divorced	885	168	3	23	45	97
Widowed	617	26	2	5	7	12
Percent distribution						
Total Hispanic men	**100.0%**	**100.0%**	**100.0%**	**100.0%**	**100.0%**	**100.0%**
Never married	39.9	62.8	97.8	76.4	49.5	27.4
Married	53.0	35.1	2.0	23.2	48.5	67.0
Divorced	5.9	2.0	0.2	0.4	1.9	5.6
Widowed	1.2	0.0	–	–	0.1	–
Total Hispanic women	**100.0**	**100.0**	**100.0**	**100.0**	**100.0**	**100.0**
Never married	29.3	51.1	91.9	60.6	32.9	19.5
Married	56.4	45.1	7.8	37.0	63.0	72.0
Divorced	8.4	3.3	0.2	1.9	3.5	7.6
Widowed	5.9	0.5	0.2	0.4	0.5	0.9

Note: (–) means sample is too small to make a reliable estimate.
Source: Bureau of the Census, detailed tables from Marital Status and Living Arrangements: March 1998, *Current Population Reports, P20-514, 1998, Internet site <www.census.gov/population/www/socdemo/ms-la.html>*

Marital Status of People Aged 15 to 34 by Sex, 1998: Whites

(number and percent distribution of whites aged 15 or older and aged 15 to 34 by marital status and sex, 1998; numbers in thousands)

		aged 15 to 34				
	total	total	15 to 19	20 to 24	25 to 29	30 to 34
Total white men	**85,219**	**31,149**	**7,945**	**7,212**	**7,743**	**8,249**
Never married	24,775	19,630	7,832	5,887	3,697	2,214
Married	51,299	10,360	100	1,193	3,688	5,379
Divorced	7,038	1,128	10	131	348	639
Widowed	2,106	29	3	–	10	16
Total white women	**89,489**	**30,258**	**7,517**	**6,956**	**7,554**	**8,231**
Never married	19,614	15,894	7,239	4,662	2,591	1,402
Married	51,410	12,802	259	2,077	4,478	5,988
Divorced	9,115	1,479	18	206	455	800
Widowed	9,351	86	2	12	30	42
Percent distribution						
Total white men	**100.0%**	**100.0%**	**100.0%**	**100.0%**	**100.0%**	**100.0%**
Never married	29.1	63.0	98.6	81.6	47.7	26.8
Married	60.2	33.3	1.3	16.5	47.6	65.2
Divorced	8.3	3.6	0.1	1.8	4.5	7.7
Widowed	2.5	0.1	0.0	–	0.1	0.2
Total white women	**100.0**	**100.0**	**100.0**	**100.0**	**100.0**	**100.0**
Never married	21.9	52.5	96.3	67.0	34.3	17.0
Married	57.4	42.3	3.4	29.9	59.3	72.7
Divorced	10.2	4.9	0.2	3.0	6.0	9.7
Widowed	10.4	0.3	0.0	0.2	0.4	0.5

Note: (–) means sample is too small to make a reliable estimate.
Source: Bureau of the Census, detailed tables from Marital Status and Living Arrangements: March 1998, *Current Population Reports, P20-514, 1998, Internet site <www.census.gov/population/www/socdemo/ms-la.html>*

7

Population

♦ Today's young adults can be divided into the Millennial generation (aged 15 to 24) and Generation X (aged 25 to 34). Between 2001 and 2010, the number of people aged 15 to 34 will increase by 5.5 million as Millennials fill the age group.

♦ Young adults are racially and ethnically diverse. Only 66 percent are non-Hispanic white, compared with 71 percent of the total population. Fifteen percent of young adults are Hispanic and 14 percent are non-Hispanic black.

♦ Young adults are more likely than the average American to have been born outside the United States. Overall, 10 percent of Americans are foreign-born, compared with 13 percent of people aged 15 to 34.

♦ Between March 1998 and March 1999, 26 percent of people aged 15 to 34 moved to a different home. Twentysomethings have the highest mobility rate, nearly one-third of them moving during the year.

Young Men Outnumber Young Women

The sex ratio reaches parity in the mid-twenties.

In 2001, 76 million young adults live in the United States. More of those young adults are men than women. Among people aged 15 to 34, men outnumber women by 576,000.

Among Americans of all ages, there are more females than males. Boys outnumber girls at birth and maintain a numerical advantage until their mid-twenties. The ratio slowly shifts in favor of women because at all ages males are more likely to die than females. Among 15-to-19-year-olds, there are 106 men per 100 women. But among 30-to-34-year-olds there are only 97 men per 100 women. The sex ratio remains roughly at parity until men and women reach their forties. After age 40, women outnumber men by a growing margin.

♦ Although men outnumber women in the 15-to-34 age group, the difference is not great enough to affect the lives of young adults.

Women begin to outnumber men among people aged 25 to 34

(number of men per 100 women by age, 2001)

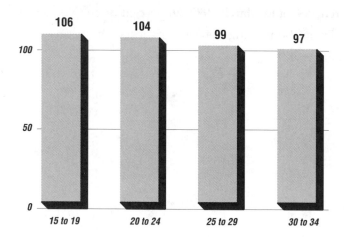

Population Aged 15 to 34 by Sex, 2001

(total number of people and number aged 15 to 34 by age and sex, and sex ratio by age, 2001; numbers in thousands)

	total	men	women	sex ratio
Total people	**277,803**	**135,795**	**142,008**	**96**
Total aged 15 to 34	**76,141**	**38,359**	**37,783**	**102**
Aged 15 to 24	39,079	19,999	19,079	105
Aged 25 to 34	37,062	18,360	18,704	98
Aged 15 to 19	20,066	10,314	9,752	106
Aged 20 to 24	19,013	9,685	9,327	104
Aged 25 to 29	17,424	8,665	8,759	99
Aged 30 to 34	19,638	9,695	9,945	97
Aged 15	3,964	2,036	1,927	106
Aged 16	3,975	2,048	1,927	106
Aged 17	3,952	2,041	1,911	107
Aged 18	3,970	2,037	1,933	105
Aged 19	4,205	2,152	2,054	105
Aged 20	4,094	2,097	1,997	105
Aged 21	4,015	2,055	1,959	105
Aged 22	3,720	1,898	1,821	104
Aged 23	3,574	1,813	1,761	103
Aged 24	3,610	1,822	1,789	102
Aged 25	3,428	1,721	1,707	101
Aged 26	3,452	1,719	1,733	99
Aged 27	3,405	1,692	1,713	99
Aged 28	3,295	1,630	1,665	98
Aged 29	3,844	1,903	1,941	98
Aged 30	4,028	1,983	2,046	97
Aged 31	3,943	1,945	1,999	97
Aged 32	3,856	1,904	1,952	98
Aged 33	3,794	1,869	1,925	97
Aged 34	4,017	1,994	2,023	99

Note: The sex ratio is the number of males per 100 females.
Source: Bureau of the Census, Internet site <www.census.gov/population/www/projections/natdet-D1A.html>; calculations by the author

The Young-Adult Population Is Expanding with the Millennial Generation

The "echo boom" is reaching adulthood and swelling the ranks of twentysomethings.

The number of people aged 15 to 34 will increase 7 percent between 2001 and 2010 as the large Millennial generation replaces small Generation X in the age group.

Today, most young adults are members of Generation X. This generation was born during the years following the baby boom, when births were declining. Consequently, it is a small cohort surrounded by much larger generations—the boomers on the older side and their children (Millennials) on the younger side. As Xers replace the larger Boomer generation in each successive age group, the number of people in the age group declines. In contrast, as the larger Millennial generation replaces Xers, it swells the age groups it enters.

Millennials already occupy most of the 15-to-24-age group. As larger birth cohorts within the generation enter the age group during the next 10 years, the number of 15-to-24-year-olds will expand by 10 percent. The number of people in their early thirties will continue to decline, however, as Generation X moves through its thirties.

♦ The entertainment and apparel industries are already banking on the growing number of young adults. Other industries providing goods and services demanded by young adults, such as apartments and household furnishings, should prosper as well during the next few years.

Population Aged 15 to 34, 2001 and 2010

(total number of people and number aged 15 to 34 by selected age groups and single-year-of-age, 2001 and 2010; numerical and percent change, 2001–10; numbers in thousands)

	2001	2010	change, 2001–10 number	change, 2001–10 percent
Total people	**277,803**	**299,862**	**22,059**	**7.9%**
Total aged 15 to 34	**76,141**	**81,673**	**5,532**	**7.3**
Aged 15 to 24	39,079	42,820	3,741	9.6
Aged 25 to 34	37,072	38,853	1,791	4.8
Aged 15 to 19	20,066	21,668	1,602	8.0
Aged 20 to 24	19,013	21,152	2,139	11.3
Aged 25 to 29	17,424	19,851	2,427	13.9
Aged 30 to 34	19,638	19,002	−636	−3.2
Aged 15	3,964	4,117	153	3.9
Aged 16	3,975	4,191	216	5.4
Aged 17	3,952	4,349	397	10.0
Aged 18	3,970	4,361	391	9.8
Aged 19	4,205	4,650	445	10.6
Aged 20	4,094	4,592	498	12.2
Aged 21	4,015	4,336	321	8.0
Aged 22	3,720	4,120	400	10.8
Aged 23	3,574	4,019	445	12.5
Aged 24	3,610	4,085	475	13.2
Aged 25	3,428	4,027	1,589	17.5
Aged 26	3,452	3,900	448	13.0
Aged 27	3,405	4,004	599	17.6
Aged 28	3,295	3,799	504	15.3
Aged 29	3,844	4,121	277	7.2
Aged 30	4,028	4,047	19	0.5
Aged 31	3,943	3,806	−137	−3.5
Aged 32	3,856	3,734	−122	−3.2
Aged 33	3,794	3,705	−89	−2.3
Aged 34	4,017	3,710	−307	−7.6

Source: Bureau of the Census, Internet site <www.census.gov/population/www/projections/natdet-D1A.html>; calculations by the author

Diversity Is Greater among the Young

Young adults are racially and ethnically more diverse than older people.

Racial and ethnic diversity among Americans has been increasing for decades. Each successive generation is more diverse than the preceding one. Young adults are more diverse than their elders, but less diverse than the nation's children.

Seventy-one percent of all Americans are non-Hispanic white, but among people aged 15 to 34, the proportion is a smaller 66 percent. More telling however is the difference in racial and ethnic composition between young adults and older Americans. Eighty-six percent of people aged 75 or older are non-Hispanic white, a share 20 percentage points greater than among 15-to-34-year-olds.

Among young adults, Hispanics now outnumber blacks. The 11.2 million Hispanics and 10.6 million non-Hispanic blacks account for 14.8 and 13.9 percent, respectively, of the 15-to-34 age group.

♦ Today's young adults grew up in a more integrated society than their elders. Their popular culture is heavily influenced by a mix of racial and ethnic groups.

Hispanics now outnumber blacks among young adults

(percent of people aged 15 to 34 by race and Hispanic origin, 2001)

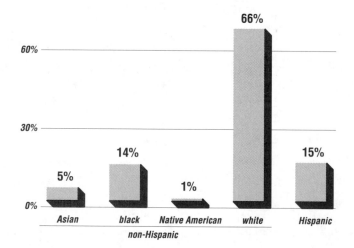

Population Aged 15 to 34 by Race and Hispanic Origin, 2001

(number and percent distribution of total people and people aged 15 to 34 by selected age groups, race, and Hispanic origin, 2001; numbers in thousands)

	total	non-Hispanic total	Asian	black	Native American	white	Hispanic
Total people	**277,803**	**244,187**	**10,990**	**33,876**	**2,072**	**197,249**	**33,616**
Total, aged 15 to 34	**76,141**	**64,907**	**3,394**	**10,554**	**682**	**50,278**	**11,232**
Aged 15 to 24	39,079	33,248	1,580	5,631	373	25,665	5,828
Aged 25 to 34	37,062	31,659	1,814	4,923	309	24,613	5,404
Aged 15 to 19	20,066	17,148	806	2,926	200	13,216	2,916
Aged 20 to 24	19,013	16,100	774	2,705	173	12,449	2,912
Aged 25 to 29	17,424	14,753	848	2,404	156	11,345	2,671
Aged 30 to 34	19,638	16,906	966	2,519	153	13,268	2,733

PERCENT DISTRIBUTION BY RACE AND HISPANIC ORIGIN

	total	non-Hispanic total	Asian	black	Native American	white	Hispanic
Total people	**100.0%**	**87.9%**	**4.0%**	**12.2%**	**0.7%**	**71.0%**	**12.1%**
Total, aged 15 to 34	**100.0**	**85.2**	**4.5**	**13.9**	**0.9**	**66.0**	**14.8**
Aged 15 to 24	100.0	85.1	4.0	14.4	1.0	65.7	14.9
Aged 25 to 34	100.0	85.4	4.9	13.3	0.8	66.4	14.6
Aged 15 to 19	100.0	85.5	4.0	14.6	1.0	65.9	14.5
Aged 20 to 24	100.0	84.7	4.1	14.2	0.9	65.5	15.3
Aged 25 to 29	100.0	84.7	4.9	13.8	0.9	65.1	15.3
Aged 30 to 34	100.0	86.1	4.9	12.8	0.8	67.6	13.9

Source: Bureau of the Census, Internet site <www.census.gov/population/www/projections/natdet-D1A.html>; calculations by the author

Hispanics Aged 15 to 34 by Race, 2001

(number and percent distribution of total Hispanics and Hispanics aged 15 to 34 by selected age groups and race, 2001; numbers in thousands)

| | Hispanic | | | | |
	total	Asian	black	Native American	white
Total people	**33,616**	**675**	**1,908**	**399**	**30,635**
Total, aged 15 to 34	**11,232**	**229**	**614**	**149**	**10,240**
Aged 15 to 24	5,828	117	318	80	5,314
Aged 25 to 34	5,404	112	296	69	4,926
Aged 15 to 19	2,916	61	164	42	2,650
Aged 20 to 24	2,912	56	154	38	2,664
Aged 25 to 29	2,671	53	140	34	2,444
Aged 30 to 34	2,733	59	156	35	2,482

PERCENT DISTRIBUTION BY RACE AND HISPANIC ORIGIN

Total people	**100.0%**	**2.0%**	**5.7%**	**1.2%**	**91.1%**
Total, aged 15 to 34	**100.0**	**2.0**	**5.5**	**1.3**	**91.2**
Aged 15 to 24	100.0	2.0	5.5	1.4	91.2
Aged 25 to 34	100.0	2.1	5.5	1.3	91.2
Aged 15 to 19	100.0	2.1	5.6	1.4	90.8
Aged 20 to 24	100.0	1.9	5.3	1.3	91.5
Aged 25 to 29	100.0	2.0	5.2	1.3	91.5
Aged 30 to 34	100.0	2.2	5.7	1.3	90.8

Source: Bureau of the Census, Internet site <www.census.gov/population/www/projections/natdet-D1A.html>; calculations by the author

Young Adults Are More Likely to Be Foreign-Born

About one in eight young adults was born in another country.

Young adults are slightly more likely than the average American to have been born in a foreign country. Thirteen percent of people aged 15 to 34 are foreign-born compared with 10 percent of all U.S. residents. Among 30-to-34-year-olds, 17 percent are foreign-born.

The proportion of young adults born in Europe is lower than average, while the proportion born in Central America (primarily Mexico, which is included in Central America in these statistics) is higher. Only 9 percent of foreign-born people aged 15 to 34 were born in Europe compared with 15 percent of the total foreign-born population. Fully 46 percent of foreign-born young adults were born in Central America compared with 35 percent of all U.S. residents.

♦ Young adults are less likely than average to be U.S. citizens. While 7 percent of all U.S. residents are not citizens, among people aged 15 to 34, the proportion is 11 percent. Many will become citizens later in life, however, if they remain in the U.S.

Among foreign-born young adults, the plurality are from Central America

(percent distribution of foreign-born people aged 15 to 34 by region of birth, 2000)

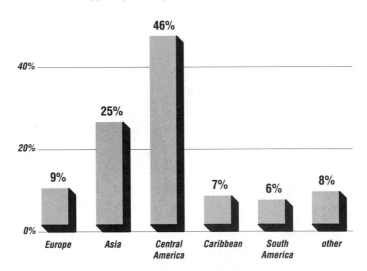

Population Aged 15 to 34 by Citizenship Status, 2000

(number and percent distribution of total people and people aged 15 to 34 by citizenship status, 2000; numbers in thousands)

	total	native-born	foreign-born total	foreign-born naturalized citizen	foreign-born not a citizen
Total people	**274,087**	**245,708**	**28,380**	**10,622**	**17,758**
Total aged 15 to 34	76,329	66,215	10,113	2,064	8,049
Aged 15 to 19	20,102	18,490	1,612	210	1,402
Aged 20 to 24	18,441	16,075	2,366	366	2,000
Aged 25 to 29	18,268	15,366	2,902	610	2,292
Aged 30 to 34	19,518	16,284	3,233	878	2,355
Percent distribution by citizenship status					
Total people	**100.0%**	**89.6%**	**10.4%**	**3.9%**	**6.5%**
Total aged 15 to 34	100.0	86.7	13.2	2.7	10.5
Aged 15 to 19	100.0	92.0	8.0	1.0	7.0
Aged 20 to 24	100.0	87.2	12.8	2.0	10.8
Aged 25 to 29	100.0	84.1	15.9	3.3	12.5
Aged 30 to 34	100.0	83.4	16.6	4.5	12.1
Percent distribution by age					
Total people	**100.0%**	**100.0%**	**100.0%**	**100.0%**	**100.0%**
Total aged 15 to 34	27.8	26.9	35.6	19.4	45.3
Aged 15 to 19	7.3	7.5	5.7	2.0	7.9
Aged 20 to 24	6.7	6.5	8.3	3.4	11.3
Aged 25 to 29	6.7	6.3	10.2	5.7	12.9
Aged 30 to 34	7.1	6.6	11.4	8.3	13.3

Source: Bureau of the Census, Internet site <www.census.gov/population/www/socdemo/foreign.html>; calculations by the author

Foreign-Born Population Aged 15 to 34, 2000

(number and percent distribution of total people and people aged 15 to 34 by foreign-born status and region of birth, 2000; numbers in thousands)

| | | foreign-born | | | | | | |
| | | | | | Latin America | | | |
	total	total	Europe	Asia	Central America	Caribbean	South America	other
Total people	**274,087**	**28,379**	**4,355**	**7,246**	**9,789**	**2,813**	**1,876**	**2,301**
Total aged 15 to 34	76,329	10,113	896	2,502	4,612	743	602	758
Aged 15 to 19	20,102	1,612	156	388	711	129	118	110
Aged 20 to 24	18,441	2,366	201	568	1,155	158	139	145
Aged 25 to 29	18,268	2,902	211	799	1,345	176	147	223
Aged 30 to 34	19,518	3,233	328	747	1,401	280	198	280

Percent distribution of foreign-born by region of birth

Total people	–	**100.0%**	**15.3%**	**25.5%**	**34.5%**	**9.9%**	**6.6%**	**8.1%**
Total aged 15 to 34	–	100.0	8.9	24.7	45.6	7.3	6.0	7.5
Aged 15 to 19	–	100.0	9.7	24.1	44.1	8.0	7.3	6.8
Aged 20 to 24	–	100.0	8.5	24.0	48.8	6.7	5.9	6.1
Aged 25 to 29	–	100.0	7.3	27.5	46.3	6.1	5.1	7.7
Aged 30 to 34	–	100.0	10.1	23.1	43.3	8.7	6.1	8.7

Percent distribution by age

Total people	**100.0%**	**100.0%**	**100.0%**	**100.0%**	**100.0%**	**100.0%**	**100.0%**	**100.0%**
Total aged 15 to 34	27.8	35.6	20.6	34.5	47.1	26.4	32.1	32.9
Aged 15 to 19	7.3	5.7	3.6	5.4	7.3	4.6	6.3	4.8
Aged 20 to 24	6.7	8.3	4.6	7.8	11.8	5.6	7.4	6.3
Aged 25 to 29	6.7	10.2	4.8	11.0	13.7	6.3	7.8	9.7
Aged 30 to 34	7.1	11.4	7.5	10.3	14.3	10.0	10.6	12.2

Note: Central America includes Mexico in these statistics; (–) means not applicable.
Source: Bureau of the Census, Internet site <www.census.gov/population/www/socdemo/foreign.html>; calculations by the author

Young Adults Are a Large Share of Immigrants

Nearly 300,000 15-to-34-year-olds immigrated to the U.S. in 1998.

More than 660,000 immigrants were admitted to the U.S. in 1998. Nearly 300,000 (44 percent) were aged 15 to 34.

The most common country of origin for U.S. immigrants in 1998 was Mexico. Overall, one out of five immigrants came from Mexico. Among young adults aged 15 to 24 the proportion is even higher—more than 25 percent. Immigrants from Mexico are overwhelmingly young. In 1998, half were aged 15 to 34.

◆ Native-born young adults are influenced by young people from other cultures. The popularity of Latino music is one manifestation of that influence.

About one-quarter of immigrants aged 15 to 29 are from Mexico

(percent of immigrants from Mexico, by age, 1998)

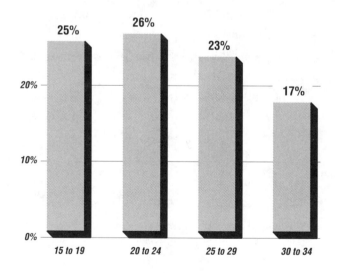

Total and Mexican Immigrants Aged 15 to 34, 1998

(number and percent distribution of total immigrants and immigrants from Mexico, by age for ages 15 to 34, and percent of immigrants from Mexico, 1998)

	total immigrants		immigrants from Mexico		
	number	percent distribution	number	percent distribution	percent of total
Total immigrants	**660,477**	**100.0%**	**131,575**	**100.0%**	**19.9%**
Total aged 15 to 34	**291,425**	**44.1**	**65,690**	**49.9**	**22.5**
Aged 15 to 19	68,319	10.3	17,285	13.1	25.3
Aged 20 to 24	59,609	9.0	15,184	11.5	25.5
Aged 25 to 29	85,432	12.9	19,985	15.2	23.4
Aged 30 to 34	78,065	11.8	13,236	10.1	17.0

Source: Immigration and Naturalization Service, 1998 Statistical Yearbook of the Immigration and Naturalization Service, *2000; calculations by the author*

States Differ in Racial and Ethnic Composition

Diversity is greater in some parts of the country.

There is considerable racial and ethnic diversity in the U.S., but it is not evenly spread throughout the nation. Among young adults, Asians and Hispanics are most common in the West. The Midwest has the largest share of non-Hispanic whites, while the South has the largest share of blacks.

In seven states at least 90 percent of young adults are non-Hispanic white. They are, in descending order, Maine, Vermont, New Hampshire, West Virginia, Iowa, North Dakota, and Kentucky. But in 23 states and the District of Columbia, minorities account for at least one-fourth of the young-adult population.

In many Southern states, non-Hispanic blacks make up a large share of the young-adult population. More than 30 percent of 15-to-34-year-olds in Alabama, Georgia, Louisiana, Maryland, and South Carolina are non-Hispanic black. Mississippi has the largest proportion of non-Hispanic blacks—42 percent. In Washington, D.C., the majority (51 percent) of young adults are non-Hispanic black, while only 34 percent are non-Hispanic white.

The majority (57 percent) of young adults in Hawaii are Asian. In California, the nation's most populous state, no racial or ethnic group accounts for the majority of young adults. Forty percent of the state's 15-to-34-year-olds are non-Hispanic white, while another 40 percent are Hispanic. Thirteen percent are Asian, and 7 percent are non-Hispanic black.

♦ Although young adults are more diverse in some states than others, the cultural influence of racial and ethnic diversity is shared by young adults everywhere.

Population Aged 15 to 34 by Region, Race, and Hispanic Origin, 2001

(number and percent distribution of total people and people aged 15 to 34 by region, race, and Hispanic origin, 2001; numbers in thousands)

	total	non-Hispanic				Hispanic	non-Hispanic				Hispanic
		Asian	black	Native American	white		Asian	black	Native American	white	
UNITED STATES, TOTAL	277,803	10,990	33,876	2,072	197,249	33,616	4.0%	12.2%	0.7%	71.0%	12.1%
Total, aged 15 to 34	76,140	3,394	10,554	682	50,278	11,232	4.5	13.9	0.9	66.0	14.8
Aged 15 to 19	20,065	806	2,926	200	13,216	2,916	4.0	14.6	1.0	65.9	14.5
Aged 20 to 24	19,012	774	2,705	173	12,449	2,912	4.1	14.2	0.9	65.5	15.3
Aged 25 to 29	17,424	848	2,404	156	11,345	2,671	4.9	13.8	0.9	65.1	15.3
Aged 30 to 34	19,639	966	2,519	153	13,268	2,733	4.9	12.8	0.8	67.6	13.9
NORTHEAST, TOTAL	52,282	2,176	5,626	114	39,274	5,092	4.2	10.8	0.2	75.1	9.7
Total, aged 15 to 34	13,488	657	1,659	36	9,539	1,598	4.9	12.3	0.3	70.7	11.8
Aged 15 to 19	3,655	152	470	10	2,601	423	4.2	12.8	0.3	71.2	11.6
Aged 20 to 24	3,264	144	406	8	2,307	399	4.4	12.4	0.2	70.7	12.2
Aged 25 to 29	2,963	168	370	8	2,046	371	5.7	12.5	0.3	69.0	12.5
Aged 30 to 34	3,606	193	414	10	2,584	405	5.4	11.5	0.3	71.7	11.2

(continued)

(continued from previous page)

| | | | non-Hispanic | | | | | | non-Hispanic | | |
	total	Asian	black	Native American	white	Hispanic	Asian	black	Native American	white	Hispanic
New England, total	**13,642**	**402**	**701**	**31**	**11,663**	**844**	**2.9%**	**5.1%**	**0.2%**	**85.5%**	**6.2%**
Total, aged 15 to 34	**3,534**	**130**	**209**	**10**	**2,903**	**282**	**3.7**	**5.9**	**0.3**	**82.2**	**8.0**
Aged 15 to 19	979	29	62	3	806	79	3.0	6.3	0.3	82.3	8.1
Aged 20 to 24	842	29	51	2	690	70	3.4	6.1	0.3	82.0	8.3
Aged 25 to 29	742	33	45	2	600	62	4.5	6.1	0.3	80.8	8.4
Aged 30 to 34	971	39	52	3	807	70	4.0	5.3	0.3	83.2	7.2
Middle Atlantic, total	**38,641**	**1,774**	**4,926**	**83**	**27,611**	**4,247**	**4.6**	**12.7**	**0.2**	**71.5**	**11.0**
Total, aged 15 to 34	**9,954**	**527**	**1,450**	**26**	**6,636**	**1,316**	**5.3**	**14.6**	**0.3**	**66.7**	**13.2**
Aged 15 to 19	2,677	123	408	7	1,795	343	4.6	15.2	0.3	67.1	12.8
Aged 20 to 24	2,422	116	355	6	1,617	329	4.8	14.6	0.2	66.8	13.6
Aged 25 to 29	2,221	134	325	6	1,446	309	6.1	14.6	0.3	65.1	13.9
Aged 30 to 34	2,635	154	362	7	1,777	334	5.9	13.7	0.3	67.4	12.7
MIDWEST, TOTAL	**63,341**	**1,218**	**6,347**	**364**	**52,715**	**2,698**	**1.9**	**10.0**	**0.6**	**83.2**	**4.3**
Total, aged 15 to 34	**17,473**	**409**	**1,978**	**126**	**14,032**	**928**	**2.3**	**11.3**	**0.7**	**80.3**	**5.3**
Aged 15 to 19	4,710	100	565	38	3,759	248	2.1	12.0	0.8	79.8	5.3
Aged 20 to 24	4,476	94	506	32	3,602	241	2.1	11.3	0.7	80.5	5.4
Aged 25 to 29	3,923	102	434	28	3,144	214	2.6	11.1	0.7	80.1	5.5
Aged 30 to 34	4,363	112	472	28	3,527	224	2.6	10.8	0.6	80.8	5.1

(continued)

(continued from previous page)

| | total | non-Hispanic | | | | Hispanic | non-Hispanic | | | | Hispanic |
		Asian	black	Native American	white		Asian	black	Native American	white	
East North Central, total	**44,414**	**885**	**5,289**	**149**	**35,923**	**2,169**	**2.0%**	**11.9%**	**0.3%**	**80.9%**	**4.9%**
Total, aged 15 to 34	**12,175**	**286**	**1,634**	**50**	**9,466**	**739**	**2.4**	**13.4**	**0.4**	**77.7**	**6.1**
Aged 15 to 19	3,266	69	467	14	2,519	198	2.1	14.3	0.4	77.1	6.1
Aged 20 to 24	3,078	66	417	12	2,391	191	2.2	13.5	0.4	77.7	6.2
Aged 25 to 29	2,727	71	358	12	2,116	170	2.6	13.1	0.4	77.6	6.2
Aged 30 to 34	3,104	80	393	12	2,440	179	2.6	12.7	0.4	78.6	5.8
West North Central, total	**18,927**	**333**	**1,058**	**215**	**16,792**	**529**	**1.8**	**5.6**	**1.1**	**88.7**	**2.8**
Total, aged 15 to 34	**5,297**	**123**	**344**	**76**	**4,566**	**189**	**2.3**	**6.5**	**1.4**	**86.2**	**3.6**
Aged 15 to 19	1,444	31	99	24	1,240	51	2.1	6.8	1.7	85.9	3.5
Aged 20 to 24	1,399	28	90	20	1,212	50	2.0	6.4	1.4	86.6	3.6
Aged 25 to 29	1,196	31	76	17	1,028	44	2.6	6.4	1.4	85.9	3.7
Aged 30 to 34	1,259	33	79	16	1,087	44	2.6	6.3	1.2	86.4	3.5
SOUTH, TOTAL	**99,226**	**1,978**	**18,900**	**591**	**67,129**	**10,627**	**2.0**	**19.0**	**0.6**	**67.7**	**10.7**
Total, aged 15 to 34	**27,345**	**621**	**5,976**	**192**	**17,049**	**3,507**	**2.3**	**21.9**	**0.7**	**62.3**	**12.8**
Aged 15 to 19	7,081	144	1,635	52	4,342	907	2.0	23.1	0.7	61.3	12.8
Aged 20 to 24	6,822	139	1,560	48	4,145	929	2.0	22.9	0.7	60.8	13.6
Aged 25 to 29	6,334	157	1,377	45	3,915	839	2.5	21.7	0.7	61.8	13.2
Aged 30 to 34	7,109	181	1,404	46	4,647	831	2.5	19.8	0.6	65.4	11.7

(continued)

(continued from previous page)

		non-Hispanic					non-Hispanic				
	total	Asian	black	Native American	white	Hispanic	Asian	black	Native American	white	Hispanic
South Atlantic, total	**51,044**	**1,145**	**10,986**	**205**	**35,128**	**3,581**	**2.2%**	**21.5%**	**0.4%**	**68.8%**	**7.0%**
Total, aged 15 to 34	**13,601**	**357**	**3,393**	**64**	**8,669**	**1,117**	**2.6**	**24.9**	**0.5**	**63.7**	**8.2**
Aged 15 to 19	3,543	82	940	17	2,227	276	2.3	26.5	0.5	62.9	7.8
Aged 20 to 24	3,286	78	864	15	2,047	281	2.4	26.3	0.5	62.3	8.6
Aged 25 to 29	3,104	90	766	15	1,963	271	2.9	24.7	0.5	63.2	8.7
Aged 30 to 34	3,667	107	823	17	2,432	289	2.9	22.4	0.5	66.3	7.9
East South Central, total	**16,839**	**138**	**3,396**	**40**	**13,080**	**185**	**0.8**	**20.2**	**0.2**	**77.7**	**1.1**
Total, aged 15 to 34	**4,668**	**45**	**1,103**	**14**	**3,442**	**64**	**1.0**	**23.6**	**0.3**	**73.7**	**1.4**
Aged 15 to 19	1,158	10	291	3	839	15	0.9	25.1	0.3	72.4	1.3
Aged 20 to 24	1,167	10	297	3	840	16	0.9	25.4	0.3	72.0	1.4
Aged 25 to 29	1,105	12	262	4	811	16	1.1	23.7	0.3	73.4	1.5
Aged 30 to 34	1,237	13	253	3	952	16	1.0	20.4	0.3	76.9	1.3
West South Central, total	**31,343**	**696**	**4,519**	**346**	**18,921**	**6,861**	**2.2**	**14.4**	**1.1**	**60.4**	**21.9**
Total, aged 15 to 34	**9,077**	**218**	**1,481**	**114**	**4,939**	**2,325**	**2.4**	**16.3**	**1.3**	**54.4**	**25.6**
Aged 15 to 19	2,380	52	404	32	1,276	615	2.2	17.0	1.3	53.6	25.9
Aged 20 to 24	2,369	50	399	30	1,258	632	2.1	16.8	1.3	53.1	26.7
Aged 25 to 29	2,124	55	349	27	1,141	552	2.6	16.4	1.3	53.7	26.0
Aged 30 to 34	2,204	61	328	26	1,263	526	2.8	14.9	1.2	57.3	23.9

(continued)

(continued from previous page)

		non-Hispanic						non-Hispanic			
	total	Asian	black	Native American	white	Hispanic	Asian	black	Native American	white	Hispanic
WEST, TOTAL	**62,953**	**5,618**	**3,002**	**1,003**	**38,131**	**15,200**	**8.9%**	**4.8%**	**1.6%**	**60.6%**	**24.1%**
Total, aged 15 to 34	**17,834**	**1,707**	**941**	**328**	**9,657**	**5,200**	**9.6**	**5.3**	**1.8**	**54.2**	**29.2**
Aged 15 to 19	4,619	410	257	100	2,513	1,338	8.9	5.6	2.2	54.4	29.0
Aged 20 to 24	4,451	397	233	84	2,395	1,343	8.9	5.2	1.9	53.8	30.2
Aged 25 to 29	4,205	421	223	74	2,240	1,247	10.0	5.3	1.8	53.3	29.6
Aged 30 to 34	4,560	480	229	70	2,509	1,273	10.5	5.0	1.5	55.0	27.9
Mountain, total	**18,245**	**406**	**523**	**581**	**13,399**	**3,337**	**2.2**	**2.9**	**3.2**	**73.4**	**18.3**
Total, aged 15 to 34	**5,246**	**132**	**170**	**196**	**3,632**	**1,116**	**2.5**	**3.2**	**3.7**	**69.2**	**21.3**
Aged 15 to 19	1,406	32	48	61	951	314	2.3	3.4	4.3	67.6	22.3
Aged 20 to 24	1,374	30	44	50	941	310	2.2	3.2	3.6	68.5	22.5
Aged 25 to 29	1,229	33	39	44	856	257	2.7	3.1	3.6	69.7	20.9
Aged 30 to 34	1,236	37	40	41	884	235	3.0	3.2	3.3	71.5	19.0
Pacific, total	**44,708**	**5,212**	**2,480**	**421**	**24,732**	**11,863**	**11.7**	**5.5**	**0.9**	**55.3**	**26.5**
Total, aged 15 to 34	**12,589**	**1,575**	**771**	**132**	**6,026**	**4,084**	**12.5**	**6.1**	**1.1**	**47.9**	**32.4**
Aged 15 to 19	3,213	378	209	39	1,563	1,024	11.8	6.5	1.2	48.6	31.9
Aged 20 to 24	3,076	367	189	34	1,454	1,033	11.9	6.1	1.1	47.3	33.6
Aged 25 to 29	2,976	388	184	30	1,384	990	13.0	6.2	1.0	46.5	33.3
Aged 30 to 34	3,324	443	189	29	1,625	1,038	13.3	5.7	0.9	48.9	31.2

Source: Projections by New Strategist

Population Aged 15 to 34 by State, Race, and Hispanic Origin, 2001

(number and percent distribution of total people and people aged 15 to 34 by state, race, and Hispanic origin, 2001)

| | non-Hispanic | | | | | | non-Hispanic | | | | |
	total	Asian	black	Native American	white	Hispanic	Asian	black	Native American	white	Hispanic
Alabama, total	**4,384,221**	**29,645**	**1,138,711**	**13,504**	**3,154,028**	**48,333**	**0.7%**	**26.0%**	**0.3%**	**71.9%**	**1.1%**
Total, aged 15 to 34	**1,209,648**	**9,157**	**367,162**	**4,840**	**812,190**	**16,300**	**0.8**	**30.4**	**0.4**	**67.1**	**1.3**
Aged 15 to 19	294,328	2,014	93,661	1,024	193,691	3,937	0.7	31.8	0.3	65.8	1.3
Aged 20 to 24	300,070	2,169	98,517	1,310	193,847	4,227	0.7	32.8	0.4	64.6	1.4
Aged 25 to 29	289,071	2,507	89,081	1,360	192,161	3,962	0.9	30.8	0.5	66.5	1.4
Aged 30 to 34	326,179	2,467	85,903	1,146	232,490	4,173	0.8	26.3	0.4	71.3	1.3
Alaska, total	**632,279**	**30,855**	**22,887**	**102,856**	**448,805**	**26,876**	**4.9**	**3.6**	**16.3**	**71.0**	**4.3**
Total, aged 15 to 34	**191,788**	**10,537**	**8,426**	**33,171**	**130,340**	**9,314**	**5.5**	**4.4**	**17.3**	**68.0**	**4.9**
Aged 15 to 19	56,872	2,809	2,168	12,312	37,181	2,402	4.9	3.8	21.6	65.4	4.2
Aged 20 to 24	51,691	2,793	1,998	9,525	34,981	2,393	5.4	3.9	18.4	67.7	4.6
Aged 25 to 29	45,758	2,811	2,397	6,891	31,170	2,489	6.1	5.2	15.1	68.1	5.4
Aged 30 to 34	37,467	2,123	1,863	4,443	27,009	2,030	5.7	5.0	11.9	72.1	5.4
Arizona, total	**5,142,570**	**101,287**	**156,590**	**249,620**	**3,398,853**	**1,236,220**	**2.0**	**3.0**	**4.9**	**66.1**	**24.0**
Total, aged 15 to 34	**1,425,046**	**32,909**	**52,177**	**83,733**	**839,616**	**416,612**	**2.3**	**3.7**	**5.9**	**58.9**	**29.2**
Aged 15 to 19	387,396	8,394	14,581	27,111	219,674	117,635	2.2	3.8	7.0	56.7	30.4
Aged 20 to 24	359,914	7,460	13,350	21,263	204,887	112,955	2.1	3.7	5.9	56.9	31.4
Aged 25 to 29	326,311	7,973	11,601	18,634	191,473	96,630	2.4	3.6	5.7	58.7	29.6
Aged 30 to 34	351,425	9,083	12,645	16,724	223,581	89,392	2.6	3.6	4.8	63.6	25.4

(continued)

(continued from previous page)

| | | non-Hispanic | | | | | | non-Hispanic | | | |
	total	Asian	black	Native American	white	Hispanic	Asian	black	Native American	white	Hispanic
Arkansas, total	**2,639,837**	**19,681**	**424,342**	**13,436**	**2,122,641**	**59,736**	**0.7%**	**16.1%**	**0.5%**	**80.4%**	**2.3%**
Total, aged 15 to 34	**733,906**	**6,591**	**143,251**	**4,235**	**558,068**	**21,760**	**0.9**	**19.5**	**0.6**	**76.0**	**3.0**
Aged 15 to 19	193,131	1,514	40,047	1,052	144,655	5,864	0.8	20.7	0.5	74.9	3.0
Aged 20 to 24	189,399	1,500	40,282	980	140,803	5,835	0.8	21.3	0.5	74.3	3.1
Aged 25 to 29	169,995	1,649	33,497	1,073	128,847	4,930	1.0	19.7	0.6	75.8	2.9
Aged 30 to 34	181,382	1,929	29,425	1,131	143,764	5,132	1.1	16.2	0.6	79.3	2.8
California, total	**33,631,107**	**3,984,000**	**2,177,927**	**180,270**	**16,199,492**	**11,089,418**	**11.8**	**6.5**	**0.5**	**48.2**	**33.0**
Total, aged 15 to 34	**9,527,935**	**1,226,706**	**667,172**	**54,088**	**3,772,625**	**3,807,344**	**12.9**	**7.0**	**0.6**	**39.6**	**40.0**
Aged 15 to 19	2,399,034	290,146	181,595	14,072	963,472	949,750	12.1	7.6	0.6	40.2	39.6
Aged 20 to 24	2,290,978	278,962	163,417	13,068	876,941	958,589	12.2	7.1	0.6	38.3	41.8
Aged 25 to 29	2,257,604	298,644	158,622	12,860	863,456	924,022	13.2	7.0	0.6	38.2	40.9
Aged 30 to 34	2,580,318	358,955	163,537	14,089	1,068,755	974,982	13.9	6.3	0.5	41.4	37.8
Colorado, total	**4,294,082**	**103,800**	**166,265**	**27,558**	**3,330,641**	**665,818**	**2.4**	**3.9**	**0.6**	**77.6**	**15.5**
Total, aged 15 to 34	**1,188,747**	**33,361**	**53,431**	**8,754**	**873,798**	**219,404**	**2.8**	**4.5**	**0.7**	**73.5**	**18.5**
Aged 15 to 19	319,895	8,186	15,022	2,403	231,173	63,111	2.6	4.7	0.8	72.3	19.7
Aged 20 to 24	310,590	7,806	14,073	2,123	224,432	62,157	2.5	4.5	0.7	72.3	20.0
Aged 25 to 29	269,812	8,125	12,391	2,031	197,701	49,564	3.0	4.6	0.8	73.3	18.4
Aged 30 to 34	288,449	9,244	11,945	2,196	220,491	44,572	3.2	4.1	0.8	76.4	15.5

(continued)

(continued from previous page)

	total	non-Hispanic					non-Hispanic				
		Asian	black	Native American	white	Hispanic	Asian	black	Native American	white	Hispanic
Connecticut, total	**3,322,822**	**89,375**	**291,787**	**6,130**	**2,631,480**	**304,050**	**2.7%**	**8.8%**	**0.2%**	**79.2%**	**9.2%**
Total, aged 15 to 34	**831,749**	**28,137**	**88,884**	**1,812**	**613,306**	**99,610**	**3.4**	**10.7**	**0.2**	**73.7**	**12.0**
Aged 15 to 19	247,568	6,784	27,145	451	184,154	29,033	2.7	11.0	0.2	74.4	11.7
Aged 20 to 24	200,542	6,180	21,899	395	147,411	24,656	3.1	10.9	0.2	73.5	12.3
Aged 25 to 29	170,287	6,861	18,455	445	123,085	21,440	4.0	10.8	0.3	72.3	12.6
Aged 30 to 34	213,353	8,312	21,385	520	158,656	24,480	3.9	10.0	0.2	74.4	11.5
Delaware, total	**775,832**	**16,920**	**151,956**	**2,107**	**574,331**	**30,518**	**2.2**	**19.6**	**0.3**	**74.0**	**3.9**
Total, aged 15 to 34	**206,211**	**4,996**	**47,113**	**667**	**142,957**	**10,478**	**2.4**	**22.8**	**0.3**	**69.3**	**5.1**
Aged 15 to 19	52,084	1,199	12,410	159	35,664	2,652	2.3	23.8	0.3	68.5	5.1
Aged 20 to 24	49,386	1,118	11,575	157	33,935	2,603	2.3	23.4	0.3	68.7	5.3
Aged 25 to 29	46,847	1,154	10,757	143	32,273	2,521	2.5	23.0	0.3	68.9	5.4
Aged 30 to 34	57,894	1,524	12,372	209	41,086	2,702	2.6	21.4	0.4	71.0	4.7
District of Columbia, total	**544,362**	**16,919**	**322,614**	**1,295**	**160,923**	**42,610**	**3.1**	**59.3**	**0.2**	**29.6**	**7.8**
Total, aged 15 to 34	**138,407**	**6,205**	**70,774**	**488**	**47,671**	**13,269**	**4.5**	**51.1**	**0.4**	**34.4**	**9.6**
Aged 15 to 19	25,220	604	18,703	57	3,531	2,325	2.4	74.2	0.2	14.0	9.2
Aged 20 to 24	25,307	855	14,135	44	7,937	2,336	3.4	55.9	0.2	31.4	9.2
Aged 25 to 29	33,931	2,115	14,174	159	13,986	3,497	6.2	41.8	0.5	41.2	10.3
Aged 30 to 34	53,948	2,631	23,762	228	22,217	5,111	4.9	44.0	0.4	41.2	9.5

(continued)

(continued from previous page)

	non-Hispanic						non-Hispanic				
	total	Asian	black	Native American	white	Hispanic	Asian	black	Native American	white	Hispanic
Florida, total	**15,532,043**	**283,693**	**2,342,519**	**44,951**	**10,386,051**	**2,474,829**	**1.8%**	**15.1%**	**0.3%**	**66.9%**	**15.9%**
Total, aged 15 to 34	**3,909,871**	**86,704**	**759,239**	**13,131**	**2,310,789**	**740,007**	**2.2**	**19.4**	**0.3**	**59.1**	**18.9**
Aged 15 to 19	1,071,642	20,835	224,241	3,710	636,910	185,946	1.9	20.9	0.3	59.4	17.4
Aged 20 to 24	965,210	19,408	200,700	3,233	553,484	188,385	2.0	20.8	0.3	57.3	19.5
Aged 25 to 29	869,274	21,229	168,657	2,982	499,513	176,893	2.4	19.4	0.3	57.5	20.3
Aged 30 to 34	1,003,745	25,232	165,642	3,206	620,881	188,783	2.5	16.5	0.3	61.9	18.8
Georgia, total	**8,230,273**	**173,994**	**2,352,884**	**15,972**	**5,420,960**	**266,463**	**2.1**	**28.6**	**0.2**	**65.9**	**3.2**
Total, aged 15 to 34	**2,313,822**	**56,466**	**745,133**	**5,057**	**1,413,561**	**93,605**	**2.4**	**32.2**	**0.2**	**61.1**	**4.0**
Aged 15 to 19	587,130	12,598	200,269	1,228	350,172	22,862	2.1	34.1	0.2	59.6	3.9
Aged 20 to 24	558,313	12,046	189,643	1,200	331,413	24,011	2.2	34.0	0.2	59.4	4.3
Aged 25 to 29	531,887	14,337	170,839	1,363	322,537	22,810	2.7	32.1	0.3	60.6	4.3
Aged 30 to 34	636,493	17,484	184,382	1,266	409,439	23,922	2.7	29.0	0.2	64.3	3.8
Hawaii, total	**1,192,110**	**721,181**	**30,354**	**4,697**	**336,790**	**99,089**	**60.5**	**2.5**	**0.4**	**28.3**	**8.3**
Total, aged 15 to 34	**320,887**	**181,992**	**12,201**	**1,370**	**92,519**	**32,805**	**56.7**	**3.8**	**0.4**	**28.8**	**10.2**
Aged 15 to 19	78,167	47,478	2,158	294	19,554	8,683	60.7	2.8	0.4	25.0	11.1
Aged 20 to 24	80,292	48,229	2,315	277	20,537	8,935	60.1	2.9	0.3	25.6	11.1
Aged 25 to 29	87,718	48,035	3,988	404	27,004	8,287	54.8	4.5	0.5	30.8	9.4
Aged 30 to 34	74,710	38,251	3,741	395	25,424	6,900	51.2	5.0	0.5	34.0	9.2

(continued)

(continued from previous page)

		non-Hispanic					non-Hispanic				
	total	Asian	black	Native American	white	Hispanic	Asian	black	Native American	white	Hispanic
Idaho, total	**1,302,182**	**14,399**	**5,235**	**14,610**	**1,163,698**	**104,240**	**1.1%**	**0.4%**	**1.1%**	**89.4%**	**8.0%**
Total, aged 15 to 34	**396,331**	**5,194**	**2,039**	**5,092**	**345,343**	**38,663**	**1.3**	**0.5**	**1.3**	**87.1**	**9.8**
Aged 15 to 19	102,033	1,126	436	1,344	88,791	10,336	1.1	0.4	1.3	87.0	10.1
Aged 20 to 24	109,317	1,164	496	1,216	95,513	10,928	1.1	0.5	1.1	87.4	10.0
Aged 25 to 29	96,129	1,382	567	1,273	83,617	9,291	1.4	0.6	1.3	87.0	9.7
Aged 30 to 34	88,852	1,523	540	1,259	77,422	8,108	1.7	0.6	1.4	87.1	9.1
Illinois, total	**12,236,810**	**419,996**	**1,826,510**	**17,816**	**8,603,296**	**1,369,192**	**3.4**	**14.9**	**0.1**	**70.3**	**11.2**
Total, aged 15 to 34	**3,315,076**	**130,753**	**550,886**	**5,526**	**2,163,187**	**464,723**	**3.9**	**16.6**	**0.2**	**65.3**	**14.0**
Aged 15 to 19	877,027	30,103	156,206	1,402	566,926	122,390	3.4	17.8	0.2	64.6	14.0
Aged 20 to 24	824,482	29,834	141,648	1,258	532,735	119,007	3.6	17.2	0.2	64.6	14.4
Aged 25 to 29	750,073	32,404	120,699	1,373	487,768	107,828	4.3	16.1	0.2	65.0	14.4
Aged 30 to 34	863,494	38,412	132,332	1,494	575,758	115,498	4.4	15.3	0.2	66.7	13.4
Indiana, total	**6,021,673**	**61,191**	**496,582**	**12,799**	**5,286,550**	**164,551**	**1.0**	**8.2**	**0.2**	**87.8**	**2.7**
Total, aged 15 to 34	**1,663,224**	**19,988**	**157,554**	**4,303**	**1,423,885**	**57,495**	**1.2**	**9.5**	**0.3**	**85.6**	**3.5**
Aged 15 to 19	432,227	4,232	44,011	1,014	368,130	14,840	1.0	10.2	0.2	85.2	3.4
Aged 20 to 24	419,409	4,516	40,908	1,047	357,848	15,091	1.1	9.8	0.2	85.3	3.6
Aged 25 to 29	377,447	5,658	34,650	1,012	322,753	13,374	1.5	9.2	0.3	85.5	3.5
Aged 30 to 34	434,140	5,581	37,984	1,231	375,154	14,189	1.3	8.7	0.3	86.4	3.3

(continued)

(continued from previous page)

		non-Hispanic					non-Hispanic				
	total	Asian	black	Native American	white	Hispanic	Asian	black	Native American	white	Hispanic
Iowa, total	**2,851,879**	**40,172**	**56,547**	**7,663**	**2,681,004**	**66,493**	**1.4%**	**2.0%**	**0.3%**	**94.0%**	**2.3%**
Total, aged 15 to 34	**791,045**	**15,383**	**19,942**	**2,654**	**728,531**	**24,535**	**1.9**	**2.5**	**0.3**	**92.1**	**3.1**
Aged 15 to 19	210,817	3,322	5,443	731	194,862	6,459	1.6	2.6	0.3	92.4	3.1
Aged 20 to 24	212,309	3,392	5,387	658	196,485	6,387	1.6	2.5	0.3	92.5	3.0
Aged 25 to 29	180,674	4,377	4,568	562	165,398	5,769	2.4	2.5	0.3	91.5	3.2
Aged 30 to 34	187,245	4,293	4,543	703	171,786	5,920	2.3	2.4	0.4	91.7	3.2
Kansas, total	**2,648,632**	**48,859**	**150,801**	**19,931**	**2,269,128**	**159,913**	**1.8**	**5.7**	**0.8**	**85.7**	**6.0**
Total, aged 15 to 34	**753,510**	**17,594**	**50,188**	**7,203**	**621,603**	**56,921**	**2.3**	**6.7**	**1.0**	**82.5**	**7.6**
Aged 15 to 19	201,499	3,823	13,783	1,725	166,624	15,544	1.9	6.8	0.9	82.7	7.7
Aged 20 to 24	200,131	3,918	13,219	1,819	165,699	15,474	2.0	6.6	0.9	82.8	7.7
Aged 25 to 29	174,462	4,797	11,819	1,958	142,976	12,911	2.7	6.8	1.1	82.0	7.4
Aged 30 to 34	177,419	5,055	11,367	1,700	146,304	12,991	2.8	6.4	1.0	82.5	7.3
Kentucky, total	**3,991,661**	**28,831**	**285,738**	**5,247**	**3,633,831**	**38,013**	**0.7**	**7.2**	**0.1**	**91.0**	**1.0**
Total, aged 15 to 34	**1,105,927**	**9,793**	**92,642**	**1,677**	**988,096**	**13,719**	**0.9**	**8.4**	**0.2**	**89.3**	**1.2**
Aged 15 to 19	271,881	2,102	23,778	340	242,698	2,962	0.8	8.7	0.1	89.3	1.1
Aged 20 to 24	277,903	2,057	24,945	356	247,166	3,379	0.7	9.0	0.1	88.9	1.2
Aged 25 to 29	267,040	2,681	22,660	493	237,404	3,802	1.0	8.5	0.2	88.9	1.4
Aged 30 to 34	289,103	2,952	21,258	488	260,828	3,577	1.0	7.4	0.2	90.2	1.2

(continued)

(continued from previous page)

		non-Hispanic					non-Hispanic				
	total	Asian	black	Native American	white	Hispanic	Asian	black	Native American	white	Hispanic
Louisiana, total	**4,406,460**	**56,147**	**1,426,667**	**17,619**	**2,782,565**	**123,462**	**1.3%**	**32.4%**	**0.4%**	**63.1%**	**2.8%**
Total, aged 15 to 34	**1,289,343**	**19,058**	**469,386**	**6,007**	**755,540**	**39,352**	**1.5**	**36.4**	**0.5**	**58.6**	**3.1**
Aged 15 to 19	334,426	4,623	130,136	1,588	188,720	9,359	1.4	38.9	0.5	56.4	2.8
Aged 20 to 24	345,702	4,914	132,891	1,623	195,792	10,482	1.4	38.4	0.5	56.6	3.0
Aged 25 to 29	308,145	4,976	112,236	1,524	179,521	9,888	1.6	36.4	0.5	58.3	3.2
Aged 30 to 34	301,069	4,544	94,123	1,272	191,506	9,623	1.5	31.3	0.4	63.6	3.2
Maine, total	**1,241,038**	**10,099**	**5,812**	**5,613**	**1,209,665**	**9,849**	**0.8**	**0.5**	**0.5**	**97.5**	**0.8**
Total, aged 15 to 34	**330,991**	**3,305**	**2,398**	**1,836**	**320,239**	**3,213**	**1.0**	**0.7**	**0.6**	**96.8**	**1.0**
Aged 15 to 19	90,677	771	509	518	88,136	744	0.9	0.6	0.6	97.2	0.8
Aged 20 to 24	84,773	770	478	487	82,293	745	0.9	0.6	0.6	97.1	0.9
Aged 25 to 29	71,514	800	634	425	68,844	810	1.1	0.9	0.6	96.3	1.1
Aged 30 to 34	84,027	964	777	405	80,965	915	1.1	0.9	0.5	96.4	1.1
Maryland, total	**5,225,461**	**217,519**	**1,464,230**	**13,343**	**3,318,656**	**211,713**	**4.2**	**28.0**	**0.3**	**63.5**	**4.1**
Total, aged 15 to 34	**1,356,667**	**63,495**	**415,396**	**3,867**	**806,024**	**67,885**	**4.7**	**30.6**	**0.3**	**59.4**	**5.0**
Aged 15 to 19	377,311	16,469	116,576	1,052	226,259	16,955	4.4	30.9	0.3	60.0	4.5
Aged 20 to 24	329,408	14,794	103,509	952	193,194	16,960	4.5	31.4	0.3	58.6	5.1
Aged 25 to 29	292,270	15,041	88,191	877	172,555	15,607	5.1	30.2	0.3	59.0	5.3
Aged 30 to 34	357,678	17,190	107,121	987	214,016	18,363	4.8	29.9	0.3	59.8	5.1

(continued)

(continued from previous page)

		non-Hispanic					non-Hispanic				
	total	Asian	black	Native American	white	Hispanic	Asian	black	Native American	white	Hispanic
Massachusetts, total	**6,230,757**	**255,901**	**350,793**	**11,452**	**5,185,448**	**427,163**	**4.1%**	**5.6%**	**0.2%**	**83.2%**	**6.9%**
Total, aged 15 to 34	**1,609,608**	**82,044**	**99,726**	**3,435**	**1,280,055**	**144,347**	**5.1**	**6.2**	**0.2**	**79.5**	**9.0**
Aged 15 to 19	428,026	17,785	29,008	889	340,189	40,156	4.2	6.8	0.2	79.5	9.4
Aged 20 to 24	370,728	17,755	24,125	760	291,931	36,158	4.8	6.5	0.2	78.7	9.8
Aged 25 to 29	344,289	21,504	21,626	807	268,243	32,109	6.2	6.3	0.2	77.9	9.3
Aged 30 to 34	466,564	25,000	24,968	979	379,692	35,925	5.4	5.4	0.2	81.4	7.7
Michigan, total	**9,754,892**	**173,910**	**1,382,026**	**53,265**	**7,855,358**	**290,332**	**1.8**	**14.2**	**0.5**	**80.5**	**3.0**
Total, aged 15 to 34	**2,683,608**	**58,206**	**431,893**	**18,413**	**2,077,513**	**97,583**	**2.2**	**16.1**	**0.7**	**77.4**	**3.6**
Aged 15 to 19	737,527	14,361	122,917	5,099	568,051	27,099	1.9	16.7	0.7	77.0	3.7
Aged 20 to 24	676,394	13,089	105,864	4,666	527,294	25,481	1.9	15.7	0.7	78.0	3.8
Aged 25 to 29	590,037	14,064	94,758	4,276	454,898	22,040	2.4	16.1	0.7	77.1	3.7
Aged 30 to 34	679,650	16,691	108,353	4,372	527,270	22,963	2.5	15.9	0.6	77.6	3.4
Minnesota, total	**4,866,164**	**145,120**	**154,660**	**58,314**	**4,405,511**	**102,559**	**3.0**	**3.2**	**1.2**	**90.5**	**2.1**
Total, aged 15 to 34	**1,359,990**	**55,524**	**52,898**	**20,639**	**1,195,053**	**35,876**	**4.1**	**3.9**	**1.5**	**87.9**	**2.6**
Aged 15 to 19	385,818	16,127	15,661	6,844	337,153	10,033	4.2	4.1	1.8	87.4	2.6
Aged 20 to 24	357,519	13,275	12,943	5,388	316,625	9,287	3.7	3.6	1.5	88.6	2.6
Aged 25 to 29	296,442	12,766	11,533	4,275	259,733	8,136	4.3	3.9	1.4	87.6	2.7
Aged 30 to 34	320,211	13,356	12,761	4,132	281,542	8,420	4.2	4.0	1.3	87.9	2.6

(continued)

(continued from previous page)

	non-Hispanic					non-Hispanic				
	total	Asian	black	Native American	white	Hispanic	Asian	black	Native American	white	Hispanic
Mississippi, total	**2,815,653**	**20,902**	**1,031,240**	**10,132**	**1,727,748**	**25,630**	**0.7%**	**36.6%**	**0.4%**	**61.4%**	**0.9%**
Total, aged 15 to 34	**829,894**	**7,446**	**348,352**	**3,486**	**461,952**	**8,659**	**0.9**	**42.0**	**0.4**	**55.7**	**1.0**
Aged 15 to 19	209,310	1,691	92,134	1,004	112,508	1,972	0.8	44.0	0.5	53.8	0.9
Aged 20 to 24	216,463	1,694	96,372	908	115,220	2,270	0.8	44.5	0.4	53.2	1.0
Aged 25 to 29	196,763	2,080	83,231	808	108,346	2,298	1.1	42.3	0.4	55.1	1.2
Aged 30 to 34	207,359	1,981	76,615	766	125,879	2,119	1.0	36.9	0.4	60.7	1.0
Missouri, total	**5,508,337**	**64,449**	**620,633**	**18,496**	**4,706,327**	**98,432**	**1.2**	**11.3**	**0.3**	**85.4**	**1.8**
Total, aged 15 to 34	**1,512,588**	**21,597**	**194,121**	**6,120**	**1,257,068**	**33,683**	**1.4**	**12.8**	**0.4**	**83.1**	**2.2**
Aged 15 to 19	408,023	4,483	56,508	1,541	337,015	8,475	1.1	13.8	0.4	82.6	2.1
Aged 20 to 24	390,033	4,754	51,189	1,481	323,793	8,816	1.2	13.1	0.4	83.0	2.3
Aged 25 to 29	339,060	5,908	42,274	1,535	281,060	8,284	1.7	12.5	0.5	82.9	2.4
Aged 30 to 34	375,471	6,452	44,149	1,563	315,200	8,108	1.7	11.8	0.4	83.9	2.2
Montana, total	**882,820**	**5,741**	**2,697**	**58,246**	**798,514**	**17,621**	**0.7**	**0.3**	**6.6**	**90.5**	**2.0**
Total, aged 15 to 34	**248,078**	**2,105**	**1,226**	**20,305**	**218,538**	**5,903**	**0.8**	**0.5**	**8.2**	**88.1**	**2.4**
Aged 15 to 19	68,421	591	264	6,609	59,406	1,550	0.9	0.4	9.7	86.8	2.3
Aged 20 to 24	70,188	488	262	5,572	62,131	1,736	0.7	0.4	7.9	88.5	2.5
Aged 25 to 29	57,874	576	376	4,469	51,069	1,384	1.0	0.6	7.7	88.2	2.4
Aged 30 to 34	51,594	450	324	3,654	45,933	1,233	0.9	0.6	7.1	89.0	2.4

(continued)

(continued from previous page)

	total	non-Hispanic				Hispanic	non-Hispanic				Hispanic
		Asian	black	Native American	white		Asian	black	Native American	white	
Nebraska, total	**1,684,819**	**23,665**	**66,897**	**14,444**	**1,496,600**	**83,213**	**1.4%**	**4.0%**	**0.9%**	**88.8%**	**4.9%**
Total, aged 15 to 34	**482,317**	**8,541**	**22,961**	**4,908**	**414,998**	**30,909**	**1.8**	**4.8**	**1.0**	**86.0**	**6.4**
Aged 15 to 19	131,178	2,067	6,644	1,525	112,489	8,454	1.6	5.1	1.2	85.8	6.4
Aged 20 to 24	129,525	1,871	6,064	1,305	112,101	8,184	1.4	4.7	1.0	86.5	6.3
Aged 25 to 29	110,704	2,252	5,134	1,105	95,228	6,986	2.0	4.6	1.0	86.0	6.3
Aged 30 to 34	110,909	2,351	5,120	973	95,180	7,285	2.1	4.6	0.9	85.8	6.6
Nevada, total	**2,023,150**	**94,375**	**140,237**	**28,871**	**1,399,984**	**359,683**	**4.7**	**6.9**	**1.4**	**69.2**	**17.8**
Total, aged 15 to 34	**532,278**	**27,566**	**43,190**	**8,826**	**332,692**	**120,004**	**5.2**	**8.1**	**1.7**	**62.5**	**22.5**
Aged 15 to 19	149,264	6,895	13,215	2,748	92,949	33,457	4.6	8.9	1.8	62.3	22.4
Aged 20 to 24	130,196	6,053	11,034	2,230	80,012	30,868	4.6	8.5	1.7	61.5	23.7
Aged 25 to 29	117,231	6,802	9,008	1,869	72,624	26,928	5.8	7.7	1.6	61.9	23.0
Aged 30 to 34	135,586	7,817	9,932	1,979	87,106	28,752	5.8	7.3	1.5	64.2	21.2
New Hampshire, total	**1,227,695**	**16,211**	**7,814**	**2,463**	**1,180,038**	**21,170**	**1.3**	**0.6**	**0.2**	**96.1**	**1.7**
Total, aged 15 to 34	**328,173**	**5,686**	**2,744**	**852**	**311,627**	**7,264**	**1.7**	**0.8**	**0.3**	**95.0**	**2.2**
Aged 15 to 19	95,592	1,305	648	222	91,403	2,015	1.4	0.7	0.2	95.6	2.1
Aged 20 to 24	80,557	1,195	681	202	76,721	1,758	1.5	0.8	0.3	95.2	2.2
Aged 25 to 29	64,533	1,371	638	178	60,683	1,663	2.1	1.0	0.3	94.0	2.6
Aged 30 to 34	87,492	1,814	777	251	82,820	1,829	2.1	0.9	0.3	94.7	2.1

(continued)

(continued from previous page)

| | non-Hispanic | | | | | | non-Hispanic | | | | |
	total	Asian	black	Native American	white	Hispanic	Asian	black	Native American	white	Hispanic
New Jersey, total	**8,233,712**	**494,767**	**1,106,547**	**14,165**	**5,538,618**	**1,079,614**	**6.0%**	**13.4%**	**0.2%**	**67.3%**	**13.1%**
Total, aged 15 to 34	**2,059,579**	**141,997**	**322,111**	**3,942**	**1,254,458**	**337,070**	**6.9**	**15.6**	**0.2**	**60.9**	**16.4**
Aged 15 to 19	574,649	35,990	89,979	1,072	360,311	87,296	6.3	15.7	0.2	62.7	15.2
Aged 20 to 24	500,360	32,891	79,813	877	302,448	84,332	6.6	16.0	0.2	60.4	16.9
Aged 25 to 29	454,026	34,091	72,486	931	267,362	79,155	7.5	16.0	0.2	58.9	17.4
Aged 30 to 34	530,544	39,024	79,833	1,063	324,337	86,287	7.4	15.0	0.2	61.1	16.3
New Mexico, total	**1,804,261**	**22,325**	**31,983**	**163,333**	**835,261**	**751,358**	**1.2**	**1.8**	**9.1**	**46.3**	**41.6**
Total, aged 15 to 34	**521,500**	**7,322**	**10,685**	**54,712**	**205,676**	**243,105**	**1.4**	**2.0**	**10.5**	**39.4**	**46.6**
Aged 15 to 19	145,853	1,785	2,766	16,637	55,408	69,256	1.2	1.9	11.4	38.0	47.5
Aged 20 to 24	144,840	1,709	2,784	13,873	55,316	71,158	1.2	1.9	9.6	38.2	49.1
Aged 25 to 29	118,778	1,818	2,664	12,234	46,957	55,104	1.5	2.2	10.3	39.5	46.4
Aged 30 to 34	112,029	2,009	2,471	11,968	47,995	47,587	1.8	2.2	10.7	42.8	42.5
New York, total	**18,506,065**	**1,066,459**	**2,685,962**	**54,345**	**11,881,393**	**2,817,905**	**5.8**	**14.5**	**0.3**	**64.2**	**15.2**
Total, aged 15 to 34	**4,807,941**	**315,193**	**792,787**	**17,526**	**2,823,285**	**859,150**	**6.6**	**16.5**	**0.4**	**58.7**	**17.9**
Aged 15 to 19	1,253,005	70,492	218,644	4,721	736,117	223,032	5.6	17.4	0.4	58.7	17.8
Aged 20 to 24	1,144,852	66,298	191,445	3,895	669,724	213,490	5.8	16.7	0.3	58.5	18.6
Aged 25 to 29	1,099,691	82,625	180,371	4,104	629,716	202,875	7.5	16.4	0.4	57.3	18.4
Aged 30 to 34	1,310,393	95,777	202,327	4,806	787,729	219,753	7.3	15.4	0.4	60.1	16.8

(continued)

(continued from previous page)

| | non-Hispanic | | | | | | non-Hispanic | | | | |
	total	Asian	black	Native American	white	Hispanic	Asian	black	Native American	white	Hispanic
North Carolina, total	**8,006,174**	**115,792**	**1,741,574**	**100,761**	**5,850,794**	**197,253**	**1.4%**	**21.8%**	**1.3%**	**73.1%**	**2.5%**
Total, aged 15 to 34	**2,166,436**	**37,054**	**539,483**	**32,419**	**1,486,848**	**70,632**	**1.7**	**24.9**	**1.5**	**68.6**	**3.3**
Aged 15 to 19	566,491	8,753	152,354	9,223	378,313	17,848	1.5	26.9	1.6	66.8	3.2
Aged 20 to 24	510,846	8,065	136,075	7,694	341,656	17,356	1.6	26.6	1.5	66.9	3.4
Aged 25 to 29	494,412	9,510	120,769	7,061	338,686	18,387	1.9	24.4	1.4	68.5	3.7
Aged 30 to 34	594,687	10,725	130,285	8,442	428,194	17,041	1.8	21.9	1.4	72.0	2.9
North Dakota, total	**625,354**	**5,555**	**3,955**	**31,983**	**575,780**	**8,080**	**0.9**	**0.6**	**5.1**	**92.1**	**1.3**
Total, aged 15 to 34	**182,800**	**2,075**	**1,652**	**11,264**	**164,532**	**3,277**	**1.1**	**0.9**	**6.2**	**90.0**	**1.8**
Aged 15 to 19	47,605	448	337	3,629	42,435	757	0.9	0.7	7.6	89.1	1.6
Aged 20 to 24	49,430	431	334	2,892	45,076	696	0.9	0.7	5.9	91.2	1.4
Aged 25 to 29	44,082	580	492	2,422	39,607	981	1.3	1.1	5.5	89.8	2.2
Aged 30 to 34	41,684	617	489	2,320	37,414	843	1.5	1.2	5.6	89.8	2.0
Ohio, total	**11,133,387**	**138,613**	**1,285,748**	**20,324**	**9,494,770**	**193,933**	**1.2**	**11.5**	**0.2**	**85.3**	**1.7**
Total, aged 15 to 34	**3,041,162**	**43,401**	**391,163**	**5,942**	**2,535,511**	**65,144**	**1.4**	**12.9**	**0.2**	**83.4**	**2.1**
Aged 15 to 19	811,849	10,183	112,551	1,560	669,814	17,740	1.3	13.9	0.2	82.5	2.2
Aged 20 to 24	768,026	10,154	101,496	1,442	637,553	17,381	1.3	13.2	0.2	83.0	2.3
Aged 25 to 29	681,212	11,356	85,599	1,407	567,968	14,881	1.7	12.6	0.2	83.4	2.2
Aged 30 to 34	780,075	11,708	91,516	1,533	660,176	15,142	1.5	11.7	0.2	84.6	1.9

(continued)

		non-Hispanic						non-Hispanic			
	total	Asian	black	Native American	white	Hispanic	Asian	black	Native American	white	Hispanic
Oklahoma, total	**3,393,941**	**46,101**	**261,693**	**255,494**	**2,681,500**	**149,153**	**1.4%**	**7.7%**	**7.5%**	**79.0%**	**4.4%**
Total, aged 15 to 34	**961,914**	**15,159**	**87,812**	**86,080**	**719,891**	**52,971**	**1.6**	**9.1**	**8.9**	**74.8**	**5.5**
Aged 15 to 19	253,888	3,381	24,317	24,572	187,121	14,497	1.3	9.6	9.7	73.7	5.7
Aged 20 to 24	253,554	3,439	24,234	22,785	188,291	14,805	1.4	9.6	9.0	74.3	5.8
Aged 25 to 29	226,152	4,265	21,294	19,680	168,408	12,504	1.9	9.4	8.7	74.5	5.5
Aged 30 to 34	228,320	4,074	17,967	19,044	176,071	11,164	1.8	7.9	8.3	77.1	4.9
Oregon, total	**3,383,144**	**116,429**	**56,341**	**40,239**	**2,935,130**	**235,005**	**3.4**	**1.7**	**1.2**	**86.8**	**6.9**
Total, aged 15 to 34	**917,461**	**38,789**	**19,070**	**13,220**	**761,319**	**85,064**	**4.2**	**2.1**	**1.4**	**83.0**	**9.3**
Aged 15 to 19	244,704	8,697	5,297	3,758	203,942	23,010	3.6	2.2	1.5	83.3	9.4
Aged 20 to 24	236,963	8,861	4,893	3,297	197,025	22,887	3.7	2.1	1.4	83.1	9.7
Aged 25 to 29	210,420	10,105	4,358	3,111	173,442	19,404	4.8	2.1	1.5	82.4	9.2
Aged 30 to 34	225,375	11,126	4,523	3,054	186,910	19,762	4.9	2.0	1.4	82.9	8.8
Pennsylvania, total	**11,900,815**	**212,698**	**1,133,085**	**14,443**	**10,190,796**	**349,794**	**1.8**	**9.5**	**0.1**	**85.6**	**2.9**
Total, aged 15 to 34	**3,086,667**	**69,829**	**334,612**	**4,444**	**2,558,003**	**119,778**	**2.3**	**10.8**	**0.1**	**82.9**	**3.9**
Aged 15 to 19	849,062	16,314	99,371	1,184	699,044	33,149	1.9	11.7	0.1	82.3	3.9
Aged 20 to 24	776,414	16,341	83,478	1,036	644,717	30,842	2.1	10.8	0.1	83.0	4.0
Aged 25 to 29	666,843	17,654	71,754	1,017	548,967	27,451	2.6	10.8	0.2	82.3	4.1
Aged 30 to 34	794,348	19,519	80,010	1,207	665,276	28,335	2.5	10.1	0.2	83.8	3.6

(continued)

(continued from previous page)

		non-Hispanic						non-Hispanic			
	total	Asian	black	Native American	white	Hispanic	Asian	black	Native American	white	Hispanic
Rhode Island, total	**1,022,464**	**24,793**	**41,553**	**4,474**	**874,816**	**76,827**	**2.4%**	**4.1%**	**0.4%**	**85.6%**	**7.5%**
Total, aged 15 to 34	**270,288**	**8,837**	**14,113**	**1,300**	**220,704**	**25,335**	**3.3**	**5.2**	**0.5**	**81.7**	**9.4**
Aged 15 to 19	72,972	2,180	4,009	365	59,296	7,122	3.0	5.5	0.5	81.3	9.8
Aged 20 to 24	63,762	2,181	3,497	280	51,740	6,064	3.4	5.5	0.4	81.1	9.5
Aged 25 to 29	57,227	2,303	3,299	267	45,880	5,476	4.0	5.8	0.5	80.2	9.6
Aged 30 to 34	76,328	2,173	3,208	387	63,787	6,674	2.8	4.3	0.5	83.6	8.7
South Carolina, total	**3,959,112**	**37,136**	**1,168,538**	**8,931**	**2,685,792**	**58,714**	**0.9**	**29.5**	**0.2**	**67.8**	**1.5**
Total, aged 15 to 34	**1,105,522**	**12,469**	**373,137**	**3,184**	**695,821**	**20,912**	**1.1**	**33.8**	**0.3**	**62.9**	**1.9**
Aged 15 to 19	273,069	2,577	99,827	702	165,315	4,649	0.9	36.6	0.3	60.5	1.7
Aged 20 to 24	270,399	2,708	97,823	745	163,860	5,264	1.0	36.2	0.3	60.6	1.9
Aged 25 to 29	262,491	3,511	87,295	868	165,174	5,643	1.3	33.3	0.3	62.9	2.1
Aged 30 to 34	299,562	3,673	88,192	870	201,472	5,356	1.2	29.4	0.3	67.3	1.8
South Dakota, total	**741,566**	**5,317**	**4,967**	**64,053**	**657,305**	**9,924**	**0.7**	**0.7**	**8.6**	**88.6**	**1.3**
Total, aged 15 to 34	**214,960**	**1,926**	**2,012**	**23,116**	**184,381**	**3,526**	**0.9**	**0.9**	**10.8**	**85.8**	**1.6**
Aged 15 to 19	58,740	474	381	7,828	49,131	925	0.8	0.6	13.3	83.6	1.6
Aged 20 to 24	59,804	421	394	6,296	51,760	933	0.7	0.7	10.5	86.6	1.6
Aged 25 to 29	50,390	497	563	4,796	43,613	921	1.0	1.1	9.5	86.6	1.8
Aged 30 to 34	46,027	534	673	4,196	39,876	747	1.2	1.5	9.1	86.6	1.6

(continued)

(continued from previous page)

| | | non-Hispanic | | | | | non-Hispanic | | | | |
	total	Asian	black	Native American	white	Hispanic	Asian	black	Native American	white	Hispanic
Tennessee, total	**5,647,268**	**58,368**	**939,824**	**11,069**	**4,564,647**	**73,359**	**1.0%**	**16.6%**	**0.2%**	**80.8%**	**1.3%**
Total, aged 15 to 34	**1,522,342**	**18,812**	**295,000**	**3,502**	**1,179,500**	**25,528**	**1.2**	**19.4**	**0.2**	**77.5**	**1.7**
Aged 15 to 19	382,492	4,243	81,473	858	289,805	6,112	1.1	21.3	0.2	75.8	1.6
Aged 20 to 24	372,672	4,321	77,070	856	283,808	6,618	1.2	20.7	0.2	76.2	1.8
Aged 25 to 29	352,564	4,843	67,339	877	273,255	6,249	1.4	19.1	0.2	77.5	1.8
Aged 30 to 34	414,613	5,406	69,118	910	332,632	6,548	1.3	16.7	0.2	80.2	1.6
Texas, total	**20,902,754**	**573,589**	**2,406,664**	**59,250**	**11,334,734**	**6,528,517**	**2.7**	**11.5**	**0.3**	**54.2**	**31.2**
Total, aged 15 to 34	**6,091,340**	**177,477**	**780,221**	**17,631**	**2,905,221**	**2,210,790**	**2.9**	**12.8**	**0.3**	**47.7**	**36.3**
Aged 15 to 19	1,598,155	42,341	209,649	4,464	755,922	585,779	2.6	13.1	0.3	47.3	36.7
Aged 20 to 24	1,580,078	40,515	201,566	4,278	733,030	600,688	2.6	12.8	0.3	46.4	38.0
Aged 25 to 29	1,419,605	44,073	182,137	4,479	664,446	524,471	3.1	12.8	0.3	46.8	36.9
Aged 30 to 34	1,493,503	50,549	186,869	4,410	751,823	499,853	3.4	12.5	0.3	50.3	33.5
Utah, total	**2,308,066**	**60,284**	**16,097**	**28,482**	**2,032,956**	**170,248**	**2.6**	**0.7**	**1.2**	**88.1**	**7.4**
Total, aged 15 to 34	**786,879**	**21,581**	**6,228**	**10,445**	**686,853**	**61,773**	**2.7**	**0.8**	**1.3**	**87.3**	**7.9**
Aged 15 to 19	194,692	4,931	1,449	3,051	169,263	15,999	2.5	0.7	1.6	86.9	8.2
Aged 20 to 24	207,110	4,812	1,624	2,577	181,422	16,675	2.3	0.8	1.2	87.6	8.1
Aged 25 to 29	207,476	5,818	1,617	2,508	182,087	15,445	2.8	0.8	1.2	87.8	7.4
Aged 30 to 34	177,601	6,019	1,537	2,310	154,081	13,654	3.4	0.9	1.3	86.8	7.7

(continued)

(continued from previous page)

| | total | non-Hispanic | | | | | non-Hispanic | | | | |
		Asian	black	Native American	white	Hispanic	Asian	black	Native American	white	Hispanic
Vermont, total	**597,053**	**5,389**	**3,002**	**1,330**	**581,891**	**5,441**	**0.9%**	**0.5%**	**0.2%**	**97.5%**	**0.9%**
Total, aged 15 to 34	**162,762**	**2,060**	**1,223**	**513**	**157,028**	**1,939**	**1.3**	**0.8**	**0.3**	**96.5**	**1.2**
Aged 15 to 19	43,842	426	273	97	42,671	376	1.0	0.6	0.2	97.3	0.9
Aged 20 to 24	41,646	495	294	108	40,190	560	1.2	0.7	0.3	96.5	1.3
Aged 25 to 29	34,386	552	291	91	32,947	505	1.6	0.8	0.3	95.8	1.5
Aged 30 to 34	42,887	587	364	218	41,220	499	1.4	0.8	0.5	96.1	1.2
Virginia, total	**7,018,920**	**274,299**	**1,389,102**	**15,712**	**5,051,800**	**288,006**	**3.9**	**19.8**	**0.2**	**72.0**	**4.1**
Total, aged 15 to 34	**1,928,181**	**87,026**	**425,542**	**4,976**	**1,313,310**	**97,327**	**4.5**	**22.1**	**0.3**	**68.1**	**5.0**
Aged 15 to 19	475,293	18,747	110,789	1,079	322,251	22,427	3.9	23.3	0.2	67.8	4.7
Aged 20 to 24	456,416	18,530	106,154	1,043	307,338	23,352	4.1	23.3	0.2	67.3	5.1
Aged 25 to 29	457,095	22,064	100,781	1,391	308,131	24,728	4.8	22.0	0.3	67.4	5.4
Aged 30 to 34	539,376	27,684	107,818	1,463	375,590	26,821	5.1	20.0	0.3	69.6	5.0
Washington, total	**5,869,110**	**359,064**	**192,157**	**93,375**	**4,811,861**	**412,653**	**6.1**	**3.3**	**1.6**	**82.0**	**7.0**
Total, aged 15 to 34	**1,630,572**	**117,391**	**64,110**	**30,497**	**1,268,910**	**149,664**	**7.2**	**3.9**	**1.9**	**77.8**	**9.2**
Aged 15 to 19	433,825	28,839	17,419	8,956	338,641	39,970	6.6	4.0	2.1	78.1	9.2
Aged 20 to 24	416,284	27,794	16,249	7,853	324,343	40,045	6.7	3.9	1.9	77.9	9.6
Aged 25 to 29	374,396	28,265	15,122	6,893	288,562	35,553	7.5	4.0	1.8	77.1	9.5
Aged 30 to 34	406,067	32,493	15,320	6,795	317,364	34,096	8.0	3.8	1.7	78.2	8.4

(continued)

(continued from previous page)

		non-Hispanic					non-Hispanic				
	total	Asian	black	Native American	white	Hispanic	Asian	black	Native American	white	Hispanic
West Virginia, total	**1,751,951**	**8,751**	**52,115**	**2,094**	**1,678,399**	**10,592**	**0.5%**	**3.0%**	**0.1%**	**95.8%**	**0.6%**
Total, aged 15 to 34	**475,638**	**2,901**	**16,841**	**683**	**451,892**	**3,321**	**0.6**	**3.5**	**0.1**	**95.0**	**0.7**
Aged 15 to 19	114,693	647	4,355	155	108,749	787	0.6	3.8	0.1	94.8	0.7
Aged 20 to 24	120,712	785	4,729	152	114,167	880	0.6	3.9	0.1	94.6	0.7
Aged 25 to 29	116,210	870	4,230	190	110,083	837	0.7	3.6	0.2	94.7	0.7
Aged 30 to 34	124,024	599	3,528	186	118,892	818	0.5	2.8	0.2	95.9	0.7
Wisconsin, total	**5,267,492**	**90,966**	**297,975**	**44,610**	**4,682,908**	**151,032**	**1.7**	**5.7**	**0.8**	**88.9**	**2.9**
Total, aged 15 to 34	**1,472,260**	**33,860**	**102,773**	**15,783**	**1,265,995**	**53,849**	**2.3**	**7.0**	**1.1**	**86.0**	**3.7**
Aged 15 to 19	407,549	10,034	30,908	4,823	346,243	15,541	2.5	7.6	1.2	85.0	3.8
Aged 20 to 24	389,376	8,656	26,962	4,031	335,210	14,518	2.2	6.9	1.0	86.1	3.7
Aged 25 to 29	328,276	7,804	21,996	3,460	282,861	12,155	2.4	6.7	1.1	86.2	3.7
Aged 30 to 34	347,059	7,365	22,908	3,469	301,681	11,636	2.1	6.6	1.0	86.9	3.4
Wyoming, total	**488,358**	**4,112**	**3,561**	**10,604**	**438,687**	**31,394**	**0.8**	**0.7**	**2.2**	**89.8**	**6.4**
Total, aged 15 to 34	**146,889**	**1,611**	**1,401**	**3,838**	**129,199**	**10,840**	**1.1**	**1.0**	**2.6**	**88.0**	**7.4**
Aged 15 to 19	38,710	403	274	1,140	33,949	2,945	1.0	0.7	2.9	87.7	7.6
Aged 20 to 24	42,145	400	345	1,055	37,026	3,319	0.9	0.8	2.5	87.9	7.9
Aged 25 to 29	35,108	373	398	870	30,949	2,518	1.1	1.1	2.5	88.2	7.2
Aged 30 to 34	30,927	436	383	774	27,275	2,058	1.4	1.2	2.5	88.2	6.7

Source: Projections by New Strategist

Twentysomethings Are on the Move

Young adults are more likely than older Americans to move.

Young adults are far more likely than their elders to move from one home to another. Fewer than 10 percent of people aged 45 or older move in a typical year, but the proportion of young adults who change homes is substantially higher. Between March 1998 and March 1999, 26 percent of people aged 15 to 34 moved to a different home. Twentysomethings have the highest mobility rate: nearly one-third moved during the year.

Of the 20 million 15-to-34-year-olds who changed residences, the majority (58 percent) remained in the same county. Twenty-one percent moved to a different county, but did not leave the state. Only 17 percent moved to a different state.

One reason for the higher mobility of young adults is that many do not have children in the household. Once children are involved, moving becomes a more difficult proposition. Among householders aged 25 to 34, one-third of those without children moved in 1998–99, compared with only one-quarter of those with children at home.

♦ With the number of young adults growing, the many businesses that serve movers will see more customers. Expect demand for apartments, home furnishings, and appliances to increase.

Geographic Mobility of People Aged 15 to 34, 1998 to 1999

(total number and percent of people aged 1 or older and aged 15 to 34 who moved between March 1998 and March 1999, by type of move; numbers in thousands)

	total	nonmover	movers						
			total	same county	different county, same state	different state, same division	different division, same region	different region	movers from abroad
Total, aged 1 or older	267,933	225,297	42,636	25,268	8,423	3,250	988	3,278	1,429
Total, aged 15 to 34	76,396	56,780	19,616	11,385	4,081	1,452	497	1,430	770
Aged 15 to 17	11,955	10,380	1,575	985	275	100	20	108	87
Aged 18 to 19	7,909	6,300	1,609	893	346	127	47	123	73
Aged 20 to 24	18,058	12,065	5,993	3,460	1,282	449	156	428	217
Aged 25 to 29	18,639	12,732	5,907	3,355	1,252	436	163	482	219
Aged 30 to 34	19,835	15,303	4,532	2,692	926	340	111	289	174
PERCENT DISTRIBUTION BY MOBILITY STATUS									
Total, aged 1 or older	100.0%	84.1%	15.9%	9.4%	3.1%	1.2%	0.4%	1.2%	0.5%
Total, aged 15 to 34	100.0	74.3	25.7	14.9	5.3	1.9	0.7	1.9	1.0
Aged 15 to 17	100.0	86.8	13.2	8.2	2.3	0.8	0.2	0.9	0.7
Aged 18 to 19	100.0	79.7	20.3	11.3	4.4	1.6	0.6	1.6	0.9
Aged 20 to 24	100.0	66.8	33.2	19.2	7.1	2.5	0.9	2.4	1.2
Aged 25 to 29	100.0	68.3	31.7	18.0	6.7	2.3	0.9	2.6	1.2
Aged 30 to 34	100.0	77.2	22.8	13.6	4.7	1.7	0.6	1.5	0.9

(continued)

(continued from previous page)

PERCENT DISTRIBUTION OF MOVERS BY TYPE OF MOVE

	total	nonmover	total	same county	different county, same state	different state, same division	different division, same region	different region	movers from abroad
							movers		
Total, aged 1 or older	–	–	**100.0%**	**59.3%**	**19.8%**	**7.6%**	**2.3%**	**7.7%**	**3.4%**
Total, aged 15 to 34	–	–	**100.0**	**58.0**	**20.8**	**7.4**	**2.5**	**7.3**	**3.9**
Aged 15 to 17	–	–	100.0	62.5	17.5	6.3	1.3	6.9	5.5
Aged 18 to 19	–	–	100.0	55.5	21.5	7.9	2.9	7.6	4.5
Aged 20 to 24	–	–	100.0	57.7	21.4	7.5	2.6	7.1	3.6
Aged 25 to 29	–	–	100.0	56.8	21.2	7.4	2.8	8.2	3.7
Aged 30 to 34	–	–	100.0	59.4	20.4	7.5	2.4	6.4	3.8

Note: (–) means not applicable.
Source: Bureau of the Census, Internet site <www.census.gov/population/socdemo/migration/p20-531/tab01.txt>; calculations by the author

POPULATION

GENERATION X **267**

Mobility of Family Householders Aged 15 to 34 by Presence of Children, 1998 to 1999

(total number and percent distribution of householders aged 15 to 34 by presence of own children under age 18 at home and mobility status between March 1998 and March 1999; numbers in thousands)

	total	nonmovers	movers total	same county	different county, same state	different state, same division	different division, same region	different region	movers from abroad
Total aged 15 to 24	**5,770**	**2,642**	**3,128**	**1,833**	**659**	**256**	**67**	**216**	**97**
No children under 18	3,776	1,612	2,164	1,164	518	189	48	165	80
With children under 18	1,994	1,030	965	669	141	68	19	51	17
Under age 6 only	1,652	832	820	554	127	52	19	51	17
Under age 6 and 6 to 17	224	131	94	77	5	12	–	–	–
Aged 6 to 17 only	118	67	51	38	9	4	–	–	–
Total aged 25 to 34	**18,826**	**13,283**	**5,543**	**3,366**	**1,089**	**399**	**146**	**385**	**158**
No children under 18	8,743	5,760	2,983	1,679	651	249	85	214	105
With children under 18	10,083	7,522	2,559	1,687	438	150	62	170	52
Under age 6 only	4,179	3,028	1,151	703	221	74	31	100	22
Under age 6 and 6 to 17	3,162	2,429	732	518	103	45	6	36	24
Aged 6 to 17 only	2,742	2,065	676	466	114	31	25	34	6

(continued)

(continued from previous page)

PERCENT DISTRIBUTION BY MOBILITY STATUS

	total	nonmovers	movers total	same county	different county, same state	different state, same division	different division, same region	different region	movers from abroad
Total aged 15 to 24	**100.0%**	**45.8%**	**54.2%**	**31.8%**	**11.4%**	**4.4%**	**1.2%**	**3.7%**	**1.7%**
No children under 18	100.0	42.7	57.3	30.8	13.7	5.0	1.3	4.4	2.1
With children under 18	100.0	51.7	48.4	33.6	7.1	3.4	1.0	2.6	0.9
Under age 6 only	100.0	50.4	49.6	33.5	7.7	3.1	1.2	3.1	1.0
Under age 6 and 6 to 17	100.0	58.5	42.0	34.4	2.2	5.4	–	–	–
Aged 6 to 17 only	100.0	56.8	43.2	32.2	7.6	3.4	–	–	–
Total aged 25 to 34	**100.0%**	**70.6%**	**29.4%**	**17.9%**	**5.8%**	**2.1%**	**0.8%**	**2.0%**	**0.8%**
No children under 18	100.0	65.9	34.1	19.2	7.4	2.8	1.0	2.4	1.2
With children under 18	100.0	74.6	25.4	16.7	4.3	1.5	0.6	1.7	0.5
Under age 6 only	100.0	72.5	27.5	16.8	5.3	1.8	0.7	2.4	0.5
Under age 6 and 6 to 17	100.0	76.8	23.1	16.4	3.3	1.4	0.2	1.1	0.8
Aged 6 to 17 only	100.0	75.3	24.7	17.0	4.2	1.1	0.9	1.2	0.2

(continued)

(continued from previous page)

PERCENT DISTRIBUTION OF MOVERS BY TYPE OF MOVE

	total	nonmovers	movers						
			total	same county	different county, same state	different state, same division	different division, same region	different region	movers from abroad
Total aged 15 to 24	–	–	**100.0%**	**58.6%**	**21.1%**	**8.2%**	**2.1%**	**6.9%**	**3.1%**
No children under 18	–	–	100.0	53.8	23.9	8.7	2.2	7.6	3.7
With children under 18	–	–	100.0	69.3	14.6	7.0	2.0	5.3	1.8
Under age 6 only	–	–	100.0	67.6	15.5	6.3	2.3	6.2	2.1
Under age 6 and 6 to 17	–	–	100.0	81.9	5.3	12.8	–	–	–
Aged 6 to 17 only	–	–	100.0	74.5	17.6	7.8	–	–	–
Total aged 25 to 34	–	–	**100.0**	**60.7**	**19.6**	**7.2**	**2.6**	**6.9**	**2.9**
No children under 18	–	–	100.0	56.3	21.8	8.3	2.8	7.2	3.5
With children under 18	–	–	100.0	65.9	17.1	5.9	2.4	6.6	2.0
Under age 6 only	–	–	100.0	61.1	19.2	6.4	2.7	8.7	1.9
Under age 6 and 6 to 17	–	–	100.0	70.8	14.1	6.1	0.8	4.9	3.3
Aged 6 to 17 only	–	–	100.0	68.9	16.9	4.6	3.7	5.0	0.9

Note: (–) means not applicable or sample too small to make a reliable estimate.
Source: Bureau of the Census, Geographical Mobility: March 1998 to March 1999 (Update), detailed tables for Current Population Report Report P20-531, 2000; Internet site <www.census.gov/population/www/socdemo/migrate.html#cps>; calculations the author

Mobility Since Age 16, 1998

"When you were 16 years old, were you living in this same city?"

(percent of people aged 18 or older responding by age, 1998)

	same city	different city	different state
Total people	39%	26%	35%
Aged 18 to 24	59	19	22
Aged 25 to 34	42	27	31
Aged 35 to 44	35	29	36
Aged 45 to 54	36	23	40
Aged 55 to 64	33	26	41
Aged 65 or older	37	26	37

Source: 1998 General Social Survey, National Opinion Research Center, University of Chicago; calculations by the author

8

Spending

♦ Spending by young adults has finally surpassed the 1990 level, after years of decline. Spending by householders under age 25, at $21,725 in 1999, was 3 percent above the 1990 level, after adjusting for inflation. Spending by householders aged 25 to 34 increased 1 percent.

♦ Although overall spending rose, young adults spent less in many categories including food, alcoholic beverages, personal care products and services, and reading materials.

♦ The youngest householders (aged 15 to 24) spend less than the average household on most categories of goods and services. They spend more than average on products and services for infants, however, and much more than average on education.

♦ Householders aged 25 to 34 are average spenders, but they spend far more than average on products and services for children. They also spend more on rent, beer, and used cars.

Spending by Young Adults Increased

Spending in some categories is lower than in 1990, however.

Americans sharply cut their spending in the early 1990s and it has only recently returned to 1990 levels. Spending by all households was 2 percent higher in 1999 than in 1990, after adjusting for inflation. Householders under age 25 spent 3 percent more and those aged 25 to 34 spent 1 percent more.

One big change for the youngest householders has been a shift in food spending. Householders under age 25 spent 12 percent more on food at home and 19 percent less on food away from home in 1999 than in 1990. They spent 9 percent less on alcoholic beverages.

Householders aged 25 to 34 cut their spending on alcohol even more—down 22 percent. Overall, their food spending is still about 2 percent less than in 1990.

Young adults spent more on housing and transportation in 1999 than in 1990. Householders under age 25 reduced their apparel spending by 10 percent while those aged 25 to 34 spent 2 percent more. Conversely, the youngest householders spent 8 percent more on entertainment while those aged 25 to 34 spent 5 percent less.

The Internet may be taking its toll on print media, at least among young adults. Spending on reading material was down 27 percent among householders under age 25 and 32 percent among those aged 25 to 34.

♦ Spending by young adults was not much higher in 1999 than in 1990. Although the slowing economy may prompt young householders to cut back, they would be hard pressed to reduce spending by much.

Average Spending of Householders under Age 35, 1990 and 1999

(average annual spending of total consumer units and consumer units headed by people under age 35, 1990 and 1999; percent change, 1990–99; in 1999 dollars)

	total consumer units			under age 25			aged 25 to 34		
	1990	1999	percent change 1990–99	1990	1999	percent change 1990–99	1990	1999	percent change 1990–99
Number of consumer units (in 000s)	96,968	108,465	11.9%	7,581	8,164	7.7%	21,287	19,332	–9.2%
Average before-tax income	$40,648	$43,951	8.1	$17,959	$18,276	1.8	$41,204	$42,470	3.1
Average annual spending	36,176	37,027	2.4	21,064	21,725	3.1	35,840	36,181	1.0
FOOD	$5,476	$5,031	–8.1%	$3,519	$3,354	–4.7%	$5,226	$5,140	–1.6%
Food at home	3,168	2,915	–8.0	1,638	1,828	11.6	2,983	2,890	–3.1
Cereals and bakery products	469	448	–4.5	233	271	16.3	423	432	2.1
Cereals and cereal products	164	160	–2.4	92	102	10.9	159	170	6.9
Bakery products	306	288	–5.9	141	169	19.9	263	262	–0.4
Meats, poultry, fish, and eggs	851	749	–12.0	377	469	24.4	800	751	–6.1
Beef	278	220	–20.9	124	155	25.0	277	221	–20.2
Pork	168	157	–6.5	75	93	24.0	145	154	6.2
Other meats	126	97	–23.0	61	61	0.0	119	95	–20.2
Poultry	138	136	–1.4	50	82	64.0	131	148	13.0
Fish and seafood	105	106	1.0	45	59	31.1	93	103	10.8
Eggs	38	32	–15.8	22	19	–13.6	37	31	–16.2

(continued)

(continued from previous page)

	total consumer units			under age 25			aged 25 to 34		
	1990	1999	percent change 1990–99	1990	1999	percent change 1990–99	1990	1999	percent change 1990–99
Dairy products	$376	$322	–14.4%	$199	$195	–2.0%	$372	$322	–13.4%
Fresh milk and cream	178	122	–31.5	103	78	–24.3	181	124	–31.5
Other dairy products	198	200	1.0	96	117	21.9	191	198	3.7
Fruits and vegetables	520	500	–3.8	240	283	17.9	467	475	1.7
Fresh fruits	162	152	–6.2	59	77	30.5	144	136	–5.6
Fresh vegetables	150	149	–0.7	73	79	8.2	131	146	11.5
Processed fruits	119	113	–5.0	61	77	26.2	108	105	–2.8
Processed vegetables	89	86	–3.4	47	49	4.3	83	87	4.8
Other food at home	951	896	–5.8	589	610	3.6	920	910	–1.1
Sugar and other sweets	120	112	–6.7	61	71	16.4	103	99	–3.9
Fats and oils	87	84	–3.4	40	54	35.0	73	80	9.6
Miscellaneous foods	428	420	–1.9	307	300	–2.3	436	463	6.2
Nonalcoholic beverages	272	242	–11.0	162	167	3.1	264	236	–10.6
Food prepared by household on trips	45	39	–13.3	19	19	0.0	45	32	–28.9
Food away from home	**2,308**	**2,116**	**–8.3**	**1,881**	**1,526**	**–18.9**	**2,243**	**2,250**	**0.3**
ALCOHOLIC BEVERAGES	**373**	**318**	**–14.7**	**405**	**369**	**–8.9**	**465**	**365**	**–21.5**
HOUSING	**11,093**	**12,057**	**8.7**	**6,176**	**6,585**	**6.6**	**11,738**	**12,520**	**6.7**
Shelter	**6,164**	**7,016**	**13.8**	**3,842**	**4,140**	**7.8**	**7,030**	**7,613**	**8.3**

(continued)

(continued from previous page)

	total consumer units			under age 25			aged 25 to 34		
	1990	1999	percent change 1990–99	1990	1999	percent change 1990–99	1990	1999	percent change 1990–99
Owned dwellings	$3,764	$4,525	20.2%	$396	$596	50.5%	$3,702	$3,936	6.3%
Mortgage interest and charges	2,316	2,547	10.0	297	311	4.7	2,882	2,694	–6.5
Property taxes	761	1,123	47.6	34	168	394.1	387	751	94.1
Maintenance, repairs, insurance, other expenses	688	855	24.3	65	117	80.0	432	490	13.4
Rented dwellings	1,954	2,027	3.7	3,192	3,296	3.3	3,111	3,447	10.8
Other lodging	445	464	4.3	255	248	–2.7	217	230	6.0
Utilities, fuels, public services	**2,409**	**2,377**	**–1.3**	**1,155**	**1,166**	**1.0**	**2,147**	**2,249**	**4.8**
Natural gas	314	270	–14.0	120	92	–23.3	254	238	–6.3
Electricity	966	899	–6.9	404	426	5.4	851	811	–4.7
Fuel oil and other fuels	127	74	–41.7	22	14	–36.4	80	47	–41.3
Telephone services	755	849	12.5	548	562	2.6	770	924	20.0
Water and other public services	246	285	15.9	61	72	18.0	191	229	19.9
Household services	**569**	**666**	**17.0**	**186**	**181**	**–2.7**	**724**	**772**	**6.6**
Personal services	279	323	15.8	127	121	–4.7	572	573	0.2
Other household services	289	343	18.7	59	60	1.7	152	199	30.9
Housekeeping supplies	**518**	**498**	**–3.9**	**227**	**221**	**–2.6**	**469**	**441**	**–6.0**
Laundry and cleaning supplies	144	121	–16.0	60	64	6.7	144	117	–18.8
Other household products	218	250	14.7	75	86	14.7	191	211	10.5
Postage and stationery	156	127	–18.6	92	71	–22.8	134	113	–15.7

(continued)

(continued from previous page)

	total consumer units			under age 25			aged 25 to 34		
	1990	1999	percent change 1990–99	1990	1999	percent change 1990–99	1990	1999	percent change 1990–99
Household furnishings and equipment	**$1,434**	**$1,499**	**4.5%**	**$766**	**$877**	**14.5%**	**$1,370**	**$1,445**	**5.5%**
Household textiles	126	114	–9.5	50	41	–18.0	101	101	0.0
Furniture	395	365	–7.6	324	283	–12.7	426	435	2.1
Floor coverings	117	44	–62.4	11	11	0.0	69	37	–46.4
Major appliances	187	183	–2.1	83	91	9.6	191	176	–7.9
Small appliances, miscellaneous housewares	96	102	6.3	51	47	–7.8	88	82	–6.8
Miscellaneous household equipment	512	692	35.2	247	405	64.0	497	615	23.7
APPAREL AND SERVICES	**2,062**	**1,743**	**–15.5**	**1,318**	**1,192**	**–9.6**	**2,003**	**2,047**	**2.2**
Men and boys	**501**	**421**	**–16.0**	**402**	**238**	**–40.8**	**500**	**519**	**3.8**
Men, aged 16 or older	413	328	–20.6	386	209	–45.9	382	387	1.3
Boys, aged 2 to 15	89	93	4.5	17	29	70.6	117	133	13.7
Women and girls	**858**	**655**	**–23.7**	**402**	**422**	**5.0**	**724**	**709**	**–2.1**
Women, aged 16 or older	747	548	–26.6	370	377	1.9	602	579	–3.8
Girls, aged 2 to 15	111	107	–3.6	33	45	36.4	122	130	6.6
Children under age 2	**89**	**67**	**–24.7**	**107**	**99**	**–7.5**	**171**	**139**	**–18.7**
Footwear	**287**	**303**	**5.6**	**120**	**234**	**95.0**	**266**	**374**	**40.6**
Other apparel products and services	**329**	**297**	**–9.7**	**288**	**199**	**–30.9**	**342**	**306**	**–10.5**

(continued)

(continued from previous page)

	total consumer units			under age 25			aged 25 to 34		
	1990	1999	percent change 1990–99	1990	1999	percent change 1990–99	1990	1999	percent change 1990–99
TRANSPORTATION	**$6,526**	**$7,011**	**7.4%**	**$4,454**	**$5,037**	**13.1%**	**$6,899**	**$7,150**	**3.6%**
Vehicle purchases	**2,714**	**3,305**	**21.8**	**2,028**	**2,859**	**41.0**	**3,086**	**3,500**	**13.4**
Cars and trucks, new	1,477	1,628	10.2	936	857	–8.4	1,602	1,377	–14.0
Cars and trucks, used	1,208	1,641	35.8	1,064	1,974	85.5	1,431	2,034	42.1
Other vehicles	28	36	28.6	29	28	–3.4	52	89	71.2
Gasoline and motor oil	**1,335**	**1,055**	**–21.0**	**920**	**708**	**–23.0**	**1,377**	**1,066**	**–22.6**
Other vehicle expenses	**2,093**	**2,254**	**7.7**	**1,277**	**1,253**	**–1.9**	**2,152**	**2,249**	**4.5**
Vehicle finance charges	382	320	–16.2	247	209	–15.4	473	402	–15.0
Maintenance and repairs	751	664	–11.6	496	402	–19.0	738	554	–24.9
Vehicle insurance	718	756	5.3	412	408	–1.0	664	705	6.2
Vehicle rental, leases, licenses, other charges	242	513	112.0	124	234	88.7	277	588	112.3
Public transportation	**385**	**397**	**3.1**	**228**	**217**	**–4.8**	**284**	**335**	**18.0**
HEALTH CARE	**1,887**	**1,959**	**3.8**	**514**	**551**	**7.2**	**1,250**	**1,170**	**–6.4**
Health insurance	741	923	24.6	135	233	72.6	498	597	19.9
Medical services	716	558	–22.1	242	184	–24.0	498	351	–29.5
Drugs	321	370	15.3	83	97	16.9	172	162	–5.8
Medical supplies	108	109	0.9	52	36	–30.8	82	60	–26.8

(continued)

(continued from previous page)

	total consumer units			under age 25			aged 25 to 34		
	1990	1999	percent change 1990–99	1990	1999	percent change 1990–99	1990	1999	percent change 1990–99
ENTERTAINMENT	**$1,813**	**$1,891**	**4.3%**	**$1,062**	**$1,149**	**8.2%**	**$1,876**	**$1,776**	**–5.3%**
Fees and admissions	473	459	–3.0	278	262	–5.8	436	395	–9.4
Television, radio, sound equipment	579	608	5.0	438	485	10.7	641	636	–0.8
Pets, toys, and playground equipment	352	346	–1.7	149	185	24.2	391	375	–4.1
Other entertainment supplies, services	409	478	16.9	198	217	9.6	409	369	–9.8
PERSONAL CARE PRODUCTS AND SERVICES	**464**	**408**	**–12.1**	**270**	**254**	**–5.9**	**402**	**381**	**–5.2**
READING	**195**	**159**	**–18.5**	**96**	**70**	**–27.1**	**171**	**116**	**–32.2**
EDUCATION	**518**	**635**	**22.6**	**1,041**	**1,277**	**22.7**	**414**	**453**	**9.4**
TOBACCO PRODUCTS AND SMOKING SUPPLIES	**349**	**300**	**–14.0**	**275**	**220**	**–20.0**	**351**	**295**	**–16.0**
MISCELLANEOUS	**1,073**	**889**	**–17.1**	**509**	**370**	**–27.3**	**1,002**	**745**	**–25.6**
CASH CONTRIBUTIONS	**1,040**	**1,190**	**14.4**	**186**	**186**	**0.0**	**524**	**589**	**12.4**
PERSONAL INSURANCE AND PENSIONS	**3,304**	**3,436**	**4.0**	**1,239**	**1,110**	**–10.4**	**3,519**	**3,433**	**–2.4**
Life and other personal insurance	440	394	–10.5	62	61	–1.6	287	238	–17.1
Pensions and Social Security	2,865	3,042	6.2	1,175	1,049	–10.7	3,233	3,195	–1.2

(continued)

(continued from previous page)

	total consumer units			under age 25			aged 25 to 34		
	1990	*1999*	*percent change 1990–99*	*1990*	*1999*	*percent change 1990–99*	*1990*	*1999*	*percent change 1990–99*
PERSONAL TAXES	**$3,763**	**$3,588**	**–4.7%**	**$1,075**	**$845**	**–21.4%**	**$3,765**	**$3,065**	**–18.6%**
Federal income taxes	2,956	2,802	–5.2	818	630	–23.0	2,925	2,316	–20.8
State and local income taxes	711	616	–13.4	245	208	–15.1	798	671	–15.9
Other taxes	96	170	77.1	13	7	–46.2	42	78	85.7
GIFTS	**1,161**	**1,083**	**–6.7**	**535**	**515**	**–3.7**	**767**	**739**	**–3.7**
Food	**121**	**83**	**–31.4**	**32**	**19**	**–40.6**	**47**	**40**	**–14.9**
Housing	**296**	**292**	**–1.4**	**120**	**139**	**15.8**	**236**	**238**	**0.8**
Housekeeping supplies	45	41	–8.9	24	14	–41.7	45	39	–13.3
Household textiles	18	17	–5.6	6	3	–50.0	14	11	–21.4
Appliances and miscellaneous housewares	34	32	–5.9	11	5	–54.5	24	19	–20.8
Major appliances	9	9	0.0	–	2	–	4	4	0.0
Small appliances and misc. housewares	25	24	–4.0	10	2	–80.0	20	15	–25.0
Miscellaneous household equipment	64	66	3.1	37	42	13.5	57	48	–15.8
Other housing	136	136	0.0	42	75	78.6	94	120	27.7
Apparel and services	**301**	**210**	**–30.2**	**157**	**118**	**–24.8**	**270**	**206**	**–23.7**
Males, aged 2 or older	78	54	–30.8	23	24	4.3	62	49	–21.0
Females, aged 2 or older	121	71	–41.3	48	35	–27.1	88	46	–47.7
Children under age 2	40	33	–17.5	27	23	–14.8	55	43	–21.8

(continued)

(continued from previous page)

	total consumer units			under age 25			aged 25 to 34		
	1990	1999	percent change 1990–99	1990	1999	percent change 1990–99	1990	1999	percent change 1990–99
Other apparel products and services	$61	$52	–14.8%	$59	$36	–39.0%	$66	$67	1.5%
Jewelry and watches	32	27	–15.6	47	22	–53.2	36	53	47.2
All other apparel products and services	29	25	–13.8	11	14	27.3	29	14	–51.7
Transportation	**68**	**63**	**–7.4**	**23**	**65**	**182.6**	**23**	**30**	**30.4**
Health care	**57**	**40**	**–29.8**	**6**	**5**	**–16.7**	**10**	**9**	**–10.0**
Entertainment	**84**	**98**	**16.7**	**41**	**63**	**53.7**	**79**	**74**	**–6.3**
Toys, games, hobbies, and tricycles	32	32	0.0	11	10	–9.1	27	23	–14.8
Other entertainment	52	66	26.9	29	53	82.8	51	51	0.0
Education	**122**	**166**	**36.1**	**29**	**42**	**44.8**	**11**	**31**	**181.8**
All other gifts	**112**	**131**	**17.0**	**127**	**65**	**–48.8**	**91**	**111**	**22.0**

Note: The Bureau of Labor Statistics uses consumer units rather than households as the sampling unit in the Consumer Expenditure Survey. For the definition of consumer unit, see the glossary. Spending on gifts is included in the preceding product and service categories.
Source: Bureau of Labor Statistics, 1990 and 1999 Consumer Expenditure Surveys, Internet site <www.bls.gov/csxhome.htm>; calculations by the author

The Youngest Householders Spend Far Less Than Average

Low incomes equal low spending.

Households headed by 15-to-24-year-olds had an average income of only $18,276 in 1999 compared with $43,951 for all households. The income gap explains why spending by the youngest householders was only 59 percent as high as that of the average household.

Householders under age 25 spend far less than average in almost every major spending category. One exception is alcoholic beverages, on which they spend 16 percent more. And in keeping with their convenience-food upbringing, their spending on fast-food meals and snacks is only slightly lower than average.

Many (but not most) are new parents, which is why they spend more than average on infants' furniture and equipment, baby food, clothing for infants and toddlers, and play-ground equipment.

Since most householders under age 25 rent their homes, they spend considerably more than average on rent. As they establish their first homes, they spend more than average on basics such as clocks and radios and close to the average on household items such as telephone answering machines and flatware.

The youngest householders need transportation, but new cars are priced far out of their reach. Consequently, they spend 20 percent more than average on used cars and trucks and only 53 percent as much on new vehicles. This may explain why they spend more than average on towing charges.

They may not have much money, but there's music in the house. The youngest householders spend 51 percent more than average on tape recorders, 46 percent more on stereos, and 41 percent more on CDs and tapes.

♦ Many of the youngest householders do not have a lot to spend because they are college students. Their investment in education will be rewarded by higher incomes and more spending in years to come.

Average and Indexed Spending of Householders under Age 25, 1999

(average annual spending of total consumer units and average annual and indexed spending of consumer units headed by people under age 25, 1999)

	total consumer units	consumer units headed by people under age 25	
		average spending	indexed spending*
Number of consumer units (in 000s)	108,465	8,164	–
Average before-tax income	$43,951	$18,276	42
Average annual spending	37,026.81	21,725.21	59
FOOD	**$5,030.53**	**$3,354.43**	**67**
FOOD AT HOME	2,914.95	1,828.05	63
Cereals and bakery products	**448.09**	**270.84**	**60**
Cereals and cereal products	159.84	102.33	64
Flour	8.84	5.07	57
Prepared flour mixes	14.42	7.90	55
Ready-to-eat and cooked cereals	89.15	55.04	62
Rice	19.87	13.34	67
Pasta, cornmeal, and other cereal products	27.56	20.98	76
Bakery products	288.24	168.50	58
Bread	82.46	48.13	58
White bread	39.14	26.53	68
Bread, other than white	43.32	21.61	50
Crackers and cookies	68.00	40.02	59
Cookies	44.26	27.21	61
Crackers	23.74	12.82	54
Frozen and refrigerated bakery products	23.22	14.03	60
Other bakery products	114.56	66.32	58
Biscuits and rolls	37.92	21.88	58
Cakes and cupcakes	35.74	22.63	63
Bread and cracker products	3.50	2.99	85
Sweetrolls, coffee cakes, doughnuts	24.10	11.27	47
Pies, tarts, turnovers	13.30	7.54	57
Meats, poultry, fish, and eggs	**748.73**	**468.99**	**63**
Beef	220.11	154.62	70
Ground beef	83.08	65.10	78

(continued)

(continued from previous page)

	total consumer units	consumer units headed by people under age 25	
		average spending	indexed spending*
Roast	$34.71	$16.24	47
Chuck roast	11.87	4.17	35
Round roast	9.82	5.63	57
Other roast	13.02	6.44	49
Steak	88.41	64.37	73
Round steak	15.59	12.04	77
Sirloin steak	25.92	21.73	84
Other steak	46.90	30.60	65
Other beef	13.90	8.90	64
Pork	156.74	92.97	59
Bacon	24.92	14.52	58
Pork chops	35.16	22.62	64
Ham	38.91	21.71	56
Ham, not canned	36.73	20.69	56
Canned ham	2.18	1.03	47
Sausage	22.99	15.55	68
Other pork	34.76	18.57	53
Other meats	97.11	60.64	62
Frankfurters	21.80	14.26	65
Lunch meats (cold cuts)	65.97	39.41	60
Bologna, liverwurst, salami	23.10	13.18	57
Other lunchmeats	42.86	26.23	61
Lamb, organ meats, and others	9.34	6.98	75
Lamb and organ meats	8.33	5.23	63
Mutton, goat, and game	1.01	1.74	172
Poultry	136.13	82.33	60
Fresh and frozen chickens	107.74	66.28	62
Fresh and frozen whole chickens	29.63	14.64	49
Fresh and frozen chicken parts	78.11	51.64	66
Other poultry	28.39	16.05	57
Fish and seafood	106.22	59.09	56
Canned fish and seafood	15.90	10.22	64
Fresh fish and shellfish	59.43	32.77	55
Frozen fish and shellfish	30.88	16.10	52
Eggs	32.43	19.33	60

(continued)

(continued from previous page)

	total consumer units	consumer units headed by people under age 25	
		average spending	indexed spending*
Dairy products	**$322.30**	**$195.25**	**61**
Fresh milk and cream	122.05	78.23	64
Fresh milk, all types	111.26	73.39	66
Cream	10.79	4.84	45
Other dairy products	200.25	117.02	58
Butter	17.68	10.18	58
Cheese	93.19	55.69	60
Ice cream and related products	56.49	29.42	52
Miscellaneous dairy products	32.90	21.74	66
Fruits and vegetables	**499.54**	**282.77**	**57**
Fresh fruits	152.49	77.29	51
Apples	28.23	17.00	60
Bananas	30.33	15.51	51
Oranges	15.48	8.75	57
Citrus fruits, excluding oranges	14.15	7.02	50
Other fresh fruits	64.30	29.02	45
Fresh vegetables	148.51	79.30	53
Potatoes	28.35	15.79	56
Lettuce	18.92	11.05	58
Tomatoes	26.91	16.22	60
Other fresh vegetables	74.33	36.24	49
Processed fruits	112.95	76.99	68
Frozen fruits and fruit juices	15.12	8.92	59
Frozen orange juice	8.56	3.99	47
Frozen fruits	1.98	0.47	24
Frozen fruit juices, excluding orange	4.59	4.46	97
Canned fruits	15.72	8.74	56
Dried fruits	5.26	2.28	43
Fresh fruit juice	23.36	19.31	83
Canned and bottled fruit juice	53.49	37.74	71
Processed vegetables	85.58	49.18	57
Frozen vegetables	25.84	11.80	46
Canned and dried vegetables and juices	59.74	37.39	63
Canned beans	11.97	8.95	75
Canned corn	7.89	6.27	79

(continued)

(continued from previous page)

	total consumer units	consumer units headed by people under age 25	
		average spending	indexed spending[*]
Canned miscellaneous vegetables	$19.03	$8.69	46
Dried peas	0.86	0.81	94
Dried beans	2.57	1.10	43
Dried miscellaneous vegetables	6.79	3.73	55
Dried processed vegetables	0.41	1.06	259
Frozen vegetable juices	0.38	0.14	37
Fresh and canned vegetable juices	9.85	6.64	67
Other food at home	**896.29**	**610.20**	**68**
Sugar and other sweets	111.52	71.16	64
Candy and chewing gum	68.42	42.92	63
Sugar	17.36	13.52	78
Artificial sweeteners	4.14	1.34	32
Jams, preserves, other sweets	21.61	13.38	62
Fats and oils	83.52	53.95	65
Margarine	11.39	5.88	52
Fats and oils	24.73	15.85	64
Salad dressings	26.46	18.54	70
Nondairy cream and imitation milk	8.86	4.01	45
Peanut butter	12.09	9.67	80
Miscellaneous foods	419.78	299.74	71
Frozen prepared foods	81.79	59.50	73
Frozen meals	24.96	11.80	47
Other frozen prepared foods	56.83	47.70	84
Canned and packaged soups	35.78	21.84	61
Potato chips, nuts, and other snacks	89.44	49.54	55
Potato chips and other snacks	71.21	42.09	59
Nuts	18.23	7.45	41
Condiments and seasonings	82.80	58.71	71
Salt, spices, other seasonings	18.63	16.53	89
Olives, pickles, relishes	9.36	4.82	51
Sauces and gravies	37.67	25.82	69
Baking needs and miscellaneous products	17.13	11.54	67
Other canned/packaged prepared foods	129.97	110.15	85
Prepared salads	17.09	8.23	48
Prepared desserts	10.43	5.78	55

(continued)

(continued from previous page)

	total consumer units	consumer units headed by people under age 25	
		average spending	indexed spending*
Baby food	$27.42	$45.33	165
Miscellaneous prepared foods	74.88	50.81	68
Nonalcoholic beverages	242.05	166.52	69
Cola	89.74	61.94	69
Other carbonated drinks	45.46	39.70	87
Coffee	37.59	13.12	35
Roasted coffee	22.92	7.34	32
Instant and freeze-dried coffee	14.67	5.78	39
Noncarbonated fruit-flavored drinks, nonfrozen lemonade	19.25	16.42	85
Tea	15.48	8.33	54
Nonalcoholic beer	0.34	–	–
Other nonalcoholic beverages and ice	34.19	27.01	79
Food prepared by household on out-of-town trips	39.42	18.82	48
FOOD AWAY FROM HOME	**2,115.58**	**1,526.39**	**72**
Meals at restaurants, carry-outs, and other	**1,705.15**	**1,273.37**	**75**
Lunch	560.84	405.25	72
Lunch at fast food, take-out, delivery, concession stands, buffet, cafeteria (other than employer, school cafeteria)	294.46	272.81	93
Lunch at full-service restaurants	191.00	95.57	50
Lunch at vending machines and mobile vendors	4.75	3.47	73
Lunch at employer and school cafeterias	70.65	33.39	47
Dinner	821.83	597.21	73
Dinner at fast food, take-out, delivery, concession stands, buffet, cafeteria (other than employer, school cafeteria)	326.42	305.63	94
Dinner at full-service restaurants	477.84	273.71	57
Dinner at vending machines and mobile vendors	7.82	5.72	73
Dinner at employer and school cafeterias	9.75	12.16	125
Snacks and nonalcoholic beverages	162.40	148.56	91
Snacks and nonalcoholic beverages at fast food, take-out, delivery, concession stands, buffet, and cafeteria (other than employer and school cafeteria)	101.35	86.76	86
Snacks and nonalcoholic beverages at full-service restaurants	19.89	13.47	68
Snacks and nonalcoholic beverages at vending machines and mobile vendors	34.14	38.70	113
Snacks and nonalcoholic beverages at employer and school cafeterias	7.01	9.62	137

(continued)

(continued from previous page)

	total consumer units	consumer units headed by people under age 25	
		average spending	indexed spending*
Breakfast and brunch	$160.08	$122.35	76
Breakfast and brunch at fast food, take-out, delivery, concession stands, buffet, and cafeteria (other than employer and school cafeteria)	75.64	68.62	91
Breakfast and brunch at full-service restaurants	77.18	48.09	62
Breakfast, brunch at vending machines, mobile vendors	2.03	0.81	40
Breakfast and brunch at employer and school cafeterias	5.23	4.84	93
Board (including at school)	**48.51**	**78.18**	**161**
Catered affairs	**71.84**	**21.55**	**30**
Food on out-of-town trips	**211.65**	**111.17**	**53**
School lunches	**58.90**	**12.68**	**22**
Meals as pay	**19.54**	**29.46**	**151**
ALCOHOLIC BEVERAGES	**$317.78**	**$369.21**	**116**
At home	**190.49**	**220.85**	**116**
Beer and ale	103.83	151.41	146
Whiskey	11.44	10.64	93
Wine	57.14	30.53	53
Other alcoholic beverages	18.08	28.27	156
Away from home	**127.29**	**148.35**	**117**
Beer and ale	62.89	82.33	131
Beer and ale at fast food, take-out, delivery, concession stands, buffet, and cafeteria	13.13	29.68	226
Beer and ale at full-service restaurants	47.51	52.23	110
Beer and ale at vending machines and mobile vendors	0.37	0.42	114
Beer and ale at catered affairs	1.87	–	–
Wine	6.64	7.27	109
Wine at fast food, take-out, delivery, concession stands, buffet, and cafeteria	1.06	2.16	204
Wine at full-service restaurants	5.25	5.08	97
Wine at vending machines and mobile vendors	0.02	0.03	150
Wine at catered affairs	0.31	–	–

(continued)

(continued from previous page)

	total consumer units	consumer units headed by people under age 25	
		average spending	indexed spending*
Other alcoholic beverages	$57.76	$58.75	102
Other alcoholic beverages at fast food, take-out, delivery, concession stands, buffet, and cafeteria	3.24	6.20	191
Other alcoholic beverages at full-service restaurants	21.16	21.88	103
Other alcoholic beverages at vending machines and mobile vendors	0.08	0.10	125
Other alcoholic beverages at catered affairs	0.84	–	–
Alcoholic beverages purchased on trips	32.45	30.58	94
HOUSING	**$12,057.31**	**$6,585.15**	**55**
Shelter	**7,016.41**	**4,140.34**	**59**
Owned dwellings**	**4,525.42**	**596.17**	**13**
Mortgage interest and charges	2,547.32	311.42	12
Mortgage interest	2,392.17	304.45	13
Interest paid, home equity loan	87.75	6.12	7
Interest paid, home equity line of credit	66.54	0.85	1
Prepayment penalty charges	0.85	–	–
Property taxes	1,123.45	167.51	15
Maintenance, repairs, insurance, other expenses	854.65	117.25	14
Homeowner's and related insurance	234.52	34.15	15
Fire and extended coverage	0.94	–	–
Homeowner's insurance	233.58	34.15	15
Ground rent	34.03	18.41	54
Maintenance and repair services	470.47	42.51	9
Painting and papering	57.44	1.61	3
Plumbing and water heating	43.05	5.02	12
Heat, air conditioning, electrical work	71.75	4.57	6
Roofing and gutters	75.39	–	–
Other repair and maintenance services	188.39	24.76	13
Repair/replacement of hard-surface flooring	32.80	6.49	20
Repair of built-in appliances	1.66	0.07	4
Maintenance and repair materials	81.80	17.56	21
Paints, wallpaper, and supplies	15.48	3.58	23
Tools/equipment for painting, wallpapering	1.66	0.38	23
Plumbing supplies and equipment	5.98	1.58	26
Electrical supplies, heating/cooling equipment	3.25	4.30	132

(continued)

(continued from previous page)

	total consumer units	consumer units headed by people under age 25	
		average spending	indexed spending*
Hard-surface flooring, repair and replacement	$7.61	$2.37	31
Roofing and gutters	7.16	1.16	16
Plaster, paneling, siding, windows, doors, screens, awnings	11.21	0.72	6
Patio, walk, fence, driveway, masonry, brick, and stucco work	1.27	–	–
Landscape maintenance	3.56	0.49	14
Miscellaneous supplies and equipment	24.64	2.98	12
Insulation, other maintenance and repair	13.79	2.82	20
Finish basement, remodel rooms, build patios, walks, etc.	10.84	0.16	1
Property management and security	28.19	3.81	14
Property management	20.94	1.94	9
Management and upkeep services for security	7.24	1.86	26
Parking	5.64	0.82	15
Rented dwellings	**2,026.61**	**3,296.26**	**163**
Rent	1,965.92	3,210.60	163
Rent as pay	31.73	70.40	222
Maintenance, insurance, and other expenses	28.96	15.26	53
Tenant's insurance	9.25	6.83	74
Maintenance and repair services	11.24	1.79	16
Repair and maintenance services	10.31	1.66	16
Repair and replacement of hard-surface flooring	0.88	–	–
Repair of built-in appliances	0.05	0.13	260
Maintenance and repair materials	8.46	6.64	78
Paint, wallpaper, and supplies	1.61	1.66	103
Equipment for painting and wallpapering	0.17	0.18	106
Plastering, paneling, roofing, gutters, etc.	0.96	1.46	152
Patio, walk, fence, driveway, masonry, brick, and stucco work	0.19	0.10	53
Plumbing supplies and equipment	0.40	0.53	133
Electrical supplies, heating and cooling equipment	0.36	0.13	36
Miscellaneous supplies and equipment	4.12	1.91	46
Insulation, other maintenance and repair	1.34	1.33	99
Additions, finishing basements, remodeling rooms	2.61	0.46	18
Construction materials for jobs not started	0.17	0.12	71

(continued)

(continued from previous page)

	total consumer units	consumer units headed by people under age 25	
		average spending	indexed spending*
Hard surface flooring	$0.41	$0.27	66
Landscape maintenance	0.24	0.42	175
Other lodging	**464.38**	**247.90**	**53**
Owned vacation homes	143.69	5.23	4
Mortgage interest and charges	44.29	1.86	4
Mortgage interest	41.99	1.86	4
Interest paid, home equity loan	1.52	–	–
Interest paid, home equity line of credit	0.78	–	–
Property taxes	75.72	3.02	4
Maintenance, insurance, and other expenses	23.68	0.35	1
Homeowner's and related insurance	5.92	–	–
Homeowner's insurance	5.84	–	–
Ground rent	2.04	0.17	8
Maintenance and repair services	9.83	0.05	1
Maintenance and repair materials	1.34	–	–
Property management and security	3.59	0.12	3
Property management	2.60	0.07	3
Management and upkeep services for security	0.99	0.06	6
Parking	0.96	–	–
Housing while attending school	75.94	162.62	214
Lodging on out-of-town trips	244.75	80.06	33
Utilities, fuels, public services	**2,377.37**	**1,166.47**	**49**
Natural gas	**270.30**	**92.24**	**34**
Natural gas (renter)	54.87	67.88	124
Natural gas (owner)	213.62	24.34	11
Natural gas (vacation)	1.81	0.02	1
Electricity	**899.20**	**426.40**	**47**
Electricity (renter)	212.61	328.25	154
Electricity (owner)	679.95	98.15	14
Electricity (vacation)	6.64	–	–
Fuel oil and other fuels	**74.35**	**13.99**	**19**
Fuel oil	36.37	6.09	17
Fuel oil (renter)	3.61	3.65	101
Fuel oil (owner)	32.21	2.44	8
Fuel oil (vacation)	0.54	–	–

(continued)

(continued from previous page)

	total consumer units	consumer units headed by people under age 25	
		average spending	indexed spending*
Coal	$0.57	–	–
Coal (renter)	0.03	–	–
Coal (owner)	0.52	–	–
Bottled/tank gas	31.57	$5.53	18
Gas (renter)	4.19	1.83	44
Gas (owner)	25.03	2.71	11
Gas (vacation)	2.34	0.99	42
Wood and other fuels	5.85	2.37	41
Wood and other fuels (renter)	0.90	1.44	160
Wood and other fuels (owner)	4.92	0.93	19
Telephone services	**848.92**	**561.75**	**66**
Telephone services in home city, excl. mobile phones	763.93	519.44	68
Telephone services for mobile phones	84.99	42.31	50
Water and other public services	**284.60**	**72.08**	**25**
Water and sewerage maintenance	209.31	56.01	27
Water and sewerage maintenance (renter)	27.29	33.82	124
Water and sewerage maintenance (owner)	180.43	22.19	12
Water and sewerage maintenance (vacation)	1.60	–	–
Trash and garbage collection	72.40	15.39	21
Trash and garbage collection (renter)	8.66	8.66	100
Trash and garbage collection (owner)	62.90	6.72	11
Trash and garbage collection (vacation)	0.84	–	–
Septic tank cleaning	2.89	0.68	24
Septic tank cleaning (renter)	0.25	0.42	168
Septic tank cleaning (owner)	2.64	0.26	10
HOUSEHOLD SERVICES	**665.92**	**180.55**	**27**
Personal services	**322.71**	**120.66**	**37**
Babysitting and child care in own home	31.32	16.15	52
Babysitting and child care in other home	37.23	33.57	90
Care for elderly, invalids, handicapped, etc.	69.34	2.73	4
Adult day care centers	2.52	0.06	2
Day care centers, nurseries, and preschools	182.29	68.15	37

(continued)

(continued from previous page)

	total consumer units	consumer units headed by people under age 25	
		average spending	indexed spending[*]
Other household services	**$343.22**	**$59.90**	**17**
Housekeeping services	97.73	2.86	3
Gardening, lawn care services	80.14	2.58	3
Water softening services	3.33	1.94	58
Nonclothing laundry and dry cleaning, sent out	1.61	0.23	14
Nonclothing laundry and dry cleaning, coin-operated	4.17	7.47	179
Termite/pest control services	10.49	0.42	4
Home security system service fee	14.46	2.27	16
Other home services	14.09	0.44	3
Termite/pest control products	0.52	0.20	38
Moving, storage, freight express	33.03	12.25	37
Appliance repair, including service center	11.28	1.48	13
Reupholstering and furniture repair	9.48	0.69	7
Repairs, rentals of lawn and garden equipment, hand and power tools, etc.	4.57	–	–
Appliance rental	3.91	2.94	75
Rental of office equipment for nonbusiness use	0.75	0.26	35
Repair of misc. household equipment and furnishings	2.15	–	–
Repair of computer systems for nonbusiness use	2.48	1.64	66
Computer information services	48.69	22.08	45
Rental, installation of dishwashers, range hoods, garbage disposals	0.35	0.15	43
HOUSEKEEPING SUPPLIES	**498.24**	**220.68**	**44**
Laundry and cleaning supplies	**121.16**	**63.78**	**53**
Soaps and detergents	70.19	40.61	58
Other laundry cleaning products	50.97	23.17	45
Other household products	**249.75**	**86.22**	**35**
Cleansing and toilet tissue, paper towels, and napkins	66.05	30.36	46
Miscellaneous household products	103.28	44.37	43
Lawn and garden supplies	80.42	11.49	14
Postage and stationery	**127.33**	**70.68**	**56**
Stationery, stationery supplies, giftwrap	62.06	51.26	83
Postage	62.48	19.42	31
Delivery services	2.79	–	–

(continued)

(continued from previous page)

	total consumer units	consumer units headed by people under age 25	
		average spending	indexed spending*
Household furnishings and equipment	**$1,499.37**	**$877.12**	**58**
Household textiles	**114.02**	**40.50**	**36**
Bathroom linens	20.28	9.84	49
Bedroom linens	50.55	17.92	35
Kitchen and dining room linens	9.31	3.66	39
Curtains and draperies	18.28	5.56	30
Slipcovers and decorative pillows	4.82	–	–
Sewing materials for household items	9.64	3.35	35
Other linens	1.14	0.18	16
Furniture	**365.22**	**282.72**	**77**
Mattresses and springs	47.53	44.16	93
Other bedroom furniture	55.31	59.67	108
Sofas	85.54	67.21	79
Living room chairs	40.97	20.44	50
Living room tables	17.60	15.09	86
Kitchen, dining room furniture	53.26	32.76	62
Infants' furniture	6.90	8.52	123
Outdoor furniture	11.86	2.33	20
Wall units, cabinets, and other furniture	46.25	32.55	70
Floor coverings	**43.67**	**11.38**	**26**
Wall-to-wall carpeting (renter)	1.54	0.29	19
Wall-to-wall carpet, replacement (owner)	28.29	5.76	20
Floor coverings, nonpermanent	12.95	5.15	40
Major appliances	**183.10**	**91.15**	**50**
Dishwashers (built-in), garbage disposals, range hoods (renter)	0.77	0.27	35
Dishwashers (built-in), garbage disposals, range hoods (owner)	13.87	3.57	26
Refrigerators and freezers (renter)	7.83	11.47	146
Refrigerators and freezers (owner)	41.09	9.56	23
Washing machines (renter)	5.09	11.06	217
Washing machines (owner)	18.56	6.25	34
Clothes dryers (renter)	3.12	8.79	282
Clothes dryers (owner)	12.45	6.20	50
Cooking stoves, ovens (renter)	2.60	1.71	66
Cooking stoves, ovens (owner)	24.32	4.91	20
Microwave ovens (renter)	2.33	7.28	312

(continued)

(continued from previous page)

	total consumer units	consumer units headed by people under age 25	
		average spending	indexed spending*
Microwave ovens (owner)	$6.07	$1.71	28
Portable dishwashers (renter)	0.11	–	–
Portable dishwashers (owner)	0.76	0.34	45
Window air conditioners (renter)	1.67	2.09	125
Window air conditioners (owner)	5.68	1.00	18
Electric floor-cleaning equipment	26.55	13.98	53
Sewing machines	4.17	–	–
Miscellaneous household appliances	**6.06**	**0.96**	**16**
Small appliances, miscellaneous housewares	101.63	46.86	46
Housewares	78.15	32.15	41
Plastic dinnerware	1.34	1.52	113
China and other dinnerware	18.50	1.92	10
Flatware	4.37	4.23	97
Glassware	12.50	5.68	45
Silver serving pieces	3.41	0.52	15
Other serving pieces	1.69	0.66	39
Nonelectric cookware	15.09	8.13	54
Tableware, nonelectric kitchenware	21.25	9.48	45
Small appliances	23.49	14.71	63
Small electric kitchen appliances	18.20	11.75	65
Portable heating and cooling equipment	5.29	2.96	56
Miscellaneous household equipment	**691.72**	**404.51**	**58**
Window coverings	15.12	4.35	29
Infants' equipment	8.01	16.05	200
Laundry and cleaning equipment	13.21	7.41	56
Outdoor equipment	26.48	2.42	9
Clocks	5.62	10.78	192
Lamps and lighting fixtures	11.50	4.94	43
Other household decorative items	138.10	71.68	52
Telephones and accessories	41.56	16.83	40
Lawn and garden equipment	44.03	9.56	22
Power tools	22.82	20.83	91
Office furniture for home use	14.21	10.31	73
Hand tools	7.85	4.12	52

(continued)

(continued from previous page)

	total consumer units	consumer units headed by people under age 25	
		average spending	indexed spending*
Indoor plants and fresh flowers	$53.88	$18.57	34
Closet and storage items	6.82	1.80	26
Rental of furniture	3.03	1.19	39
Luggage	9.36	3.38	36
Computers and computer hardware, nonbusiness use	192.13	163.73	85
Computer software and accessories, nonbusiness use	22.28	14.38	65
Telephone answering devices	2.71	2.57	95
Calculators	1.98	3.66	185
Business equipment for home use	2.08	0.20	10
Other hardware	12.99	5.21	40
Smoke alarms (owner)	0.64	0.05	8
Smoke alarms (renter)	0.06	0.08	133
Other household appliances (owner)	7.73	0.42	5
Other household appliances (renter)	1.20	1.97	164
Miscellaneous household equipment and parts	26.32	8.01	30
APPAREL AND SERVICES	**$1,742.72**	**$1,191.66**	**68**
MEN AND BOYS	**421.01**	**238.39**	**57**
Men, aged 16 or older	**328.00**	**209.09**	**64**
Suits	34.28	11.65	34
Sportcoats and tailored jackets	4.16	–	–
Coats and jackets	30.69	41.72	136
Underwear	14.79	7.34	50
Hosiery	12.12	3.61	30
Nightwear	3.03	1.54	51
Accessories	25.76	13.93	54
Sweaters and vests	11.83	12.46	105
Active sportswear	15.41	11.53	75
Shirts	84.42	44.56	53
Pants	72.11	50.40	70
Shorts and shorts sets	13.05	8.48	65
Uniforms	2.65	1.42	54
Costumes	3.72	0.44	12
Boys, aged 2 to 15	**93.00**	**29.30**	**32**
Coats and jackets	6.35	1.67	26
Sweaters	2.76	0.90	33

(continued)

(continued from previous page)

	total consumer units	consumer units headed by people under age 25	
		average spending	indexed spending*
Shirts	$23.08	$5.38	23
Underwear	4.32	0.65	15
Nightwear	3.15	0.98	31
Hosiery	4.73	1.50	32
Accessories	5.85	2.02	35
Suits, sportcoats, and vests	2.52	1.60	63
Pants	23.19	7.31	32
Shorts and shorts sets	8.47	6.39	75
Uniforms	3.34	0.34	10
Active sportswear	3.33	0.21	6
Costumes	1.90	0.35	18
WOMEN AND GIRLS	**654.97**	**422.04**	**64**
Women, aged 16 or older	**547.58**	**377.14**	**69**
Coats and jackets	34.74	14.32	41
Dresses	86.01	53.81	63
Sportcoats and tailored jackets	4.27	1.61	38
Vests and sweaters	37.93	15.12	40
Shirts, tops, and blouses	82.52	77.49	94
Skirts	16.20	15.17	94
Pants	74.17	52.24	70
Shorts and shorts sets	21.78	31.42	144
Active sportswear	24.34	15.88	65
Sleepwear	31.17	18.95	61
Undergarments	38.82	22.81	59
Hosiery	20.49	15.88	78
Suits	35.10	15.00	43
Accessories	31.35	22.91	73
Uniforms	2.97	2.62	88
Costumes	5.70	1.91	34
Girls, aged 2 to 15	**107.38**	**44.89**	**42**
Coats and jackets	7.05	1.89	27
Dresses and suits	16.72	14.07	84
Shirts, blouses, and sweaters	24.31	8.53	35
Skirts and pants	21.05	6.50	31
Shorts and shorts sets	8.70	2.64	30

(continued)

(continued from previous page)

	total consumer units	consumer units headed by people under age 25	
		average spending	indexed spending*
Active sportswear	$6.70	$3.03	45
Underwear and sleepwear	6.98	2.40	34
Hosiery	4.45	4.03	91
Accessories	5.26	0.63	12
Uniforms	3.51	0.69	20
Costumes	2.66	0.48	18
CHILDREN UNDER AGE 2	**66.87**	**98.85**	**148**
Coats, jackets, and snowsuits	2.88	2.73	95
Dresses and outerwear	14.34	19.83	138
Underwear	39.08	63.78	163
Nightwear and loungewear	3.64	4.72	130
Accessories	6.92	7.79	113
FOOTWEAR	**303.07**	**233.83**	**77**
Men's	101.98	64.23	63
Boys'	30.18	12.10	40
Women's	140.85	138.43	98
Girls'	30.07	19.07	63
OTHER APPAREL PRODUCTS AND SERVICES	**296.80**	**198.55**	**67**
Material for making clothes	6.80	2.09	31
Sewing patterns and notions	6.47	2.04	32
Watches	19.11	13.63	71
Jewelry	139.18	73.28	53
Shoe repair and other shoe services	2.03	0.65	32
Coin-operated apparel laundry and dry cleaning	36.82	74.72	203
Apparel alteration, repair, and tailoring services	5.92	2.25	38
Clothing rental	2.84	4.01	141
Watch and jewelry repair	4.61	2.00	43
Professional laundry and dry cleaning	72.67	23.61	32
Clothing storage	0.37	0.28	76
TRANSPORTATION	**$7,011.25**	**$5,036.66**	**72**
VEHICLE PURCHASES	**3,305.35**	**2,858.74**	**86**
Cars and trucks, new	**1,627.93**	**856.75**	**53**
New cars	883.19	588.75	67
New trucks	744.75	268.00	36

(continued)

(continued from previous page)

	total consumer units	consumer units headed by people under age 25	
		average spending	indexed spending*
Cars and trucks, used	$1,641.36	$1,973.73	120
Used cars	1,003.15	1,247.83	124
Used trucks	638.21	725.89	114
Other vehicles	**36.06**	**28.26**	**78**
New motorcycles	23.86	–	–
Used motorcycles	12.20	28.26	232
GASOLINE AND MOTOR OIL	**1,054.71**	**708.11**	**67**
Gasoline	952.95	636.90	67
Diesel fuel	8.46	0.60	7
Gasoline on out-of-town trips	80.43	60.18	75
Gasohol	0.76	–	–
Motor oil	11.31	9.82	87
Motor oil on out-of-town trips	0.81	0.61	75
OTHER VEHICLE EXPENSES	**2,253.81**	**1,252.88**	**56**
Vehicle finance charges	**320.45**	**209.04**	**65**
Automobile finance charges	168.61	138.42	82
Truck finance charges	132.13	69.18	52
Motorcycle and plane finance charges	2.03	0.07	3
Other vehicle finance charges	17.68	1.38	8
Maintenance and repairs	**664.14**	**401.76**	**60**
Coolant, additives, brake, transmission fluids	4.11	3.58	87
Tires	83.45	45.96	55
Parts, equipment, and accessories	51.30	40.04	78
Vehicle audio equipment	7.85	0.29	4
Vehicle products	3.93	2.24	57
Miscellaneous auto repair, servicing	33.88	14.40	43
Body work and painting	32.45	25.73	79
Clutch, transmission repair	46.87	38.73	83
Drive shaft and rear-end repair	4.81	1.22	25
Brake work, including adjustments	56.15	36.60	65
Repair to steering or front-end	16.27	15.46	95
Repair to engine cooling system	21.33	8.30	39
Motor tune-up	39.54	17.20	44
Lube, oil change, and oil filters	58.37	38.69	66

(continued)

(continued from previous page)

	total consumer units	consumer units headed by people under age 25	
		average spending	indexed spending*
Front-end alignment, wheel balance, rotation	$10.18	$5.23	51
Shock absorber replacement	4.80	3.15	66
Gas tank repair, replacement	6.73	4.67	69
Tire repair and other repair work	31.42	18.15	58
Vehicle air conditioning repair	18.96	9.07	48
Exhaust system repair	13.07	9.23	68
Electrical system repair	31.18	17.04	55
Motor repair, replacement	79.78	45.58	57
Auto repair service policy	7.10	1.20	17
Vehicle insurance	**756.38**	**407.99**	**54**
Vehicle rental, leases, licenses, other charges	**512.84**	**234.09**	**46**
Leased and rented vehicles	345.83	147.28	43
Rented vehicles	43.31	15.41	36
Auto rental	9.66	5.54	57
Auto rental, out-of-town trips	27.46	6.19	23
Truck rental	2.12	2.00	94
Truck rental, out-of-town trips	3.80	1.69	44
Motorcycle rental, out-of-town trips	0.05	–	–
Aircraft rental, out-of-town trips	0.19	–	–
Leased vehicles	302.52	131.86	44
Car lease payments	161.36	61.36	38
Cash down payment (car lease)	12.69	12.61	99
Termination fee (car lease)	1.02	0.07	7
Truck lease payments	115.43	50.87	44
Cash down payment (truck lease)	11.18	6.96	62
Termination fee (truck lease)	0.85	–	–
State and local registration	94.34	41.62	44
Driver's license	8.40	5.26	63
Vehicle inspection	9.00	4.76	53
Parking fees	25.32	22.63	89
Parking fees in home city, excluding residence	21.50	20.65	96
Parking fees, out-of-town trips	3.83	1.97	51
Tolls	12.18	1.51	12
Tolls on out-of-town trips	4.13	3.14	76
Towing charges	5.37	6.27	117
Automobile service clubs	8.27	1.63	20

(continued)

(continued from previous page)

	total consumer units	consumer units headed by people under age 25	
		average spending	indexed spending*
PUBLIC TRANSPORTATION	**$397.38**	**$216.93**	**55**
Airline fares	253.03	124.19	49
Intercity bus fares	14.84	10.06	68
Intracity mass transit fares	47.28	38.62	82
Local transportation on out-of-town trips	11.73	6.31	54
Taxi fares and limousine service on trips	6.89	3.71	54
Taxi fares and limousine service	12.16	15.68	129
Intercity train fares	17.87	8.95	50
Ship fares	32.34	8.65	27
School bus	1.25	0.76	61
HEALTH CARE	**$1,958.85**	**$551.12**	**28**
HEALTH INSURANCE	**922.59**	**233.31**	**25**
Commercial health insurance	**185.03**	**64.65**	**35**
Traditional fee-for-service health plan (not BCBS)	82.11	29.78	36
Preferred-provider health plan (not BCBS)	102.93	34.87	34
Blue Cross, Blue Shield	**210.07**	**44.76**	**21**
Traditional fee-for-service health plan	51.28	8.49	17
Preferred-provider health plan	54.69	10.38	19
Health maintenance organization	57.84	21.26	37
Commercial Medicare supplement	40.98	4.19	10
Other health insurance	5.27	0.44	8
Health maintenance plan (not BCBS)	**246.12**	**97.14**	**39**
Medicare payments	**162.93**	**9.57**	**6**
Commercial Medicare supplements/ other health insurance	**118.43**	**17.20**	**15**
Commercial Medicare supplement (not BCBS)	77.51	10.86	14
Other health insurance (not BCBS)	40.92	6.34	15
MEDICAL SERVICES	**557.70**	**184.13**	**33**
Physician's services	134.16	56.43	42
Dental services	223.10	53.55	24
Eyecare services	41.98	19.24	46
Services by professionals other than physicians	36.68	4.75	13
Lab tests, x-rays	25.14	5.00	20
Hospital room	27.21	7.35	27

(continued)

(continued from previous page)

	total consumer units	consumer units headed by people under age 25	
		average spending	*indexed spending[*]*
Hospital services other than room	$34.50	$16.65	48
Care in convalescent or nursing home	18.86	0.56	3
Repair of medical equipment	0.71	–	–
Other medical services	15.37	20.60	134
DRUGS	**369.97**	**97.30**	**26**
Nonprescription drugs	72.41	35.62	49
Nonprescription vitamins	38.72	12.87	33
Prescription drugs	258.84	48.81	19
MEDICAL SUPPLIES	**108.59**	**36.37**	**33**
Eyeglasses and contact lenses	56.87	23.57	41
Hearing aids	15.46	0.04	0
Topicals and dressings	27.07	12.28	45
Medical equipment for general use	2.20	0.26	12
Supportive, convalescent medical equipment	5.45	0.08	1
Rental of medical equipment	0.64	0.15	23
Rental of supportive, convalescent medical equipment	0.89	–	–
ENTERTAINMENT	**$1,890.92**	**$1,149.14**	**61**
FEES AND ADMISSIONS	**458.78**	**261.83**	**57**
Recreation expenses, out-of-town trips	23.50	11.83	50
Social, recreation, civic club memberships	91.76	43.76	48
Fees for participant sports	71.46	33.97	48
Participant sports, out-of-town trips	29.44	13.07	44
Movie, theater, opera, ballet	89.85	82.78	92
Movie, other admissions, out-of-town trips	43.36	22.51	52
Admission to sporting events	34.07	22.80	67
Admission to sports events, out-of-town trips	14.45	7.50	52
Fees for recreational lessons	37.37	11.79	32
Other entertainment services, out-of-town trips	23.50	11.83	50
TELEVISION, RADIO, SOUND EQUIPMENT	**608.10**	**484.62**	**80**
Television	**443.00**	**280.14**	**63**
Community antenna or cable TV	302.52	151.32	50
Black and white TV sets	0.74	0.21	28
Color TV, console	26.28	23.19	88
Color TV, portable/table model	43.58	40.57	93

(continued)

(continued from previous page)

	total consumer units	consumer units headed by people under age 25	
		average spending	indexed spending*
VCRs and video disc players	$25.51	$24.70	97
Video cassettes, tapes, and discs	20.12	19.10	95
Video game hardware and software	19.68	17.73	90
Repair of TV, radio, and sound equipment	4.13	1.95	47
Rental of television sets	0.45	1.38	307
Radios, sound equipment	**165.10**	**204.48**	**124**
Radios	6.80	4.20	62
Tape recorders and players	4.98	7.50	151
Sound components and component systems	28.00	40.97	146
Miscellaneous sound equipment	1.27	–	–
Sound equipment accessories	3.12	0.98	31
Satellite dishes	3.33	3.27	98
Compact disc, tape, record, and video mail order clubs	10.37	12.01	116
Records, CDs, audio tapes, needles	40.37	56.95	141
Rental of VCR, radio, sound equipment	0.36	0.12	33
Musical instruments and accessories	24.39	31.45	129
Rental and repair of musical instruments	1.88	–	–
Rental of video cassettes, tapes, films, discs	40.21	47.03	117
PETS, TOYS, PLAYGROUND EQUIPMENT	**345.67**	**185.38**	**54**
Pets	**213.11**	**93.76**	**44**
Pet food	92.40	31.39	34
Pet purchase, supplies, medicine	40.31	37.81	94
Pet services	19.77	3.92	20
Veterinary services	60.62	20.64	34
Toys, games, hobbies, and tricycles	**128.56**	**72.41**	**56**
Playground equipment	**4.01**	**19.21**	**479**
OTHER ENTERTAINMENT SUPPLIES, EQUIPMENT, SERVICES	**478.37**	**217.31**	**45**
Unmotored recreational vehicles	**40.95**	**11.02**	**27**
Boat without motor and boat trailers	8.15	0.97	12
Trailer and other attachable campers	32.80	10.05	31
Motorized recreational vehicles	**170.91**	**31.75**	**19**
Motorized camper	90.80	–	–
Other vehicle	21.58	7.71	36
Boat with motor	58.52	24.04	41

(continued)

(continued from previous page)

	total consumer units	consumer units headed by people under age 25	
		average spending	indexed spending*
Rental of recreational vehicles	**$2.87**	**$1.00**	**35**
Outboard motors	**3.63**	**–**	**–**
Docking and landing fees	**6.86**	**0.09**	**1**
Sports, recreation, and exercise equipment	**145.08**	**104.56**	**72**
Athletic gear, game tables, and exercise equipment	52.91	19.88	38
Bicycles	14.04	12.27	87
Camping equipment	14.73	8.62	59
Hunting and fishing equipment	29.50	41.81	142
Winter sports equipment	7.71	6.14	80
Water sports equipment	7.95	3.41	43
Other sports equipment	15.11	11.28	75
Rental and repair of miscellaneous sports equipment	3.12	1.15	37
Photographic equipment, supplies, and services	**84.77**	**53.09**	**63**
Film	21.59	14.01	65
Other photographic supplies	0.61	–	–
Film processing	31.62	20.55	65
Repair and rental of photographic equipment	0.57	0.06	11
Photographic equipment	18.69	13.35	71
Photographer fees	11.68	5.12	44
Fireworks	**5.29**	**–**	**–**
Souvenirs	**0.44**	**–**	**–**
Visual goods	**0.28**	**–**	**–**
Pinball, electronic video games	**17.30**	**15.80**	**91**
PERSONAL CARE PRODUCTS, SERVICES	**$408.28**	**$253.88**	**62**
Personal care products	**248.82**	**184.76**	**74**
Hair care products	52.78	42.90	81
Nonelectric articles for the hair	6.90	3.61	52
Wigs and hairpieces	1.52	2.88	189
Oral hygiene products	25.64	14.46	56
Shaving products	12.97	11.90	92
Cosmetics, perfume, and bath products	113.84	76.19	67
Deodorants, feminine hygiene, miscellaneous products	27.42	24.06	88
Electric personal care appliances	7.75	8.77	113

(continued)

	total consumer units	consumer units headed by people under age 25	
		average spending	indexed spending*
Personal care services	**$159.46**	**$69.11**	**43**
Personal care service for females	107.28	48.22	45
Personal care service for males	52.18	20.89	40
READING	**$159.38**	**$70.30**	**44**
Newspaper subscriptions	50.69	7.72	15
Newspapers, nonsubscription	14.27	7.12	50
Magazine subscriptions	20.91	10.28	49
Magazines, nonsubscription	10.91	11.14	102
Books purchased through book clubs	9.36	2.81	30
Books not purchased through book clubs	52.32	30.29	58
Encyclopedia and other reference book sets	0.85	0.95	112
EDUCATION	**$634.62**	**$1,276.88**	**201**
College tuition	355.50	951.55	268
Elementary/high school tuition	104.11	4.17	4
Other school tuition	29.52	20.51	69
Other school expenses including rentals	27.65	21.68	78
Books, supplies for college	51.53	245.30	476
Books, supplies for elementary, high school	14.97	1.16	8
Books, supplies for day care, nursery school	4.23	3.97	94
Miscellaneous school expenses and supplies	47.12	28.54	61
TOBACCO PRODUCTS, SMOKING SUPPLIES	**$300.09**	**$220.46**	**73**
Cigarettes	272.87	195.23	72
Other tobacco products	24.27	21.91	90
Smoking accessories	2.96	3.31	112
FINANCIAL PRODUCTS AND SERVICES	**$888.76**	**$370.30**	**42**
Miscellaneous fees, gambling losses	37.10	17.58	47
Legal fees	120.37	57.44	48
Funeral expenses	69.82	6.84	10
Safe deposit box rental	5.36	0.42	8
Checking accounts, other bank service charges	21.12	16.63	79
Cemetery lots, vaults, maintenance fees	13.15	0.43	3
Accounting fees	68.78	8.32	12
Miscellaneous personal services	55.48	39.25	71

(continued)

(continued from previous page)

	total consumer units	consumer units headed by people under age 25	
		average spending	indexed spending*
Finance charges excluding mortgage and vehicle	$272.05	$175.31	64
Occupational expenses	93.79	36.79	39
Expenses for other properties	126.77	10.04	8
Interest paid, home equity line of credit (other property)	0.61	–	–
Credit card memberships	4.37	1.23	28
CASH CONTRIBUTIONS	**$1,190.11**	**$186.09**	**16**
Cash contributions to nonhousehold members, including students, alimony, and child support	279.71	39.85	14
Gifts of cash, stocks, bonds to nonhousehold members	244.91	16.32	7
Contributions to charities	134.44	10.51	8
Contributions to religious organizations	454.77	106.12	23
Contributions to educational organizations	58.68	11.97	20
Contributions to political organizations	6.63	0.19	3
Other contributions	10.96	1.12	10
PERSONAL INSURANCE AND PENSIONS	**$3,436.22**	**$1,109.92**	**32**
Life and other personal insurance	**394.42**	**61.35**	**16**
Life, endowment, annuity, other personal insurance	382.04	60.40	16
Other nonhealth insurance	12.38	0.95	8
Pensions and Social Security	**3,041.79**	**1,048.57**	**34**
Deductions for government retirement	67.62	4.75	7
Deductions for railroad retirement	3.04	–	–
Deductions for private pensions	387.89	55.32	14
Nonpayroll deposit to retirement plans	476.51	25.42	5
Deductions for Social Security	2,106.73	963.08	46
PERSONAL TAXES	**$3,587.97**	**$844.68**	**24**
Federal income tax	2,801.76	630.10	22
State and local income tax	615.84	207.98	34
Other taxes	170.36	6.59	4
GIFTS***	**1,083.33**	**514.88**	**48**
Food	**82.92**	**19.44**	**23**
Cakes and cupcakes	2.87	–	–
Candy and chewing gum	8.51	5.49	65

(continued)

(continued from previous page)

	total consumer units	consumer units headed by people under age 25	
		average spending	indexed spending*
Board (including at school)	$27.97	$7.64	27
Catered affairs	26.05	0.66	3
HOUSING	**291.88**	**138.51**	**47**
Housekeeping supplies	**40.60**	**14.09**	**35**
Laundry and cleaning supplies	2.24	0.84	38
Miscellaneous household products	7.06	1.01	14
Lawn and garden supplies	3.07	0.95	31
Stationery, stationery supplies, giftwrap	19.45	10.00	51
Postage	6.42	1.04	16
Household textiles	**16.83**	**2.58**	**15**
Bathroom linens	3.45	0.20	6
Bedroom linens	8.94	1.99	22
Appliances and miscellaneous housewares	**32.34**	**4.71**	**15**
Major appliances	8.60	2.26	26
Electric floor cleaning equipment	2.66	–	–
Small appliances and miscellaneous housewares	23.75	2.45	10
China and other dinnerware	5.44	–	–
Glassware	4.01	0.04	1
Nonelectric cookware	3.85	0.19	5
Tableware, nonelectric kitchenware	4.21	0.10	2
Small electric kitchen appliances	2.89	1.29	45
Miscellaneous household equipment	**66.17**	**42.07**	**64**
Infants' equipment	2.26	3.25	144
Other household decorative items	22.60	13.38	59
Power tools	3.10	2.70	87
Indoor plants and fresh flowers	15.75	8.87	56
Computers and computer hardware, nonbusiness use	9.01	1.92	21
Other housing expenses	**135.94**	**75.07**	**55**
Repair or maintenance services	3.48	0.27	8
Housing while attending school	45.15	19.65	44
Lodging on out-of-town trips	2.64	1.77	67
Natural gas (renter)	3.08	1.88	61
Electricity (renter)	12.50	10.32	83
Telephone services in home city, excl. mobile phones	13.34	31.70	238

(continued)

(continued from previous page)

	total consumer units	consumer units headed by people under age 25 average spending	consumer units headed by people under age 25 indexed spending[*]
Water and sewerage maintenance (renter)	$2.32	$2.40	103
Babysitting and child care in other home	2.48	–	–
Day care centers, nurseries, and preschools	22.04	3.04	14
Housekeeping services	3.18	–	–
Gardening, lawn care service	2.17	0.03	1
Moving, storage, freight express	3.09	0.01	0
APPAREL AND SERVICES	**209.67**	**117.75**	**56**
Males, aged 2 or older	**54.13**	**23.83**	**44**
Men's coats and jackets	3.10	–	–
Men's accessories	4.01	3.34	83
Men's sweaters and vests	3.88	4.89	126
Men's active sportswear	2.59	3.99	154
Men's shirts	13.12	3.78	29
Men's pants	6.17	1.16	19
Boys' shirts	3.60	1.35	38
Boys' pants	2.87	1.14	40
Females, aged 2 or older	**70.91**	**35.21**	**50**
Women's coats and jackets	4.37	–	–
Women's dresses	9.71	2.38	25
Women's vests and sweaters	4.46	–	–
Women's shirts, tops, and blouses	8.28	5.00	60
Women's pants	4.48	2.52	56
Women's shorts and shorts sets	2.36	6.15	261
Women's sleepwear	5.03	5.24	104
Women's undergarments	3.21	0.82	26
Women's suits	2.18	2.44	112
Women's accessories	3.32	0.59	18
Girls' dresses and suits	4.13	–	–
Girls' shirts, blouses, and sweaters	5.39	3.55	66
Girls' skirts and pants	2.78	0.17	6
Children under age 2	**32.98**	**22.65**	**69**
Infant dresses, outerwear	9.41	4.24	45
Infant underwear	16.01	12.77	80
Infant accessories	4.05	2.67	66

(continued)

	total consumer units	consumer units headed by people under age 25	
		average spending	indexed spending*
Other apparel products and services	**$51.64**	**$36.06**	**70**
Watches	2.37	1.96	83
Jewelry	24.25	20.19	83
Men's footwear	6.80	9.32	137
Boys' footwear	4.02	–	–
Women's footwear	7.31	3.67	50
Girls' footwear	4.99	0.64	13
TRANSPORTATION	**63.22**	**64.64**	**102**
Used cars	17.43	40.30	231
Gasoline on out-of-town trips	12.77	6.04	47
Airline fares	9.43	11.75	125
Ship fares	3.18	0.19	6
HEALTH CARE	**40.10**	**4.52**	**11**
Traditional fee-for-service health plan (not BCBS)	2.36	–	–
Physician's services	2.11	1.20	57
Dental services	5.14	0.75	15
Hospital room	2.30	–	–
Care in convalescent or nursing home	12.51	–	–
Nonprescription vitamins	2.40	–	–
Prescription drugs	2.02	0.53	26
ENTERTAINMENT	**98.17**	**63.12**	**64**
Toys, games, hobbies, tricycles	31.87	9.65	30
Other entertainment	66.30	53.47	81
Movie, other admissions, out-of-town trips	9.03	3.35	37
Admission to sports events, out-of-town trips	3.01	1.12	37
Community antenna or cable TV	4.05	4.23	104
Color TV, portable/table model	2.56	1.86	73
VCRs and video disc players	2.02	0.58	29
Video game hardware and software	2.35	1.38	59
Veterinary services	2.28	0.92	40
Athletic gear, game tables, and exercise equipment	10.19	–	–
Hunting and fishing equipment	7.32	32.62	446
Pinball, electronic video games	2.72	–	–

(continued)

(continued from previous page)

	total consumer units	consumer units headed by people under age 25	
		average spending	indexed spending*
EDUCATION	**$166.20**	**$41.62**	**25**
College tuition	122.76	27.34	22
Elementary and high school tuition	12.75	0.77	6
Other school tuition	6.41	0.52	8
Other school expenses including rentals	6.94	0.78	11
Books and supplies for college	10.01	9.66	97
Books and supplies for elementary/high school	2.10	0.64	30
ALL OTHER GIFTS	**131.18**	**65.29**	**50**
Gifts of out-of-town trip expenses	47.98	16.16	34

* The index compares the spending of consumer units headed by people under age 25 with the spending of the average consumer unit by dividing the spending of people under age 25 by average spending in each category and multiplying by 100. An index of 100 means the spending of people under age 25 equals average spending. An index of 130 means the spending of people under age 25 is 30 percent above average, while an index of 70 means it is 30 percent below average.
** This figure does not include the amount paid for mortgage principle, which is considered an asset.
*** Expenditures on gifts are also included in the preceding product and service categories. Food spending, for example, includes the amount spent on food gifts. Only gift categories with spending of $2.00 or more by the average consumer unit are shown.
Note: The Bureau of Labor Statistics uses consumer units rather than households as the sampling unit in the Consumer Expenditure Survey. For the definition of consumer unit, see the glossary; (–) means the sample is too small to make a reliable estimate.
Source: Bureau of Labor Statistics, unpublished data from the 1999 Consumer Expenditure Survey; calculations by the author

Householders Aged 25 to 34 Are Average Spenders

They spend more than average on children, fast food, and rental housing.

The spending of households headed by people aged 25 to 34 almost matches spending by the average household. In 1999, householders aged 25 to 34 spent $42,470, slightly less than the $43,951 spent by the average household.

Judged by their spending patterns, the diets of young adults include a lot of quick, inexpensive meals and plenty of beer and snacks. Householders aged 25 to 34 spend 20 to 30 percent more than average on meals from fast-food, take-out, and delivery places. They spend 21 percent more than average on snacks and nonalcoholic drinks, 37 percent more on beer and ale at home, and 27 percent more on beer and ale away from home.

Most clearly reflected in the spending data is their status as parents. The spending of households headed by people aged 25 to 34 far exceeds the average for products and services for young children. These householders spend more than twice the average on infants' clothing, baby food, toys, babysitting, and day care centers.

Most householders in the age group cannot yet afford to buy a home. Consequently, their spending on rent is 70 percent more than average. They also spend more than average on furniture rental and the purchase of some home furnishings as they settle into family life.

Young adults also have difficulty affording new vehicles. They spend only 85 percent as much as the average household on new cars and trucks, but 24 percent more than average on used vehicles.

♦ The incomes of young adults don't leave much room for extravagance, and the need to buy for children limits them further.

Average and Indexed Spending of Householders Aged 25 to 34, 1999

(average annual spending of total consumer units and average annual and indexed spending of consumer units headed by people aged 25 to 34, 1999)

	total consumer units	consumer units headed by 25-to-34-year-olds	
		average spending	indexed spending*
Number of consumer units (in 000s)	108,465	19,332	–
Average before-tax income	$43,951	$42,470	97
Average annual spending	37,026.81	36,181.41	98
FOOD	**$5,030.53**	**$5,140.12**	**102**
FOOD AT HOME	2,914.95	2,889.67	99
Cereals and bakery products	**448.09**	**432.07**	**96**
Cereals and cereal products	159.84	169.58	106
Flour	8.84	6.91	78
Prepared flour mixes	14.42	13.44	93
Ready-to-eat and cooked cereals	89.15	97.88	110
Rice	19.87	22.37	113
Pasta, cornmeal, and other cereal products	27.56	28.98	105
Bakery products	288.24	262.49	91
Bread	82.46	75.30	91
White bread	39.14	37.98	97
Bread, other than white	43.32	37.32	86
Crackers and cookies	68.00	59.85	88
Cookies	44.26	40.42	91
Crackers	23.74	19.43	82
Frozen and refrigerated bakery products	23.22	22.21	96
Other bakery products	114.56	105.13	92
Biscuits and rolls	37.92	31.90	84
Cakes and cupcakes	35.74	37.32	104
Bread and cracker products	3.50	3.01	86
Sweetrolls, coffee cakes, doughnuts	24.10	21.33	89
Pies, tarts, turnovers	13.30	11.56	87
Meats, poultry, fish, and eggs	**748.73**	**751.29**	**100**
Beef	220.11	220.54	100
Ground beef	83.08	95.73	115

(continued)

(continued from previous page)

	total consumer units	consumer units headed by 25-to-34-year-olds	
		average spending	indexed spending*
Roast	$34.71	$28.05	81
Chuck roast	11.87	10.44	88
Round roast	9.82	7.48	76
Other roast	13.02	10.12	78
Steak	88.41	84.45	96
Round steak	15.59	14.30	92
Sirloin steak	25.92	24.26	94
Other steak	46.90	45.89	98
Other beef	13.90	12.31	89
Pork	156.74	153.57	98
Bacon	24.92	22.67	91
Pork chops	35.16	40.25	114
Ham	38.91	36.90	95
Ham, not canned	36.73	35.78	97
Canned ham	2.18	1.12	51
Sausage	22.99	20.60	90
Other pork	34.76	33.15	95
Other meats	97.11	95.14	98
Frankfurters	21.80	22.28	102
Lunch meats (cold cuts)	65.97	65.05	99
Bologna, liverwurst, salami	23.10	23.34	101
Other lunchmeats	42.86	41.71	97
Lamb, organ meats, and others	9.34	7.81	84
Lamb and organ meats	8.33	6.38	77
Mutton, goat, and game	1.01	1.43	142
Poultry	136.13	147.56	108
Fresh and frozen chickens	107.74	118.96	110
Fresh and frozen whole chickens	29.63	31.57	107
Fresh and frozen chicken parts	78.11	87.39	112
Other poultry	28.39	28.60	101
Fish and seafood	106.22	103.42	97
Canned fish and seafood	15.90	12.53	79
Fresh fish and shellfish	59.43	60.45	102
Frozen fish and shellfish	30.88	30.44	99
Eggs	32.43	31.06	96

(continued)

(continued from previous page)

	total consumer units	consumer units headed by 25-to-34-year-olds	
		average spending	indexed spending*
Dairy products	**$322.30**	**$321.69**	**100**
Fresh milk and cream	122.05	123.61	101
Fresh milk, all types	111.26	113.09	102
Cream	10.79	10.52	97
Other dairy products	200.25	198.08	99
Butter	17.68	15.79	89
Cheese	93.19	94.22	101
Ice cream and related products	56.49	51.27	91
Miscellaneous dairy products	32.90	36.80	112
Fruits and vegetables	**499.54**	**474.60**	**95**
Fresh fruits	152.49	136.27	89
Apples	28.23	26.43	94
Bananas	30.33	27.78	92
Oranges	15.48	14.60	94
Citrus fruits, excluding oranges	14.15	12.53	89
Other fresh fruits	64.30	54.93	85
Fresh vegetables	148.51	146.31	99
Potatoes	28.35	27.06	95
Lettuce	18.92	18.25	96
Tomatoes	26.91	27.96	104
Other fresh vegetables	74.33	73.05	98
Processed fruits	112.95	104.76	93
Frozen fruits and fruit juices	15.12	14.40	95
Frozen orange juice	8.56	7.39	86
Frozen fruits	1.98	1.55	78
Frozen fruit juices, excluding orange	4.59	5.46	119
Canned fruits	15.72	12.82	82
Dried fruits	5.26	3.59	68
Fresh fruit juice	23.36	20.24	87
Canned and bottled fruit juice	53.49	53.71	100
Processed vegetables	85.58	87.26	102
Frozen vegetables	25.84	25.84	100
Canned and dried vegetables and juices	59.74	61.41	103
Canned beans	11.97	12.65	106
Canned corn	7.89	9.74	123

(continued)

	total consumer units	consumer units headed by 25-to-34-year-olds	
		average spending	indexed spending*
Canned miscellaneous vegetables	$19.03	$17.71	93
Dried peas	0.86	0.67	78
Dried beans	2.57	2.20	86
Dried miscellaneous vegetables	6.79	7.43	109
Dried processed vegetables	0.41	0.18	44
Frozen vegetable juices	0.38	0.25	66
Fresh and canned vegetable juices	9.85	10.58	107
Other food at home	**896.29**	**910.02**	**102**
Sugar and other sweets	111.52	98.55	88
Candy and chewing gum	68.42	58.27	85
Sugar	17.36	17.96	103
Artificial sweeteners	4.14	2.20	53
Jams, preserves, other sweets	21.61	20.12	93
Fats and oils	83.52	80.28	96
Margarine	11.39	9.66	85
Fats and oils	24.73	26.70	108
Salad dressings	26.46	25.49	96
Nondairy cream and imitation milk	8.86	6.82	77
Peanut butter	12.09	11.62	96
Miscellaneous foods	419.78	463.40	110
Frozen prepared foods	81.79	83.74	102
Frozen meals	24.96	25.21	101
Other frozen prepared foods	56.83	58.53	103
Canned and packaged soups	35.78	34.01	95
Potato chips, nuts, and other snacks	89.44	89.09	100
Potato chips and other snacks	71.21	76.66	108
Nuts	18.23	12.43	68
Condiments and seasonings	82.80	87.89	106
Salt, spices, other seasonings	18.63	18.77	101
Olives, pickles, relishes	9.36	9.78	104
Sauces and gravies	37.67	41.00	109
Baking needs and miscellaneous products	17.13	18.33	107
Other canned/packaged prepared foods	129.97	168.68	130
Prepared salads	17.09	15.95	93
Prepared desserts	10.43	9.61	92

(continued)

(continued from previous page)

	total consumer units	consumer units headed by 25-to-34-year-olds	
		average spending	indexed spending*
Baby food	$27.42	$56.11	205
Miscellaneous prepared foods	74.88	86.99	116
Nonalcoholic beverages	242.05	236.11	98
Cola	89.74	88.64	99
Other carbonated drinks	45.46	50.51	111
Coffee	37.59	26.46	70
Roasted coffee	22.92	16.57	72
Instant and freeze-dried coffee	14.67	9.89	67
Noncarbonated fruit-flavored drinks, nonfrozen lemonade	19.25	22.07	115
Tea	15.48	15.30	99
Nonalcoholic beer	0.34	0.44	129
Other nonalcoholic beverages and ice	34.19	32.69	96
Food prepared by household on out-of-town trips	39.42	31.68	80
FOOD AWAY FROM HOME	**2,115.58**	**2,250.45**	**106**
Meals at restaurants, carry-outs, and other	**1,705.15**	**1,945.71**	**114**
Lunch	560.84	630.51	112
Lunch at fast food, take-out, delivery, concession stands, buffet, cafeteria (other than employer, school cafeteria)	294.46	372.50	127
Lunch at full-service restaurants	191.00	181.36	95
Lunch at vending machines and mobile vendors	4.75	3.91	82
Lunch at employer and school cafeterias	70.65	72.75	103
Dinner	821.83	953.20	116
Dinner at fast food, take-out, delivery, concession stands, buffet, cafeteria (other than employer, school cafeteria)	326.42	425.28	130
Dinner at full-service restaurants	477.84	509.24	107
Dinner at vending machines and mobile vendors	7.82	8.43	108
Dinner at employer and school cafeterias	9.75	10.25	105
Snacks and nonalcoholic beverages	162.40	196.68	121
Snacks and nonalcoholic beverages at fast food, take-out, delivery, concession stands, buffet, and cafeteria (other than employer and school cafeteria)	101.35	121.96	120
Snacks and nonalcoholic beverages at full-service restaurants	19.89	20.91	105
Snacks and nonalcoholic beverages at vending machines and mobile vendors	34.14	45.15	132
Snacks and nonalcoholic beverages at employer and school cafeterias	7.01	8.66	124

(continued)

(continued from previous page)

	total consumer units	consumer units headed by 25-to-34-year-olds	
		average spending	indexed spending*
Breakfast and brunch	$160.08	$165.33	103
Breakfast and brunch at fast food, take-out, delivery, concession stands, buffet, and cafeteria (other than employer and school cafeteria)	75.64	91.50	121
Breakfast and brunch at full-service restaurants	77.18	66.68	86
Breakfast, brunch at vending machines, mobile vendors	2.03	2.37	117
Breakfast and brunch at employer and school cafeterias	5.23	4.78	91
Board (including at school)	**48.51**	**9.73**	**20**
Catered affairs	**71.84**	**42.28**	**59**
Food on out-of-town trips	**211.65**	**168.85**	**80**
School lunches	**58.90**	**53.93**	**92**
Meals as pay	**19.54**	**29.96**	**153**
ALCOHOLIC BEVERAGES	**$317.78**	**$365.17**	**115**
At home	**190.49**	**215.65**	**113**
Beer and ale	103.83	142.23	137
Whiskey	11.44	6.44	56
Wine	57.14	49.45	87
Other alcoholic beverages	18.08	17.52	97
Away from home	**127.29**	**149.52**	**117**
Beer and ale	62.89	79.65	127
Beer and ale at fast food, take-out, delivery, concession stands, buffet, and cafeteria	13.13	19.04	145
Beer and ale at full-service restaurants	47.51	59.61	125
Beer and ale at vending machines and mobile vendors	0.37	0.45	122
Beer and ale at catered affairs	1.87	0.56	30
Wine	6.64	7.71	116
Wine at fast food, take-out, delivery, concession stands, buffet, and cafeteria	1.06	1.53	144
Wine at full-service restaurants	5.25	6.09	116
Wine at vending machines and mobile vendors	0.02	0.03	150
Wine at catered affairs	0.31	0.06	19

(continued)

(continued from previous page)

	total consumer units	consumer units headed by 25-to-34-year-olds	
		average spending	indexed spending*
Other alcoholic beverages	$57.76	$62.15	108
Other alcoholic beverages at fast food, take-out, delivery, concession stands, buffet, and cafeteria	3.24	4.65	144
Other alcoholic beverages at full-service restaurants	21.16	26.99	128
Other alcoholic beverages at vending machines and mobile vendors	0.08	0.10	125
Other alcoholic beverages at catered affairs	0.84	0.25	30
Alcoholic beverages purchased on trips	32.45	30.16	93
HOUSING	**$12,057.31**	**$12,520.28**	**104**
SHELTER	**7,016.41**	**7,613.05**	**109**
Owned dwellings**	**4,525.42**	**3,936.12**	**87**
Mortgage interest and charges	2,547.32	2,694.42	106
Mortgage interest	2,392.17	2,614.46	109
Interest paid, home equity loan	87.75	58.51	67
Interest paid, home equity line of credit	66.54	21.34	32
Prepayment penalty charges	0.85	0.11	13
Property taxes	1,123.45	751.31	67
Maintenance, repairs, insurance, other expenses	854.65	490.39	57
Homeowner's and related insurance	234.52	160.56	68
Fire and extended coverage	0.94	0.41	44
Homeowner's insurance	233.58	160.15	69
Ground rent	34.03	30.69	90
Maintenance and repair services	470.47	208.63	44
Painting and papering	57.44	30.68	53
Plumbing and water heating	43.05	27.09	63
Heat, air conditioning, electrical work	71.75	40.68	57
Roofing and gutters	75.39	30.72	41
Other repair and maintenance services	188.39	59.03	31
Repair/replacement of hard-surface flooring	32.80	19.74	60
Repair of built-in appliances	1.66	0.69	42
Maintenance and repair materials	81.80	66.64	81
Paints, wallpaper, and supplies	15.48	13.86	90
Tools/equipment for painting, wallpapering	1.66	1.49	90
Plumbing supplies and equipment	5.98	4.24	71
Electrical supplies, heating/cooling equipment	3.25	1.38	42

(continued)

(continued from previous page)

	total consumer units	consumer units headed by 25-to-34-year-olds	
		average spending	indexed spending*
Hard surface flooring, repair and replacement	$7.61	$3.45	45
Roofing and gutters	7.16	4.45	62
Plaster, paneling, siding, windows, doors, screens, awnings	11.21	4.31	38
Patio, walk, fence, driveway, masonry, brick and stucco work	1.27	1.36	107
Landscape maintenance	3.56	2.79	78
Miscellaneous supplies and equipment	24.64	29.32	119
Insulation, other maintenance and repair	13.79	15.10	109
Finish basement, remodel rooms, build patios, walks, etc.	10.84	14.22	131
Property management and security	28.19	19.73	70
Property management	20.94	15.86	76
Management and upkeep services for security	7.24	3.87	53
Parking	5.64	4.14	73
Rented dwellings	**2,026.61**	**3,447.01**	**170**
Rent	1,965.92	3,348.10	170
Rent as pay	31.73	54.65	172
Maintenance, insurance, and other expenses	28.96	44.26	153
Tenant's insurance	9.25	15.16	164
Maintenance and repair services	11.24	9.55	85
Repair and maintenance services	10.31	8.69	84
Repair and replacement of hard-surface flooring	0.88	0.82	93
Repair of built-in appliances	0.05	0.04	80
Maintenance and repair materials	8.46	19.55	231
Paint, wallpaper, and supplies	1.61	1.71	106
Equipment for painting and wallpapering	0.17	0.18	106
Plastering, paneling, roofing, gutters, etc.	0.96	2.64	275
Patio, walk, fence, driveway, masonry, brick, and stucco work	0.19	0.07	37
Plumbing supplies and equipment	0.40	0.23	58
Electrical supplies, heating and cooling equipment	0.36	0.68	189
Miscellaneous supplies and equipment	4.12	13.32	323
Insulation, other maintenance and repair	1.34	1.16	87
Additions, finishing basements, remodeling rooms	2.61	11.69	448
Construction materials for jobs not started	0.17	0.48	282

(continued)

(continued from previous page)

	total consumer units	consumer units headed by 25-to-34-year-olds	
		average spending	indexed spending*
Hard surface flooring	$0.41	$0.23	56
Landscape maintenance	0.24	0.49	204
Other lodging	**464.38**	**229.92**	**50**
Owned vacation homes	143.69	47.65	33
Mortgage interest and charges	44.29	19.03	43
Mortgage interest	41.99	17.81	42
Interest paid, home equity loan	1.52	1.22	80
Interest paid, home equity line of credit	0.78	–	–
Property taxes	75.72	18.15	24
Maintenance, insurance, and other expenses	23.68	10.47	44
Homeowner's and related insurance	5.92	3.64	61
Homeowner's insurance	5.84	3.64	62
Ground rent	2.04	0.20	10
Maintenance and repair services	9.83	4.09	42
Maintenance and repair materials	1.34	0.18	13
Property management and security	3.59	2.24	62
Property management	2.60	2.01	77
Management and upkeep services for security	0.99	0.23	23
Parking	0.96	0.12	13
Housing while attending school	75.94	23.09	30
Lodging on out-of-town trips	244.75	159.18	65
UTILITIES, FUELS, PUBLIC SERVICES	**2,377.37**	**2,249.37**	**95**
Natural gas	**270.30**	**238.09**	**88**
Natural gas (renter)	54.87	94.11	172
Natural gas (owner)	213.62	143.51	67
Natural gas (vacation)	1.81	0.47	26
Electricity	**899.20**	**811.30**	**90**
Electricity (renter)	212.61	368.69	173
Electricity (owner)	679.95	440.54	65
Electricity (vacation)	6.64	2.07	31
Fuel oil and other fuels	**74.35**	**46.70**	**63**
Fuel oil	36.37	20.93	58
Fuel oil (renter)	3.61	4.68	130
Fuel oil (owner)	32.21	16.01	50
Fuel oil (vacation)	0.54	0.25	46

(continued)

(continued from previous page)

	total consumer units	consumer units headed by 25-to-34-year-olds	
		average spending	indexed spending*
Coal	$0.57	$0.12	21
Coal (renter)	0.03	0.06	200
Coal (owner)	0.52	0.06	12
Bottled/tank gas	31.57	22.18	70
Gas (renter)	4.19	7.15	171
Gas (owner)	25.03	13.52	54
Gas (vacation)	2.34	1.52	65
Wood and other fuels	5.85	3.46	59
Wood and other fuels (renter)	0.90	1.28	142
Wood and other fuels (owner)	4.92	2.18	44
Telephone services	**848.92**	**924.28**	**109**
Telephone services in home city, excl. mobile phones	763.93	816.17	107
Telephone services for mobile phones	84.99	108.11	127
Water and other public services	**284.60**	**229.00**	**80**
Water and sewerage maintenance	209.31	171.38	82
Water and sewerage maintenance (renter)	27.29	46.53	171
Water and sewerage maintenance (owner)	180.43	124.43	69
Water and sewerage maintenance (vacation)	1.60	0.43	27
Trash and garbage collection	72.40	56.82	78
Trash and garbage collection (renter)	8.66	13.62	157
Trash and garbage collection (owner)	62.90	42.92	68
Trash and garbage collection (vacation)	0.84	0.28	33
Septic tank cleaning	2.89	0.79	27
Septic tank cleaning (renter)	0.25	–	–
Septic tank cleaning (owner)	2.64	0.79	30
HOUSEHOLD SERVICES	**665.92**	**771.83**	**116**
Personal services	**322.71**	**572.58**	**177**
Babysitting and child care in own home	31.32	63.14	202
Babysitting and child care in other home	37.23	102.51	275
Care for elderly, invalids, handicapped, etc.	69.34	1.03	1
Adult day care centers	2.52	–	–
Day care centers, nurseries, and preschools	182.29	405.90	223

(continued)

(continued from previous page)

	total consumer units	consumer units headed by 25-to-34-year-olds	
		average spending	indexed spending*
Other household services	**$343.22**	**$199.25**	**58**
Housekeeping services	97.73	39.30	40
Gardening, lawn care services	80.14	28.23	35
Water softening services	3.33	2.51	75
Nonclothing laundry and dry cleaning, sent out	1.61	1.38	86
Nonclothing laundry and dry cleaning, coin-operated	4.17	6.88	165
Termite/pest control services	10.49	5.49	52
Home security system service fee	14.46	11.77	81
Other home services	14.09	8.56	61
Termite/pest control products	0.52	0.29	56
Moving, storage, freight express	33.03	26.98	82
Appliance repair, including service center	11.28	5.49	49
Reupholstering and furniture repair	9.48	4.49	47
Repairs, rentals of lawn and garden equipment, hand and power tools, etc.	4.57	1.14	25
Appliance rental	3.91	3.87	99
Rental of office equipment for nonbusiness use	0.75	0.90	120
Repair of misc. household equipment and furnishings	2.15	0.73	34
Repair of computer systems for nonbusiness use	2.48	1.67	67
Computer information services	48.69	49.31	101
Rental, installation of dishwashers, range hoods, garbage disposals	0.35	0.24	69
Housekeeping Supplies	**498.24**	**440.67**	**88**
Laundry and cleaning supplies	**121.16**	**116.53**	**96**
Soaps and detergents	70.19	66.69	95
Other laundry cleaning products	50.97	49.84	98
Other household products	**249.75**	**211.49**	**85**
Cleansing and toilet tissue, paper towels, and napkins	66.05	55.40	84
Miscellaneous household products	103.28	97.01	94
Lawn and garden supplies	80.42	59.07	73
Postage and stationery	**127.33**	**112.66**	**88**
Stationery, stationery supplies, giftwrap	62.06	59.00	95
Postage	62.48	50.62	81
Delivery services	2.79	3.04	109

(continued)

(continued from previous page)

	total consumer units	consumer units headed by 25-to-34-year-olds	
		average spending	indexed spending*
HOUSEHOLD FURNISHINGS AND EQUIPMENT	$1,499.37	$1,445.36	96
Household textiles	**114.02**	**100.56**	**88**
Bathroom linens	20.28	16.45	81
Bedroom linens	50.55	47.97	95
Kitchen and dining room linens	9.31	7.38	79
Curtains and draperies	18.28	17.49	96
Slipcovers and decorative pillows	4.82	6.43	133
Sewing materials for household items	9.64	4.21	44
Other linens	1.14	0.63	55
Furniture	**365.22**	**435.22**	**119**
Mattresses and springs	47.53	54.06	114
Other bedroom furniture	55.31	73.84	134
Sofas	85.54	110.70	129
Living room chairs	40.97	39.40	96
Living room tables	17.60	21.10	120
Kitchen, dining room furniture	53.26	58.92	111
Infants' furniture	6.90	13.41	194
Outdoor furniture	11.86	11.27	95
Wall units, cabinets, and other furniture	46.25	52.52	114
Floor coverings	**43.67**	**36.69**	**84**
Wall-to-wall carpeting (renter)	1.54	3.17	206
Wall-to-wall carpet, replacement (owner)	28.29	15.13	53
Floor coverings, nonpermanent	12.95	17.43	135
Major appliances	**183.10**	**176.05**	**96**
Dishwashers (built-in), garbage disposals, range hoods (renter)	0.77	0.71	92
Dishwashers (built-in), garbage disposals, range hoods (owner)	13.87	6.68	48
Refrigerators and freezers (renter)	7.83	15.23	195
Refrigerators and freezers (owner)	41.09	32.46	79
Washing machines (renter)	5.09	9.76	192
Washing machines (owner)	18.56	17.26	93
Clothes dryers (renter)	3.12	8.39	269
Clothes dryers (owner)	12.45	12.05	97
Cooking stoves, ovens (renter)	2.60	4.44	171
Cooking stoves, ovens (owner)	24.32	15.52	64

(continued)

(continued from previous page)

	total consumer units	consumer units headed by 25-to-34-year-olds	
		average spending	indexed spending*
Microwave ovens (renter)	$2.33	$3.48	149
Microwave ovens (owner)	6.07	4.96	82
Portable dishwashers (renter)	0.11	0.15	136
Portable dishwashers (owner)	0.76	0.60	79
Window air conditioners (renter)	1.67	3.94	236
Window air conditioners (owner)	5.68	2.98	52
Electric floor-cleaning equipment	26.55	29.38	111
Sewing machines	4.17	2.26	54
Miscellaneous household appliances	**6.06**	**5.82**	**96**
Small appliances, miscellaneous housewares	101.63	81.51	80
Housewares	78.15	65.40	84
Plastic dinnerware	1.34	1.36	101
China and other dinnerware	18.50	10.89	59
Flatware	4.37	3.08	70
Glassware	12.50	6.62	53
Silver serving pieces	3.41	3.17	93
Other serving pieces	1.69	1.08	64
Nonelectric cookware	15.09	15.51	103
Tableware, nonelectric kitchenware	21.25	23.69	111
Small appliances	23.49	16.11	69
Small electric kitchen appliances	18.20	12.43	68
Portable heating and cooling equipment	5.29	3.68	70
Miscellaneous household equipment	**691.72**	**615.32**	**89**
Window coverings	15.12	12.75	84
Infants' equipment	8.01	14.85	185
Laundry and cleaning equipment	13.21	12.56	95
Outdoor equipment	26.48	14.31	54
Clocks	5.62	1.85	33
Lamps and lighting fixtures	11.50	9.89	86
Other household decorative items	138.10	142.45	103
Telephones and accessories	41.56	33.75	81
Lawn and garden equipment	44.03	33.82	77
Power tools	22.82	17.00	74
Office furniture for home use	14.21	14.55	102
Hand tools	7.85	8.34	106

(continued)

	total consumer units	consumer units headed by 25-to-34-year-olds	
		average spending	indexed spending*
Indoor plants and fresh flowers	$53.88	$39.14	73
Closet and storage items	6.82	6.63	97
Rental of furniture	3.03	5.13	169
Luggage	9.36	10.25	110
Computers and computer hardware, nonbusiness use	192.13	179.12	93
Computer software and accessories, nonbusiness use	22.28	19.07	86
Telephone answering devices	2.71	2.85	105
Calculators	1.98	1.17	59
Business equipment for home use	2.08	1.67	80
Other hardware	12.99	6.73	52
Smoke alarms (owner)	0.64	0.51	80
Smoke alarms (renter)	0.06	0.08	133
Other household appliances (owner)	7.73	3.65	47
Other household appliances (renter)	1.20	0.76	63
Miscellaneous household equipment and parts	26.32	22.44	85
APPAREL AND SERVICES	**$1,742.72**	**$2,047.14**	**117**
MEN AND BOYS	**421.01**	**519.46**	**123**
Men, aged 16 or older	**328.00**	**386.63**	**118**
Suits	34.28	37.97	111
Sportcoats and tailored jackets	4.16	7.35	177
Coats and jackets	30.69	34.57	113
Underwear	14.79	13.93	94
Hosiery	12.12	14.49	120
Nightwear	3.03	1.81	60
Accessories	25.76	30.14	117
Sweaters and vests	11.83	15.91	134
Active sportswear	15.41	22.52	146
Shirts	84.42	90.54	107
Pants	72.11	91.40	127
Shorts and shorts sets	13.05	16.78	129
Uniforms	2.65	5.06	191
Costumes	3.72	4.16	112
Boys, aged 2 to 15	**93.00**	**132.83**	**143**
Coats and jackets	6.35	6.18	97
Sweaters	2.76	2.42	88

(continued)

(continued from previous page)

	total consumer units	consumer units headed by 25-to-34-year-olds	
		average spending	indexed spending*
Shirts	$23.08	$37.25	161
Underwear	4.32	8.29	192
Nightwear	3.15	5.11	162
Hosiery	4.73	6.29	133
Accessories	5.85	5.93	101
Suits, sportcoats, and vests	2.52	4.85	192
Pants	23.19	32.53	140
Shorts and shorts sets	8.47	12.28	145
Uniforms	3.34	3.50	105
Active sportswear	3.33	5.01	150
Costumes	1.90	3.20	168
WOMEN AND GIRLS	**654.97**	**708.94**	**108**
Women, aged 16 or older	**547.58**	**578.90**	**106**
Coats and jackets	34.74	41.99	121
Dresses	86.01	96.78	113
Sportcoats and tailored jackets	4.27	3.41	80
Vests and sweaters	37.93	43.23	114
Shirts, tops, and blouses	82.52	92.15	112
Skirts	16.20	22.61	140
Pants	74.17	79.27	107
Shorts and shorts sets	21.78	23.09	106
Active sportswear	24.34	19.69	81
Sleepwear	31.17	30.65	98
Undergarments	38.82	39.37	101
Hosiery	20.49	21.97	107
Suits	35.10	27.02	77
Accessories	31.35	28.22	90
Uniforms	2.97	4.63	156
Costumes	5.70	4.82	85
Girls, aged 2 to 15	**107.38**	**130.04**	**121**
Coats and jackets	7.05	8.78	125
Dresses and suits	16.72	20.56	123
Shirts, blouses, and sweaters	24.31	21.71	89
Skirts and pants	21.05	31.34	149
Shorts and shorts sets	8.70	13.60	156

(continued)

	total consumer units	consumer units headed by 25-to-34-year-olds	
		average spending	indexed spending*
Active sportswear	$6.70	$4.73	71
Underwear and sleepwear	6.98	9.15	131
Hosiery	4.45	5.20	117
Accessories	5.26	6.64	126
Uniforms	3.51	4.14	118
Costumes	2.66	4.20	158
CHILDREN UNDER AGE 2	**66.87**	**139.32**	**208**
Coats, jackets, and snowsuits	2.88	4.82	167
Dresses and outerwear	14.34	23.77	166
Underwear	39.08	86.86	222
Nightwear and loungewear	3.64	8.33	229
Accessories	6.92	15.54	225
FOOTWEAR	**303.07**	**373.55**	**123**
Men's	101.98	155.86	153
Boys'	30.18	53.69	178
Women's	140.85	123.02	87
Girls'	30.07	40.98	136
OTHER APPAREL PRODUCTS AND SERVICES	**296.80**	**305.87**	**103**
Material for making clothes	6.80	3.83	56
Sewing patterns and notions	6.47	2.65	41
Watches	19.11	15.39	81
Jewelry	139.18	132.42	95
Shoe repair and other shoe services	2.03	1.85	91
Coin-operated apparel laundry and dry cleaning	36.82	61.67	167
Apparel alteration, repair, and tailoring services	5.92	5.25	89
Clothing rental	2.84	3.52	124
Watch and jewelry repair	4.61	2.36	51
Professional laundry and dry cleaning	72.67	76.73	106
Clothing storage	0.37	0.21	57
TRANSPORTATION	**$7,011.25**	**$7,150.41**	**102**
VEHICLE PURCHASES	**3,305.35**	**3,500.05**	**106**
Cars and trucks, new	**1,627.93**	**1,377.14**	**85**
New cars	883.19	648.98	73
New trucks	744.75	728.16	98

(continued)

(continued from previous page)

	total consumer units	consumer units headed by 25-to-34-year-olds	
		average spending	indexed spending*
Cars and trucks, used	**$1,641.36**	**$2,033.61**	**124**
Used cars	1,003.15	1,166.64	116
Used trucks	638.21	866.98	136
Other vehicles	**36.06**	**89.30**	**248**
New motorcycles	23.86	66.88	280
Used motorcycles	12.20	22.43	184
GASOLINE AND MOTOR OIL	**1,054.71**	**1,066.17**	**101**
Gasoline	952.95	975.30	102
Diesel fuel	8.46	6.00	71
Gasoline on out-of-town trips	80.43	71.42	89
Gasohol	0.76	–	–
Motor oil	11.31	12.72	112
Motor oil on out-of-town trips	0.81	0.72	89
OTHER VEHICLE EXPENSES	**2,253.81**	**2,249.10**	**100**
Vehicle finance charges	**320.45**	**401.99**	**125**
Automobile finance charges	168.61	212.10	126
Truck finance charges	132.13	170.12	129
Motorcycle and plane finance charges	2.03	3.31	163
Other vehicle finance charges	17.68	16.46	93
Maintenance and repairs	**664.14**	**553.95**	**83**
Coolant, additives, brake, transmission fluids	4.11	3.89	95
Tires	83.45	84.58	101
Parts, equipment, and accessories	51.30	53.96	105
Vehicle audio equipment	7.85	9.87	126
Vehicle products	3.93	5.57	142
Miscellaneous auto repair, servicing	33.88	17.43	51
Body work and painting	32.45	21.27	66
Clutch, transmission repair	46.87	40.67	87
Drive shaft and rear-end repair	4.81	3.58	74
Brake work, including adjustments	56.15	49.50	88
Repair to steering or front-end	16.27	9.45	58
Repair to engine cooling system	21.33	16.34	77
Motor tune-up	39.54	33.73	85
Lube, oil change, and oil filters	58.37	51.97	89

(continued)

(continued from previous page)

	total consumer units	consumer units headed by 25-to-34-year-olds	
		average spending	indexed spending*
Front-end alignment, wheel balance, rotation	$10.18	$8.72	86
Shock absorber replacement	4.80	3.89	81
Gas tank repair, replacement	6.73	2.52	37
Tire repair and other repair work	31.42	22.72	72
Vehicle air conditioning repair	18.96	12.51	66
Exhaust system repair	13.67	10.72	78
Electrical system repair	31.18	19.87	64
Motor repair, replacement	79.78	68.68	86
Auto repair service policy	7.10	2.50	35
Vehicle insurance	**756.38**	**705.47**	**93**
Vehicle rental, leases, licenses, other charges	**512.84**	**587.68**	**115**
Leased and rented vehicles	345.83	425.54	123
Rented vehicles	43.31	46.09	106
Auto rental	9.66	16.23	168
Auto rental, out-of-town trips	27.46	22.30	81
Truck rental	2.12	3.15	149
Truck rental, out-of-town trips	3.80	4.06	107
Motorcycle rental, out-of-town trips	0.05	0.14	280
Aircraft rental, out-of-town trips	0.19	0.22	116
Leased vehicles	302.52	379.45	125
Car lease payments	161.36	184.93	115
Cash down payment (car lease)	12.69	8.14	64
Termination fee (car lease)	1.02	2.25	221
Truck lease payments	115.43	170.98	148
Cash down payment (truck lease)	11.18	13.16	118
Termination fee (truck lease)	0.85	–	–
State and local registration	94.34	91.31	97
Driver's license	8.40	7.63	91
Vehicle inspection	9.00	8.07	90
Parking fees	25.32	26.93	106
Parking fees in home city, excluding residence	21.50	23.52	109
Parking fees, out-of-town trips	3.83	3.41	89
Tolls	12.18	14.98	123
Tolls on out-of-town trips	4.13	3.77	91
Towing charges	5.37	5.48	102
Automobile service clubs	8.27	3.98	48

(continued)

(continued from previous page)

	total consumer units	consumer units headed by 25-to-34-year-olds	
		average spending	indexed spending*
PUBLIC TRANSPORTATION	**$397.38**	**$335.10**	**84**
Airline fares	253.03	199.10	79
Intercity bus fares	14.84	8.48	57
Intracity mass transit fares	47.28	60.23	127
Local transportation on out-of-town trips	11.73	8.95	76
Taxi fares and limousine service on trips	6.89	5.25	76
Taxi fares and limousine service	12.16	17.36	143
Intercity train fares	17.87	13.39	75
Ship fares	32.34	19.85	61
School bus	1.25	2.49	199
HEALTH CARE	**$1,958.85**	**$1,170.41**	**60**
HEALTH INSURANCE	**922.59**	**597.31**	**65**
Commercial health insurance	**185.03**	**148.23**	**80**
Traditional fee-for-service health plan (not BCBS)	82.11	46.42	57
Preferred-provider health plan (not BCBS)	102.93	101.81	99
Blue Cross, Blue Shield	**210.07**	**144.59**	**69**
Traditional fee-for-service health plan	51.28	29.55	58
Preferred-provider health plan	54.69	43.14	79
Health maintenance organization	57.84	58.89	102
Commercial Medicare supplement	40.98	9.60	23
Other health insurance	5.27	3.40	65
Health maintenance plan (not BCBS)	**246.12**	**245.27**	**100**
Medicare payments	**162.93**	**13.05**	**8**
Commercial Medicare supplements/ other health insurance	**118.43**	**46.18**	**39**
Commercial Medicare supplement (not BCBS)	77.51	27.60	36
Other health insurance (not BCBS)	40.92	18.58	45
MEDICAL SERVICES	**557.70**	**351.19**	**63**
Physician's services	134.16	105.71	79
Dental services	223.10	132.69	59
Eyecare services	41.98	31.78	76
Services by professionals other than physicians	36.68	19.08	52
Lab tests, x-rays	25.14	11.29	45
Hospital room	27.21	21.42	79

(continued)

(continued from previous page)

	total consumer units	consumer units headed by 25-to-34-year-olds	
		average spending	indexed spending*
Hospital services other than room	$34.50	$25.38	74
Care in convalescent or nursing home	18.86	0.43	2
Repair of medical equipment	0.71	–	–
Other medical services	15.37	3.41	22
DRUGS	**369.97**	**161.86**	**44**
Nonprescription drugs	72.41	45.92	63
Nonprescription vitamins	38.72	29.28	76
Prescription drugs	258.84	86.66	33
MEDICAL SUPPLIES	**108.59**	**60.05**	**55**
Eyeglasses and contact lenses	56.87	32.46	57
Hearing aids	15.46	0.83	5
Topicals and dressings	27.07	24.01	89
Medical equipment for general use	2.20	0.42	19
Supportive, convalescent medical equipment	5.45	1.90	35
Rental of medical equipment	0.64	0.16	25
Rental of supportive, convalescent medical equipment	0.89	0.27	30
ENTERTAINMENT	**$1,890.92**	**$1,775.57**	**94**
FEES AND ADMISSIONS	**458.78**	**394.91**	**86**
Recreation expenses, out-of-town trips	23.50	20.20	86
Social, recreation, civic club memberships	91.76	63.86	70
Fees for participant sports	71.46	59.80	84
Participant sports, out-of-town trips	29.44	26.04	88
Movie, theater, opera, ballet	89.85	86.38	96
Movie, other admissions, out-of-town trips	43.36	37.54	87
Admission to sporting events	34.07	34.98	103
Admission to sports events, out-of-town trips	14.45	12.51	87
Fees for recreational lessons	37.37	33.39	89
Other entertainment services, out-of-town trips	23.50	20.20	86
TELEVISION, RADIO, SOUND EQUIPMENT	**608.10**	**636.41**	**105**
Television	**443.00**	**456.73**	**103**
Community antenna or cable TV	302.52	302.80	100
Black and white TV sets	0.74	1.01	136
Color TV, console	26.28	29.03	110
Color TV, portable/table model	43.58	45.20	104

(continued)

(continued from previous page)

	total consumer units	consumer units headed by 25-to-34-year-olds	
		average spending	indexed spending[*]
VCRs and video disc players	$25.51	$27.91	109
Video cassettes, tapes, and discs	20.12	24.57	122
Video game hardware and software	19.68	22.65	115
Repair of TV, radio, and sound equipment	4.13	2.82	68
Rental of television sets	0.45	0.73	162
Radios, sound equipment	**165.10**	**179.68**	**109**
Radios	6.80	4.98	73
Tape recorders and players	4.98	3.14	63
Sound components and component systems	28.00	34.46	123
Miscellaneous sound equipment	1.27	1.21	95
Sound equipment accessories	3.12	1.60	51
Satellite dishes	3.33	4.62	139
Compact disc, tape, record, and video mail order clubs	10.37	9.32	90
Records, CDs, audio tapes, needles	40.37	47.14	117
Rental of VCR, radio, sound equipment	0.36	0.52	144
Musical instruments and accessories	24.39	16.09	66
Rental and repair of musical instruments	1.88	1.89	101
Rental of video cassettes, tapes, films, discs	40.21	54.71	136
PETS, TOYS, PLAYGROUND EQUIPMENT	**345.67**	**375.49**	**109**
Pets	**213.11**	**191.50**	**90**
Pet food	92.40	78.82	85
Pet purchase, supplies, medicine	40.31	49.01	122
Pet services	19.77	12.48	63
Veterinary services	60.62	51.19	84
Toys, games, hobbies, and tricycles	**128.56**	**177.39**	**138**
Playground equipment	**4.01**	**6.60**	**165**
OTHER ENTERTAINMENT SUPPLIES, EQUIPMENT, SERVICES	**478.37**	**368.76**	**77**
Unmotored recreational vehicles	**40.95**	**18.55**	**45**
Boat without motor and boat trailers	8.15	14.73	181
Trailer and other attachable campers	32.80	3.82	12
Motorized recreational vehicles	**170.91**	**57.27**	**34**
Motorized camper	90.80	–	–
Other vehicle	21.58	19.58	91
Boat with motor	58.52	37.69	64

(continued)

(continued from previous page)

	total consumer units	consumer units headed by 25-to-34-year-olds	
		average spending	indexed spending[*]
Rental of recreational vehicles	**$2.87**	**$3.71**	**129**
Outboard motors	**3.63**	**1.22**	**34**
Docking and landing fees	**6.86**	**1.66**	**24**
Sports, recreation, and exercise equipment	**145.08**	**183.71**	**127**
Athletic gear, game tables, and exercise equipment	52.91	54.95	104
Bicycles	14.04	17.72	126
Camping equipment	14.73	16.27	110
Hunting and fishing equipment	29.50	56.52	192
Winter sports equipment	7.71	6.43	83
Water sports equipment	7.95	16.17	203
Other sports equipment	15.11	14.34	95
Rental and repair of miscellaneous sports equipment	3.12	1.31	42
Photographic equipment, supplies, and services	**84.77**	**90.87**	**107**
Film	21.59	22.57	105
Other photographic supplies	0.61	0.86	141
Film processing	31.62	34.90	110
Repair and rental of photographic equipment	0.57	0.55	96
Photographic equipment	18.69	18.39	98
Photographer fees	11.68	13.60	116
Fireworks	**5.29**	**1.05**	**20**
Souvenirs	**0.44**	**0.04**	**9**
Visual goods	**0.28**	**–**	**–**
Pinball, electronic video games	**17.30**	**10.70**	**62**
PERSONAL CARE PRODUCTS, SERVICES	**$408.28**	**$381.36**	**93**
Personal care products	**248.82**	**247.25**	**99**
Hair care products	52.78	61.85	117
Nonelectric articles for the hair	6.90	7.56	110
Wigs and hairpieces	1.52	0.56	37
Oral hygiene products	25.64	22.59	88
Shaving products	12.97	12.50	96
Cosmetics, perfume, and bath products	113.84	107.05	94
Deodorants, feminine hygiene, miscellaneous products	27.42	28.25	103
Electric personal care appliances	7.75	6.89	89

(continued)

(continued from previous page)

	total consumer units	consumer units headed by 25-to-34-year-olds	
		average spending	indexed spending*
Personal care services	**$159.46**	**$134.11**	**84**
Personal care service for females	107.28	88.87	83
Personal care service for males	52.18	45.24	87
READING	**$159.38**	**$116.00**	**73**
Newspaper subscriptions	50.69	20.69	41
Newspapers, nonsubscription	14.27	14.02	98
Magazine subscriptions	20.91	16.11	77
Magazines, nonsubscription	10.91	11.14	102
Books purchased through book clubs	9.36	7.30	78
Books not purchased through book clubs	52.32	46.24	88
Encyclopedia and other reference book sets	0.85	0.50	59
EDUCATION	**$634.62**	**$453.14**	**71**
College tuition	355.50	255.73	72
Elementary/high school tuition	104.11	58.55	56
Other school tuition	29.52	20.01	68
Other school expenses including rentals	27.65	22.39	81
Books, supplies for college	51.53	44.03	85
Books, supplies for elementary, high school	14.97	11.61	78
Books, supplies for day care, nursery school	4.23	4.24	100
Miscellaneous school expenses and supplies	47.12	36.58	78
TOBACCO PRODUCTS, SMOKING SUPPLIES	**$300.09**	**$294.51**	**98**
Cigarettes	272.87	264.28	97
Other tobacco products	24.27	28.71	118
Smoking accessories	2.96	1.52	51
FINANCIAL PRODUCTS AND SERVICES	**$888.76**	**$744.69**	**84**
Miscellaneous fees, gambling losses	37.10	31.06	84
Legal fees	120.37	92.09	77
Funeral expenses	69.82	43.81	63
Safe deposit box rental	5.36	1.77	33
Checking accounts, other bank service charges	21.12	21.16	100
Cemetery lots, vaults, maintenance fees	13.15	4.80	37
Accounting fees	68.78	31.41	46
Miscellaneous personal services	55.48	58.65	106

(continued)

(continued from previous page)

	total consumer units	consumer units headed by 25-to-34-year-olds	
		average spending	indexed spending*
Finance charges excluding mortgage and vehicle	$272.05	$295.61	109
Occupational expenses	93.79	90.64	97
Expenses for other properties	126.77	70.84	56
Interest paid, home equity line of credit (other property)	0.61	–	–
Credit card memberships	4.37	2.84	65
CASH CONTRIBUTIONS	**$1,190.11**	**$589.38**	**50**
Cash contributions to nonhousehold members, including students, alimony, and child support	279.71	127.38	46
Gifts of cash, stocks, bonds to nonhousehold members	244.91	82.38	34
Contributions to charities	134.44	49.49	37
Contributions to religious organizations	454.77	297.03	65
Contributions to educational organizations	58.68	22.30	38
Contributions to political organizations	6.63	3.21	48
Other contributions	10.96	7.58	69
PERSONAL INSURANCE AND PENSIONS	**$3,436.22**	**$3,433.23**	**100**
Life and other personal insurance	**394.42**	**238.29**	**60**
Life, endowment, annuity, other personal insurance	382.04	232.81	61
Other nonhealth insurance	12.38	5.48	44
Pensions and Social Security	**3,041.79**	**3,194.94**	**105**
Deductions for government retirement	67.62	50.67	75
Deductions for railroad retirement	3.04	1.10	36
Deductions for private pensions	387.89	397.72	103
Nonpayroll deposit to retirement plans	476.51	323.59	68
Deductions for Social Security	2,106.73	2,421.85	115
PERSONAL TAXES	**$3,587.97**	**$3,065.05**	**85**
Federal income tax	2,801.76	2,316.18	83
State and local income tax	615.84	671.01	109
Other taxes	170.36	77.83	46
GIFTS***	**$1,083.33**	**$738.71**	**68**
Food	**82.92**	**39.57**	**48**
Cakes and cupcakes	2.87	7.53	262
Candy and chewing gum	8.51	5.12	60

(continued)

(continued from previous page)

	total consumer units	consumer units headed by 25-to-34-year-olds	
		average spending	indexed spending*
Board (including at school)	$27.97	$1.45	5
Catered affairs	26.05	4.43	17
HOUSING	**291.88**	**237.52**	**81**
Housekeeping supplies	**40.60**	**39.32**	**97**
Laundry and cleaning supplies	2.24	2.14	96
Miscellaneous household products	7.06	6.20	88
Lawn and garden supplies	3.07	1.64	53
Stationery, stationery supplies, giftwrap	19.45	19.09	98
Postage	6.42	8.39	131
Household textiles	**16.83**	**11.37**	**68**
Bathroom linens	3.45	1.87	54
Bedroom linens	8.94	6.34	71
Appliances and miscellaneous housewares	**32.34**	**19.36**	**60**
Major appliances	8.60	4.01	47
Electric floor cleaning equipment	2.66	–	–
Small appliances and miscellaneous housewares	23.75	15.35	65
China and other dinnerware	5.44	1.97	36
Glassware	4.01	2.35	59
Nonelectric cookware	3.85	2.85	74
Tableware, nonelectric kitchenware	4.21	5.30	126
Small electric kitchen appliances	2.89	1.12	39
Miscellaneous household equipment	**66.17**	**47.93**	**72**
Infants' equipment	2.26	1.78	79
Other household decorative items	22.60	23.78	105
Power tools	3.10	0.40	13
Indoor plants and fresh flowers	15.75	9.80	62
Computers and computer hardware, nonbusiness use	9.01	1.77	20
Other housing expenses	**135.94**	**119.55**	**88**
Repair or maintenance services	3.48	1.71	49
Housing while attending school	45.15	4.77	11
Lodging on out-of-town trips	2.64	1.03	39
Natural gas (renter)	3.08	3.80	123
Electricity (renter)	12.50	15.30	122
Telephone services in home city, excl. mobile phones	13.34	18.41	138

(continued)

	total consumer units	consumer units headed by 25-to-34-year-olds	
		average spending	indexed spending*
Water and sewerage maintenance (renter)	$2.32	$2.65	114
Babysitting and child care in other home	2.48	6.04	244
Day care centers, nurseries, and preschools	22.04	41.91	190
Housekeeping services	3.18	0.52	16
Gardening, lawn care service	2.17	0.40	18
Moving, storage, freight express	3.09	1.25	40
APPAREL AND SERVICES	**209.67**	**205.76**	**98**
Males, aged 2 or older	**54.13**	**49.00**	**91**
Men's coats and jackets	3.10	6.50	210
Men's accessories	4.01	3.77	94
Men's sweaters and vests	3.88	3.64	94
Men's active sportswear	2.59	2.16	83
Men's shirts	13.12	5.21	40
Men's pants	6.17	5.86	95
Boys' shirts	3.60	5.89	164
Boys' pants	2.87	2.15	75
Females, aged 2 or older	**70.91**	**46.33**	**65**
Women's coats and jackets	4.37	0.56	13
Women's dresses	9.71	4.79	49
Women's vests and sweaters	4.46	3.12	70
Women's shirts, tops, and blouses	8.28	8.44	102
Women's pants	4.48	2.75	61
Women's shorts and shorts sets	2.36	2.83	120
Women's sleepwear	5.03	1.80	36
Women's undergarments	3.21	2.19	68
Women's suits	2.18	0.62	28
Women's accessories	3.32	2.31	70
Girls' dresses and suits	4.13	0.01	0
Girls' shirts, blouses, and sweaters	5.39	4.39	81
Girls' skirts and pants	2.78	2.53	91
Children under age 2	**32.98**	**43.48**	**132**
Infant dresses, outerwear	9.41	8.44	90
Infant underwear	16.01	25.10	157
Infant accessories	4.05	6.77	167

(continued)

(continued from previous page)

	total consumer units	consumer units headed by 25-to-34-year-olds	
		average spending	indexed spending*
Other apparel products and services	**$51.64**	**$66.95**	**130**
Watches	2.37	1.89	80
Jewelry	24.25	50.98	210
Men's footwear	6.80	3.45	51
Boys' footwear	4.02	5.02	125
Women's footwear	7.31	3.74	51
Girls' footwear	4.99	1.12	22
TRANSPORTATION	**63.22**	**30.47**	**48**
Used cars	17.43	7.97	46
Gasoline on out-of-town trips	12.77	9.40	74
Airline fares	9.43	4.96	53
Ship fares	3.18	1.09	34
HEALTH CARE	**40.10**	**9.25**	**23**
Traditional fee-for-service health plan (not BCBS)	2.36	–	–
Physician's services	2.11	0.81	38
Dental services	5.14	0.53	10
Hospital room	2.30	0.04	2
Care in convalescent or nursing home	12.51	–	–
Nonprescription vitamins	2.40	2.20	92
Prescription drugs	2.02	0.97	48
ENTERTAINMENT	**98.17**	**73.97**	**75**
Toys, games, hobbies, tricycles	31.87	23.46	74
Other entertainment	66.30	50.51	76
Movie, other admissions, out-of-town trips	9.03	9.39	104
Admission to sports events, out-of-town trips	3.01	3.13	104
Community antenna or cable TV	4.05	5.20	128
Color TV, portable/table model	2.56	1.00	39
VCRs and video disc players	2.02	0.54	27
Video game hardware and software	2.35	1.84	78
Veterinary services	2.28	2.12	93
Athletic gear, game tables, and exercise equipment	10.19	3.68	36
Hunting and fishing equipment	7.32	6.78	93
Pinball, electronic video games	2.72	0.10	4

(continued)

(continued from previous page)

	total consumer units	consumer units headed by 25-to-34-year-olds	
		average spending	indexed spending*
EDUCATION	**$166.20**	**$30.74**	**18**
College tuition	122.76	10.50	9
Elementary and high school tuition	12.75	7.77	61
Other school tuition	6.41	2.04	32
Other school expenses including rentals	6.94	1.83	26
Books and supplies for college	10.01	3.40	34
Books and supplies for elementary/high school	2.10	0.95	45
ALL OTHER GIFTS	**131.18**	**111.41**	**85**
Gifts of out-of-town trip expenses	47.98	29.10	61

*The index compares the spending of consumer units headed by 25-to-34-year-olds with the spending of the average consumer unit by dividing the spending of 25-to-34-year-olds by average spending in each category and multiplying by 100. An index of 100 means the spending of 25-to-34-year-olds equals average spending. An index of 125 means the spending of 25-to-34-year-olds is 25 percent above average, while an index of 75 means it is 25 percent below average.

** This figure does not include the amount paid for mortgage principle, which is considered an asset.

*** Expenditures on gifts are also included in the preceding product and service categories. Food spending, for example, includes the amount spent on food gifts. Only gift categories with spending of $2.00 or more by the average consumer unit are shown.

Note: The Bureau of Labor Statistics uses consumer units rather than households as the sampling unit in the Consumer Expenditure Survey. For the definition of consumer unit, see the glossary; (–) means the sample is too small to make a reliable estimate.

Source: Bureau of Labor Statistics, unpublished data from the 1999 Consumer Expenditure Survey; calculations by the author

9

Wealth

♦ During the 1990s, a strong economy boosted the net worth of the average household. But young adults did not share in the gains. The median net worth of households headed by people under age 35 fell from $9,900 to $9,000 between 1989 and 1998.

♦ The median value of financial assets owned by householders under age 35 grew 37 percent between 1989 and 1998, to a modest $4,500 after adjusting for inflation. This increase was much less than the 64 percent gain enjoyed by the average household.

♦ The median value of nonfinancial assets owned by young adults stood at $22,700 in 1998, well below the $97,800 held by the average household.

♦ The debt of householders under age 35 rose only half as fast as that of the average household between 1989 and 1998, up 33 percent to a median of $19,200.

♦ The proportion of workers under age 35 covered by a pension plan ranges from a low of 5 percent among those under age 20 to 45 percent among those aged 25 to 34.

Young Adults Have Lowest Net Worth

The net worth of young adults fell despite the strong economy of the 1990s.

During the 1990s, a strong economy boosted the net worth of the average household. Young adults, however, did not share in these gains. The median net worth of households headed by people under age 35 was $9,000 in 1998, down from $9,900 in 1989. In contrast, the median net worth of the average household rose from $59,700 to $71,600 during those years. (Net worth is what remains after a household's debts are subtracted from its assets.)

The net worth of young adults is much lower than that of older householders primarily because fewer of the young own homes, which account for the largest share of the net worth of Americans. And while rising stock values were behind some of the rise in the net worth of older householders, young adults own few stocks and therefore did not benefit much from the booming market.

Young adults also typically carry educational loans, car loans, and credit card balances which reduce their net worth. Net worth rises in middle age as people buy homes and pay off debts.

♦ The net worth of young adults will always be lower than that of older householders. Their low incomes, coupled with the costs of setting up a household and starting a family, leave young adults with little money for saving.

Net worth rises with age

(median net worth of households by age of householder, 1998)

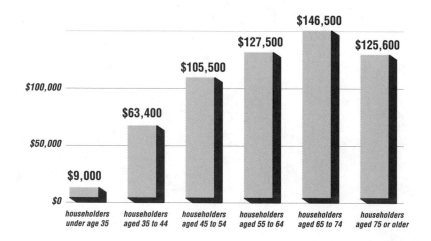

Net Worth of Households by Age of Householder, 1989 and 1998

(median net worth of households by age of householder, 1989 and 1998; percent change, 1989–98; in 1998 dollars)

	1998	1989	percent change 1989–98
Total households	**$71,600**	**$59,700**	**19.9%**
Under age 35	9,000	9,900	−9.1
Aged 35 to 44	63,400	71,800	−11.7
Aged 45 to 54	105,500	125,700	−16.1
Aged 55 to 64	127,500	124,600	2.3
Aged 65 to 74	146,500	97,100	50.9
Aged 75 or older	125,600	92,200	36.2

Source: Federal Reserve Board, Recent Changes in U.S. Family Finances: Results from the 1998 Survey of Consumer Finances, *Federal Reserve Bulletin, January 2000; calculations by the author*

Most Young Adults Own Financial Assets

The value of those assets grew during the 1990s.

The value of financial assets owned by householders under age 35 grew 37 percent between 1989 and 1998, after adjusting for inflation. The increase was considerably less than the 64 percent gain in asset value for the average household. The median value of the financial assets owned by young adults stood at just $4,500 in 1998 compared with $22,400 for the average household.

Behind the rise in financial asset values during the 1990s was the soaring stock market. Forty-one percent of householders under age 35 own stock. But those stocks were worth a median of only $7,000 in 1998. Householders under age 35 who own stock are better off financially than the average young adult, with a median of $25,000 in financial assets in 1999, according to the Investment Company Institute and the Securities Industry Association.

Mutual fund ownership is lowest among householders under age 25, at 23 percent. Among householders aged 25 to 34, however, nearly half own mutual funds. At all ages, stock equity funds are the most commonly held type of mutual fund. Fourteen percent of householders under age 25 and 33 percent of those aged 25 to 34 own equity funds.

♦ The financial assets of young householders will grow if the stock market continues to make gains.

The financial assets of young adults are worth little

(median financial assets of total households and householders under age 35, 1998)

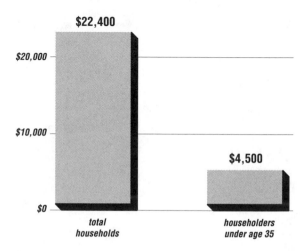

Financial Assets of Households by Age of Householder, 1989 and 1998

(percentage of households owning financial assets and median value of assets for owners, by age of householder, 1989 and 1998; percentage point change in ownership and percent change in value of assets, 1989–98; in 1998 dollars)

	percent owning any financial asset			median value of financial assets		
	1998	**1989**	**percentage point change 1989–98**	**1998**	**1989**	**percent change 1989–98**
Total households	**92.9%**	**87.5%**	**5.4**	**$22,400**	**$13,671**	**63.9%**
Under age 35	88.6	82.2	6.4	4,500	3,286	36.9
Aged 35 to 44	93.3	88.4	4.9	22,900	14,722	55.5
Aged 45 to 54	94.9	90.4	4.5	37,800	19,060	98.3
Aged 55 to 64	95.6	87.5	8.1	45,600	26,290	73.4
Aged 65 to 74	95.6	91.5	4.1	45,800	23,924	91.4
Aged 75 or older	92.1	90.6	1.5	36,600	27,605	32.6

Source: Federal Reserve Board, Recent Changes in U.S. Family Finances: Results from the 1998 Survey of Consumer Finances, *Federal Reserve Bulletin, January 2000; and* Changes in Family Finances from 1983 to 1989: Evidence from the Survey of Consumer Finances, *Federal Reserve Bulletin, January 1992; calculations by the author*

Financial Assets of Householders under Age 35, 1998

(percent of total households and householders under age 35 owning financial assets, and median value of assets for owners, by type of asset, 1998)

	total households	householders under age 35
Percent owning asset		
Any financial asset	**92.9%**	**88.6%**
Transaction accounts	90.5	84.6
Certificates of deposit	15.3	6.2
Savings bonds	19.3	17.2
Bonds	3.0	1.0
Stocks	19.2	13.1
Mutual funds	16.5	12.2
Retirement accounts	48.8	39.8
Life insurance	29.6	18.0
Other managed assets	5.9	1.9
Other financial assets	9.4	10.1
Median value of asset		
Any financial asset	**$22,400**	**$4,500**
Transaction accounts	3,100	1,500
Certificates of deposit	15,000	2,500
Savings bonds	1,000	500
Bonds	44,800	3,000
Stocks	17,500	5,000
Mutual funds	25,000	7,000
Retirement accounts	24,000	7,000
Life insurance	7,300	2,700
Other managed assets	31,500	19,400
Other financial assets	3,000	1,000

Source: Federal Reserve Board, Recent Changes in U.S. Family Finances: Results from the 1998 Survey of Consumer Finances, *Federal Reserve Bulletin, January 2000*

Stock Ownership by Age of Householder, 1998

(percentage of households owning stocks directly or indirectly, median value of stocks for owners, and share of total household financial assets accounted for by stock holdings, by age of householder, 1998)

	percent owning stock	median value of owners' stock	stock as a share of total financial assets
Total households	**48.8%**	**$25,000**	**53.9%**
Under age 35	40.7	7,000	44.8
Aged 35 to 44	56.5	20,000	54.7
Aged 45 to 54	58.6	38,000	55.7
Aged 55 to 64	55.9	47,000	58.3
Aged 65 to 74	42.6	56,000	51.3
Aged 75 or older	29.4	60,000	48.7

Source: Federal Reserve Board, Recent Changes in U.S. Family Finances: Results from the 1998 Survey of Consumer Finances, *Federal Reserve Bulletin, January 2000*

Profile of Stock Owners by Age, 1999

(selected characteristics of equity owners by age, 1999)

	19 to 35	*36 to 54*	*55 to 74*	*75 or older*
Median age	29	44	61	78
Median household income	$47,000	$62,500	$53,000	$30,000
Median household financial assets	25,000	88,000	200,000	200,000
Median household financial assets in equities	20,000	50,000	85,000	74,000
Number of individual stocks and stock mutual funds owned	3	4	5	5
Percent owning individual stock	**45%**	**52%**	**58%**	**63%**
Inside employer-sponsored retirement plans	21	23	17	6
Outside employer-sponsored retirement plans	35	43	51	59
Percent owning stock mutual funds	**83**	**88**	**84**	**80**
Inside employer-sponsored retirement plans	64	67	47	12
Outside employer-sponsored retirement plans	45	57	62	72

Source: Investment Company Institute and the Securities Industry Association, Equity Ownership in America, *Fall 1999; Internet site <www.sia.com>*

Mutual Fund Ownership by Age of Householder and Type of Fund, 2000

(percent of households owning mutual funds by age of householder and type of fund, 2000)

	any mutual fund	equity funds	bond funds	hybrid funds	money market funds
Total households	**49%**	**35%**	**16%**	**12%**	**24%**
Under age 25	23	14	7	2	8
Aged 25 to 34	49	33	12	10	23
Aged 35 to 44	58	44	17	12	26
Aged 45 to 54	59	42	20	16	30
Aged 55 to 64	54	37	17	15	29
Aged 65 or older	32	21	14	11	19

Note: Numbers will not add to total because households may own more than one type of mutual fund.
Source: Investment Company Institute, Fundamentals, *August 2000; Internet site <www.ici.org>*

Young Adults Made Gains in Nonfinancial Assets

But the value of their nonfinancial assets is well below average.

Between 1989 and 1998, the value of nonfinancial assets owned by householders under age 35 rose 11 percent, after adjusting for inflation—matching the national increase. The median value of nonfinancial assets owned by young adults stood at $22,700 in 1998, well below the $97,800 median for all households.

Young adults have modest nonfinancial assets because few own a home, and home values account for the bulk of nonfinancial assets. Young adults are almost as likely as the average American to own a vehicle, however. Seventy-eight percent of householders under age 35 owned a vehicle in 1998, only 5 percentage points less than among all households.

♦ If the economy remains strong and the labor market tight, more young adults will become homeowners—boosting their nonfinancial assets.

Nonfinancial assets of young adults are modest

(median value of nonfinancial assets owned by total householders and householders under age 35, 1998)

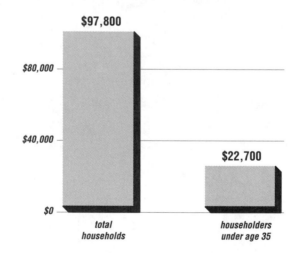

Nonfinancial Assets of Households by Age of Householder, 1989 and 1998

(percentage of households owning nonfinancial assets and median value of assets for owners, by age of householder, 1989 and 1998; percentage point change in ownership and percent change in value of assets, 1989–98; in 1998 dollars)

	percent owning any nonfinancial asset			median value of nonfinancial assets		
	1998	1989	percentage point change 1989–98	1998	1989	percent change 1989–98
Total households	**89.9%**	**90.2%**	**–0.3**	**$97,800**	**$87,677**	**11.5%**
Under age 35	83.3	84.4	–1.1	22,700	20,375	11.4
Aged 35 to 44	92.0	92.8	–0.8	103,500	106,869	–3.2
Aged 45 to 54	92.9	93.3	–0.4	126,800	138,417	–8.4
Aged 55 to 64	93.8	92.1	1.7	126,900	123,432	2.8
Aged 65 to 74	92.0	93.8	–1.8	109,900	82,945	32.5
Aged 75 or older	87.2	87.3	–0.1	96,100	68,354	40.6

Source: Federal Reserve Board, Recent Changes in U.S. Family Finances: Results from the 1998 Survey of Consumer Finances, *Federal Reserve Bulletin, January 2000; and* Changes in Family Finances from 1983 to 1989: Evidence from the Survey of Consumer Finances, *Federal Reserve Bulletin, January 1992; calculations by the author*

Nonfinancial Assets of Householders under Age 35, 1998

(percent of total households and householders under age 35 owning nonfinancial assets, and median value of assets for owners, by type of asset, 1998)

	total households	householders under age 35
Percent owning asset		
Any nonfinancial asset	**89.9%**	**83.3%**
Vehicles	82.8	78.3
Primary residence	66.2	38.9
Other residential property	12.8	3.5
Equity in nonresidential property	8.6	2.7
Business equity	11.5	7.2
Other nonfinancial assets	8.5	7.3
Median value of asset		
Any nonfinancial asset	**$97,800**	**$22,700**
Vehicles	10,800	8,900
Primary residence	100,000	84,000
Other residential property	65,000	42,500
Equity in nonresidential property	38,000	25,000
Business equity	60,000	34,000
Other nonfinancial assets	10,000	5,000

Source: Federal Reserve Board, Recent Changes in U.S. Family Finances: Results from the 1998 Survey of Consumer Finances, *Federal Reserve Bulletin, January 2000*

Homeownership Rate, 1990 and 2000

(percent of householders who own their home, by age of householder, 1990 and 2000; percentage point change, 1990-2000)

	2000	1990	percentage point change 1990–2000
Total households	**67.4%**	**63.9%**	**3.5**
Under age 25	21.7	15.7	6.0
Aged 25 to 29	38.1	35.2	2.9
Aged 30 to 34	54.6	51.8	2.8
Aged 35 to 39	65.0	63.0	2.0
Aged 40 to 44	70.6	69.8	0.8
Aged 45 to 49	74.7	73.9	0.8
Aged 50 to 54	78.5	76.8	1.7
Aged 55 to 59	80.4	78.8	1.6
Aged 60 to 64	80.3	79.8	0.5
Aged 65 to 69	83.0	80.0	3.0
Aged 70 to 74	82.6	78.4	4.2
Aged 75 or older	77.7	72.3	5.4

Source: Bureau of the Census, Internet site <www.census.gov/hhes/www/hvs.html>; calculations by the author

Young Adults Have Substantial Debts

But they owe less than older householders.

The debt of householders under age 35 rose only half as fast as that of the average household between 1989 and 1998, up 33 percent to a median of $19,200. While young adults are more likely than average to be in debt, the median amount they owe is less than the $33,300 owed by the average household.

Since young adults are less likely to own a home, they are less likely to have mortgage debt. But those who do have mortgages owe more than average for their mortgage—a median of $71,000 compared with $62,000 for all households with mortgage debt. Younger householders are more recent home buyers and have had less time to pay down their mortgage debt.

Sixty percent of young adults have installment debt—typically, car loans. In contrast, only 44 percent of all households have installment debt. Half of householders under age 35 carry a balance on their credit cards, owing a median of $1,500.

♦ Many young adults get financial help from their parents, but most still borrow money to get the things they want and need.

Young adults owe less than the average household

(median amount of debt held by total households and householders under age 35, 1998)

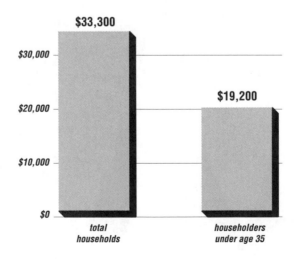

Debt of Households by Age of Householder, 1989 and 1998

(percentage of households with debts and median amount of debt for debtors, by age of house-holder, 1989 and 1998; percentage point change in households with debt and percent change in amount of debt, 1989–98; in 1998 dollars)

	percent with debt			median amount of debt		
	1998	1989	percentage point change 1989–98	1998	1989	percent change 1989–98
Total households	**74.1%**	**72.7%**	**1.4**	**$33,300**	**$19,980**	**66.7%**
Under age 35	81.2	79.5	1.7	19,200	14,460	32.8
Aged 35 to 44	87.6	89.6	–2.0	55,700	40,881	36.2
Aged 45 to 54	87.0	85.9	1.1	48,400	31,154	55.4
Aged 55 to 64	76.4	74.0	2.4	34,600	14,197	143.7
Aged 65 to 74	51.4	47.9	3.5	11,900	6,573	81.1
Aged 75 or older	24.6	23.8	0.8	8,000	3,944	102.9

Source: Federal Reserve Board, Recent Changes in U.S. Family Finances: Results from the 1998 Survey of Consumer Finances, *Federal Reserve Bulletin, January 2000; and* Changes in Family Finances from 1983 to 1989: Evidence from the Survey of Consumer Finances, *Federal Reserve Bulletin, January 1992; calculations by the author*

Debt of Householders under Age 35, 1998

(percent of total households and householders under age 35 with debt, and median value of debt for those with debts, by type of debt, 1998)

	total households	householders under age 35
Percent with debt		
Any debt	**74.1%**	**81.2%**
Mortgage and home equity	43.1	33.2
Installment	43.7	60.0
Other lines of credit	2.3	2.4
Credit card	44.1	50.7
Other residential property	5.1	2.0
Other debt	8.8	9.6
Median value of debt		
Any debt	**$33,300**	**$19,200**
Mortgage and home equity	62,000	71,000
Installment	8,700	9,100
Other lines of credit	2,500	1,000
Credit card	1,700	1,500
Other residential property	40,000	55,000
Other debt	3,000	1,700

Source: Federal Reserve Board, Recent Changes in U.S. Family Finances: Results from the 1998 Survey of Consumer Finances, *Federal Reserve Bulletin, January 2000*

Most Young Adults Do Not Have Pension Coverage

But their coverage rates are higher than in the early 1990s.

Overall, fewer than half of the nation's workers (47 percent) are covered by a pension plan, but the rate is higher than in 1992, when only 43 percent had pension plans. Among workers under age 35, the proportion covered by a pension plan ranges from a low of 5 percent for those under age 20 to 45 percent for those aged 25 to 34.

Young adults are less likely than older workers to be included in an employer's pension plan. They may not have had enough years of service to be vested in a plan or may work only part-time or for companies that do not offer pension benefits.

The pension coverage rate rises with age, so the low coverage rate of young adults is not a serious concern. The majority of workers aged 35 to 64 are covered by pension plans.

♦ Retirement benefits may not be an obvious lure to attract young workers, but with so much talk about the need to save for retirement, many young adults might consider a pension plan a worthy benefit.

Pension Coverage by Age, 1992 and 1998

(percent of workers covered by a pension plan, by age, 1992 and 1998; percentage point change, 1992–98)

	1998	1992	percentage point change
Total workers	**46.7%**	**42.6%**	**4.1**
Aged 20 and under	4.8	3.5	1.3
Aged 21 to 24	21.1	18.1	3.0
Aged 25 to 34	44.5	41.0	3.5
Aged 35 to 44	56.9	53.9	3.0
Aged 45 to 54	64.3	60.5	3.8
Aged 55 to 64	58.1	55.5	2.6
Aged 65 or older	30.1	27.2	2.9

Source: Employee Benefit Research Institute, "Pension Coverage: Examining CPS Data," EBRI Notes, September 2000; calculations by the author

A Note on 2000 Census Data

Generation X: Americans Aged 18 to 34 does not include 2000 census data, which have only begun to be released—a process that will take at least three years to complete. Consequently, most of the population and household data in *Generation X: Americans Aged 18 to 34* are based on the Census Bureau's Current Population Survey, which is benchmarked each decade to census numbers. The benchmarking of the CPS follows the census by two or three years.

Because the 2000 census found more people in the U.S. than the Census Bureau had estimated, the CPS estimates and projections of populations and households are too low. The bureau estimated there were 275 million people in the U.S. in 2000, for example, while the 2000 census counted 281 million. Rather than the U.S. population growing a projected 10 percent during the 1990s, it grew a considerably larger 13 percent.

Such a gap between estimates and reality has occurred before. The 1980 census found millions more people than had been estimated by the bureau. It took the agency until 1983 to benchmark the CPS to match census figures. This is the situation again today, and researchers will have to wait a few years before CPS and census are once more in alignment.

Users of demographic statistics should keep in mind that the figures in this and other demographic reference books now being published are somewhat below the actual numbers. The trends described in *Generation X: Americans Aged 18 to 34*, however, are not affected by the census count. And it is the trends—not the exact numbers—that are most important in demographic research. Trends reveal opportunities, numbers tell you their size. Just bear in mind that the many opportunities described in *Generation X: Americans Aged 18 to 34* are even bigger than the numbers suggest.

For more information about 2000 census data, including the release schedule, see Internet site <www.census.gov/dmd/www/2khome.htm>.

For More Information

The federal government is a rich source of data on almost every aspect of American life. Below are the Internet addresses of agencies collecting the data analyzed in this book. Also shown are the phone numbers of subject specialists, organized alphabetically by topic. A list of State Data Centers and Small Business Development Centers is also below to help you track down demographic and economic information for your state or local area. E-mail addresses are shown when available.

Internet Addresses

Bureau of the Census .... <www.census.gov>
Bureau of Justice Statistics .... <www.ojp.usdoj.gov/bjs>
Bureau of Labor Statistics .... <www.bls.gov>
Consumer Expenditure Survey ....<www.bls.gov/csxhome>
Current Population Survey .... <www.bls.census.gov/cps>
Department of Agriculture, Food Surveys
Research Group ....<www.barc.usda.gov/bhnrc/foodsurvey/home.htm>
Immigration and Naturalization Service ....
.... <www.ins.usdoj.gov/graphics/aboutins/statistics/index.htm>
Investment Company Institute .... <www.ici.org>
National Center For Education Statistics .... <http://nces.ed.gov/>
National Center For Health Statistics .... <www.cdc.gov/nchs>
National Endowment for the Arts .... <www.ntia.doc.gov>
National Opinion Research Center .... <www.norc.uchicago.edu>
National Telecommunications and Information Administration .... <www.ntia.doc.gov>
Security Industries Association .... <www.sia.com>
Survey of Consumer Finances .... <www.federalreserve.gov/pubs/OSS/oss2/scfindex.html>
U.S. Substance Abuse and Mental Health Services Administration .... <www.samhsa.gov>

Subject Specialists

Absences from work, Staff 202-691-6378
Aging population, Staff 301-457-2422
Ancestry, Staff 301-457-2403
Apportionment, Ed Byerly 301-457-2381
Bureau of Justice Statistics, 202-307-0765; .... askbjs@ojp.usdoj.gov
Business expenditures, Sheldon Ziman 301-457-3315
Business investment, Charles Funk 301-457-3324
Census Bureau customer service, Staff 301-457-4100
Census 2000
• Address list, Joel Sobel 301-457-1106
• Aging population, Staff 301-457-2378
• American Community Survey, Larry McGinn 301-457-8050
• Am. Indian and Alaska Native Program, Sydnee Chattin-Reynolds 301-457-2032

- Annexations/boundary changes, Joe Marinucci 301-457-1099
- Apportionment/redistricting, Edwin Byerly 301-457-2381
- Armed forces, Staff 301-457-2422
- Census history, Dave Pemberton 301-457-1167
- Census in schools, Kim Crews 301-457-3626
- Census operations, Mike Stump 301-457-3577
- Citizenship, Diane Schmidley 301-457-2403
- Commuting and place of work, Gloria Swieczkowski 301-457-2454
- Confidentiality and privacy, Jerry Gates 301-457-2515
- Count review, Paul Campbell 301-457-2390
- Data dissemination, Customer Services 301-457-4100
- Disability, Jack McNeil 301-457-8520
- Education, Staff 301-457-2464
- Emigration, Staff 301-457-2438
- Employment projections, demographic, Howard Fullerton 202-691-5711
- Employment/unemployment, Staff 301-457-3242
- Foreign born, Dianne Schmidley 301-457-2403
- Geographic entities, Staff 301-457-1099
- Group quarters population, Denise Smith 301-457-2378
- Hispanic origin, ethnicity, ancestry, Kevin Deardorff/Roberto Ramirez 301-457-2403
- Homeless, Edison Gore 301-457-3998
- Housing, Staff 301-457-3242
- Immigration, Dianne Schmidley 301-457-2403
- Income, Kirby Posey 301-457-3243
- Labor force status/work experience, Thomas Palumbo 301-457-3220
- Language spoken in home, Wendy Bruno 301-457-2464
- Living arrangements, Staff 301-457-2465
- Metropolitan areas, concepts and standards, Michael Ratcliffe 301-457-2419
- Microdata files, Amanda Shields 301-457-1326
- Migration, Kris Hansen/Carol Faber 301-457-2454
- Occupation/industry, Staff 301-457-3210
- Outlying areas, Idabelle Hovland 301-457-8443
- Persons without conventional housing, Edison Gore 301-457-3998
- Population (general information), Staff 301-457-2422
- Questionnaire content, Louisa Miller 301-457-2073
- Race, Staff 301-457-2402
- Residence rules, Karen Mills 301-457-2390
- Response rates, Staff 301-457-3691
- Sampling, Rajendra Singh 301-457-4199
- Service based enumeration, Annetta Clark Smith 301-457-2378
- Special places/group quarters, Denise Smith 301-457-2378
- Special populations, Staff 301-457-2378
- Special tabulations, Marie Pees 301-457-2447
- Undercount, Rajendra Singh 301-457-4199
- Demographic, Greg Robinson 301-457-2103
  - Urban/rural, Ryan Short 301-457-1099
- U.S. citizens abroad, Staff 301-457-2422

Occupational Projections:
- Computer, Carolyn Veneri 202-691-5714
- Construction, Doug Braddock 202-691-5695
- Education, Arlene Dohm 202-691-5727
- Engineering, Doug Braddock 202-691-5695
- Food and lodging, Carolyn Veneri 202-691-5714
- Health, Theresa Cosca 202-691-5712
- Legal, Tina Shelley 202-691-5726
- Mechanics and repairers, Theresa Cosca 202-691-5712
- Sales, Doug Braddock 202-691-5695
- Scientific, Tina Shelley 202-691-5726
Older workers, Staff 202-691-6378
Outlying areas, population, Michael Levin 301-457-1444
Part-time workers, Staff 202-691-6378
Place of birth, Kristin Hansen/Carol Faber 301-457-2454
Population information, Staff 301-457-2422
Poverty statistics, Staff 301-457-3242
Prisoner surveys, Marilyn Monahan 301-457-3925
Puerto Rico, Idabelle Hovland 301-457-8443
Quarterly Financial Report, Ronald Horton 301-457-3343
Race, concepts and interpretation, Staff 301-457-2402
Race statistics, Staff 301-457-2422
Reapportionment and redistricting, Marshall Turner, Jr. 301-457-4015
Retail Trade:
- Advance monthly, Scott Scheleur 301-457-2713
- Economic census, Fay Dorsett 301-457-2687
- Monthly sales and inventory, Nancy Piesto 301-457-2706
- Quarterly Financial Report, Ronald Horton 301-457-3343
Sampling methods, census, Rajendra Singh 301-457-4199
School enrollment, Staff 301-457-2464
Seasonal adjustment methodology, labor, Robert McIntire 202-691-6345
Security Industries Association .... 212-608-1604; info@sia.com
Services:
- Current Reports, Ruth Bramblett 301-457-2766
- Economic census, Jack Moody 301-457-2689
- Services information, Staff 800-541-8345
Small area population estimates, Staff 301-457-3242
Special censuses, Josephine Ruffin 301-457-1429
Special surveys, Ron Dopkowski 301-457-3801
Special tabulations, Marie Pees 301-457-2447
State populations and projections, Staff 301-457-2422
Statistics of U.S. businesses, Melvin Cole 301-457-3320
Survey of Income and Program Participation (SIPP), Staff 301-457-3242
Transportation:
- Commodity Flow Survey, John Fowler 301-457-2108
- Economic census, Pam Palmer 301-457-2811
- Vehicle inventory and use, Kim Moore 301-457-2797
- Warehousing and trucking, Ruth Bramblett 301-457-2766

Undercount, demographic analysis, Gregg Robinson 301-457-2103
Union membership, Staff 202-691-6378
Urban/rural population, Michael Ratcliff/Rodger Johnson 301-457-2419
Veterans, characteristics, Staff 301-457-3242
Veterans in labor force, Staff 202-691-6378
Voters, characteristics, Staff 301-457-2445
Voting age population, Jennifer Day 301-457-2464
Weekly earnings, Staff 202-691-6378
Wholesale Trade:
• Current sales and inventories, Scott Scheleur 301-457-2713
• Economic census, Donna Hambric 301-457-2725
• Quarterly Financial Report, Ronald Horton 301-457-3343
Women, Staff 301-457-2378
Women in the labor force, Staff 202-691-6378

Census Regional Offices

Information specialists in the Census Bureau's 12 regional offices answer thousands of questions each year. If you have questions about the Census Bureau's products and services, you can contact the regional office that serves your state. The states served by each regional office are listed in parentheses.

• **Atlanta** (AL, FL, GA) .... 404-730-3833; atlanta.regional.office@census.gov
• **Boston** (CT, MA, ME, NH, NY, RI, VT) .... 617-424-0510; boston.regional.office@census.gov
• **Charlotte** (KY, NC, SC, TN, VA) .... 704-344-6144; charlotte.regional.office@census.gov
• **Chicago** (IL, IN, WI) .... 312-353-9747; chicago.regional.office@census.gov
• **Dallas** (LA, MS, TX) .... 214-655-3050; dallas.regional.office@census.gov
• **Denver** (AZ, CO, MT, NE, ND, NM, NV, SD, UT, WY) ....
.... 303-969-7750; denver_regional_office@census.gov
• **Detroit** (MI, OH, WV) .... 313-259-1875; detroit.regional.office@census.gov
• **Kansas City** (AR, IA, KS, MN, MO, OK) .... 913-551-6711; kansas.regional.office@census.gov
• **Los Angeles** (CA southern, HI) .... 818-904-6339; la.regional.office@census.gov
• **New York** (NY, NJ selected counties) .... 212-264-4730; ny.regional.office@census.gov
• **Philadelphia** (DE, DC, MD, NJ selected counties, PA) ....
.... 215-656-7578; philly.regional.office@census.gov
• **Seattle** (CA northern, AK, ID, OR, WA) .... 206-553-5835; seattle.regional.office@census.gov
• **Puerto Rico** and the **U.S. Virgin Islands** are serviced by the Boston regional office. All other outlying areas are serviced by the Los Angeles regional office.

State Data Centers and Business and Industry Data Centers

For demographic and economic information about states and local areas, contact your State Data Center (SDC) or Business and Industry Data Center (BIDC). Every state has a State Data Center. Below are listed the leading centers for each state-usually a state government agency, university, or library that heads a network of affiliate centers. Asterisks (*) identify states that also have BIDCs. In some states, one agency serves as the lead for both the SDC and the BIDC. The BIDC is listed separately if a separate agency serves as the lead.

Alabama, Annette Watters, University of Alabama .... 205-348-619; awatters@cba.ua.edu
Alaska, Kathryn Lizik, Department of Labor .... 907-465-2437; kathryn_lizik@labor.state.ak.us

American Samoa, Vaitoelav Filiga, Dept. of Commerce ....684-633-5155; vfiliga@samotelco.com

* **Arizona**, Betty Jeffries, Dept. of Economic Security .... 602-542-5984; popstats@de.state.az.us

Arkansas, Sarah Breshears, Univ. of Arkansas/Little Rock.... 501-569-8530; sgbreshears@ualr.edu

California, Linda Gage, Department of Finance...........................916-323-4086; filgage@dof.ca.gov

Colorado, Rebecca Picaso, Dept. of Local Affairs ....303-866-2156; rebecca.picaso@state.co

Connecticut, Bill Kraynak, Office of Policy and Management ....

.... 860-418-6230; william.kraynak@po.state.ct.us

* **Delaware**, O'Shell Howell, Economic Development Office .... 302-739-427; oshowell@state.de.us

District of Columbia, Herb Bixhorn, Mayor's Office of Planning ....

....202-442-7603; hbixhorn@dcgov.com

* **Florida**, Pam Schenker, Dept. of Labor and Employment Security ....

.... 850-488-1048; pamela_schenker@awi.state.fl.us

Georgia, Robert Giacomini, Office of Planning and Budget ....

.... 404-463-1115; robert.giacomini@sdrc.gadata.org

Guam, Eugene Yungi Li, Department of Commerce . 671-475-0205; e-mail unavailable at this time

Hawaii, Jan Nakamoto, Dept. of Business, Ec. Dev., and Tourism ....

.... 808-586-2493; jnakamot@dbedt.hawaii.gov

Idaho, Alan Porter, Department of Commerce ....208-334-2470; aporter@idoc.state.id.us

Illinois, Suzanne Ebetsch, Bureau of the Budget .... 217-782-1381; sebetsch@commerce.state.il.us

* **Indiana**, Roberta Brooker, State Library .... 317-232-3733; rbooker@statelib.lib.in.us

Indiana BIDC, Carol Rogers, Business Research Center .... 317-274-2205; rogersc@iupui.edu

Iowa, Beth Henning, State Library .... 515-281-4350; b.henning@lib.state.ia.us

Kansas, Marc Galbraith, State Library .... 785-296-3296; ksstl3lb@ink.org

* **Kentucky**, Ron Crouch, University of Louisville .... 502-852-7990; rtcrou01gwise@louisville.edu

Louisiana, Karen Paterson, Office of Planning and Budget...

.... 225-219-4025; webmaster@doa.state.la.us

* **Maine**, Eric VonMagnus, State Planning Office .... 207-287-2989; eric.vonmagnus@state.me.us

* **Maryland**, Jane Traynham, Office of Planning .... 410-767-4450; jtraynham@mdp.state.md.us

* **Massachusetts**, John Gaviglio, Institute for Social and Ec. Research ....

.... 413-545-3460; miser@miser.umass.edu

Michigan, Carolyn Lauer, Dept. of Management and Budget .... 517-373-7910; Lauerc@state.mi.us

* **Minnesota**, David Birkholz, State Demographer's Office ....

.... 651-297-2360; david.birkholz@mnplan.state.mm.us

Minnesota BIDC, Barbara Ronningen, State Demographer's Office ....

.... 651-296-4886; barbara.ronningen@mnplan.state.mm.us

* **Mississippi**, Rachel McNeely, University of Mississippi .... 662-915-7288; rmcneely@olemiss.edu

Mississippi BIDC, Deloise Tate, Dept. of Ec. and Comm. Dev. ....

.... 601-359-3593; dtate@mississippi.org

* **Missouri**, Debra Pitts, State Library .... 573-526-7648; pittsd@mail.sos.state.mo.us

Missouri BIDC, Fred Goss, Small Business Devel. Center............. 573-341-4559; fredgoss@umr.edu

* **Montana**, Allan B. Cox, Department of Commerce .... 406-444-4393; jclack@state.mt.us

Nebraska, Jerome Deichert, University of Nebraska at Omaha ....

.... 402-554-2134; jerome_deichert@unomaha.edu

Nevada, Joyce M. Cox, State Library and Archives .... 775-684-3303; jmcox@clan.lib.nv.us

New Hampshire, Thomas Duffy, Office of State Planning .. 603-271-2155; t_duffy@osp.state.nh.us

* **New Jersey**, David Joye, Department of Labor .... 609-984-2595; djoye@dol.state.nj.us

* **New Mexico**, Kevin Kargacin, University of New Mexico .... 505-277-6626; kargacin@unm.edu

New Mexico BIDC, Karma Shore, Econ. Development Dept. .... 505-827-0264; kshore@unm.edu

* **New York**, Staff, Department of Economic Development ....
.... 518-292-5300; rscardamalia@empire.state.ny.us

* **North Carolina**, Staff, State Library .... 919-733-3270; francine@ospl.state.nc.us

North Dakota, Richard Rathge, State Univ. .... 701-231-8621; richard_rathge@ndsu.nodak.edu

Northern Mariana Islands, Diego Sasamoto, Dept. of Commerce ....
.... 670-664-3034; cad@itecnmi.com

* **Ohio**, Barry Bennett, Department of Development .... 614-466-2115; bbennett@odod.state.oh.us

* **Oklahoma**, Jeff Wallace, Department of Commerce ... 405-815-5184; jeff_wallace@odoc.state.ok.us

Oregon, George Hough, Portland State University .... 503-725-5159; houghg@mail.pdx.edu

* **Pennsylvania**, Diane Shoop, Pennsylvania State Univ./Harrisburg ....
.... 717-948-6096; des102@psu.edu

Puerto Rico, Lillian Torres Aguirre, Planning Bd. .... 787-728-4430; torres_l@jp.prstar.net

Rhode Island, Mark Brown, Dept. of Admin. .... 401-222-6183 mbrown@planning.state.ri.us

South Carolina, Mike MacFarlane, Budget and Control Board ....
.... 803-734-3780; mmacfarl@drss.state.sc.us

South Dakota, Nancy Nelson, Univ. of South Dakota .... 605-677-5287; nnelson@usd.edu

Tennessee, Betty Vickers, University of Tennessee .... 423-974-6080; bvickers@utk.edu

* **Texas**, Steve Murdock, Texas A&M Univ. .... 409-845-5115/5332; smurdock@rsocsun.tamu.edu

Texas BIDC, Donna Osborne, Dept. of Economic Dev. .... 512-936-0223; donna@ded.state.tx.us

* **Utah**, Lisa Hillman, Office of Planning and Budget .... 801-537-9013; lhillman@gov.state.ut.us

Vermont, Sharon Whitaker, Univ. of Vermont .... 802-656-3021; sharon.whitaker@uvm.edu

Virgin Islands, Frank Mills, Univ. of the Virgin Islands .... 340-693-1027; fmills@uvi.edu

* **Virginia**, Don Lillywhite, Virginia Employment Commission ....
.... 804-786-8026; dlillywhite@vec.state.va.us

* **Washington**, Yi Zhao, Office of Financial Management .... 360-902-0599; yi.zhao@ofm.wa.gov

* **West Virginia**, Delphine Coffey, Office of Comm. and Ind. Dev. 304-558-4010; dcoffey@wvdo.org

West Virginia BIDC, Randy Childs, Center for Economic Research ....
.... 304-293-6524; childs@be.wvu.edu

* **Wisconsin**, Robert Naylor, Dept of Administration .... 608-266-1927; bob.naylor@doa.state.wi.us

Wisconsin BIDC, Dan Veroff, Univ. of Wisconsin .... 608-265-9545; dlveroff@facstaff.wisc.edu

Wyoming, Wenlin Liu, Dept. of Admin. and Information .... 307-766-2925; wliu@state.wy.us

Glossary

adjusted for inflation Income or a change in income that has been adjusted for the rise in the cost of living, or the consumer price index (CPI-U-XI).

American Housing Survey The AHS collects national and metropolitan-level data on the nation's housing, including apartments, single-family homes, and mobile homes. The national survey, with a sample of 55,000 homes, is conducted by the Census Bureau for the Department of Housing and Urban Development every other year.

Asian In this book, the term "Asian" includes both Asians and Pacific Islanders.

baby boom Americans born between 1946 and 1964. Baby boomers were aged 37 to 55 in 2001.

baby bust Americans born between 1965 and 1976, also known as Generation X. In 2001, baby busters were aged 25 to 36.

central cities The largest city in a metropolitan area is called the central city. The balance of the metropolitan area outside the central city is regarded as the "suburbs."

Consumer Expenditure Survey The Consumer Expenditure Survey (CEX) is an ongoing study of the day-to-day spending of American households administered by the Bureau of Labor Statistics. The survey is used to update prices for the Consumer Price Index. The CEX includes an interview survey and a diary survey. The average spending figures shown in this book are the integrated data from both the diary and interview components of the survey. Two separate, nationally representative samples are used for the interview and diary surveys. For the interview survey, about 5,000 consumer units are interviewed on a rotating panel basis each quarter for five consecutive quarters. For the diary survey, 5,000 consumer units keep weekly diaries of spending for two consecutive weeks.

consumer unit (on Spending tables only) For convenience, the terms consumer unit and household are used interchangeably in the spending tables of this book, although consumer units are somewhat different from the Census Bureau's households. Consumer units are all related members of a household, or financially independent members of a household. A household may include more than one consumer unit.

1994–96 Continuing Survey of Food Intakes by Individuals This survey was conducted by the Agricultural Research Service of the U.S. Department of Agriculture to measure the food consumption of individuals. In taking the survey, a nationally representative sample of 21,700 people of all ages and 11,800 children aged 0 to 19 were asked to provide information on their food intakes for two nonconsecutive days.

Current Population Survey A nationally representative survey of the civilian noninstitutional population aged 15 or older. It is taken monthly by the Census Bureau for the Bureau of Labor Statistics, collecting information from 50,000 households on employment and unemployment. In March of each year, the survey includes a demographic supplement which is the source of most national data on the characteristics of Americans, such as their educational attainment, living arrangements, and incomes.

1994–96 Diet and Health Knowledge Survey This survey was conducted by the Agricultural Research Service of the U.S. Department of Agriculture to measure the public's knowledge about healthy eating. It was designed as a follow-up to the 1994-96 Continuing Survey of Food Intakes by Individuals, with telephone interviews placed to 5,800 individuals who had taken part in the Continuing Survey of Food Intakes about two weeks earlier.

dual-earner couple A married couple in which both husband and wife are in the labor force.

earnings A type of income, earnings is the amount of money a person receives from his or her job. See also Income.

employed All civilians who did any work as a paid employee or farmer/self-employed worker, or who worked 15 hours or more as an unpaid farm worker or in a family-owned business, during the reference period. All those who have jobs but who are temporarily absent from their jobs due to illness, bad weather, vacation, labor management dispute, or personal reasons are considered employed.

expenditure The transaction cost including excise and sales taxes of goods and services acquired during the survey period. The full cost of each purchase is recorded even though full payment may not have been made at the date of purchase. Average expenditure figures may be artificially low for infrequently purchased items such as cars because figures are calculated using all consumer units within a demographic segment rather than just purchasers. Expenditure estimates include money spent on gifts for others.

family A group of two or more people (one of whom is the householder) related by birth, marriage, or adoption and living in the same household.

family household A household maintained by a householder who lives with one or more people related to him or her by blood, marriage, or adoption.

female/male householder A woman or man who maintains a household without a spouse present. May head family or nonfamily households.

full-time employment Full-time is 35 or more hours of work per week during a majority of the weeks worked during the preceding calendar year.

full-time, year-round Indicates 50 or more weeks of full-time employment during the previous calendar year.

General Social Survey The General Social Survey (GSS) is a biennial survey of the attitudes of Americans taken by the University of Chicago's National Opinion Research Center (NORC). NORC conducts the GSS through face-to-face interviews with an independently drawn, representative sample of 1,500 to 3,000 noninstitutionalized English-speaking people aged 18 or older who live in the United States.

Generation X Americans born between 1965 and 1976, also known as the baby-bust generation. Generation Xers were aged 25 to 36 in 2001.

Hispanic People or householders who identify their origin as Mexican, Puerto Rican, Central or South American, or some other Hispanic origin. People of Hispanic origin may be of any race. In other words, there are Asian Hispanics, black Hispanics, Native American Hispanics, and white Hispanics.

household All the persons who occupy a housing unit. A household includes the related family members and all the unrelated persons, if any, such as lodgers, foster children, wards, or employees who share the housing unit. A person living alone is counted as a household. A group of unrelated people who share a housing unit as roommates or unmarried partners is also counted as a household. Households do not include group quarters such as college dormitories, prisons, or nursing homes.

household, race/Hispanic origin of Households are categorized according to the race or Hispanic origin of the householder only.

householder The householder is the person (or one of the persons) in whose name the housing unit is owned or rented or, if there is no such person, any adult member. With married couples, the householder may be either the husband or wife. The householder is the reference person for the household.

householder, age of The age of the householder is used to categorize households into age groups such as those used in this book. Married couples, for example, are classified according to the age of either the husband or wife, depending on which one identified him or herself as the householder.

housing unit A housing unit is a house, an apartment, a group of rooms, or a single room occupied or intended for occupancy as separate living quarters. Separate living quarters are those in which the occupants do not live and eat with any other persons in the structure and that have direct access from the outside of the building or through a common hall that is used or intended for use by the occupants of another unit or by the general public. The occupants may be a single family, one person living alone, two or more families living together, or any other group of related or unrelated persons who share living arrangements.

immigration The relatively permanent movement (change of residence) of persons into the country of reference.

income Money received in the preceding calendar year by each person aged 15 or older from each of the following sources: (1) earnings from longest job (or self-employment); (2) earnings from jobs other than longest job; (3) unemployment compensation; (4) workers' compensation; (5) Social Security; (6) Supplemental Security income; (7) public assistance; (8) veterans' payments; (9) survivor benefits; (10) disability benefits; (11) retirement pensions; (12) interest; (13) dividends; (14) rents and royalties or estates and trusts; (15) educational assistance; (16) alimony; (17) child support; (18) financial assistance from outside the household, and other periodic income. Income is reported in several ways in this book. Household income is the combined income of all household members. Income of persons is all income accruing to a person from all sources. Earnings is the amount of money a person receives from his or her job.

labor force The labor force tables in this book show the civilian labor force only. The labor force includes both the employed and the unemployed (people who are looking for work). People are counted as in the labor force if they were working or looking for work during the reference week in which the Census Bureau fields the Current Population Survey.

labor force participation rate The percent of a population that is in the labor force, which includes both the employed and unemployed. Labor force participation rates may be shown for sex-age groups or other special populations such as mothers of children of a given age.

married couples with or without children under age 18 Refers to married couples with or without children under age 18 living in the same household. Couples without children under age 18 may be parents of grown children who live elsewhere, or they could be childless couples.

median The median is the amount that divides the population or households into two equal portions: one below and one above the median. Medians can be calculated for income, age, and many other characteristics.

median income The amount that divides the income distribution into two equal groups, half having incomes above the median, half having incomes below the median. The medians for households or families are based on all households or families. The median for persons are based on all persons aged 15 or older with income.

metropolitan area An area qualifies for recognition as a metropolitan area if it includes a city of at least 50,000 population, or it includes a Census Bureau defined urbanized area of at least 50,000 with a total metropolitan population of at least 100,000 (75,000 in New England). In addition to the county containing the main city or urbanized area, a metropolitan area may include other counties having strong commuting ties to the central county.

millennial generation Americans born between 1977 and 1994. Millennials were aged 7 to 24 in 2001.

National Ambulatory Medical Care Survey The NAMCS is an annual survey of visits to nonfederally employed office-based physicians who are primarily engaged in direct patient care. Data are collected from physicians rather than patients, with each physician assigned a one-week reporting period. During that week, a systematic random sample of visit characteristics are recorded by the physician or office staff.

National Health Interview Survey The NHIS is a continuing nationwide sample survey of the civilian noninstitutional population of the U.S. conducted by the Census Bureau for the National Center for Health Statistics. Each year, data are collected from more than 100,000 people about their illnesses, injuries, impairments, chronic and acute conditions, activity limitations, and the use of health services.

net worth The amount of money left over after a household's debts are subtracted from its assets.

nonfamily household A household maintained by a householder who lives alone or who lives with people to whom he or she is not related.

nonfamily householder A householder who lives alone or with nonrelatives.

nonmetropolitan area Counties that are not classified as metropolitan areas.

occupation Occupational classification is based on the kind of work a person did at his or her job during the previous calendar year. If a person changed jobs during the year, the data refer to the occupation of the job held the longest during that year.

occupied housing units A housing unit is classified as occupied if a person or group of people is living in it or if the occupants are only temporarily absent-on vacation, example. By definition, the count of occupied housing units is the same as the count of households.

outside central city The portion of a metropolitan county or counties that falls outside of the central city or cities; generally regarded as the suburbs.

own children Own children are sons and daughters, including stepchildren and adopted children, of the householder. The totals include never-married children living away from home in college dormitories.

owner occupied A housing unit is "owner occupied" if the owner lives in the unit, even if it is mortgaged or not fully paid for. A cooperative or condominium unit is "owner occupied" only if the owner lives in it. All other occupied units are classified as "renter occupied."

part-time employment Part-time employment is less than 35 hours of work per week in a majority of the weeks worked during the year.

percent change The change (either positive or negative) in a measure that is expressed as a proportion of the starting measure. When median income changes from $20,000 to $25,000, for example, this is a 25 percent increase.

percentage point change The change (either positive or negative) in a value which is already expressed as a percentage. When a labor force participation rate changes from 70 percent of 75 percent, for example, this is a 5 percentage point increase.

poverty level The official income threshold below which families and persons are classified as living in poverty. The threshold rises each year with inflation and varies depending on family size and age of householder.

proportion or share The value of a part expressed as a percentage of the whole. If there are 4 million people aged 25 and 3 million of them are white, then the white proportion is 75 percent.

race Race is self-reported and appears in four categories in this book: Asian, black, Native American, and white. A household is assigned the race of the householder.

regions The four major regions and nine census divisions of the United States are the state groupings as shown below:

Northeast:
–New England: Connecticut, Maine, Massachusetts, New Hampshire, Rhode Island, and Vermont

–Middle Atlantic: New Jersey, New York, and Pennsylvania

Midwest:
–East North Central: Illinois, Indiana, Michigan, Ohio, and Wisconsin
–West North Central: Iowa, Kansas, Minnesota, Missouri, Nebraska, North Dakota, and South Dakota

South:
–South Atlantic: Delaware, District of Columbia, Florida, Georgia, Maryland, North Carolina, South Carolina, Virginia, and West Virginia
–East South Central: Alabama, Kentucky, Mississippi, and Tennessee
–West South Central: Arkansas, Louisiana, Oklahoma, and Texas

West:
–Mountain: Arizona, Colorado, Idaho, Montana, Nevada, New Mexico, Utah, and Wyoming
–Pacific: Alaska, California, Hawaii, Oregon, and Washington

renter occupied   *See* Owner occupied.

rounding   Percentages are rounded to the nearest tenth of a percent; therefore, the percentages in a distribution do not always add exactly to 100.0 percent. The totals, however, are always shown as 100.0. Moreover, individual figures are rounded to the nearest thousand without being adjusted to group totals, which are independently rounded; percentages are based on the unrounded numbers.

self-employment   A person is categorized as self-employed if he or she was self-employed in the job held longest during the reference period. Persons who report self-employment from a second job are excluded, but those who report wage-and-salary income from a second job are included. Unpaid workers in family businesses are excluded. Self-employment statistics exclude people who work for themselves in an incorporated business.

sex ratio   The number of men per 100 women.

suburbs   The portion of a metropolitan area that is outside the central city.

Survey of Consumer Finances   The Survey of Consumer Finances is a triennial survey taken by the Federal Reserve Board. It collects data on the assets, debts, and net worth of American households. For the 1998 survey, the Federal Reserve Board interviewed a random sample of 2,813 households and a supplemental sample of 1,496 wealthy households based on tax-return data.

unemployed   Unemployed people are those who, during the survey period, had no employment but were available and looking for work. Those who were laid off from their jobs and were waiting to be recalled are also classified as unemployed.

Bibliography

Bureau of the Census
>   Internet site <www.census.gov>
>   —2000 Current Population Survey, unpublished data
>   —*Educational Attainment in the United States: March 2000*, detailed tables from Current Population Reports, P20-536, 2000
>   —*Geographic Mobility: March 1998 to March 1999*, Current Population Reports, P20-531, 2000
>   —*Household and Family Characteristics: March 1998*, detailed tables from Current Population Reports, P20-515, 1998
>   —Housing Vacancy Surveys, unpublished data
>   —*Marital Status and Living Arrangements: March 1998*, Current Population Reports, P20-514, 1998
>   —*Money Income in the United States: 1999*, Current Population Reports, P60-209, 2000
>   —*Population Projections of the United States by Age, Sex, Race, and Hispanic Origin: 1995 to 2050*, Current Population Reports, P25-1130, 1996
>   —*Poverty in the United States: 1999*, Current Population Reports, P60-210, 2000
>   —*School Enrollment: Social and Economic Characteristics of Students: October 1999*, detailed tables from Current Population Reports, P20-533, 2001
>   —*Statistical Abstract of the United States: 1999* (119th edition) Washington, DC 1999
>   —*Statistical Abstract of the United States: 2000* (120th edition) Washington, DC 2001

Bureau of Labor Statistics
>   Internet site <www.bls.gov>
>   —1990 and 1999 Consumer Expenditure Surveys, unpublished data
>   —2000 Current Population Survey, unpublished data
>   —*Contingent and Alternative Employment Arrangements*, February 1999
>   —*Employment and Earnings*, January 1991
>   —*Employment and Earnings*, January 2001
>   —*Handbook of Labor Statistics*, Bulletin 2340, 1989
>   —*Monthly Labor Review*, November 1999
>   —*Work at Home in 1997*, USDL 98-93

Federal Reserve Board
>   Internet site <www.federalreserve.gov/pubs/OSS/oss2/scfindex.html>
>   —Recent Change in U.S. Family Finance: Results from the 1998 Survey of Consumer Finances, *Federal Reserve Bulletin*, January 2000

Immigration and Naturalization Service
>   Internet site <www.ins.usdoj.gov/graphics/aboutins/statistics/index.htm>
>   —*1998 Statistical Yearbook of the Immigration and Naturalization Service*, 2000

Investment Company Institute
>   Internet site <www.ici.org>
>   —*Fundamentals*, August 2000

National Center for Education Statistics
Internet site <http://nces.ed.gov>
National Household Education Survey 1999, unpublished data

National Center for Health Statistics
Internet site <www.cdc.gov/nchs>
—*Births: Final Data for 1998*, National Vital Statistics Report, Vol. 48, No. 3, 2000
—*Births: Preliminary Data for 1999*, National Vital Statistics Report, Vol. 48, No. 14, 2000
—*Current Estimates from the National Health Interview Survey, 1996*, Series 10, No. 200, 1999
—*Deaths: Final Data for 1998*, National Vital Statistics Report, Vol. 48, No. 11, 2000
—*Health, United States*, 2000
—National Ambulatory Medical Care Survey: 1998 Summary, Advance Data No. 315, 2000

National Opinion Research Center
Internet site <www.norc.uchicago.edu>
—General Social Surveys, unpublished data

National Telecommunications and Information Administration
Internet site <www.ntia.doc.gov>
—*Falling through the Net: Toward Digital Inclusion—A Report on Americans' Access to Technology Tools*, October 2000

Security Industries Association and Investment Company Institute
Internet site <www.sia.com>
—*Equity Ownership in America*, Fall 1999

U.S. Department of Agriculture, Food Surveys Research Group
Internet site <www.barc.usda.gov/bhnrc/foodsurvey/home.htm>
—ARS Food Surveys Research Group, 1994–96 Continuing Survey of Food Intakes by Individuals
—ARS Food Surveys Research Group, 1994–96 Diet and Health Knowledge Survey

U.S. Substance Abuse and Mental Health Services Administration
Internet site <www.samhsa.gov>
—National Household Survey on Drug Abuse, 1999

Index